AMERICA'S —

TEST KITCHEN

ALSO BY AMERICA'S TEST KITCHEN

FOR A FULL LISTING OF ALL OUR BOOKS

CooksIllustrated.com

AmericasTestKitchen.com

THE BEST OF

AMERICA'S TEST KITCHEN

BEST RECIPES, EQUIPMENT REVIEWS, AND TASTINGS

2022

AMERICA'S TEST KITCHEN

AMERICA'S TEST KITCHEN
21 Drydock Avenue, Boston, MA 02210

THE BEST OF AMERICA'S TEST KITCHEN 2022
Best Recipes, Equipment Reviews, and Tastings

ISBN: 978-1-948703-78-9
ISSN: 1940-3925

Printed in Canada
10 9 8 7 6 5 4 3 2 1

Distributed by Penguin Random House Publisher Services
Tel: 800-733-3000

EDITORIAL DIRECTOR, BOOKS: Adam Kowit
EXECUTIVE MANAGING EDITORS: Debra Hudak and Todd Meier
DEPUTY EDITOR: Megan Ginsberg
ASSISTANT EDITORS: Tess Berger and Sara Zatopek
DESIGN DIRECTOR: Lindsey Timko Chandler
DEPUTY ART DIRECTOR: Courtney Lentz
PHOTOGRAPHY DIRECTOR: Julie Bozzo Cote
PHOTOGRAPHY PRODUCER: Meredith Mulcahy
SENIOR STAFF PHOTOGRAPHERS: Steve Klise and Daniel J. van Ackere
PHOTOGRAPHER: Kevin White
ADDITIONAL PHOTOGRAPHY: Carl Tremblay and Joseph Keller
FOOD STYLING: Catrine Kelty, Chantal Lambeth, Kendra McKnight, Ashley Moore, Christie Morrison, Marie Piraino, Elle Simone Scott, Kendra Smith, and Sally Staub
PHOTOSHOOT KITCHEN TEAM
    PHOTO TEAM MANAGER: Alli Berkey
    LEAD TEST COOK: Eric Haessler
    TEST COOKS: Hannah Fenton, Jacqueline Gochenouer, and Gina McCreadie
    ASSISTANT TEST COOKS: Christa West
ILLUSTRATION: John Burgoyne, Sophie Greenspan, and Jay Layman
SENIOR MANAGER, PUBLISHING OPERATIONS: Taylor Argenzio
IMAGING MANAGER: Lauren Robbins
PRODUCTION AND IMAGING COORDINATOR: Amanda Yong
PRODUCTION AND IMAGING SPECIALISTS: Tricia Neumyer and Dennis Noble
LEAD COPY EDITOR: Rachel Schowalter
COPY EDITORS: Christine Campbell and April Poole
PROOFREADER: Vicki Rowland
INDEXER: Elizabeth Parson

CHIEF CREATIVE OFFICER: Jack Bishop
EXECUTIVE EDITORIAL DIRECTORS: Julia Collin Davison and Bridget Lancaster

PICTURED ON FRONT COVER: Nutella Rugelach (page 259)

CONTENTS

WELCOME TO AMERICA'S TEST KITCHEN

The recipes in this book have been tested, written, and edited by the folks at America's Test Kitchen, where curious cooks become confident cooks. Located in Boston's Seaport District in the historic Innovation and Design Building, it features 15,000 square feet of kitchen space, including multiple photography and video studios. It is the home of *Cook's Illustrated* magazine and *Cook's Country* magazine and is the workday destination for more than 60 test cooks, editors, and cookware specialists. Our mission is to empower and inspire confidence, community, and creativity in the kitchen.

We start the process of testing a recipe with a complete lack of preconceptions, which means that we accept no claim, no technique, and no recipe at face value. Instead, we seek out as many versions of a dish as possible, prepare a half dozen of the most promising recipes, and taste the results blind. We then construct our own recipe and continue to test it, varying ingredients, techniques, and cooking times until we reach a consensus. As we like to say in the test kitchen, "We make the mistakes so that you don't have to." The result, we hope, is the best version of a particular recipe, but we realize that only you can be the final judge of our success (or failure). We use the same rigorous approach when we test equipment and taste ingredients.

All of this would not be possible without a belief that good cooking, much like good music, is based on a foundation of objective technique. Some people like spicy foods and others don't, but we believe that there is a right way to sauté, there is a best way to cook a pot roast, and there are measurable scientific principles involved in producing perfectly beaten, stable egg whites. Our ultimate goal is to investigate the fundamental principles of cooking to give you the techniques, tools, and ingredients you need to become a better cook. It is as simple as that.

To see what goes on behind the scenes at America's Test Kitchen, check out our social media channels for kitchen snapshots, exclusive content, video tips, and much more. You can watch us work (in our actual test kitchen) by tuning in to *America's Test Kitchen* or *Cook's Country* on public television or on our websites. Download our award-winning podcast *Proof*, which goes beyond recipes to solve food mysteries (AmericasTestKitchen.com/proof), or listen in to test kitchen experts on public radio (SplendidTable.org) to hear insights that illuminate the truth about real home cooking. Want to hone your cooking skills or finally learn how to bake—with an America's Test Kitchen test cook? Enroll in one of our online cooking classes. And you can engage the next generation of home cooks with kid-tested, kid-approved recipes from America's Test Kitchen Kids.

Our community of home recipe testers provides valuable feedback on recipes under development by ensuring that they are foolproof. You can help us investigate the how and why behind successful recipes from your home kitchen. (Sign up at AmericasTestKitchen.com/recipe_testing.)

However you choose to visit us, we welcome you into our kitchen, where you can stand by our side as we test our way to the best recipes in America.

facebook.com/AmericasTestKitchen
twitter.com/TestKitchen
youtube.com/AmericasTestKitchen
instagram.com/TestKitchen
pinterest.com/TestKitchen

AmericasTestKitchen.com
CooksIllustrated.com
CooksCountry.com
OnlineCookingSchool.com
AmericasTestKitchen.com/kids

WARM SPELT SALAD WITH PICKLED FENNEL, PEA GREENS, AND MINT

SOUPS, SALADS, AND STARTERS

CHICKEN PHO, YOUR WAY

✔ **WHY THIS RECIPE WORKS** Phở gà is the chicken version of Vietnam's famous beef noodle soup, named for its slippery rice noodles, or bánh phở. We made ours by breaking down a whole bird into parts that packed more snugly into our Dutch oven and lessened the amount of water needed to cover the chicken, which shortened the time it took to reduce the liquid to a concentrated broth. With parts, we could also remove the white meat when it was cooked. Covering the pot for the majority of the cooking time prevented evaporation. To keep the broth clear, we skimmed the scum from the broth, simmered it gently, and strained it through cheesecloth. The soup is flavored differently in northern and southern Vietnam, so we made both styles. In keeping with northern Vietnam's preference for a savory and lightly spiced broth, we flavored ours with coriander seeds and clove, adding the spices after we removed the chicken breasts from the pot. And for southern Vietnam's sweet and highly spiced broth, we incorporated sugar, star anise, cinnamon, coriander seeds, and cloves, adding the spices after we removed the chicken breasts from the pot. Before cooking, we soaked our pho noodles to remove starch from their surfaces so that they wouldn't stick together. Finally, we offered an assortment of garnishes so that every diner could personalize their bowl.

You'd never know it, but phở gà started out playing second fiddle. It wasn't until the Vietnamese government restricted beef slaughter in the 1930s that Hanoi cooks turned to chicken to make their brothy noodle soup. Of course, the poultry version was soon a triumph in its own right: clear; silky with gelatin; fragrant with spices and sweet-savory charred aromatics; and, above all, deeply, supremely chicken-y. Over time, street vendors and pho shops throughout Vietnam dedicated themselves to crafting it, seasoning the broth with fish sauce and submerging nests of slippery rice strands (bánh phở) in each bowl along with pulled chicken and shaved onion. Diners mounded herbs over the top, a veritable crown of freshness and vibrancy.

Like the beef-based original, phở gà became a quintessential breakfast for slurping down on the street but also a comfort food for savoring anytime, day or night. It saw the country through foreign occupation, civil war, separation, and reunification. Then, when the dish traveled to the United States during the waves of immigration in the '70s and '80s, more cooks made it at home.

"You would show up after church, and the smell of chicken fat and star anise and cinnamon were so in the air," said Soleil Ho, restaurant critic for the *San Francisco Chronicle*, recalling how her grandmother would wake early on Sunday mornings to start simmering the broth.

I don't have memories of my family cooking pho from scratch; it was more of an occasional treat on our weekly treks to the Vietnamese grocery store. But I've always wanted to learn the process for myself, and I recently decided to do just that. I pored over recipes and consulted experts, all the while keeping an eye out for places to streamline. I wanted a rendition that would do justice to this famous noodle soup but also be simple enough to feed my frequent cravings.

Everything about phở gà hinges on the quality of the broth. Many Vietnamese cooks like to load up the pot with a whole bird (if it's still got the collagen-rich feet attached, all the better) along with extra wings to give the broth a lip-sticking viscosity. But I found that a 4-pound chicken provided plenty of fat and collagen for a rich taste and nice body, and I also made sure to include the giblets for a hint of minerality, as Vietnamese cooks do. I broke down my chicken into parts that fit more snugly in the Dutch oven and added just enough water to cover them, which minimized the time needed to reduce the broth to concentrate it. With parts, I could also pull out the white meat early to keep it tender and moist.

NOTES FROM THE TEST KITCHEN

A DIFFERENT TASTE IN EVERY SPOONFUL
Part of the pleasure of digging into a bowl of phở gà is how customizable it is. For starters, you can choose which broth to make—the more savory northern style or the sweeter, more warmly spiced southern iteration. Then it's your decision which and what quantity of garnishes particular to each version to place in your bowl. That's not all: You can engineer each bite to be exactly the same—or mix it up by favoring a different element with every taste. Either way, as you slurp down the soup, pay attention to how heat from the piping-hot broth mellows the sharpness of the onion and scallions and triggers an outpouring of aromatic compounds from the herbs. Dip the chicken into the sauces or stir them into the broth (but do try a sip before tinkering—a customary courtesy in pho shops).

A crystal-clear broth is critical. Many cooks achieve this by first blanching the chicken in boiling water to wash away proteins that can cloud the liquid. I found it easier to skim the scum as it rose to the surface and then hold the liquid at a gentle simmer. As long as I avoided aggressive boiling, the clumps I didn't manage to capture stayed intact and were easily removed when I strained the broth through cheesecloth.

Traditionally, the ginger and onions that give backbone to the broth are roasted over a brazier and the blackened skins are discarded, leaving their outermost layers with a subtle sweetness. But charring, cooling, and peeling an onion and a stub of ginger took 30 minutes—and while the nuance these roasted vegetables contributed was pleasant, I liked the broth just as well when I added raw aromatics to the pot.

There are two main approaches to seasoning the broth and then accessorizing it with garnishes at the table. In the north, where pho was born, cooks like to keep the broth simple and purely savory. In the south, where northerners fleeing the Communists in the 1950s helped popularize the soup, it has a different character. In this agriculturally rich and historically more prosperous region, cooks took to sweetening the broth with sugar and warming it with additional spices. More embellishments also made it into the bowl, including bottled condiments that were unavailable in the north.

Among Vietnamese diners, passions still run high over which style is best. Though my family is from the south, I couldn't pledge myself solely to that version—I love them both. And luckily, it couldn't be more straightforward to switch their flavor profiles: Twenty minutes into the cooking, after I took the white meat out, I added one or the other seasoning to the broth. For a northern soup, I opted for coriander and cloves. For a southern pho, I augmented these two spices with cinnamon, star anise, and a teaspoon of sugar. I let the pot simmer for another hour and then strained the broth.

Whichever way I seasoned it, it was a lovely broth—golden and limpid when I strained it and even more savory-tasting once I stirred in ¼ cup of fish sauce. I kept it warm on the stove as I pulled the cooled chicken into bite-size shreds.

The broth is the essence of pho, but the rice noodles provide the ballast, and their plain taste and sleek texture are ultrasoothing in their own right. Noodle stalls serve fresh bánh phở, but the dried kind are almost as good and are widely available. The trick is to treat them just right: First, I soaked the dried rice noodles in tap water, which removed their surface starches so that the cooked strands wouldn't fuse together. This also gave them a head start on hydrating. Then, I dunked them in boiling water so that they were just cooked through. I drained them and mounded them in serving bowls along with some pulled chicken and sliced onion and scallions and poured the piping-hot broth over the top.

When serving the northern soup, I provided the standard greenery for that style—cilantro and green chiles—along with slivers of aromatic lime leaves that Vietnamese cooking authority Andrea Nguyen, author of *The Pho Cookbook* (2017), told me adorn more elaborate bowls in the north. Though not traditional, I also stirred together the gingery dipping sauce called nước mắm gừng—an idea I got from chatting with An Nguyen Xuan, who served the sauce with pho at his recently closed chicken-focused restaurant, Bếp Gà, in New York's Chinatown. For the southern pho, I again put out cilantro and green chile, along with heaps of bean sprouts and Thai basil, as well as hoisin and sriracha.

Choose one style of soup, or do as I do and enjoy them both. After all, it's the diner who is ultimately in charge of how phở gà tastes. "There's a pho bowl for everyone," said Nguyen. "It's part of Vietnam's welcoming table."

—LAN LAM, *Cook's Illustrated*

Phở Gà Miến Bắc (Northern Vietnamese–Style Chicken Pho)
SERVES 6 TO 8

Prepare the garnishes while the broth simmers. Makrut lime leaves are sometimes sold as kaffir lime leaves. If you prefer a milder sauce, omit the Thai chile. Look for rice noodles labeled as bánh phở; if they're unavailable, substitute ⅛-inch-wide flat rice noodles or rice vermicelli. The broth will taste overseasoned on its own but will be balanced by the unsalted noodles and garnishes. Serve in large, deep soup bowls. The dipping sauce is not traditional, but some Vietnamese cooks like to include it.

PHỞ GÀ MIỀN BẮC (NORTHERN VIETNAMESE–STYLE CHICKEN PHO)

BROTH

- 1 (4-pound) whole chicken, neck and giblets reserved, liver discarded
- 1 onion, halved
- 1 (3-inch) piece ginger, peeled and halved lengthwise
- 2 teaspoons table salt
- 1 tablespoon coriander seeds
- 2 whole cloves
- ¼ cup fish sauce

SAUCE

- ⅓ cup fish sauce
- ¼ cup lime juice (2 limes)
- 3 tablespoons sugar
- 1 tablespoon grated fresh ginger
- 2 garlic cloves, minced
- 1 Thai chile, stemmed and minced (optional)

PHO

- 12 ounces dried rice noodles
- ½ small onion, sliced thin
- 2 scallions, sliced thin
- 6 makrut lime leaves, middle vein removed and leaves sliced thin
  Fresh cilantro leaves and stems
  Thinly sliced serrano chiles

1. FOR THE BROTH: Place chicken breast side down on cutting board. Using kitchen shears, cut through bones on either side of backbone. Reserve backbone. Using sharp chef's knife, cut straight down through breastbone to make 2 halves. Working with 1 half at a time, separate leg quarter and wing from each breast.

2. Transfer chicken parts, backbone, neck, and giblets to Dutch oven. Add 12 cups water, onion, ginger, and salt and bring to boil over high heat. Reduce heat to maintain gentle simmer. Cook, skimming off any scum that rises to surface, until breasts register 160 to 165 degrees, 15 to 20 minutes. Transfer breasts to plate. Add coriander seeds and cloves to broth, cover, and continue to simmer for 1 hour (check broth occasionally and adjust heat as necessary to maintain gentle simmer).

3. FOR THE SAUCE: While broth simmers, stir ⅔ cup hot water; fish sauce; lime juice; sugar; ginger; garlic; and Thai chile, if using, in bowl until sugar dissolves.

4. Transfer leg quarters to plate with breasts. Discard wings, backbone, neck, giblets, and onion. Strain broth through fine-mesh strainer lined with double layer of cheesecloth. Rinse pot well and return broth to pot. (You should have about 12 cups broth.) Stir in fish sauce, cover, and keep warm over low heat.

5. FOR THE PHO: Place noodles in large bowl and cover with water. Let sit until noodles are pliable, about 20 minutes. While noodles soak, shred chicken, discarding skin and bones. Bring 2 quarts water to boil in large pot. Drain noodles. Return broth to boil.

6. Add noodles to boiling water and cook, stirring frequently, until almost tender, 30 to 60 seconds. Drain immediately and divide among serving bowls. Place ⅓ cup chicken in each bowl (save remaining chicken for another use). Divide onion, scallions, and lime leaves among bowls. Add broth until chicken and noodles are covered by ½ inch, about 2 cups per bowl (save remaining broth for later use). Provide each diner with small bowl of dipping sauce and serve pho immediately, passing cilantro and serranos separately.

TO MAKE AHEAD: Prepare recipe through step 4 and refrigerate chicken and broth for up to 3 days. To serve, let chicken come to room temperature while reheating broth and cooking noodles.

NOTES FROM THE TEST KITCHEN

HOW TO BREAK DOWN THE CHICKEN

Breaking down the chicken allows it to fit more snugly in the pot so that we can use less water and have less liquid to reduce for a concentrated broth. Plus, we can take out the white meat early so that it won't overcook.

1. Place chicken breast side down on cutting board. Using kitchen shears, cut through bones on either side of backbone.

2. Using sharp chef's knife, cut straight down through breastbone to make 2 halves.

3. Working with 1 half at a time, separate leg quarter and wing from each breast.

Phở Gà Miến Nam (Southern Vietnamese–Style Chicken Pho)

SERVES 6 TO 8

Prepare the garnishes while the broth simmers. Look for rice noodles labeled as bánh phở; if they're unavailable, substitute ⅛-inch-wide flat rice noodles or rice vermicelli. The broth will taste overseasoned on its own but will be balanced by the unsalted noodles and garnishes. Serve in large, deep soup bowls, passing the bean sprouts, herbs, lime, serranos, and sauces separately to allow each diner to customize their soup.

BROTH

1 (4-pound) whole chicken, neck and giblets reserved, liver discarded
1 onion, halved
1 (3-inch) piece ginger, peeled and halved lengthwise
2 teaspoons table salt
1 teaspoon sugar
1 tablespoon coriander seeds
1 cinnamon stick
1 star anise pod
2 whole cloves
¼ cup fish sauce

PHO

12 ounces dried rice noodles
½ small onion, sliced thin
2 scallions, sliced thin
Bean sprouts
Fresh cilantro leaves and stems
Fresh Thai basil leaves
Lime wedges
Thinly sliced serrano chiles
Hoisin sauce
Sriracha

1. FOR THE BROTH: Place chicken breast side down on cutting board. Using kitchen shears, cut through bones on either side of backbone. Reserve backbone. Using sharp chef's knife, cut straight down through breastbone to make 2 halves. Working with 1 half at a time, separate leg quarter and wing from each breast.

2. Transfer chicken parts, backbone, neck, and giblets to Dutch oven. Add 12 cups water, onion, ginger, salt, and sugar and bring to boil over high heat. Reduce heat to maintain gentle simmer. Cook, skimming off any scum that rises to surface, until breasts register 160 to 165 degrees, 15 to 20 minutes. Transfer breasts to plate. Add coriander seeds, cinnamon stick, star anise, and cloves to broth; cover; and continue to simmer for 1 hour (check broth occasionally and adjust heat as necessary to maintain gentle simmer).

3. Transfer leg quarters to plate with breasts. Discard wings, backbone, neck, giblets, and onion. Strain broth through fine-mesh strainer lined with double layer of cheesecloth. Rinse pot well and return broth to pot. (You should have about 12 cups broth.) Stir in fish sauce, cover, and keep warm over low heat.

4. FOR THE PHO: Place noodles in large bowl and cover with water. Let sit until noodles are pliable, about 20 minutes. While noodles soak, shred chicken, discarding skin and bones. Bring 2 quarts water to boil in large pot. Drain noodles. Return broth to boil.

5. Add noodles to boiling water and cook, stirring frequently, until almost tender, 30 to 60 seconds. Drain immediately and divide among serving bowls. Place ⅓ cup chicken in each bowl (save remaining chicken for another use). Divide onion and scallions among bowls. Add broth until chicken and noodles are covered by ½ inch, about 2 cups per bowl (save remaining broth for later use). Serve immediately, passing bean sprouts, cilantro, Thai basil, lime wedges, serranos, hoisin, and sriracha separately.

TO MAKE AHEAD: Prepare recipe through step 3 and refrigerate chicken and broth for up to 3 days. To serve, let chicken come to room temperature while reheating broth and cooking noodles.

KOREAN-INSPIRED SPICY FISH STEW

✓ WHY THIS RECIPE WORKS If you're looking for a fiery soup to warm you up, look no further than maeuntang, a traditional Korean spicy fish soup that brings the heat. This soup gets its fire from both gochujang (a funky fermented chili, soybean, and rice paste that has sweet, spicy, and salty flavors) and gochugaru (red chile pepper flakes that bring bright but nuanced heat). Traditionally made with anchovy stock, we tried re-creating maeuntang using more readily available chicken broth, which gave the soup the rich body and round flavor it needed. We found that adding ginger; garlic; scallions; and a typical side accompaniment, kimchi (for acidity and fermented flavors) to the stock and simmering chunks of red snapper in it created a rich, flavorful, and complex broth that tasted like the sea and nothing like chicken soup. Adding cubes of tofu and slices of zucchini—traditional mix-ins for this soup—provided mild bites to counteract the heat of our fiery broth.

Although the Korean word "maeuntang" translates as "spicy soup," it's most closely associated with a spicy fish stew. This version is a favorite for a reason: The stew is brimming with pieces of fresh fish and vegetables and seasoned generously with gochujang and gochugaru. Savory and spicy, with a deep-red color and satisfying body, maeuntang is just the thing to restore and invigorate you on a cold, dreary day. I was inspired to create a quick fish stew that would provide me with the same warm comfort.

I started with the fish. Maeuntang can be made with a wide variety of fish and seafood; my research yielded recipes that called for red snapper, sea bass, cod, pollack, flounder, and fluke. I landed on red snapper for its flaky texture and mild flavor, which played well with the stew's assertive seasonings. Meatier white fish such as halibut, mahi-mahi, and swordfish made fine substitutes.

In traditional maeuntang, a whole fish is cut into several pieces before being cooked in the broth. (In Korea, many restaurants that serve the stew allow diners to pick their fish from an aquarium.) The collagen from the bones and fat from the skin melt into the broth as it simmers, creating an unctuous stew. I was after a quick meal, so I chose a skinless red snapper fillet for easier prep. I'd have to find another way to achieve a broth with a similarly rich texture.

Many Korean soups and stews start with anchovy stock, which is made by boiling dried anchovies in water. Some cooks like to add radish, seaweed, and/or aromatics to the pot as well. I wondered if I could use store-bought ingredients to supply these savory flavors in less time. One of the recipes I encountered in my research called for clams in addition to the fish, so I opened up a bottle of clam juice and stirred it into the pot along with anchovy paste and water. It wasn't the quick fix I'd hoped for: The fish flavor was weak, and the broth was much too thin. I had better luck with chicken broth, which provided enough gelatin and

meatiness to make the broth satisfyingly rich. Once simmered with the fish, it didn't taste like chicken at all.

The broth was still missing the brininess from the anchovies, so I turned to a common accompaniment to maeuntang: kimchi. A full cup added salinity and funk, and the chopped pieces contributed welcome bites of crunch. The kimchi also bolstered the stew's spiciness.

Maeuntang is a fiery dish, featuring heat from two sources: red chile flakes known as gochugaru and the fermented soybean, rice, and chile paste called gochujang. Many cooks add fresh chiles to the pot, too. I played with the amounts of gochugaru and gochujang until I was satisfied with the spice level: Just 1 tablespoon of each delivered enough bright heat to perk me up and open my nasal passages, but not so much that it overpowered the delicate flavor of the fish.

With the fish and broth settled, I wanted to bulk up the stew. Many of the recipes I found in my research called for zucchini and tofu; I loved how their mildness contrasted with the stew's savory and spicy flavors, and they offered cooling bites between sips of the fiery broth. I chose firm tofu so that it would hold its shape during cooking, and I cut it into easy-to-eat 1-inch pieces. I sliced the zucchini into thin half-moons, the perfect shape to cradle with a soupspoon.

The zucchini contributed freshness and a pleasing green color amid the red stew, but I thought the dish could use even more of both. Scallions are popular in maeuntang, so I cut four of them into substantial 1-inch lengths and stirred them in with the fish, tofu, and zucchini. Sprinkling the finished stew with a hefty amount of fresh cilantro evoked the grassy notes of chrysanthemum leaves, a traditional addition.

My hearty stew was filled with chunks of flaky red snapper, cubes of tofu, and slices of zucchini, and its briny, savory flavors balanced a nuanced heat. What's more, it was a snap to prepare. I started by briefly sautéing garlic and ginger in a Dutch oven and then added the chicken broth, kimchi, and seasonings. Once the mixture came to a simmer, I stirred in the red snapper, tofu, zucchini, and scallions. The delicate fish took no more than 4 minutes to cook through. Both bracing and comforting, this fast, flavorful stew will warm me up on the coldest of days.

—CAMILA CHAPARRO, *America's Test Kitchen Books*

Korean-Inspired Spicy Fish Stew
SERVES 6

If you cannot find Korean chile flakes, substitute ¾ teaspoon paprika and ¼ teaspoon red pepper flakes. Serve with lime wedges, if desired.

> 1 tablespoon vegetable oil
> 4 garlic cloves, minced
> 1 tablespoon grated fresh ginger
> 6 cups chicken or vegetable broth
> 1 cup cabbage kimchi, drained and coarsely chopped
> 1 tablespoon gochujang
> 1 tablespoon Korean chile flakes (gochugaru)
> ½ teaspoon pepper
> 1 (1½-pound) skinless red snapper fillet, 1 inch thick, cut into 2-inch pieces
> 7 ounces firm tofu, cut into 1-inch pieces
> 1 small zucchini, halved lengthwise and sliced ¼ inch thick
> 4 scallions, cut into 1-inch lengths
> ½ cup fresh cilantro leaves

1. Heat oil in Dutch oven over medium heat until shimmering. Add garlic and ginger and cook until fragrant, about 30 seconds. Stir in broth, kimchi, gochujang, chile flakes, and pepper, then bring to simmer.

2. Stir in red snapper, tofu, zucchini, and scallions. Return to gentle simmer, then reduce heat to medium-low; cover; and cook until fish flakes apart when gently prodded with paring knife, 3 to 4 minutes. Sprinkle with cilantro and serve.

SPICED WILD RICE AND COCONUT SOUP

✔ WHY THIS RECIPE WORKS Wild rice can be tricky to cook properly, but the pressure cooker turns this grain tender with just the right amount of chew in this earthy soup that pairs vibrant turmeric with bold garam masala. Along with the spices, we added tomato paste, a serrano chile, and ginger to a combination of vegetable broth and rich coconut milk. We tried putting everything in the pot all at once, but the flavors dulled while cooking, so we reserved half of the coconut milk and some ginger to stir in after cooking. For fresh texture, we stirred in Swiss chard until just wilted, letting it maintain its pleasant bite. Some chopped tomato added just the right amount of sweetness and acidity and a sprinkle of cilantro provided a bright finish.

For one-pot cooking, the Instant Pot is a superstar. It's the perfect vessel for a speedy, streamlined meal that will be on the table quickly and leave minimal cleanup afterward. As such, it was a natural fit for recipes in *The Complete One Pot*, so I turned to it to develop this hearty, warming, naturally gluten-free, vegetarian soup. The recipe takes just over an hour; leaves only one pot to clean; and much of the cooking is hands off, making it a great meal for an easy dinner or a "meatless Monday." I wanted to create a different take on a rice soup from the typical chicken and rice soups that we often see, so I turned to wild rice and added warm Indian spices such as turmeric and garam masala. My goals were layered flavor, streamlined one-pot cooking, varied textures, and a more inventive vegetarian soup.

Over the past couple of years, the Instant Pot has become perhaps the biggest food and cooking trend with numerous cookbooks, blog posts, and social media posts spotlighting its versatility and benefits. Here in the test kitchen, we love the Instant Pot for its abilities to speed up cooking and create streamlined one-pot meals, plus its convenience and approachability. In this recipe, I use the Instant Pot to speed up the cooking of wild rice, which can often take 40 minutes to an hour to cook on the stovetop but which cooks in just 30 hands-off minutes in the Instant Pot. Wild rice can be difficult to cook consistently, but in the Instant Pot it cooks quickly and reliably. However, there are some downsides to cooking in the Instant Pot. It can often dull flavors if ingredients are not added strategically, and without careful timing, it can be easy to overcook ingredients. For this recipe, I did extensive testing to make sure that we came out with a foolproof recipe that avoids these potential Instant Pot pitfalls.

Another benefit of the Instant Pot is its numerous cooking settings. In this dish, I employ both the sauté function and the pressure-cook function. Using the sauté mode allowed me to get a jump start on softening the onions and the Swiss chard stems so that they dissolved into the soup and fully incorporated into the dish. It also allowed me to bloom and activate the spices, tomato paste, ginger, garlic, and serrano chile to open up their flavors and give the soup more depth of flavor.

KOREAN-INSPIRED SPICY FISH STEW

Blooming the spices helps them become more full-bodied and helps them stand out more in the final dish.

My main goal was a multilayered, complexly flavored dish, and every ingredient was chosen to achieve that goal. Turmeric and garam masala contributed curry flavor and warmth to the dish, and since garam masala is a blend of spices, this single ingredient contributed deep flavor. Slightly wilted Swiss chard added body, texture, and a modest bitterness. I chose the star of the dish, wild rice, for its heartiness and for a change from typical rice-based soups. Technically the seed of a type of aquatic grass, wild rice is gluten-free and high in protein and fiber, which made it the perfect, filling choice for this vegetarian, gluten-free dish, making this soup into a full meal.

Developing this recipe, I came across a few stumbling blocks that needed to be faced in order to create a truly foolproof dish. First was the cooking of the wild rice. Finding the cooking-time sweet spot for the ideal wild rice was a bit of a challenge. I started with a 15-minute cooking time and ended up with undercooked and still-crunchy rice. However, when I increased the cooking time too much, I got rice that overcooked during the last stages of cooking. Thirty minutes was optimal, resulting in perfectly cooked rice.

Another challenge came with the Instant Pot's tendency to dull flavors; this affected both the coconut milk and the fresh ginger in this recipe, which became muted if added in their entirety before pressure cooking. To rectify this issue, I split the addition of both ingredients, adding half the coconut milk before pressure cooking and half after, and adding two-thirds of the ginger before pressure cooking and one-third after. Adding before pressure cooking helped provide a base of flavor, and the second addition after pressure cooking gave a sharper hit of flavor in the final dish. I also staggered the additions of the Swiss chard, adding the stems before pressure cooking to soften them and adding the leaves at the end so that they were just wilted and still had a slight bite to them.

Finally, with the addition of tomato and cilantro for brightness and freshness and lime wedges on the side for acidity, I had a filling one-pot soup with complex flavor. The textures of the rice and Swiss chard were perfect, and it was the ideal warming soup to whip up for a weeknight dinner or for a quick vegetarian meal.

—SARAH EWALD, *America's Test Kitchen Books*

Spiced Wild Rice and Coconut Soup

SERVES 6 TO 8

Do not use quick-cooking or presteamed wild rice (read the ingredient list on the package to determine this) in this recipe. The test kitchen's favorite garam masala is McCormick Gourmet Collection Garam Masala.

- 2 tablespoons vegetable oil
- 2 onions, chopped fine
- 8 ounces Swiss chard, stems chopped fine, leaves cut into 1½-inch pieces, divided
- ¾ teaspoon table salt
- 6 garlic cloves, minced
- 2 tablespoons grated fresh ginger, divided
- 1 serrano chile, stemmed, seeded, and minced
- 1 tablespoon tomato paste
- 2 teaspoons ground turmeric
- 1½ teaspoons garam masala
- 4 cups vegetable or chicken broth
- 2 (14-ounce) cans coconut milk, divided
- 1 cup wild rice, picked over and rinsed
- 1 tomato, cored and chopped
- ¼ cup chopped fresh cilantro
  Lime wedges

1. Using highest sauté or browning function, heat oil in electric pressure cooker until shimmering. Add onions, chard stems, and salt and cook until softened, 3 to 5 minutes. Stir in garlic, 4 teaspoons ginger, serrano, tomato paste, turmeric, and garam masala and cook until fragrant, about 1 minute. Stir in broth and 1 can coconut milk, scraping up any browned bits, then stir in rice.

2. Lock lid in place and close pressure release valve. Select high pressure cook function and cook for 30 minutes. Turn off pressure cooker and quick-release pressure. Carefully remove lid, allowing steam to escape away from you.

3. Stir remaining can coconut milk and chard leaves into soup and cook, using highest sauté or browning function, until chard leaves are wilted, about 5 minutes. Turn off pressure cooker. Stir in tomato and remaining 2 teaspoons ginger and let sit until heated through, about 2 minutes. Stir in cilantro and season with salt and pepper to taste. Serve with lime wedges.

HORIATIKI SALATA (HEARTY GREEK SALAD)

✓ **WHY THIS RECIPE WORKS** Imagine bites of sweet tomatoes, briny olives, savory onion, crunchy cucumber, and tangy feta—without any lettuce filler—and you've got horiatiki salata, the original Greek salad. As with any ingredient-driven dish, sourcing high-quality components and bringing out their best was a must. Ripe, sweet tomatoes are loaded with juice that can flood the salad, so we tossed halved wedges (which allowed for chunky but manageable bites) with salt and set them in a colander to drain for 30 minutes. Soaking the onion slices in ice water lessened their hot bite by washing away thiosulfinates while maintaining their fresh, crisp texture. A creamy Greek feta, which must be made with at least 70 percent fatty sheep's milk, brought richness to the lean vegetables. When we tried subbing in fresh oregano for the traditional dried, we understood why the dried herb is preferred: Its more delicate flavor complemented—but didn't upstage—the vegetables. Vinaigrette is never used to dress horiatiki salata, but we did tweak the custom of drizzling the salad separately with oil and vinegar by tossing the vegetables with each component, ensuring that the mixture was lightly but evenly dressed.

Greek salad is an old-fashioned immigrant story—an imported original nudged into an alternate version of itself so that it fell more in line with mainstream American expectations.

The traditional Greek version, known as horiatiki salata, is a colorful, chunky mix of raw tomatoes, cucumbers, green bell peppers, and onions; briny kalamata olives and (sometimes) capers; and thick slabs of rich, sheepy feta. These components are drizzled with extra-virgin olive oil and maybe lemon juice or vinegar and sprinkled with dried oregano. A staple accompaniment at Greek meals, this simple, hearty dish (also called "village salad") made its way to the United States during the 19th- and 20th-century waves of Hellenic migration and landed on the menus of many Greek-run diners and pizzerias. When the dish didn't gain much traction with American consumers, restaurateurs turned it into a recognizable (to Americans) salad by diluting the vegetables with lettuce (iceberg or romaine), crumbling the feta, and tossing the whole affair in a thick vinaigrette. That Greek American adaptation balanced familiarity and

intrigue, eventually earning such a following that it became a standard not just at diners and pizzerias but also at chain restaurants, pubs, delis, and even convenience stores nationwide.

The popularity of Greek salad rages on, but in recent years American interest in more traditional Greek fare has started to catch up. That's good news for horiatiki fans such as myself, who've always preferred the original version of the dish—without the lettuce filler and vinaigrette bath, every element comes into bright, sharp, saline focus—and I took it as an excuse to hone my own version. I looked for ripe tomatoes and good-quality olives, feta, and olive oil, since that's best practice for any ingredient-driven dish. But it would be just as important to figure out the best way to prepare each item so that it was the best version of itself and the jumble of flavors and textures would hang together in perfect balance. Here's a component-by-component deep dive into my testing notes.

There's nothing like raw onion to add sharp, savory bite and crunch to a salad, as long as it's used in moderation. Even just half an onion's worth of thin slices tasted harsh, so I tried soaking the slices in three different liquids to temper their bite. In each case, the soak drew out the onion's harsh-tasting sulfur compounds (thiosulfinates), but only ice water did so without introducing new, distracting flavors.

Ripe, sweet tomatoes are a must for horiatiki, but they're also loaded with juice that flooded the salad when I added them directly to the mix. So my first step was to toss the tomatoes (halved wedges, for chunky but reasonable bites) with salt and set them in a colander to drain for 30 minutes. The salt pulled out a whopping ½ cup of juice, preventing all that liquid from saturating the other vegetables; plus, it seasoned the tomatoes more deeply and evenly than I could have by simply seasoning the salad before serving.

It's not just folklore that Greeks make great feta. Of the eight different fetas we tasted from Greece, France, and the United States, the Greek ones boasted almost universally superior flavor and texture—and for several good reasons, which stem from Greek government regulations that control the feta-making process.

First, the milk itself is rich and complex: At least 70 percent of it must be sheep's milk, which contains twice as much fat as cow's milk; any remainder must be goat's milk. Because Greek sheep and goats eat uniquely diverse diets, their milks contain fatty acids

HORIATIKI SALATA (HEARTY GREEK SALAD)

that impart distinctively gamy, savory flavors to the feta. Second, Greek feta is produced via a slower, more methodical process that encourages the development of exceptionally complex flavors. Our favorite fetas, made by Real Greek Feta and Dodoni, work equally well in our salad. Avoid crumbled fetas, which are produced from cow's milk and lack the complexity and rich, dense texture of the real deal.

Greeks cook extensively with oregano, particularly the dried leaves, which they use in cooked applications and as a finishing touch for meat, fish, vegetables, legumes, and salads such as horiatiki. The woodsy, floral profile of dried oregano leaves is subtler and more complex than that of fresh leaves, but it's still fragrant because oregano is a hardy herb that retains much of its flavor and aroma when dried. We found that subtlety ideal for horiatiki when we tasted the salad sprinkled with both fresh and dried oregano, noting that the dried herb's more delicate flavor paired well with—but didn't upstage—the vegetables.

Even if you don't care for the grassy, vegetal, faintly bitter flavor of green bell pepper, consider using one here. Those qualities (which are due to flavor compounds in unripe peppers called methoxypyrazines) uniquely balance the horiatiki, complementing the fresh, sweet, briny, and rich flavors of the other components.

—STEVE DUNN, *Cook's Illustrated*

Horiatiki Salata (Hearty Greek Salad)
SERVES 4 AS A MAIN DISH OR 6 TO 8 AS A SIDE DISH

Soaking the sliced onion in ice water tempers its heat and bite. Use only large, round tomatoes here, not Roma or cherry varieties, and use the ripest in-season tomatoes you can find. A fresh, fruity, peppery olive oil works well here if you have it. We prefer to use feta by Real Greek Feta or Dodoni in this recipe. The salad can be served with crusty bread as a light meal for four.

1¾ **pounds tomatoes, cored**

1¼ **teaspoons table salt, divided**

½ **red onion, sliced thin**

2 **tablespoons red wine vinegar**

1 **teaspoon dried oregano, plus extra for seasoning**

½ **teaspoon pepper**

1 **English cucumber, quartered lengthwise and cut into ¾-inch chunks**

1 **green bell pepper, stemmed, seeded, and cut into 2 by ½-inch strips**

1 **cup pitted kalamata olives**

2 **tablespoons capers, rinsed**

5 **tablespoons extra-virgin olive oil, divided**

1 **(8-ounce) block feta cheese, sliced into ½-inch-thick triangles**

NOTES FROM THE TEST KITCHEN

THE BEST WAY TO MELLOW THE ONION'S BITE

BAKING SODA SOLUTION	**VINEGAR AND SALT**	**ICE WATER**
Left a chemical aftertaste, even after we rinsed the onion three times	Essentially quick-pickled the onion, wilting the slices so that they lacked crunch and infusing them with distracting sourness	Mellowed the onion's harsh bite without dulling its crunch

1. Cut tomatoes into ½-inch-thick wedges. Cut wedges in half crosswise. Toss tomatoes and ½ teaspoon salt together in colander set in large bowl. Let drain for 30 minutes. Place onion in small bowl, cover with ice water, and let sit for 15 minutes. Whisk vinegar, oregano, pepper, and remaining ¾ teaspoon salt together in second small bowl.

2. Discard tomato juice and transfer tomatoes to now-empty bowl. Drain onion and add to bowl with tomatoes. Add vinegar mixture, cucumber, bell pepper, olives, and capers and toss to combine. Drizzle with ¼ cup oil and toss gently to coat. Season with salt and pepper to taste. Transfer to serving platter and top with feta. Season each slice of feta with extra oregano to taste. Drizzle feta with remaining 1 tablespoon oil. Serve.

SWEET POTATO SALAD WITH CUMIN, SMOKED PAPRIKA, AND ALMONDS

✔ **WHY THIS RECIPE WORKS** Sweet potatoes are often mashed or roasted. We wanted a fresher, more vibrant take on the average sweet potato side. To achieve this goal, we started by peeling and cutting the sweet potatoes into bite-size pieces. Cooking them in a hot oven (450 degrees) developed golden exteriors while the insides baked up fluffy and tender. We let the roasted sweet potatoes cool down (to protect their structural integrity) before tossing them with a vinaigrette made with scallions, minced jalapeño, lime juice, garlic, and warm spices. We finished the dressed sweet potatoes with fresh cilantro plus toasted almonds for a nutty crunch, making a great salad to serve alongside any fall-favorite main dish.

We love sweet potatoes for their deep earthy flavor, and we've prepared them in myriad ways, from roasting and baking to mashing and frying, but this year I wanted to take them in a fresh new direction inspired by simple, vinaigrette-based potato salads. My goal was a combination of bright, fresh, lively flavors anchored by the trusty sweet potato that we all love.

I started by cutting up a few sweet potatoes into ¾-inch pieces. I found that it doesn't matter if the pieces are all exactly the same shape as long as they're about the same size; this is necessary for them to cook at the same rate. I gave the sweet potato pieces a quick toss in extra-virgin olive oil, sprinkled them with salt, arranged them in a single layer on a baking sheet, and then slid them into a 450-degree oven to roast and cook through. Thirty minutes later (with a quick stir halfway through the roasting time), the sweet potatoes were perfectly tender. I set them aside to cool completely and scanned the pantry for inspiration.

I like strong flavors, so I assembled a rogues' gallery of my favorites: sharp scallions, punchy lime juice, spicy minced jalapeño (I chose to remove the seeds to keep the heat in check, but if you love heat, you can include them, too), ground cumin to amplify the earthiness of the sweet potatoes, smoked paprika, black pepper, pungent minced garlic, and ground allspice for its unbeatable complexity. I combined these ingredients with a bit more extra-virgin olive oil in a large bowl to make my flavorful dressing.

Once the sweet potatoes had cooled completely, I tossed them with the dressing and added chopped fresh cilantro leaves and stems. The mixture tasted bright and fresh, but the dish was missing some texture. I wanted to incorporate a little something to offset the soft texture of the sweet potatoes.

The answer? Some toasted almonds. I had some almonds in the pantry already, so after I quickly toasted them (3 to 5 minutes in a dry skillet over medium heat was all they needed), I chopped them up and added them into the mix. This was the crunch and contrast I had been missing.

After a few more run-throughs, I got the ratio of nuts to sweet potatoes right. And I also learned that I could roast the sweet potatoes and stir together the dressing ahead of time and store them in the refrigerator separately until I needed them. (The potatoes need about an hour out of the refrigerator to take the chill off before serving; don't dress them until you're ready to serve them.)

I was so happy with this salad that I decided to create another version of it. I made another punchy dressing, this time with soy sauce, spicy sriracha, a little sugar, and some grated fresh ginger in place of the cumin, smoked paprika, pepper, and allspice in my original dressing. I also swapped in some more complementary-flavored peanuts for the almonds.

I'll always have room in my heart for a marshmallow-topped sweet potato casserole, but this year, I'm making room for these fresh takes.

—MARK HUXSOLL, *Cook's Country*

Sweet Potato Salad with Cumin, Smoked Paprika, and Almonds
SERVES 6 TO 8

A high-quality extra-virgin olive oil will add depth and complexity here. The test kitchen's favorite ground cumin is Simply Organic Ground Cumin.

- 3 pounds sweet potatoes, peeled and cut into ¾-inch pieces
- 3 tablespoons plus ¼ cup extra-virgin olive oil, divided
- 2 teaspoons table salt
- 3 scallions, sliced thin
- 3 tablespoons lime juice (2 limes)
- 1 jalapeño chile, stemmed, seeded, and minced
- 1 teaspoon ground cumin
- 1 teaspoon smoked paprika
- 1 teaspoon pepper
- 1 garlic clove, minced
- ½ teaspoon ground allspice
- ½ cup fresh cilantro leaves and stems, chopped coarse
- ½ cup whole almonds, toasted and chopped

1. Adjust oven rack to middle position and heat oven to 450 degrees. Toss potatoes with 3 tablespoons oil and salt in bowl. Transfer to rimmed baking sheet and spread into even layer. Roast until potatoes are tender and just beginning to brown, 30 to 40 minutes, stirring halfway through roasting. Let potatoes cool for 30 minutes.

2. Meanwhile, combine scallions, lime juice, jalapeño, cumin, paprika, pepper, garlic, allspice, and remaining ¼ cup oil in large bowl. (Cooled sweet potatoes and scallion mixture can be refrigerated, separately, for up to 24 hours; let both come to room temperature before proceeding with recipe.)

3. Add cilantro, almonds, and potatoes to bowl with scallion mixture and toss to combine. Serve.

VARIATION

Sweet Potato Salad with Soy Sauce, Sriracha, and Peanuts

Substitute 1 tablespoon soy sauce, 1 tablespoon sriracha, 1 teaspoon sugar, and 1 teaspoon grated fresh ginger for cumin, smoked paprika, pepper, and allspice. Substitute salted dry-roasted peanuts for almonds.

SHOWSTOPPER MELON SALADS

✔ **WHY THIS RECIPE WORKS** Melon salads are ideal hot-weather fare, but they're prone to some common pitfalls: namely, watered-down dressings and garnishes that slide to the bottom of the salad bowl. We set out to make three melon salads, each featuring a different melon: cantaloupe, honeydew, or watermelon. Because melons vary in sweetness, we started by tasting the melons to determine how much honey or sugar to incorporate into our dressings. To counter the abundant water contributed by the melons, we made intense dressings with assertive ingredients, but we skipped the oil, which would only be repelled by the water on the surface of the melon. To avoid watering down the dressing in each salad, we left the melons in large chunks, which freed less juice and accentuated the contrast between the well-seasoned exteriors and the sweet, juicy interiors.

I crave melon in the summer, and it turns out the urge might be physiological: We're drawn to water-rich foods in hot weather because they keep us hydrated and because they require less energy to digest than high-fat or high-protein foods. But after weeks of melon wedges, slices, cubes, and balls, I find myself wanting something more exciting, with a bit more texture and even salty, savory flavors. Enter melon salad.

At its root, it's a pretty old concept. Greeks have been combining watermelon with salty feta cheese for centuries or perhaps millennia, and the pairing is genius: The sweetness of the fruit balances the brininess of the cheese, and the salty, crumbly cheese makes the melon seem even sweeter and more explosively juicy.

Somewhere along the line, cooks began to riff off this concept, pairing melon with all sorts of other salty, savory, and/or creamy ingredients and drizzling the whole thing with oil and vinegar. But these innovations can be problematic. Often the components don't fully meld—or, worse, they overpower the melon—and the dressing can taste watered-down.

My mission was to rethink melon salad to make it more cohesive and balanced and to devise some enticing combinations that could be eaten as refreshing side dishes. I created three salads, each featuring a melon, either cantaloupe, honeydew, or watermelon. In addition to incorporating salty and savory elements into my melon salads, I came up with some best practices. First,

I decided to keep the salads melon-focused. Other sweet, juicy fruits competed with the melon, while additions such as tomatoes and cucumbers were distractingly similar to underripe melon. Leaving the melon in large pieces with fewer cut surfaces meant that less liquid would be exuded to water down the dressing. Larger pieces also accentuated the contrast between the melon's well-seasoned exterior and sweet, juicy interior.

Next, I found it best to keep secondary components small. In my tests, chunky pieces fell to the bottom of the bowl, but smaller ones clung to the melon and held on to the dressing while they did so, ensuring that each piece was coated with flavor and texture.

Finally, for the best flavor, I decided to add some heat, incorporate richness, and brighten the salads with lots of herbal essence. A touch of fresh or dried chile added an interesting dimension to the ripe melons, which—though luscious—lacked zing. Nuts, seeds, cheese, and even olives all worked well to balance the leanness of the fruit. And the fresh, grassy, aromatic flavors of herbs complemented the sweet fruit.

I tied each salad together with an oil-free, citrusy dressing, after finding that oil just slipped off the wet surface of the melons. I crafted dressings that were bright and intense and coated the salad components. I preferred the fruitiness of lemon or lime juice to vinegar, which tasted a little harsh with the melons. Now I had three exciting melon salads to turn to all summer long.

—ANDREA GEARY, *Cook's Illustrated*

Cantaloupe Salad with Olives and Red Onion

SERVES 4 TO 6

Taste your melon as you cut it up: If it's very sweet, omit the honey; if it's less sweet, add the honey to the dressing. We like the gentle heat and raisiny sweetness of ground dried Aleppo pepper here, but if it's unavailable, substitute ¾ teaspoon of paprika and ¼ teaspoon of cayenne pepper. This salad makes a light and refreshing accompaniment to grilled meat or fish and couscous or steamed white rice.

- ½ red onion, sliced thin
- ⅓ cup lemon juice (2 lemons)
- 1–3 teaspoons honey (optional)
- 1 teaspoon ground dried Aleppo pepper
- ½ teaspoon table salt
- 1 cantaloupe, peeled, halved, seeded and cut into 1½-inch chunks (6 cups)
- 5 tablespoons chopped fresh parsley, divided
- 5 tablespoons chopped fresh mint, divided
- ¼ cup finely chopped pitted oil-cured olives, divided

Combine onion and lemon juice in large bowl and let sit for 5 minutes. Stir in honey, if using; Aleppo pepper; and salt. Add cantaloupe, ¼ cup parsley, ¼ cup mint, and 3 tablespoons olives and stir to combine. Transfer to shallow serving bowl. Sprinkle with remaining 1 tablespoon parsley, remaining 1 tablespoon mint, and remaining 1 tablespoon olives and serve.

Honeydew Salad with Peanuts and Lime

SERVES 4 TO 6

Taste your melon as you cut it up: If it's very sweet, omit the sugar; if it's less sweet, add the sugar to the dressing. This salad makes a light and refreshing accompaniment to grilled meat or fish and steamed white rice.

- ⅓ cup lime juice (3 limes)
- 1 shallot, sliced thin
- 2 Thai chiles, stemmed, seeded, and minced
- 1 garlic clove, minced
- ½ teaspoon table salt
- 1–2 tablespoons sugar (optional)
- 1 tablespoon fish sauce
- 1 honeydew melon, peeled, halved, seeded, and cut into 1½-inch chunks (6 cups)
- 5 tablespoons chopped fresh cilantro, divided
- 5 tablespoons chopped fresh mint, divided
- 5 tablespoons salted dry-roasted peanuts, chopped fine, divided

1. Combine lime juice and shallot in large bowl. Using mortar and pestle (or on cutting board using flat side of chef's knife), mash Thai chiles, garlic, and salt to fine paste. Add chile paste; sugar, if using; and fish sauce to lime juice mixture and stir to combine.

2. Add honeydew, ¼ cup cilantro, ¼ cup mint, and ¼ cup peanuts and toss to combine. Transfer to shallow serving bowl. Sprinkle with remaining 1 tablespoon cilantro, remaining 1 tablespoon mint, and remaining 1 tablespoon peanuts and serve.

SHOWSTOPPER MELON SALADS

Watermelon Salad with Cotija and Serrano Chiles

SERVES 4 TO 6

Taste your melon as you cut it up: If it's very sweet, omit the sugar; if it's less sweet, add the sugar to the dressing. Jalapeños can be substituted for the serranos. If cotija cheese is unavailable, substitute feta cheese. This salad makes a light and refreshing accompaniment to grilled meat or fish.

⅓ cup lime juice (3 limes)

2 scallions, white and green parts separated and sliced thin

2 serrano chiles, stemmed, halved, seeded, and sliced thin crosswise

1–2 tablespoons sugar (optional)

¾ teaspoon table salt

6 cups 1½-inch seedless watermelon pieces

3 ounces cotija cheese, crumbled (¾ cup), divided

5 tablespoons chopped fresh cilantro, divided

5 tablespoons chopped roasted, salted pepitas, divided

Combine lime juice, scallion whites, and serranos in large bowl and let sit for 5 minutes. Stir in sugar, if using, and salt. Add watermelon, ½ cup cotija, ¼ cup cilantro, ¼ cup pepitas, and scallion greens and stir to combine. Transfer to shallow serving bowl. Sprinkle with remaining ¼ cup cotija, remaining 1 tablespoon cilantro, and remaining 1 tablespoon pepitas and serve.

CHARRED CHICKEN CAESAR SALAD

✔ **WHY THIS RECIPE WORKS** Skip the old wilted lettuce, stale croutons, and bottled dressing for this mouthwatering charred chicken Caesar salad—straight from your toaster oven. While "toaster oven" and "salad" may not be synonymous, this recipe will convince you otherwise. Crisp, charred romaine lettuce hearts (brushed with a creamy homemade dressing), moist chicken breasts, and garlicky baguette chunks emerge from your toaster oven to give you a hearty and unexpectedly exciting meal. To give our croutons a leg up on anything premade, we tossed cubes of fresh baguette with olive oil and fresh garlic paste before crisping them up in the toaster oven. Baking the boneless, skinless chicken breasts with a simple rub of olive oil, salt, and pepper kept them moist in the 400-degree oven. Finally, whisking up our own creamy dressing and brushing some on the romaine halves before putting them in the oven produced a beautifully charred and deeply satisfying base for our crunchy croutons and warm chicken. A final drizzle of dressing was all we needed to achieve a wonderfully warm and filling charred chicken Caesar salad dinner.

What is it about char? The siren song of summer grilling, stovetop searing, and oven broiling, char can transform familiar favorites—fruits, meats, vegetables, and more—into something altogether otherworldly. Searing heat and a bit of time add countless new dimensions of flavor to foods, along with layers of smokiness, complexity, and textural interest. Here in the test kitchen, we've used char to our advantage in myriad recipes, from Grilled Stone Fruit to Skillet-Charred Green Beans, Homemade Naan, and Char-Grilled Steaks. But charring a salad? That gave me pause. Introducing scorching heat to a defenseless head of leafy, cooling lettuce seemed like a recipe for disaster.

That is, of course, until I tried our recipe for Grilled Caesar Salad. That first recipe, developed by my colleagues at *Cook's Country* a few years back, represents such a delicious blend of flavors and textures that I couldn't help but be instantly smitten when I tried it. The rich, tangy Caesar dressing, with the raw bite of fresh garlic and a burst of bright lemon, perfectly complemented the refreshing, crispy, smoky lettuce, and crunchy grilled croutons added heft and substance to the delicious side dish. Wanting to develop a version that would serve as a meal unto itself, I planned to add chicken into the mix, and I wanted a version that I could make indoors so that I could linger in the world of char and smoky goodness even when summer grilling days were gone. I was already developing a slew of recipes for our *Toaster Oven Perfection* book, so I got to work harnessing the power of that appliance in pursuit of the perfect char.

Knowing that my primary obstacle would be getting the lettuce just right, and wanting to preserve the dish's classic flavor profile, I first whipped up a traditional Caesar dressing, tinkering with the proportions until I struck the right balance of richness (from mayonnaise, olive oil, and grated Parmesan) and acidity (from lemon juice, mustard, and white wine vinegar). Worcestershire sauce and an optional minced anchovy fillet rounded out the dressing with umami complexity. As for the chicken, boneless, skinless chicken breasts were easy to work with and would be simple to slice and plate. Knowing the punchy dressing would do most of the heavy lifting flavorwise, I kept the chicken seasoning simple, adding some olive oil and a bit of salt and pepper before baking the chicken in a 400-degree oven. Baguette pieces tossed with additional olive oil and a paste of minced garlic toasted up crispy, crunchy, and substantial in a matter of minutes, and I could finally turn to the main event: the lettuce.

I started by halving a pair of romaine hearts lengthwise (to reveal the most surface area for browning) and popping them, unadorned, into the still-hot toaster oven. Romaine is traditional in Caesar salad, and its fresh crunch and clean, cooling flavor profile are key in balancing out the richness of the fatty dressing. Compact hearts are sturdier than leafier full heads, and without any loose outer leaves, there would be fewer rogue edges for potential overbrowning. Plus, though I sometimes needed to do a bit of trimming, the smaller hearts were the perfect size for sliding into a toaster oven, and this manageable amount would be just right for a meal serving two people. Unfortunately, my first few attempts revealed something I'd already suspected: Without the benefit of an open flame, charring lettuce in a toaster oven was going to take some work. Even at a high temperature, the cut surface of the romaine took so long to brown that the rest of the leaves and base turned limp, wilted, and rubbery—not exactly the results I was looking for.

So I turned to the toaster oven's most powerful heating source—the broiler. Broiling in a toaster oven actually offers a surprising advantage; because of the oven's smaller size, the cut surfaces of the romaine hearts sit just a few inches from the heating element. With heat primarily emanating from the hot broiler above, I found that I could finally achieve browning on the cut sides of the romaine hearts before the rest of the lettuce cooked through, keeping the hearts crisp and fresh-tasting. However, though I was moving in the right direction, the browning I did get was spotty and inconsistent. I'd need to add something to the surface that would pick up browning more readily and evenly; brushing on a generous swipe of the Caesar dressing did the trick. (Mayonnaise, a key element in the dressing, has been shown to improve Maillard browning, and the milk solids in the Parmesan picked

up a golden-brown color under the hot broiler, too.) With all the elements of my indoor marvel cooked to perfection, all that was left was to assemble the salads on individual plates—with a generous drizzle of the remaining dressing and a sprinkle of Parmesan cheese—and dig in.

—RUSSELL SELANDER, *America's Test Kitchen Books*

Charred Chicken Caesar Salad
SERVES 2

Depending on the size of your baking sheet, you may need to trim the tops of your romaine hearts to fit. The test kitchen's favorite mayonnaises are Blue Plate Real Mayonnaise and Hellmann's Real Mayonnaise.

- 1 (6-inch) piece baguette, cut into ¾-inch pieces
- 3 tablespoons extra-virgin olive oil, divided
- 2 small garlic cloves, minced to paste, divided
- 1 pound boneless, skinless chicken breasts, trimmed
- ½ teaspoon pepper, divided
- ¼ teaspoon table salt
- 3 tablespoons mayonnaise
- 3 tablespoons grated Parmesan cheese, plus extra for serving
- 1½ teaspoons lemon juice
- 1½ teaspoons white wine vinegar
- 1½ teaspoons Worcestershire sauce
- 1½ teaspoons Dijon mustard
- 1 anchovy fillet, rinsed and minced (optional)
- 2 romaine lettuce hearts (6 ounces each), halved lengthwise through cores

1. Adjust toaster oven rack to middle position and heat oven to 400 degrees. Toss baguette pieces, 1 tablespoon oil, and half of garlic together in bowl. Arrange baguette pieces in single layer on small rimmed baking sheet and bake until light golden brown and crisp, 6 to 8 minutes. Transfer croutons to bowl and season with salt and pepper to taste; set aside.

2. Pound thicker end of chicken breasts between 2 sheets of plastic wrap to uniform thickness. Pat chicken dry with paper towels and sprinkle with ¼ teaspoon pepper and salt. Arrange chicken on now-empty sheet and bake until chicken registers 160 degrees, 18 to 23 minutes, flipping halfway through baking. Transfer chicken to cutting board, tent with aluminum foil, and let rest while preparing dressing and lettuce.

3. Wipe sheet clean with paper towels. Select highest broiler function and heat broiler. Whisk mayonnaise; Parmesan; lemon juice; vinegar; Worcestershire; mustard; anchovy, if using; remaining 2 tablespoons oil; remaining garlic; and remaining ¼ teaspoon pepper in bowl until smooth.

4. Brush cut sides of each romaine half with 1 tablespoon dressing. Place romaine cut side up on again-empty sheet and broil until lightly charred, 5 to 7 minutes.

5. Slice chicken thin crosswise. Arrange romaine halves on individual plates and drizzle with remaining dressing. Top with chicken and croutons and sprinkle with extra Parmesan. Serve.

HOW TO COOK WHOLE GRAINS

✔ **WHY THIS RECIPE WORKS** With more varieties of whole grains, such as wheat berries, spelt, and kamut, becoming easier to find at supermarkets, we wanted to create recipes that made these ingredients shine. We started by figuring out the right cooking method. Grains are typically cooked using either the pilaf method—simmering a measured amount of grain in a measured amount of water—or the pasta method—boiling the grains in water and then draining them. After some tests, we found the pasta method more consistent. With the cooking method down, we developed a couple of salads and a side dish featuring various whole grains.

Wide selections of whole grains, including wheat berries, spelt, and kamut, are becoming more available at supermarkets and online—and that's great news for cooks. Whole grains, or grains that have been minimally processed and still contain their bran and germ, are a livelier (and more nutritious) alternative to rice or pasta, lending a satisfying chew and earthy, nutty depth to casseroles, soups, and sides. Keep a stash of them on hand, and you'll have a wholesome base for countless dishes. I selected nine varieties of hearty grains and got to work to find a simple cooking method that would suit them all.

Whole-grain cookery typically falls into two categories: the pilaf method and the pasta method. The former calls for simmering a measured amount of grain in a specific amount of water in a covered pot until the water is absorbed and the grains are tender; the latter involves boiling the grains in an abundance of water that is later drained off.

I quickly discovered that the pilaf method was frustratingly inconsistent: It worked well for shorter-cooking choices such as einkorn, but longer-cooking grains such as triticale turned out uneven. Because the kernels soaked up most of the liquid early in the cooking process, only those that fully hydrated at the start softened completely, while those that didn't initially absorb enough liquid remained firm.

The pasta method offered significant improvements. With 2 quarts of boiling salted water in the pot, the liquid could penetrate the grains evenly from all sides, softening them uniformly. Plus, since the large volume of water allowed the grains to absorb water more readily than the small amount of water used in the pilaf method, these grains cooked faster. And for even speedier results, a pressure cooker is the way to go: Using one reduced the cooking times by at least 50 percent.

One more thing: If you have the time (and the forethought), it's a good idea to soak the raw kernels overnight. In addition to speeding up the cooking time, this step helps prevent blowouts. A bag of grains is likely to contain kernels with different moisture levels, and soaking equalizes the amount of liquid in each grain, so they stay intact during cooking.

With cooked grains on hand, it was easy to come up with a couple of interesting salads and a hearty side dish where their earthy, nutty flavors could shine.

—KEITH DRESSER, *Cook's Illustrated*

Warm Wheat Berry Salad with Radicchio, Dried Cherries, and Pecans
SERVES 4 TO 6

Soaking the wheat berries in water overnight will shorten the cooking time to 45 minutes to 1 hour. If using refrigerated grains, let them come to room temperature before making the salad. Any variety of radicchio can be used.

WARM WHEAT BERRY SALAD WITH RADICCHIO, DRIED CHERRIES, AND PECANS

GUIDE TO WHOLE GRAIN COOKERY

This chart contains all you need to know to cook some of our favorite hearty whole grains. The grains featured here are largely interchangeable—while we've provided recommendations in the accompanying recipes, feel free to swap in whichever grain you may have on hand. The recipes can be scaled up by increasing the amounts proportionally. The cooking times will remain the same. Note that pressure cooking is not recommended for einkorn and soaked emmer, as they cook too quickly.

STOVETOP METHOD: Rinse and drain grains before cooking. Bring 2 quarts water to boil in large saucepan. Stir in 1 cup of grain and 2 teaspoons table salt. Return to boil, reduce heat, and gently boil until tender, following times given. Drain well. Spread on rimmed baking sheet and let cool for at least 15 minutes before using.

PRESSURE COOKER METHOD: Rinse and drain grains before cooking. Combine 1 cup grains with 1 quart water, 1 tablespoon vegetable oil (this helps prevent foaming), and 1 teaspoon table salt. Bring to high pressure over high heat. Reduce heat to maintain high pressure and cook following times given.

Remove from heat and allow pressure to drop naturally, about 10 minutes. Check for doneness. If grains are still firm, return to a simmer and cook until tender. Drain well. Spread on rimmed baking sheet and let cool for at least 15 minutes before using.

STORAGE: Store raw grains in the freezer. Cooked grains can be refrigerated for up to two days or frozen for up to three months.

SOAKING (OPTIONAL, REDUCES COOKING TIME): Cover the grains with water and soak for at least 8 hours at room temperature.

Grain		Stovetop, Unsoaked	Stovetop, Soaked	Pressure Cooker, Unsoaked	Pressure Cooker, Soaked	Yield
	Einkorn (Farro Piccolo)	20–35 minutes	15–20 minutes	–	–	2½ cups
	Emmer (Farro Medio)	30–45 minutes	20–30 minutes	8 minutes	–	2½ cups
	Spelt (Farro Grande)	50–65 minutes	35–50 minutes	27 minutes	18 minutes	2¾ cups
	Hulled Barley	50–65 minutes	35–50 minutes	22 minutes	13 minutes	2¾ cups
	Rye	50–70 minutes	40–55 minutes	25 minutes	15 minutes	2¾ cups
	Triticale	45–60 minutes	40–55 minutes	26 minutes	18 minutes	2¾ cups
	Oat Berries	35–50 minutes	25–40 minutes	25 minutes	17 minutes	2½ cups
	Wheat Berries	60–80 minutes	45–60 minutes	31 minutes	20 minutes	2¾ cups
	Kamut (Khorasan)	55–75 minutes	35–50 minutes	25 minutes	15 minutes	2¾ cups

COOKING TIMES

1 cup wheat berries, rinsed and drained

½ teaspoon table salt, plus salt for cooking wheat berries

3 tablespoons extra-virgin olive oil

2 tablespoons red wine vinegar

1 small shallot, minced

½ teaspoon pepper

1 cup chopped Chioggia radicchio

1 cup loosely packed fresh parsley leaves

½ cup pecans, toasted and chopped coarse, divided

¼ cup dried cherries

1 ounce blue cheese, crumbled (¼ cup)

1. Bring 2 quarts water to boil in large saucepan. Stir in wheat berries and 2 teaspoons salt. Return to boil; reduce heat; and simmer until tender, 1 hour to 1 hour 20 minutes. Drain well. Spread on rimmed baking sheet and let cool for at least 15 minutes (wheat berries can be refrigerated in airtight container for up to 2 days).

2. Whisk oil, vinegar, shallot, pepper, and salt together in large bowl. Add wheat berries, radicchio, parsley, half of pecans, and cherries to dressing and toss to combine. Season with salt and pepper to taste and transfer to serving bowl. Sprinkle salad with blue cheese and remaining pecans. Serve.

Warm Spelt Salad with Pickled Fennel, Pea Greens, and Mint

SERVES 4 TO 6

Soaking the spelt in water overnight will shorten the cooking time to 35 to 50 minutes. If using refrigerated grains, let them come to room temperature before making the salad. Pea tendrils are also called pea greens or pea shoots. Watercress can be used in place of the pea tendrils. Pickle the fennel while cooking the spelt. The fennel can be pickled up to three days in advance and stored in an airtight container in the refrigerator.

1 cup spelt, rinsed and drained

½ teaspoon table salt, divided, plus salt for cooking spelt

⅓ cup cider vinegar

2 tablespoons sugar

1 small fennel bulb, 1 tablespoon fronds minced, stalks discarded, bulb halved, cored, and sliced thin

3 tablespoons extra-virgin olive oil

2 tablespoons lemon juice

1 small shallot, minced

¼ teaspoon pepper

2 ounces pea tendrils, torn into bite-size pieces (2 cups)

¼ cup torn fresh mint

1 ounce feta cheese, crumbled (¼ cup)

1. Bring 2 quarts water to boil in large saucepan. Stir in spelt and 2 teaspoons salt. Return to boil; reduce heat; and simmer until tender, 50 minutes to 1 hour 5 minutes. Drain well. Spread on rimmed baking sheet and let cool for at least 15 minutes (spelt can be refrigerated in airtight container for up to 2 days).

2. Bring vinegar, sugar, and ¼ teaspoon salt to simmer in small saucepan over medium-high heat, stirring occasionally, until sugar dissolves. Off heat, add fennel pieces and stir to combine. Cover and let cool completely, about 30 minutes. Drain and discard liquid.

3. Whisk oil, lemon juice, shallot, pepper, and remaining ¼ teaspoon salt together in large bowl. Add pea tendrils, mint, fennel fronds, spelt, and ½ cup pickled fennel (reserve remaining pickled fennel for another use) to dressing and toss to combine. Season with salt and pepper to taste and transfer to serving bowl. Sprinkle salad with feta and serve.

Warm Kamut with Carrots and Pomegranate

SERVES 4 TO 6

Soaking the kamut in water overnight will shorten the cooking time to 35 to 50 minutes. Kamut is also sold as khorasan wheat. Serve as a side dish with meat or poultry.

1 cup kamut, rinsed and drained

¼ teaspoon table salt, plus salt for cooking kamut

2 tablespoons vegetable oil

2 carrots, peeled and cut into ¼-inch pieces

2 garlic cloves, minced

¾ teaspoon garam masala

¼ cup pistachios, toasted and chopped coarse, divided

3 tablespoons chopped fresh cilantro, divided

1 teaspoon lemon juice

¼ cup pomegranate seeds

1. Bring 2 quarts water to boil in large saucepan. Stir in kamut and 2 teaspoons salt. Return to boil; reduce heat; and simmer until tender, 55 minutes to 1¼ hours. Drain well. Spread on rimmed baking sheet and let cool for at least 15 minutes (kamut can be refrigerated in airtight container for up to 2 days).

SKORDALIA (GREEK GARLIC-POTATO PUREE)

2. Heat oil in 12-inch skillet over medium heat until shimmering. Add carrots and salt and cook, stirring frequently, until carrots are softened and lightly browned, 4 to 6 minutes. Add garlic and garam masala and cook, stirring constantly, until fragrant, about 1 minute. Add kamut and cook until warmed through, 2 to 5 minutes. Off heat, stir in half of pistachios, 2 tablespoons cilantro, and lemon juice. Season with salt and pepper to taste. Transfer to serving bowl and sprinkle with pomegranate seeds, remaining pistachios, and remaining 1 tablespoon cilantro. Serve.

SKORDALIA (GREEK GARLIC-POTATO PUREE)

✔ WHY THIS RECIPE WORKS Skordalia is meant to be a bold condiment, but we didn't want the garlic flavor to be fiery. We tempered the bite of the garlic by soaking it in acidic lemon juice for 10 minutes to neutralize its alliinase, the enzyme that creates garlic's harsh flavor. Choosing an all-potato base rather than oft-used day-old bread helped achieve the smooth, spreadable texture that we sought. Sliced almonds not only added a touch of earthy sweetness but also contributed richness for a puree that was luxuriously dense and creamy. Whizzing all the ingredients except the potato in the blender produced a smooth, emulsified puree, and adding more water and lemon juice than many recipes call for yielded a puree that remained spreadable and dippable even when it cooled to room temperature.

Most countries along the Mediterranean enjoy a robust garlic sauce as part of their cuisine. The French and Spanish have aioli and allioli, respectively; the Lebanese have toum; and the Turks, tarator. But of all the great garlic sauces throughout Western cultures, the Greek contribution to this lineup, skordalia, might be the most versatile.

It's cobbled together from the simplest of ingredients: Start with a starchy base of riced boiled potatoes or day-old bread soaked in liquid (ground nuts are sometimes added, too). Add fresh lemon juice (or wine vinegar) and a liberal amount of minced raw garlic, and then vigorously whisk in extra-virgin olive oil until an emulsion forms. The resulting blend, with a heady aroma and fresh acidity, is used in myriad ways, making it an irreplaceable fixture of Greek cookery.

In crafting my own take on skordalia, I would need to determine the intensity of garlic flavor I wanted, as well as the consistency of the mixture, since both vary a good deal. After trying a handful of published recipes, I went after a well-rounded, bold, and bright garlic profile—nothing fiery or overpowering. To temper the bite of the garlic, I briefly steeped the minced cloves in lemon juice, since the acid in the juice deactivates alliinase, the enzyme that creates garlic's harsh notes. Just a 10-minute soak in the lemon juice cushioned some of the garlic's sharpness while maintaining its underlying gutsiness.

The consistency of skordalia ranges from thin and silky to thick and chunky. I preferred a texture suitable for dipping (along the lines of hummus) and found that using earthy russet potatoes rather than bread worked best. I also added some water to loosen the mixture a bit. When I experimented with nuts (almonds and walnuts are common), I liked the richness they contributed, making the dip creamier and denser. I settled on almonds, as I preferred the ivory color of the dip made with the paler nuts.

Following the lead of a modern-day recipe from Boston-area chef and restaurateur Ana Sortun, making the skordalia couldn't have been easier: Instead of emulsifying the mixture by hand, I whizzed the olive oil, sliced almonds, lemon-soaked garlic, some lemon zest (to double down on the citrusy notes), water, and salt in the blender. Once the mixture was thick and creamy, I folded it into freshly boiled and riced potatoes to yield a vibrant, luxuriously smooth puree (adding the potatoes to the blender would burst their swollen starch granules, which would form a sticky gel and create a gluey mess). Served warm, as is common, the skordalia had a consistency that worked well as both a dip and a spread. But as it cooled to room temperature, as it's also frequently served, everything changed. At that point, it became barely spreadable.

It turned out that the mixture was underhydrated, so over time the starch in the potatoes and the soluble proteins in the nuts (almonds are particularly high in these proteins) continued to absorb water until the puree seized up. To achieve a workable viscosity, I slowly lowered the amounts of potato and oil while increasing the water and lemon juice until I had a dip with a hummus-like consistency, no matter the temperature. Here was a skordalia that could proudly grace any table.

—STEVE DUNN, *Cook's Illustrated*

Skordalia (Greek Garlic-Potato Puree)

SERVES 8 TO 10 (MAKES 2 CUPS)

You'll need a blender for this recipe. To make a puree with the smoothest texture, you'll need a potato ricer or food mill equipped with a fine disk; if these aren't available, you can mash the potato thoroughly with a potato masher, but the dip will have a more rustic texture. We prefer a russet potato for its earthier flavor, but a Yukon Gold works well, too. If a single large potato is unavailable, it's fine to use two smaller potatoes that total 12 ounces. You can use either blanched or skin-on almonds. A rasp-style grater makes quick work of turning the garlic into a paste. Serve as a dip with crudités, spread on crackers or bread, or as an accompaniment to fish or meat.

- 1 large russet potato (12 ounces), peeled and sliced ½ inch thick
- 4 garlic cloves, peeled
- 2 teaspoons grated lemon zest plus ¼ cup juice (2 lemons)
- ⅔ cup sliced almonds
- ½ cup extra-virgin olive oil, plus extra for drizzling
- ¾ teaspoon table salt
- 2 teaspoons minced fresh chives or parsley

1. Place potato in medium saucepan and add cold water to cover by 1 inch. Bring to boil over high heat. Adjust heat to maintain simmer and cook until paring knife can be easily slipped into and out of potato, 18 to 22 minutes.

2. While potato cooks, mince garlic to fine paste. Transfer 1 tablespoon garlic paste to small bowl; discard remaining garlic paste. Combine lemon juice with garlic paste and let sit for 10 minutes.

3. Process garlic mixture, lemon zest, almonds, oil, ½ cup water, and salt in blender until very smooth, about 45 seconds.

4. Drain potato. Set ricer or food mill over medium bowl. Working in batches, transfer hot potato to hopper and process. Stir garlic mixture into potato until smooth. Season with salt and pepper to taste and transfer to serving bowl. Drizzle with extra oil and sprinkle with chives. Serve warm or at room temperature. (Skordalia can be refrigerated for up to 3 days. Let sit, covered, at room temperature for 30 minutes before serving.)

SMOKED SALMON DIP

WHY THIS RECIPE WORKS For a well-rounded dip that could be enjoyed anytime, we balanced the flavors of rich smoked salmon with complementary ingredients. To create a cohesive and easily scoopable dip, we started with softened cream cheese; added smoked salmon, lemon zest and juice, and pepper; and blended them all in a food processor until the mixture was smooth. In just 30 seconds, we had a flavor-packed, scoopable dip that was ready for an array of flavorful toppings that really made it sing: briny, pungent capers; fresh dill; and a bit of minced shallot, which had just enough oniony flavor but not too much. We drizzled extra-virgin olive oil on top to smooth out the texture and tie the dip together.

I love a fully loaded bagel on a weekend morning. I'm talking a schmear of cream cheese, smoked salmon, sliced onions, briny capers, fresh dill—the whole nine yards. It's a perfect combination of flavors, so I wanted to bring it to cocktail hour, too. I set my sights on a dip that would highlight the subtle sweet and smoky flavors of the salmon, with a boost from a few complementary ingredients.

I started with an 8-ounce block of chilled cream cheese, which I cut into eight pieces. Then, in the food processor, I layered 4 ounces of smoked salmon on top of the cream cheese, added lemon zest and juice, and seasoned it with a twist of freshly ground black pepper (because smoked salmon is already salted, there was no need to add more salt here). The lemon helped cut the richness of the fatty salmon and cream cheese without disguising their flavors.

NOTES FROM THE TEST KITCHEN

SAUCE, DIP, OR SPREAD?
Skordalia is as all-purpose as a condiment gets. Its consistency can range from mashed-potato thick to mayonnaise-like depending on the ratio of binders to liquid in the mix, and its goes-with-everything flavor profile makes it endlessly useful in Greek cuisine. Garlic-forward, bright with lemon, rich, and smooth, it's just the thing to spread on pita, scoop up with crudités, or serve alongside fried fish or grilled meat or vegetables.

SMOKED SALMON DIP

But my dip wasn't dippable: Crackers kept breaking in half. What's more, the lemon and smoked salmon weren't evenly distributed. So I decided to start with softened cream cheese, which meant taking it out of the refrigerator 30 minutes before processing it (or microwaving it—out of the foil package—for 20 to 30 seconds). This gave me a much more cohesive and easily scoopable dip that was ready for an array of flavorful toppings.

Briny, pungent capers and chopped fresh dill were definitely in, but the raw red onion was overwhelming the other flavors in the dip. After a few taste tests, I found the delicate flavor of a shallot—which contributed the perfect amount of oniony flavor—to be less harsh and more appealing. A finishing drizzle of extra-virgin olive oil helped smooth out the texture and tied everything together.

—AMANDA LUCHTEL, *Cook's Country*

Smoked Salmon Dip
SERVES 4 TO 6 (MAKES ABOUT 1½ CUPS)

To soften the cream cheese quickly, microwave it in a large bowl for 20 to 30 seconds. This recipe can easily be doubled. Serve the dip with cucumber slices, crackers, toasted baguette, and/or our Bagel Chips (recipe follows).

- 8 ounces cream cheese, cut into 8 pieces and softened
- 4 ounces smoked salmon
- 1 teaspoon grated lemon zest plus 1 tablespoon juice
- ¼ teaspoon pepper
- 1 tablespoon minced shallot
- 1 tablespoon capers, rinsed
- 1 tablespoon coarsely chopped fresh dill
- 1 tablespoon extra-virgin olive oil

1. Process cream cheese, salmon, lemon zest and juice, and pepper in food processor until smooth, about 30 seconds, scraping down sides of bowl as needed. Transfer to serving dish and spread into even layer.

2. Sprinkle with shallot, capers, and dill. Drizzle with oil and serve.

TO MAKE AHEAD: Dip can be made through step 1, covered with plastic wrap, and refrigerated for up to 3 days. Let come to room temperature before proceeding with step 2.

Bagel Chips
SERVES 4 TO 6

Any type of savory bagel can be used in this recipe. Look for unsliced bagels, which are often available in the bakery section of the grocery store. This recipe can easily be doubled; to do so, divide the slices between two baking sheets and bake one sheet at a time.

- 2 (4- to 5-inch) bagels
- ¼ cup extra-virgin olive oil, divided
- ¼ teaspoon kosher salt, divided

1. Adjust oven rack to middle position and heat oven to 350 degrees. Place bagels on cutting board. Using serrated knife, slice bagels vertically, ¼ inch thick (slices will vary in length). Cut any slices that barely hang together in center (from bagel's hole) in half.

2. Spread slices in single layer on rimmed baking sheet. Brush tops with 2 tablespoons oil and sprinkle with ⅛ teaspoon salt. Flip slices and repeat brushing and sprinkling on second side with remaining 2 tablespoons oil and remaining ⅛ teaspoon salt.

3. Bake until crisp and light golden brown, 13 to 17 minutes. Let cool on sheet for 5 minutes. Serve. (Chips can be stored in airtight container for up to 3 days.)

PAJEON (KOREAN SCALLION PANCAKE)

✓ **WHY THIS RECIPE WORKS** Pajeon, a Korean scallion pancake, is a cheap, quick-to-make snack that comes together with pantry ingredients and loads of scallions and suits any occasion. Our dry mix starts with all-purpose flour and potato starch, a pure starch that equips the batter with more material for crisping up; its unique chemical makeup also helps keep the starch molecules separate after cooling so that the crust stays crisp. Using ice water in the batter minimized the hydration of the starches, thus allowing the batter to dry out and crisp more easily during frying. A little baking soda raised the pH of the batter and boosted browning; pressing the pancake against the skillet after flipping it also encouraged color development. Adding baking powder to the batter opened up the crumb so that it was pleasantly dense and moist, not gummy. We used about five scallions per pancake and cut them into

2-inch lengths so that they formed a nest-like structure glued together by the viscous batter. A combination of soy sauce, rice vinegar, and sugar made for a savory, tart, faintly sweet condiment that complemented the heartiness of the pancake. A little gochugaru and sesame oil added heat and nutty depth, respectively.

Pajeon, Korea's ubiquitous scallion pancake, strikes that ideal balance between pragmatism and sheer pleasure. One of the simplest and most popular forms of jeon, a broader term for battered and pan-fried foods, it's cheap and quick to make by mixing up a flour-and-water-based batter, loading it up with scallions, and pan-frying it into one big round. The filling-to-batter ratio is high, and the scallions are typically cut into lengths, so the effect is a nest of verdant stalks glued together by a viscous batter. As it sizzles in a well-oiled skillet, the pancake crisps and browns and the interior sets up soft and dense, with—as Beverly Kim, chef and co-owner of Parachute, an acclaimed Korean American restaurant in Chicago, described—"mochi-like" chew. It's a no-fuss, substantial snack that's best eaten right off the pan with a soy sauce–based dipping sauce.

"It's very comforting food, and it can be for any occasion," said Nanam Myszka, a Seoul native who co-owns Epiphany Farms Hospitality Group in Bloomington, Illinois. Pajeon can be celebratory fare for festive occasions such as weddings or Chuseok, the annual autumn harvest festival, or a clean-out-the-fridge preparation that uses up scallions and any other vegetables, meat or seafood, or kimchi. Most delightfully, it's a popular snack to make on rainy days.

Given how regularly Koreans eat pajeon, many households stock buchim garu, a just-add-water seasoned pancake mix that's widely sold in Korean markets. Some cooks combine that with twuigim garu, a mix that also requires nothing but water and is primarily used to coat food for frying (its relatively high proportion of pure starch helps it boost crispness). But both products contain mostly pantry ingredients (flours, starch, leaveners), so plenty of cooks make their own batter. That route appealed to me: I was a chemist before I was a cook, so sorting out formulas is right up my alley. Plus, I don't usually have the commercial stuff on hand but wanted the option to whip up pajeon any time the mood (or the occasion, or the weather) strikes.

My first batters were basic: equal parts all-purpose flour and water, salt, and a little sugar to encourage browning. I made enough of it to produce two large pancakes, and it was quite thick, so I used a rubber spatula to fold in 10 scallions that I'd cut into 2-inch lengths. Then I dragged the spatula blade down the middle of the bowl and scraped half the batter into a hot skillet that I'd coated with oil, spreading the batter into an evenly thick round that stopped an inch or so short of the sides to give me room to flip it. Over the next few minutes, I shook the pan periodically so that the oil spread evenly beneath the pancake and encouraged browning and watched for the surface bubbles in the center to burst—the visual cue that it was time to flip, according to recipes I'd seen. As soon as I turned the pancake, I added more oil to the pan and pressed the pancake against it to help crisp and brown the second side and then drained it on a paper towel while I cooked off the rest of the batter.

I knew I'd be able to gauge the crispness of the pancake by the sound it made when I pushed the knife through the crust—and when I heard almost nothing, it was clear that this batch lacked interior-exterior contrast. So I reread the commercial pancake and frying mix labels to see what I might be missing.

NOTES FROM THE TEST KITCHEN

PAJEON: A RECIPE FOR A RAINY DAY

South Koreans have never needed a good excuse to eat pajeon, but everyone seems to have one. Most notably: rain.

"Whenever it's a rainy day, people say, 'Oh, this is time to eat pajeon and makgeolli,'" Nanam Myszka said of the cuisine's popular scallion pancake. "My mom will say it, my grandma will say it."

Myszka, who grew up in Seoul and co-owns Epiphany Farms Hospitality Group with her husband, Ken, in Bloomington, Illinois, explained that the association is about sound: The sputter and sizzle of the pajeon batter crisping in oil echoes the light, rhythmic tapping of rainfall—and in a part of the world that experiences significant precipitation, the response is downright Pavlovian. Sales of pancake ingredients and makgeolli, the so-called farmer's liquor made from fermented rice, reportedly surge, and crowds flood pajeon shops.

There are other inclement weather–related associations, too, such as the theory that flour-based foods boost serotonin and blood sugar during gloomy, low-pressure spells, and the popular tale of Korean farmers who once fried up jeon when it was too rainy to work in the fields. The ingredients were accessible, and the crispy, glutinously chewy sustenance was just the thing to eat with cheap, milky makgeolli.

PAJEON (KOREAN SCALLION PANCAKES)

The most glaring omission was a second starch—corn or potato. I tried both, and each made the pancakes more crisp. The potato starch batch, though, was exceptionally good. The unique chemical makeup of potato starch helps keep the starch molecules separate after cooling, so the crust stays crisp.

I also added both baking soda and baking powder to the batter. The powder appears in most commercial mixes, opening up the crumb so that the texture is pleasantly glutinous—but not gummy. The soda, a less common addition, was there to boost browning, which occurs most readily in high pH (basic) environments.

There were a couple other tips that I picked up from the commercial mix labels and anecdotally. The first was adding minced garlic and pepper to the batter to give it more complexity and to underscore the scallions' allium-ness. The second was using cold water to make the pancakes more crisp. Won Chung, Kim's nephew and a chef at the Michelin-rated Onjium in Seoul, said that some cooks actually add ice. Kim said her mother would even chop and add still-frozen shellfish to her haemul (seafood) pajeon batter to keep it cold.

Here's why: Fried foods crisp when their starch molecules absorb water; form a gel; and then eject that water as steam during frying, leaving behind an open, dry matrix. The trick is getting the starch to absorb the right amount of water: enough to create a gel but not so much that the gel is too dense and sodden to lose its moisture during frying. Using cold water helps because starch absorbs it relatively slowly, meaning there's less gel formation and less water to force out.

I ran a side-by-side test just to confirm that a cold-water batter makes a noticeable difference to the pancakes' texture (it does). Along the way, I also heeded advice from Kim, Chung, and others to carefully monitor the temperature of the pan.

"Because you are cooking in such a hot pan," said Chung, "the pajeon can burn. But if you make the mistake of turning down the heat too much, the pancake has a tendency to become oily."

That made sense: Starchy batters fried at relatively low temperatures turn greasy because the water they contain doesn't get hot enough to forcefully blow off steam, repel the oil, and prevent it from seeping in. So what I needed to do was keep the oil at a gentle sizzle, adjusting the heat as needed to keep it hot but just shy of smoking. As long as I did that, the pancakes cooked up evenly brown and crisp.

After that, I just needed to work out the dipping sauce: a soy sauce–based concoction that should be savory and tart, with just a hint of sweetness. I thinned mine with a little water and stirred in rice vinegar and a bit of sugar, as well as gochugaru and toasted sesame oil for a backdrop of heat and nutty depth. It soaked into the crisp-chewy, oniony pancake wedges that I'd cut from the communal disk, and the effect was sheer pleasure.

—ANDREW JANJIGIAN, *Cook's Illustrated*

NOTES FROM THE TEST KITCHEN

HOW TO BROWN AND CRISP PAJEON

1. Spread batter into evenly thick 8-inch round, making sure scallions are distributed in single layer.

2. Shake skillet to distribute oil beneath pancake. Cook, adjusting heat to maintain gentle sizzle, until underside is golden brown, 3 to 5 minutes.

3. Flip pancake and press firmly into skillet with back of spatula to flatten. Add 1 tablespoon oil to edges of skillet and continue to cook pancake.

4. Press pancake occasionally to flatten, until second side is spotty golden brown, 2 to 4 minutes.

Pajeon (Korean Scallion Pancakes)

SERVES 4

Be sure to purchase the coarse variety of gochugaru (Korean chile flakes), which is sometimes labeled "coarse powder." Use a full teaspoon if you prefer a spicier dipping sauce. If gochugaru is unavailable, substitute ⅛ to ¼ teaspoon of red pepper flakes. Potato starch is available at Asian markets and some supermarkets; we like the crisp exterior that it produces in these pancakes, but you can substitute cornstarch.

SAUCE

- 2 tablespoons soy sauce
- 1 tablespoon water
- 2 teaspoons unseasoned rice vinegar
- 1 teaspoon toasted sesame oil
- ½–1 teaspoon gochugaru
- ½ teaspoon sugar

PANCAKES

- 10 scallions
- 1 cup (5 ounces) all-purpose flour
- ¼ cup potato starch
- 1 teaspoon sugar
- 1 teaspoon baking powder
- ¼ teaspoon baking soda
- ½ teaspoon pepper
- ¼ teaspoon table salt
- 1 cup ice water
- 2 garlic cloves, minced
- 6 tablespoons vegetable oil, divided

1. FOR THE SAUCE: Whisk all ingredients together in small bowl; set aside.

2. FOR THE PANCAKES: Line large plate with double layer of paper towels and set aside. Separate green tops of scallions from white and light green parts. Halve white and light green parts lengthwise. Cut all scallion parts into 2-inch lengths and set aside. Whisk flour, potato starch, sugar, baking powder, baking soda, pepper, and salt together in medium bowl. Add ice water and garlic and whisk until smooth. Using rubber spatula, fold in scallions until mixture is evenly combined.

3. Heat 2 tablespoons oil in 10-inch nonstick or carbon-steel skillet over medium-high heat until just smoking. Stir batter to recombine. Run blade of spatula through center of batter to halve and scrape half of batter into center of skillet. Spread into 8-inch round of even thickness, using spatula or tongs to move scallions so they are evenly distributed in single layer. Shake skillet to distribute oil beneath pancake and cook, adjusting heat as needed to maintain gentle sizzle (reduce heat if oil begins to smoke), until bubbles at center of pancake burst and leave holes in surface and underside is golden brown, 3 to 5 minutes. Flip pancake and press firmly into skillet with back of spatula to flatten. Add 1 tablespoon oil to edges of skillet and continue to cook, pressing pancake occasionally to flatten, until second side is spotty golden brown, 2 to 4 minutes longer. Transfer to prepared plate.

4. Repeat with remaining 3 tablespoons oil and remaining batter. Drain second pancake on prepared plate for 2 minutes. Cut each pancake into 6 wedges and transfer to platter. Serve, passing sauce separately.

CRISPY FRIED SHRIMP

✔ WHY THIS RECIPE WORKS Our goal for these fried shrimp was perfectly seasoned, crispy, tender morsels with an irresistible dipping sauce. Because shrimp can overcook quickly, we chose to use extra-large shrimp (21 to 25 per pound), which could withstand enough time in the hot oil for the crispy coating to get good browning. After peeling and deveining enough shrimp for four people (leaving the tails on contributed to a nice look and provided a handle for dipping), we seasoned them with salt, pepper, granulated garlic, and cayenne to ensure that the finished product would be thoroughly flavorful inside and out. For a breading that would adhere perfectly to the shrimp and get golden and crispy quickly, we dipped the seasoned shrimp in a light batter of seasoned flour, egg, and water and then into ultracrispy panko bread crumbs. A brief stint in the fridge while our oil heated up got the shrimp nice and cold, providing further insurance against overcooking. While we heated 6 cups of oil to 350 degrees (the minimum temperature we needed to ensure that it didn't drop too low when we added the shrimp), we put together the sauce. Combining ketchup and horseradish with mayo, Worcestershire, lemon juice, cayenne, and Old Bay seasoning created a delectable spicy-creamy hybrid of the classic cocktail and tartar sauces that are typically served with fried shrimp.

CRISPY FRIED SHRIMP

I have a list of must-haves when it comes to fried shrimp: shrimp that are tender and juicy (not rubbery and overcooked), a coating that comes out of the fryer crispy (not soggy or greasy) and stays that way until the last shrimp is gone, and a sauce so good that I can't stop myself from dipping.

That's exactly what I was after when I set out to develop my own fried shrimp recipe. First, I focused on the shrimp themselves. Since shrimp cook so quickly, I knew that I'd need to use large specimens that wouldn't overcook in the hot oil before the breading could get crispy and golden brown. I opted for extra-large shrimp (21 to 25 per pound), since they're more common and slightly less expensive per pound than jumbo.

I peeled and deveined enough for four hungry people, leaving the tails on the shrimp because I like how they look and I enjoy using the tail as a little handle for dipping the shrimp into sauce. Then I patted the shrimp dry and seasoned them with my go-to mix of salt, pepper, granulated garlic, and cayenne pepper.

Next, I needed a breading that would get crispy and golden brown quickly. When I tried frying shrimp that I'd coated using a typical three-step breading process—dipping them into flour, then beaten egg, and then flour again—the coating was soggy and still pale when the shrimp finished cooking. Instead, I combined the egg and seasoned flour (plus a little water) into a light batter, and then I reached for supercrispy panko bread crumbs.

I grabbed the shrimp by their tails and dipped them first into the batter and then into the panko, which clung beautifully to the sticky batter. Once the shrimp were all breaded, I popped them into the refrigerator to make sure that they'd be cold when I put them in the hot oil, one more safeguard against overcooked shrimp. While I heated 6 cups of oil to 350 degrees, I put together my sauce.

Fried shrimp served in restaurants typically come with cocktail sauce and tartar sauce. I always dip my shrimp in both sauces, so I decided to make a hybrid of the two. I did so by combining ketchup and horseradish with mayonnaise, Worcestershire sauce, lemon juice, cayenne, and Old Bay seasoning. Delicious—especially when hugging a hot, crispy, perfectly tender fried shrimp.

—MATTHEW FAIRMAN, *Cook's Country*

NOTES FROM THE TEST KITCHEN

WHAT DOES "EXTRA-LARGE" MEAN?

Shrimp are sorted by size, specifically by how many of a specific size make a pound. We call for extra-large shrimp here, which are known as "21-25s" because 21 to 25 of them make 1 pound. Jumbo shrimp (16-20s) will also work in this recipe.

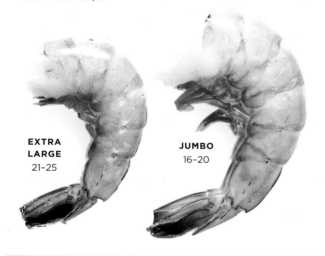

EXTRA LARGE
21–25

JUMBO
16–20

Crispy Fried Shrimp

SERVES 4 TO 6

For this recipe, we like using extra-large shrimp (21 to 25 per pound), but jumbo shrimp (16 to 20 per pound) will also work. We prefer untreated shrimp—those not treated with sodium or additives such as sodium tripolyphosphate (STPP). Most frozen E-Z peel shrimp have been treated (the ingredient list should tell you). If you're using treated shrimp, reduce the salt sprinkled on the shrimp in step 3 to ¼ teaspoon. Use a Dutch oven that holds 6 quarts or more. The test kitchen's favorite panko bread crumbs are Kikkoman Panko Japanese Style Bread Crumbs. Serve the shrimp with lemon wedges.

SAUCE

- ½ cup ketchup
- ½ cup mayonnaise
- ¼ cup prepared horseradish
- 2 teaspoons Worcestershire sauce
- 1 teaspoon lemon juice
- ½ teaspoon Old Bay seasoning
- ½ teaspoon cayenne pepper

SHRIMP

½ cup all-purpose flour

½ cup water

2 large eggs

1¼ teaspoons table salt, divided

½ teaspoon pepper, divided

2 cups panko bread crumbs

1 teaspoon granulated garlic

¼ teaspoon cayenne pepper

1½ pounds extra-large shrimp (21 to 25 per pound), peeled, deveined, and tails left on

1½ quarts vegetable oil for frying

1. FOR THE SAUCE: Whisk all ingredients in bowl until combined; set aside.

2. FOR THE SHRIMP: Whisk flour, water, eggs, ½ teaspoon salt, and ¼ teaspoon pepper in bowl until no lumps remain. Spread panko in shallow dish.

3. Combine granulated garlic, cayenne, remaining ¾ teaspoon salt, and remaining ¼ teaspoon pepper in small bowl. Pat shrimp dry with paper towels and sprinkle with spice mixture.

4. Working with 1 shrimp at a time, hold shrimp by tail and dip into batter, letting excess drip back into bowl, then coat with panko, pressing gently to adhere. Arrange breaded shrimp on rimmed baking sheet. Refrigerate while heating oil (breaded shrimp can be refrigerated for up to 2 hours).

5. Line platter with triple layer of paper towels. Add oil to large Dutch oven until it measures about 1 inch deep and heat over medium-high heat to 350 degrees. Add one-third of shrimp, one at a time, to hot oil. Fry, stirring gently to prevent shrimp from sticking together, until shrimp are golden brown, 1 to 2 minutes after adding last shrimp.

6. Transfer shrimp to prepared platter. Return oil to 350 degrees and repeat with remaining shrimp in 2 more batches. Serve shrimp immediately with sauce.

TO MAKE AHEAD: At end of step 4, freeze breaded shrimp on sheet until firm, then transfer to zipper-lock bag and freeze for up to 1 month. Do not thaw before cooking; increase cooking time in step 5 by 1 to 2 minutes.

PIGS IN BLANKETS

✔ WHY THIS RECIPE WORKS For our pigs in blankets recipe, we wanted a slightly more sophisticated version of the retro-campy childhood classic. So in place of the traditional refrigerated crescent roll dough, we turned to puff pastry, which is just as easy to use as the crescent roll dough but imparts a more-grown-up, flakier texture. We unrolled the sheet of puff pastry and, using a pizza wheel, sliced it into 32 equal strips. Then we rolled a little cocktail frank in each strip and placed them all, seam side down, on a parchment paper–lined baking sheet, with a little space between the bundles to allow for the inevitable puffing. Next, we brushed each li'l piggy with egg wash and sprinkled on a generous amount of grated Parmesan cheese for a savory punch. For more flavor and texture, we opted to add a little bit of our Everything Bagel Seasoning to the Parmesan, along with some pepper. We transferred the bundles to the oven to bake, and while they slowly turned golden brown, we stirred together a simple, pantry-friendly dipping sauce with yellow mustard, cider vinegar, brown sugar, ketchup, Worcestershire sauce, and hot sauce.

Pigs in blankets are a cocktail-hour standby and a childhood classic, but the tasty little nuggets can feel outdated to some. I disagree! Sure, the little treats are retro-campy in a midcentury way, but I'm an unapologetic fan of them.

Most "pigs" I've encountered have been wrapped in refrigerated crescent roll dough and served with yellow mustard for dipping, but I wanted to go for something slightly more sophisticated (to the extent that these savory little pop-'ems can really be sophisticated).

So I turned to puff pastry, which is just as easy to use as refrigerated crescent roll dough (albeit without the exciting pop that comes when you open the tube) but imparts a more-grown-up, flakier—and dare I say more sophisticated—texture. I unrolled one sheet of puff pastry and, using a pizza wheel, sliced it into 32 equal strips. (If your puff pastry comes in a package of two and you have to thaw both sheets to unroll them, you can reroll and refreeze the extra sheet.) I rolled a cocktail frank in each strip of puff pastry and placed all the bundles seam side down on a parchment paper–lined baking sheet, with a little space between the bundles to allow for the inevitable puffing.

Next, I brushed each li'l piggy with egg wash and sprinkled on a generous amount of grated Parmesan cheese for a savory punch. These pigs were good, but my tasters and I thought they could use something more. A bit of our Everything Bagel Seasoning, a mixture of sesame seeds, poppy seeds, dried minced garlic, dried onions, and kosher salt, added textural and visual interest plus an extra pop of flavor. I transferred these dressed-up bundles to the oven to bake, and while they slowly turned golden brown, I stirred together a simple mustardy dipping sauce with a few pantry ingredients: yellow mustard, cider vinegar, brown sugar, ketchup, Worcestershire sauce, hot sauce, and pepper.

My new recipe for this retro favorite is fancy enough for grown-ups but still totally kid appropriate. All that was left to do was mix up something refreshing with which to wash them down. Oh, and to mark my calendar for April 24, National Pigs in a Blanket Day.

—CECELIA JENKINS, *Cook's Country*

Pigs in Blankets

SERVES 8 TO 10 (MAKES 32 PIECES)

To thaw frozen puff pastry, let it sit either in the refrigerator for 24 hours or on the counter for 30 minutes to 1 hour. One 10- to 13-ounce package of cocktail franks usually contains 32 franks. This recipe can easily be doubled; bake the pigs in blankets on two separate baking sheets, one sheet at a time. The test kitchen's favorite yellow mustard is Heinz Yellow Mustard, and our favorite cider vinegar is Heinz Filtered Apple Cider Vinegar.

PIGS

1   (9½ by 9-inch) sheet puff pastry, thawed
1   large egg, beaten with 1 tablespoon water
32 cocktail franks, patted dry
¼   cup grated Parmesan cheese
2   teaspoons Everything Bagel Seasoning (recipe follows)
½   teaspoon pepper

MUSTARD SAUCE

⅓   cup yellow mustard
2   tablespoons cider vinegar
2   tablespoons packed brown sugar
1   tablespoon ketchup
½   teaspoon Worcestershire sauce
½   teaspoon hot sauce
¼   teaspoon pepper

1. FOR THE PIGS: Adjust oven rack to middle position and heat oven to 400 degrees. Line rimmed baking sheet with parchment paper. Unfold puff pastry on lightly floured counter and roll into 12 by 9-inch rectangle with short side parallel to edge of counter, flouring top of dough as needed.

2. Using pizza wheel or chef's knife, trim dough to 12 by 8-inch rectangle. Cut dough lengthwise into eight 1-inch strips. Cut dough crosswise at three 3-inch intervals. (You should have thirty-two 3 by 1-inch dough strips.)

3. Lightly brush 1 row of dough strips with egg wash. Roll 1 frank in each dough strip and transfer bundle, seam side down, to prepared sheet. Repeat with remaining dough strips and franks, spacing bundles ½ inch apart.

4. Combine Parmesan, bagel seasoning, and pepper in bowl. Working with a few bundles at a time, brush tops with egg wash and sprinkle with Parmesan mixture. Bake until pastry is golden brown, about 23 minutes.

5. FOR THE MUSTARD SAUCE: Meanwhile, whisk all ingredients together in bowl.

6. Let pigs cool on sheet for 10 minutes. Serve with mustard sauce.

TO MAKE AHEAD: Unbaked pigs can be prepared through step 3, covered with plastic wrap, and refrigerated for up to 24 hours. Bake as directed.

Everything Bagel Seasoning

MAKES 5 TEASPOONS

In addition to using this seasoning blend to flavor our Pigs in Blankets, you can sprinkle it on eggs; macaroni and cheese; dinner rolls; and, of course, homemade bagels. The blend can also be used to season chicken and pork.

1   teaspoon sesame seeds
1   teaspoon poppy seeds
1   teaspoon dried minced garlic
1   teaspoon dried onion flakes
1   teaspoon kosher salt

Combine all ingredients in bowl.

PIGS IN BLANKETS

TORN AND FRIED POTATOES

SIDE DISHES

SKILLET-ROASTED GREEN BEANS

✓ **WHY THIS RECIPE WORKS** We wanted skillet-roasted green beans that were perfectly seasoned and fully tender (not wet or mushy) and that had lots of caramelization. We also wanted a recipe that was quick and easy. Since green beans cooked with only dry heat (in the oven or sautéed on the stovetop) tend to turn leathery by the time they brown and those cooked with lots of water or steam never get much browning, we decided to use a hybrid wet/dry method. We filled a skillet with green beans; added water, oil, salt, and pepper; and then placed the lid on and turned the burner to medium-high to let the beans steam for a bit. Once the beans were bright green and nearly tender, we uncovered them to cook off any remaining water so that the beans would get good browning. Adding sliced onion and minced garlic to the skillet after taking off the lid rounded out the flavors with sweet and savory complexity, and a final flourish of vibrant lemon juice and shaved Pecorino Romano cheese made these skillet-roasted green beans truly irresistible.

Whether we're talking about brussels sprouts, butternut squash, broccoli, or beets, my go-to method for cooking most vegetables is to toss them with olive oil, salt, and pepper and then roast them in the oven. The high, dry heat gives them deep browning and concentrates their flavors by cooking off some of the vegetables' moisture. But I've never really gotten great results from oven-roasting green beans; they usually turn out dry and leathery. You can sauté green beans in a skillet on the stovetop, but it's hard to not overcook them into mush by the time you get good color (unless you precook the beans first, and who wants to add a step?).

Undeterred, I set out to achieve the ideal roasted green beans. I wanted them to be fully tender but not wet or mushy, and I wanted lots of caramelization. I also wanted a recipe that was relatively quick and easy. Since green beans cooked with only dry heat (in the oven or sautéed on the stovetop) tend to turn leathery by the time they brown and those cooked with lots of water or steam never get much browning, I began to think of ways to use a hybrid wet/dry method. If I could steam the beans with a little bit of water and then uncover them and open them up to dry heat at just the right moment, I could count on the moisture cooking off to let the browning begin.

I began playing with oven methods first. I tossed the beans on a baking sheet with a little water, olive oil, salt, and pepper; covered them with foil; and popped them into a 450-degree oven. After they steamed for a little while, I uncovered them so that they could brown. And the beans did get some nice, spotty browning. But I wanted more, so I turned to the stovetop.

I filled a skillet with green beans; added water, oil, salt, and pepper; and then placed the lid on and turned the burner to medium-high to let them steam. Once the beans were bright green and nearly tender, I uncovered them to cook off any remaining water and see if I could get some good caramelization. Just a few minutes later, they were sizzling and starting to brown. I continued to cook them, without stirring, for 2 more minutes to get a really nice sear, and then I stirred them and let them cook undisturbed again to get even more browning. After a few more minutes they were fully tender, and I gave them a taste. They were a bit plain, but they were cooked to perfection: tender and juicy, with all the complex flavors of caramelization.

On my next two attempts, I nailed down the timing as well as the ratio of water to oil, and I gussied up the beans a bit by adding onion, garlic, lemon, and Pecorino Romano for my main recipe and bacon, black bean garlic sauce, and tahini for a supersavory (and irresistible) variation. Oven roasting will still be my preferred method for lots of vegetables, but if it's green beans I'm having, I'm never making them any other way.

—MATTHEW FAIRMAN, *Cook's Country*

Skillet-Roasted Green Beans with Garlic and Pecorino Romano

SERVES 4

You will need a 12-inch nonstick skillet with a tight-fitting lid for this recipe.

- 1½ **pounds green beans, trimmed**
- 3 **tablespoons extra-virgin olive oil**
- 2 **tablespoons water**
- 1 **teaspoon table salt**
- ½ **teaspoon pepper**
- ½ **cup thinly sliced red onion**
- 2 **garlic cloves, minced**
- 2 **teaspoons lemon juice**
- 2 **ounces Pecorino Romano cheese, shaved with vegetable peeler**

SKILLET-ROASTED GREEN BEANS WITH GARLIC AND PECORINO ROMANO

1. Combine green beans, oil, water, salt, and pepper in 12-inch nonstick skillet. Cover and cook over medium-high heat until green beans are nearly tender, about 8 minutes, shaking skillet occasionally to redistribute green beans.

2. Stir green beans and continue to cook, uncovered, until water has evaporated and green beans are just beginning to brown in spots, about 5 minutes longer.

3. Add onion and cook until onion is just softened and green beans are spotty brown and fully tender, 2 to 4 minutes, stirring often. Stir in garlic and cook until fragrant, about 1 minute. Off heat, stir in lemon juice. Transfer to serving platter. Sprinkle with Pecorino and serve.

VARIATION

Skillet-Roasted Green Beans with Bacon, Black Bean Garlic Sauce, and Tahini

Reduce salt to ¼ teaspoon. Add 2 tablespoons black bean garlic sauce and 2 tablespoons water with lemon juice in step 3. After transferring to serving platter, drizzle green beans with 1 tablespoon tahini. Substitute ¼ cup crumbled cooked bacon (3 slices) and 2 teaspoons toasted sesame seeds for Pecorino.

ROASTED FENNEL

✔ **WHY THIS RECIPE WORKS** For our roasted fennel recipe, we began by cutting the bulbs into wedges, which had two benefits: It provided good surface area for browning, and the attached core kept the pieces intact. Covering the pieces of fennel with aluminum foil for most of the cooking time allowed them to steam and turn creamy; we then removed the foil for the last 10 minutes of roasting so that they could turn golden and deliciously caramelized. We also tossed the wedges with salted water before covering them, which provided moisture for steaming and helped get seasoning between their layers. Arranging the pieces on the long sides of a rimmed baking sheet ensured that all the pieces got equal exposure to the heat and browned evenly.

Fennel sparks controversy. You either love its intense anise flavors—or hate them. To those in the latter camp, I like to ask: Have you tried fennel roasted? While heat of any kind mellows this bulbous vegetable's licorice notes and turns its fibrous texture luxuriously creamy, roasting coaxes out hidden flavors, recalibrating how it tastes. The result: a nutty, savory-sweet vegetable that's the perfect accompaniment to almost any dish.

Fennel's multilayered structure presents challenges, and I began my recipe development by figuring out how to prep the vegetable (which, incidentally, comes from a different variety of the fennel plant than the one that produces fennel seeds). Cutting the bulb crosswise into thick rounds caused the layers to fall apart into random-size pieces. Lengthwise slices were better, but if they were too thin, they dried out in the oven, which emphasized the fennel's stringiness. The best method was slicing the bulb into wedges, which provided flat surfaces for browning and tidy pieces attached at the core that stayed intact.

I also found that simply coating the pieces of fennel with oil and roasting them in a hot oven charred their exteriors before their insides turned creamy. The solution: I drizzled the wedges with water and covered them with aluminum foil so that they steamed for the first 20 minutes of cooking. After that I removed the foil, and in 10 minutes the fennel turned golden brown and deliciously caramelized.

There was another benefit to adding water. When I dissolved salt in the water first, it was a great way to get seasoning into the pieces' interiors. I had one more tweak: Since the wedges in the middle of the baking sheet didn't get as browned, I arranged the pieces on the long sides of the sheet, where they'd all get equal exposure to the heat.

Sprinkling these beautifully golden-brown wedges with the chopped fennel fronds made a satisfying side dish, but since their mild anise notes have such an affinity for other flavors, I created some optional toppings: a floral vinaigrette made with white wine vinegar and honey as well as orange juice (and zest); briny oil-cured black olives quickly crisped in the microwave; crunchy panko bread crumbs mixed with umami-rich Parmesan cheese and a touch of red pepper flakes; and chopped cashews toasted with a slew of bold-flavored spices, including cumin seeds, mustard seeds, and nigella seeds.

—KEITH DRESSER, *Cook's Illustrated*

Roasted Fennel

Look for fennel bulbs that measure 3½ to 4 inches in diameter and weigh around 1 pound with the stalks (12 to 14 ounces without); trim the bases very lightly so that the bulbs remain intact.

  2 **fennel bulbs, bases lightly trimmed, 2 tablespoons fronds chopped coarse, stalks discarded**
  2 **tablespoons water**
  1 **teaspoon kosher salt**
  3 **tablespoons vegetable oil**
  ¼ **teaspoon pepper**
  1 **recipe topping (optional) (recipes follow)**

1. Adjust oven rack to lower-middle position and heat oven to 450 degrees. Spray rimmed baking sheet with vegetable oil spray.

2. Cut each fennel bulb lengthwise through core into 8 wedges (do not remove core). Whisk water and salt in large bowl until salt is dissolved. Add fennel wedges to bowl and toss gently to coat. Drizzle with oil, sprinkle with pepper, and toss gently to coat. Arrange fennel wedges cut side down along 2 longer sides of prepared sheet. Drizzle any water in bowl evenly over fennel wedges. Cover sheet tightly with aluminum foil and roast for 20 minutes.

3. Remove foil from sheet and continue to roast until side of fennel touching sheet is browned, 5 to 8 minutes longer, rotating sheet halfway through roasting. Flip each fennel wedge to second cut side. Continue to roast until second side is browned, 3 to 5 minutes longer. Transfer to plate; sprinkle with topping, if using, and fennel fronds; and serve.

Orange-Honey Dressing

MAKES ¼ CUP

Vinegar boosts the acidity in this dressing.

  1 **tablespoon extra-virgin olive oil**
  2 **teaspoons honey**
  1½ **teaspoons white wine vinegar**
  ⅛ **teaspoon grated orange zest plus 1 tablespoon juice**
     Pinch kosher salt

Whisk all ingredients together in bowl.

Crunchy Oil-Cured Olives

MAKES 2 TABLESPOONS

The olives will crisp as they cool.

  2 **tablespoons coarsely chopped pitted oil-cured black olives**
  ¼ **teaspoon grated lemon zest**

Line plate with double layer of paper towels. Spread olives on towels. Microwave, stirring every 30 seconds, until olives start to dry and no longer clump together, 2½ to 3 minutes. Let cool for 10 minutes. Transfer olives to cutting board, sprinkle with lemon zest, and chop until olives are finely chopped and mixture is homogeneous.

Parmesan Bread Crumbs

MAKES ⅓ CUP

Parmesan contributes umami to the bread crumbs.

  ¼ **cup panko bread crumbs**
  2 **teaspoons extra-virgin olive oil**
  ¼ **cup grated Parmesan cheese**
  ⅛ **teaspoon red pepper flakes**
  ⅛ **teaspoon kosher salt**

Combine panko and oil in 8-inch nonstick skillet and toast over medium heat, stirring frequently, until golden brown, 3 to 4 minutes. Transfer panko to bowl and let cool for 5 minutes. Stir in Parmesan, pepper flakes, and salt. Let cool completely, about 10 minutes.

Spiced Cashews

MAKES ⅓ CUP

Yellow mustard seeds can be used instead of brown. Nigella seeds are sometimes called black cumin or kalonji.

  1 **teaspoon water**
  ½ **teaspoon brown sugar**
  ¼ **cup coarsely chopped raw cashews**
  2 **teaspoons vegetable oil**
  ½ **teaspoon cumin seeds**
  ½ **teaspoon brown mustard seeds**
  ½ **teaspoon fennel seeds**
  ½ **teaspoon nigella seeds**
  ½ **teaspoon fenugreek seeds**
  ⅛ **teaspoon kosher salt**

Stir water and sugar in small bowl until sugar is dissolved; set aside. Heat cashews and oil in 8-inch nonstick skillet over medium heat, stirring constantly, until cashews are fragrant and just starting to turn golden, 3 to 4 minutes. Add cumin seeds, mustard seeds, fennel seeds, nigella seeds, and fenugreek seeds and continue to cook, stirring constantly, until spices are fragrant, 1 to 2 minutes longer. Add water mixture and continue to cook, stirring constantly, until water has evaporated and cashews are toasty, 1 to 2 minutes longer. Transfer to bowl and toss with salt. Let cool completely, about 10 minutes. Transfer to cutting board and chop fine.

BRAISED RED CABBAGE

✓ **WHY THIS RECIPE WORKS** Red cabbage is usually cooked with an acidic liquid such as wine, citrus juice, or vinegar, and that's no accident. This cabbage variety gets its hue from pH-sensitive plant pigments called anthocyanins, and if the cooking liquid skews alkaline, the cabbage can turn an unappetizing bluish color. Acid lowers the pH, keeping things rosy. The problem? Acid also strengthens the pectin that holds the cell walls together, which extends the time it takes for the cabbage to soften. In our recipe, we added the red wine vinegar only after the cabbage had softened, which cut the cooking time nearly in half. Bacon did double duty in this dish: Its fat imbued the cabbage with a subtle smoky meatiness, and the crispy bacon bits sprinkled on top after plating contributed textural interest. A grated sweet apple, along with a small amount of sugar, balanced the sourness of the vinegar, and a dollop of mustard added a hint of piquancy.

Red cabbage is inexpensive, long storing, widely available, and strikingly beautiful. Because it takes longer to mature than other varieties, it's also impressively sturdy. For that reason, a quick sauté can leave it unappealingly tough, so I prefer a tenderizing braise. The cabbage not only turns silky but also melts into a uniform and vivid bright purple, making it a cheerful dish to enjoy in late fall and winter, when food tends toward the brown and beige sections of the color wheel.

As I cast my mind back over the many braised red cabbage recipes I'd eaten and made, a theme emerged: The dish always has a sweet-and-sour profile. Research revealed that this isn't a coincidence. Red cabbage gets its color from pH-sensitive compounds called anthocyanins, and if the cooking liquid skews even a little alkaline (tap water rarely comes in at a perfect 7 on the pH scale), the cabbage can turn an unappetizing blue color. A little acid in the form of wine, vinegar, or citrus juice keeps things rosy, and then some sugar balances it out.

My usual cooking method is to fry some chopped bacon, reserve it as a garnish, and then sauté some alliums (often shallots) in the leftover fat. Then I add the thinly sliced cabbage and water or stock with a shot of acidic liquid (typically vinegar). It's a simple way to do things, but I find that it generally takes more than an hour for the cabbage to fully soften.

Years ago, I learned that adding some acid to the cooking water can keep vegetables firm by strengthening the pectin in their cell walls. It's a handy trick if you're boiling potatoes for a salad, but now it occurred to me that adding the color-preserving vinegar to my cabbage at the outset was probably slowing the cooking.

I tried braising the cabbage in water without any vinegar, and sure enough it took just 30 minutes to soften. But now, unsurprisingly, the cabbage was blue. Would adding vinegar at this point correct the color? I poured a glug of red wine vinegar into the pot to find out, and happily, the bright-purple color returned instantly.

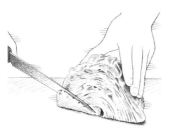

BRAISED RED CABBAGE WITH APPLE, BACON, AND SHALLOTS

The bacon and shallots provided plenty of savory backbone, and the sugar and vinegar supplied the right sweet-and-sour profile, but the cabbage cried out for a couple finishing touches. A grated apple added toward the end of cooking contributed freshness, and a generous spoonful of Dijon mustard gave the dish a subtle but pervasive piquancy. A handful of bright-green chopped fresh parsley accented the deep purple of the cabbage nicely. And that's how I raised my braising game.

—ANDREA GEARY, *Cook's Illustrated*

Braised Red Cabbage with Apple, Bacon, and Shallots

SERVES 6

Red cabbage is the sturdiest variety of cabbage. Do not substitute another variety—the cooking time will be different. To make grating easier, peel the apple and then grate all around the core. Don't worry if the cabbage takes on a bluish cast in step 1; the addition of vinegar in step 2 will correct the color. This cabbage makes a great accompaniment to rich meats such as pork and beef.

    4 slices bacon, chopped
    2 shallots, minced
    1 head red cabbage (2 pounds), quartered, cored,
       and sliced ¼ inch thick
    1 cup water
 1¼ teaspoons table salt
    1 Pink Lady or Gala apple
    3 tablespoons red wine vinegar, plus extra for
       seasoning
    2 teaspoons sugar
    2 teaspoons Dijon mustard
    2 tablespoons chopped fresh parsley, divided
    ¼ teaspoon pepper

1. Cook bacon in Dutch oven over medium heat, stirring occasionally, until fat is rendered and bacon is browned and crispy, 8 to 10 minutes. Using slotted spoon, transfer bacon to paper towel–lined plate; let cool. Add shallots to fat left in pot and cook, stirring occasionally, until golden and slightly softened, 2 to 3 minutes. Add cabbage, water, and salt; increase heat to high; and bring to boil. Adjust heat to maintain simmer. Cover and cook until cabbage is tender but still intact, about 30 minutes, stirring halfway through cooking. While cabbage cooks, peel apple and grate on large holes of box grater.

2. Stir apple, vinegar, sugar, and mustard into cabbage. Increase heat to high and continue to cook, uncovered, stirring occasionally, until liquid has evaporated, 2 to 5 minutes longer. Off heat, stir in 1 tablespoon parsley and pepper and season with salt and extra vinegar to taste. Transfer to shallow serving bowl, sprinkle with bacon and remaining 1 tablespoon parsley, and serve.

CELERY ROOT PUREE

✓ **WHY THIS RECIPE WORKS** For celery root puree with a clean, pure flavor, we processed chunks of the peeled root, along with russet potato for body, in the food processor to create tiny pieces that would cook quickly in small amounts of water and unsalted butter. To help the celery root and potato cook even more quickly, we added a touch of baking soda to the cooking liquid. This created an alkaline cooking environment that sped up their breakdown. Once the vegetables had cooked into a thick mush, we returned the mixture to the food processor and buzzed it with some heavy cream to form a smooth puree.

I adore celery root. Its ivory flesh cooks up earthy and nutty-sweet, with celery-like undertones (celery root is the same plant species as stalk celery but a different variety grown for its roots) and a light texture. Puree the cooked root with touches of butter and cream, and you've got a dish that's neutral enough to stand in for mashed potatoes yet still offers plenty of personality.

Working with peeled chunks of celery root, I ran a few tests and found that braising the chunks in small amounts of water and unsalted butter produced the purest taste. And yet I soon found myself in a conundrum: It took 45 minutes for the pieces to turn fully tender, but cooking times longer than 30 minutes produced less celery flavor and more slightly cabbagey sourness. I needed to cook the root as quickly as possible.

Small pieces of celery root would soften faster, so I changed course and used the food processor to blitz the large, dense chunks into tiny bits. I also added a touch of baking soda to the cooking water, because an alkaline environment would help the root break down more quickly. Indeed, after just 15 minutes, the mixture had cooked into a mush. I processed the mushy mixture with a pour of heavy cream until it formed a smooth puree.

The flavor of the puree was delightful, with a mellow vegetal backbone, but since celery root contains only 5 or 6 percent starch, the consistency was loose. Many celery root puree recipes call for thickening the puree with potato. I gave it a try and, sure enough, a small starchy russet provided just enough body. Finally, I whipped up a couple savory, herb-forward toppings to give the simple dish some pizzazz: the first featured bacon, garlic, and parsley and the second shallot, sage, and black pepper.

—JULIA COLLIN DAVISON, *Cook's Illustrated*

Celery Root Puree

SERVES 4 TO 6

When buying celery root, look for one with few roots for easy peeling and minimal waste. Once it's prepped, you should have about 1½ pounds of celery root. If desired, garnish the puree with Bacon, Garlic, and Parsley Topping or Shallot, Sage, and Black Pepper Topping (recipes follow); make the topping while the celery root cooks. (If you're making the puree in advance, make the topping as close to serving as possible.) Alternatively, garnish the puree with 1 tablespoon of minced fresh herbs such as chives, parsley, chervil, or tarragon.

1¾–2 pounds celery root, peeled and cut into 2-inch chunks
1 russet potato (6 ounces), peeled and cut into 2-inch chunks
2 tablespoons unsalted butter
1 cup water
½ teaspoon table salt
¼ teaspoon baking soda
⅓ cup heavy cream

1. Working in 2 batches, pulse celery root and potato in food processor until finely chopped, about 20 pulses per batch; transfer to bowl. (You should have about 4½ cups chopped vegetables.)

2. Melt butter in large saucepan over medium heat. Stir in celery root–potato mixture, water, salt, and baking soda. Cover and cook, stirring often (mixture will stick but cleans up easily), until vegetables are very soft and translucent and mixture resembles applesauce, 15 to 18 minutes.

3. Uncover and cook, stirring vigorously to further break down vegetables and thicken remaining cooking liquid, about 1 minute. Transfer vegetable mixture to clean, dry processor. Add cream and process until smooth, about 40 seconds. Season with salt to taste. Transfer to bowl and serve. (Puree can be cooled and refrigerated for up to 2 days. Before serving, microwave puree on medium-high power in covered bowl, stirring often, until hot throughout, 7 to 10 minutes.)

Bacon, Garlic, and Parsley Topping

MAKES ABOUT ¼ CUP

If desired, freeze the bacon for 15 minutes to make it easier to chop.

2 slices bacon, chopped fine
¼ cup water
4 garlic cloves, sliced thin
1 tablespoon minced fresh parsley

Combine bacon, water, and garlic in 8-inch nonstick skillet and cook over medium-high heat until water has evaporated and bacon and garlic are browned and crispy, 8 to 10 minutes. Off heat, stir in parsley.

Shallot, Sage, and Black Pepper Topping

MAKES ABOUT 3 TABLESPOONS

For the best results, do not substitute dried sage.

2 tablespoons unsalted butter
1 small shallot, minced
1 tablespoon minced fresh sage
¼ teaspoon pepper
   Pinch table salt

Melt butter in 8-inch nonstick skillet over medium-high heat. Add shallot and sage; cook, stirring frequently, until shallot is golden and sage is crisp, about 3 minutes. Off heat, stir in pepper and salt.

GOBI MANCHURIAN

GOBI MANCHURIAN

✔ **WHY THIS RECIPE WORKS** Gobi Manchurian, a multinational dish with roots in Chinese immigrant communities in Kolkata, India, features cauliflower florets battered and fried until crisp and then served with or tossed in a flavorful, spicy sauce. In recent years the dish has proven popular in Indian restaurants across the United States for its powerful flavors and mix of crisp and soft textures. Fans love it as a side dish or shared snack. For our version, we coated cauliflower florets in a light batter (made of water, cornstarch, flour, baking powder, and salt) that was wonderfully crisp when fried. The fried cauliflower was able to stay crispy even after being dressed in a spicy, tangy sauce made from ketchup, chili-garlic sauce, garlic, ginger, scallions, and enough freshly squeezed lime juice to brighten the whole dish.

Gobi Manchurian is a beautiful, complex dish with roots in the Chinese community of Kolkata, India. It's a popular dish in cities across the United States, too, including Asheville, North Carolina, where chef Meherwan Irani serves a version at his restaurant Chai Pani. Gobi Manchurian features cauliflower florets that are battered, fried, and then served with a spicy-sweet sauce. Its powerful mix of textures and flavors makes it a popular vegetarian dish that's served as a meal or a snack.

Gobi Manchurian comes in at least two styles. The "dry" style features fried cauliflower florets with a vibrant dipping sauce on the side, while the "wet" style marries the florets and the sauce in the same dish. The recipe here, inspired by the version served at Chai Pani, is the "wet" style.

The first order of business is to fry the cauliflower. Ideally, the fried pieces will have crisp exteriors and creamy centers. To achieve this, you create a thick, sticky batter of cornstarch, flour, and water, plus a bit of baking powder to create a lighter, crispier texture.

After dunking the florets in the batter and ensuring that they are completely coated, you fry them for about 5 minutes in oil heated to 375 degrees; the florets emerge perfectly crisp. Keep an eye on the oil temperature after you add the florets to make sure that it doesn't dip too low. (Peanut or vegetable oil works best here.) Once the coating is golden and firm, use a spider skimmer to carefully transfer the florets to a paper towel–lined baking sheet to drain.

Next up, the sauce. While sauces vary from kitchen to kitchen, most include a mixture of alliums, spices, citrus, and tomato sauce or ketchup for a balanced mix of heat, sweetness, and depth. The first step is to cook aromatic scallions, garlic, and ginger gently in a saucepan until they are soft and fragrant; then you stir in a mixture of ingredients including chili-garlic sauce, lime juice, soy sauce, and cumin. After a short time on the stove, the flavors come together and the mixture thickens into a sauce that clings perfectly to the fried florets. Once you toss the fried cauliflower and sauce together, be ready to eat! While the crisp exterior will keep its crunch for a little while, it won't last forever.

Simple to make, packed with flavor, and featuring a beautiful range of textures, Gobi Manchurian is best enjoyed with good friends and cold drinks.

—MARK HUXSOLL, *Cook's Country*

NOTES FROM THE TEST KITCHEN

HOW TO PREP CAULIFLOWER
Here's how to cut the cauliflower into florets.

1. Cut the stem flush with the base of the head, and then snap off the leaves.

2. Place the head on the cutting board, rounded side down. Using a paring knife, cut down through the floret stems, rotating the head after each cut.

3. Pull off the loose florets, and then continue cutting until all the florets are removed. Cut the florets into 1½-inch pieces.

Gobi Manchurian

SERVES 4

A whole 2½-pound head of cauliflower should yield 1 pound of florets. You can also buy precut florets if available. Use a Dutch oven that holds 6 quarts or more.

CAULIFLOWER

- 1 cup water
- ⅔ cup cornstarch
- ⅔ cup all-purpose flour
- 1 teaspoon table salt
- 1 teaspoon baking powder
- 1 pound (1½-inch) cauliflower florets (4 cups)
- 2 quarts peanut or vegetable oil for frying

SAUCE

- ¼ cup ketchup
- 3 tablespoons water
- 2 tablespoons soy sauce
- 1 tablespoon Asian chili-garlic sauce
- 2 teaspoons lime juice, plus lime wedges for serving
- ¾ teaspoon pepper
- ½ teaspoon ground cumin
- 2 tablespoons vegetable oil
- 3 scallions, white and green parts separated and sliced thin
- 1 tablespoon grated fresh ginger
- 3 garlic cloves, minced

1. FOR THE CAULIFLOWER: Whisk water, cornstarch, flour, salt, and baking powder in large bowl until smooth. Add cauliflower florets to batter and toss with rubber spatula to evenly coat; set aside.

2. Line baking sheet with triple layer of paper towels. Add oil to large Dutch oven until it measures about 1½ inches deep and heat over medium-high heat to 375 degrees.

3. Using tongs, add florets to hot oil 1 piece at a time. Cook, stirring occasionally to prevent florets from sticking, until coating is firm and very lightly golden, about 5 minutes. (Adjust burner, if necessary, to maintain oil temperature between 300 and 325 degrees.) Using spider skimmer, transfer florets to prepared sheet.

4. FOR THE SAUCE: Combine ketchup, water, soy sauce, chili-garlic sauce, lime juice, pepper, and cumin in bowl. Heat oil in small saucepan over medium-high heat until shimmering. Add scallion whites, ginger, and garlic and cook, stirring frequently, until fragrant, about

1½ minutes. Stir in ketchup mixture and bring to simmer, scraping up any bits of ginger mixture from bottom of saucepan. Transfer sauce to clean large bowl.

5. Add cauliflower and scallion greens to bowl with sauce and toss to combine. Transfer to platter and serve with lime wedges.

MARINATED ZUCCHINI

✓ **WHY THIS RECIPE WORKS** We wanted to add some pop to notoriously mild zucchini by marinating it in a punchy Italian-inspired dressing. Cooking the zucchini in large pieces drove off some of the squash's water and built flavor by lightly caramelizing the outside without turning the squash to mush. After searing the zucchini, we cut it into bite-size pieces and let it marinate for an hour (or longer) in a flavorful vinaigrette of olive oil, shallot, lemon juice, thyme, garlic, and red pepper flakes. Shaved Parmesan cheese added before serving gave extra richness and nutty savoriness.

Growing up, the only way I would eat zucchini was doused in bottled Italian dressing. I loved how the mild, porous zucchini soaked up that tangy, salty, herbed vinaigrette.

My tastes have (thankfully) evolved, but I wanted to see if I could create something similar—just a little more grown-up. This wasn't a unique idea, as I found tons of recipes that called for marinating either raw or cooked zucchini in an Italian-inspired dressing. I made a handful of those recipes and dug in.

A few of the recipes called for tossing raw, bite-size pieces of zucchini in the dressing and letting the acid and salt in the dressing do the work of softening it. But the squash released a lot of water, and these samples became too diluted. And bite-size pieces of zucchini that were cooked before or after marinating ended up mushy. I knew I needed to precook the zucchini to drive off some of its water, but I needed to cook it gently enough that it didn't turn to mush when dressed.

To strike the right balance, I cut three medium zucchini in half lengthwise, patted them dry (to minimize splatter), and seared the halves in a hot skillet. Cooking the zucchini this way drove off some of the squash's water and built flavor by lightly caramelizing the outside without cooking it through.

Once the zucchini was seared, I cut it into bite-size pieces; tossed it with a dressing of olive oil, shallot, lemon juice, fresh thyme, garlic, and red pepper flakes; and let it sit for an hour. The zucchini soaked up the flavorful marinade without releasing too much water. Sprinkling the dish with some shaved Parmesan cheese added richness and nutty savoriness.

—MORGAN BOLLING, *Cook's Country*

Marinated Zucchini

SERVES 4 TO 6

You will need one medium shallot to yield the 3 table-spoons called for here. Buy medium zucchini that weigh about 8 ounces each.

5	tablespoons extra-virgin olive oil, divided
3	tablespoons minced shallot
1½	tablespoons lemon juice
1½	teaspoons table salt
1	teaspoon chopped fresh thyme
1	garlic clove, minced
⅛	teaspoon red pepper flakes
1½	pounds zucchini, trimmed and halved lengthwise
1½	ounces Parmesan cheese, shaved with vegetable peeler

1. Combine ¼ cup oil, shallot, lemon juice, salt, thyme, garlic, and pepper flakes in medium bowl.

2. Pat zucchini dry with paper towels. Heat remaining 1 tablespoon oil in 12-inch nonstick skillet over medium heat until shimmering. Add half of zucchini to skillet cut side down and cook until browned, about 3 minutes. Flip and cook until skin side is spotty brown, about 3 minutes. Transfer to large plate. Repeat with remaining zucchini. Let cool for 5 minutes.

3. Slice zucchini crosswise ¼ inch thick. Transfer zucchini to bowl with oil mixture and toss to evenly coat. Marinate for at least 1 hour or up to 24 hours. (If marinating longer than 1 hour, cover with plastic wrap and refrigerate. Let sit at room temperature for 1 hour before serving.)

4. Season zucchini with salt to taste. Transfer zucchini to shallow platter and sprinkle with Parmesan. Serve.

KANSAS CITY–STYLE CHEESY CORN

WHY THIS RECIPE WORKS For this more-cheese-than-corn barbecue side, we turned to cream cheese for a rich, tangy base and combined it in a saucepan with corn, milk (to smooth out the mixture), granulated garlic, and a pinch of cayenne pepper for savoriness and a gentle kick. Once the cheese melted and the mixture heated through, the corn kernels softened to give the dish pleasant pops of sweetness. Stirring in shredded yellow cheddar gave our version the right look and kicked up the cheesy flavor. Lastly, we studded the mixture with juicy cubes of ham steak and chewy bits of salty bacon (a nod to the bits of leftover smoked meats that barbecue joints stir into theirs) and then popped it under the broiler for attractive spotty-brown color.

To be fair, the barbecue-style cheesy corn in Kansas City is more cheese than corn. As Executive Food Editor Bryan Roof discovered on a recent visit to Missouri, it is so cheesy that you eat it with a spoon. In addition, its pleasant pops of bright, sweet corn and savory nubs of meat provide a creamy, stick-to-your-ribs counterpoint to a barbecue lunch tray of smoked meat.

To mimic the meaty spread it goes with (and since barbecue joints often stir barky bits of leftover smoked meats into it), I started re-creating this cheese-packed side by rendering two strips' worth of cut-up bacon in a saucepan, a shortcut substitute for those chewy, smoky, meaty morsels of leftover barbecue scraps.

Once the bacon was crispy and its fat had rendered, I dumped in 3 cups of corn kernels (kernels freshly cut from the cob are best, but frozen corn works well here, too), cream cheese for a rich and tangy base, and milk to thin it out (we found that this added just enough richness; cream was a little too much), plus granulated garlic and cayenne pepper for a kick.

By the time the cream cheese was melted and smooth, the fresh corn kernels had softened to give the dish a pleasant, tender, sweet pop. Shredded yellow cheddar cheese (which we preferred to less flavorful varieties such as American and mozzarella) stirred in gave it the right look and topped off the cheesy flavor. As I ladled out rich, molten pools of cheese dotted with corn and bacon, the approving nods from my teammates told me I was nearly there.

The question arose: Were two strips of bacon enough meat? When I swapped in cubed ham steak for the bacon, my tasters were excited to sink their teeth into the plump, juicy squares of ham poking through the veil of cheese on their spoons . . . but they missed the smoky flavor and chewy texture the bacon provided. Did we have to choose? Using both meats gave us the perfect varied combination of meaty flavors and textures. This is a corn dish that will stick to your ribs.

–CECELIA JENKINS, *Cook's Country*

Kansas City–Style Cheesy Corn

SERVES 6 TO 8

Frozen corn can be substituted for the fresh corn, if desired. A 14-ounce bag of frozen kernels will yield 3 cups. You will need a broiler-safe 1½-quart baking dish for this recipe. Do not use a Pyrex dish; it is not broiler-safe.

- 2 slices bacon, cut into ½-inch pieces
- 4 ears corn, kernels cut from cobs (3 cups)
- 4 ounces ham steak, cut into ½-inch pieces
- 1 cup whole milk
- 8 ounces cream cheese
- 1 teaspoon granulated garlic
- ½ teaspoon table salt
- ½ teaspoon pepper
- ¼ teaspoon cayenne pepper
- 6 ounces yellow cheddar cheese, shredded (1½ cups), divided

1. Adjust oven rack 6 inches from broiler element and heat broiler. Cook bacon in large saucepan over medium heat until crispy, 5 to 7 minutes. Add corn, ham, milk, cream cheese, granulated garlic, salt, pepper, and cayenne to saucepan, breaking up cream cheese with heat-resistant rubber spatula. Cook, stirring occasionally, until cream cheese is melted and mixture just begins to bubble at edges of saucepan, 8 to 10 minutes (mixture will be liquid-y).

2. Off heat, stir in 1 cup cheddar until melted, about 30 seconds. Transfer corn mixture to 1½-quart broiler-safe baking dish and top with remaining ½ cup cheddar. Broil until cheese is spotty brown, about 3 minutes. Serve immediately.

SKILLET SQUASH CASSEROLE

✓ **WHY THIS RECIPE WORKS** The typical combination that makes up squash casserole—mild summer squash, melted cheese, mayonnaise or sour cream, and a crunchy Ritz Cracker topping—sounds great. But yellow squash is, by nature, a watery vegetable, and if you throw it in a casserole dish with salt, which pulls out moisture, it often turns out bland and wet. For a better, more flavorful version, we cooked the squash (along with some onions) in a skillet to drive off moisture and soften the vegetables. Rather than switching to a separate baking dish (why dirty another dish?), we stirred cheese, mayonnaise, and scallions directly into the skillet with the softened squash. We sprinkled crushed Ritz Crackers on top and moved the skillet to the oven to melt the cheese and brown the topping. Using a mix of intense sharp cheddar and creamy, silky American cheese created a rich, smooth sauce. Two peppers, black and cayenne, added just enough heat to contrast the sweet squash.

Her squash casserole almost made us break up.

You see, a man I was dating knew about my disapproval of this side dish and brought me home to try his mother's rendition. She was a great cook, and when he described her squash casserole—mild summer squash, melted cheese, sour cream, and a crunchy Ritz Cracker topping—it sounded great. But it was not. It was watery and sad.

I was young and hadn't yet learned that there are times when you can be too honest. And one of those times is a face-to-face assessment of a Southern mom's cooking.

I apologized and we got past it. He and I didn't last in the long run (maybe the squash scars were too deep), but his mom was fighting an uphill battle. Yellow squash is, by nature, a watery vegetable. Throw it in a casserole dish with salt, which pulls out moisture, and it's no wonder things turn out bland and wet. I wanted to give this dish another shot to live up to its full potential by making something deliciously rich and cheesy, pleasantly moist but not wet, and finished with buttery crackers on top.

After researching and making half a dozen existing recipes from Southern sources, I cobbled together my own. I started by cooking sliced onions and squash in a skillet with plenty of salt to drive off moisture and soften the squash. Rather than switching to a separate baking dish (why dirty another dish?), I stirred cheese, sour cream, and scallions directly into the skillet with the softened squash. I scattered crushed Ritz Crackers

SKILLET SQUASH CASSEROLE

over top and moved the skillet to the oven to melt the cheese and brown the topping.

The texture was good, but the flavor was bland. I swapped in mayonnaise for the sour cream (both are common here) because mayonnaise has a more savory flavor. I increased the amount of cheese (a mix of intense sharp cheddar and creamy, silky American cheese) to create a rich, smooth sauce. Two kinds of pepper, black and cayenne, added just enough heat to contrast the sweet squash.

This was a squash casserole that I was excited to eat. If you read this, Mrs. Chapman, I hope all is forgiven.

—MORGAN BOLLING, *Cook's Country*

Skillet Squash Casserole

SERVES 6 TO 8

The skillet will be full when you add the squash in step 2. This is OK; the squash will shrink as it cooks.

- 2 tablespoons extra-virgin olive oil
- 3 cups thinly sliced onion (3 onions)
- 1 teaspoon table salt, divided
- 2 pounds yellow summer squash, halved lengthwise and sliced ¼ inch thick
- 2 garlic cloves, minced
- 6 ounces sharp cheddar cheese, shredded (1½ cups)
- 2 ounces American cheese, chopped (½ cup)
- ½ cup mayonnaise
- 4 scallions, sliced thin
- ½ teaspoon pepper
  Pinch cayenne pepper
- 30 Ritz Crackers, crushed coarse

1. Adjust oven rack to middle position and heat oven to 375 degrees. Heat oil in 12-inch ovensafe skillet over medium-high heat until shimmering. Add onions and ¼ teaspoon salt and cook until onions are lightly browned, about 6 minutes.

2. Add squash, garlic, and remaining ¾ teaspoon salt and cook until any liquid exuded by squash has evaporated and squash is tender, about 10 minutes. Reduce heat to low and stir in cheddar cheese, American cheese, mayonnaise, scallions, pepper, and cayenne until fully combined, about 2 minutes.

HOW RITZ CRACKERS GOT THEIR NAME

In 1934, the National Biscuit Company (now known as Nabisco) needed a name and a marketing hook for its newest snack, a crisp round cracker with ridged edges, so it turned to employee Sydney Stern. His pitch: Ritz. Executives were concerned that the snazzy (even ritzy) name was out of touch with Depression-era America, but customers loved it. The name stuck. Since then, it's remained one of the best-selling crackers in the country.

3. Off heat, use rubber spatula to scrape down sides of skillet. Scatter crackers over top. Transfer skillet to oven and bake until bubbling around edges and hot throughout, about 18 minutes. Let cool for 10 minutes. Serve.

TO MAKE AHEAD: At end of step 2, transfer mixture to 8-inch square baking pan and let cool completely. Cover with aluminum foil and refrigerate for up to 24 hours. To serve, keep covered and bake until casserole is heated through, about 20 minutes. Uncover, top with crackers, and continue to bake 15 minutes longer.

SWEET POTATO FRITTERS

✓ **WHY THIS RECIPE WORKS** We were after lightly crisp sweet potato fritters with savory exteriors and creamy, sweet insides. We started by following a test kitchen method for making mashed sweet potatoes that calls for steaming the spuds in a small amount of water (rather than boiling them in an abundance of water, which dilutes their flavor). After cooking the potatoes, we mashed them, purposefully leaving a few small chunks for contrasting texture. Adding eggs and flour to the mash made the fritters fluffier, with extra-crunchy edges. Shallow frying was easier to manage—and clean up—than deep frying. Sliced scallions, chopped fresh cilantro and dill, and some briny feta cheese made each bite of these fritters exciting.

I had just wrapped up frying a few batches of battered shrimp, and as my hand reached out to shut off the burner under the oil, I paused and thought, Is there anything else in my refrigerator to fry? (We test cooks are a strange breed.) As I held the refrigerator door open, I briefly considered the cookie dough on the second shelf before training my eyes on a more promising ingredient: leftover mashed sweet potatoes. With one eyebrow raised, I carefully dropped a few spoonfuls of the cold mashed sweet potatoes into the hot oil and peered into the pot.

After a few minutes, the blobby, orange spoonfuls transformed into little bronze nuggets. I pulled them out of the oil and then drained and salted them before taking a bite. The fritters had lightly crisp, savory exteriors and creamy, sweet insides. The idea had potential! That said, they could have used a boost of flavor, and I wanted them to be fluffier. My idea needed a bit of fine-tuning.

I made another batch of mashed sweet potatoes, this time following a *Cook's Country* method that calls for steaming the spuds in a small amount of water (rather than boiling them in an abundance of water, which dilutes their flavor). After cooking the sweet potatoes until they were tender, I mashed them, purposefully leaving a few small chunks for contrasting texture. I stirred in sliced scallions, chopped fresh cilantro and dill, and some crumbled briny feta cheese. For this go-round, instead of setting up a whole pot of oil as I had for the shrimp, I added just ½ cup of oil to a 12-inch nonstick skillet. This shallow-frying method was much easier to manage—and much easier to clean up after.

While I loved the bold, fresh flavor of this batch, the fritters' texture was still a bit more dense than I'd like. Thankfully, I was not the first chef to attempt turning mashed sweet potatoes into fritters. Some research led me to try adding a couple eggs, which definitely made the fritters fluffier. Unfortunately, the eggs also made the mixture too loose to work with—not something you want to deal with while standing over hot oil. The solution was to add a little flour; ½ cup was enough to make the mixture more firm and workable, and the added starch made the edges of the fried fritters extra-crunchy.

Now, what else can I find in my kitchen to fry?

—MORGAN BOLLING, *Cook's Country*

Sweet Potato Fritters with Feta, Dill, and Cilantro

SERVES 4 TO 6

Using two spatulas to flip the fritters helps prevent the oil from splattering.

- 1½ **pounds sweet potatoes, peeled and sliced ¼ inch thick**
- ¼ **cup water**
- 1½ **teaspoons table salt**
- 3 **ounces feta cheese, crumbled (¾ cup)**
- ½ **cup all-purpose flour**
- 2 **large eggs**
- 4 **scallions, sliced thin**
- ¼ **cup chopped fresh cilantro**
- ¼ **cup chopped fresh dill**
- 1 **teaspoon ground cumin**
- ½ **teaspoon pepper**
- ½ **cup peanut or vegetable oil for frying**
- **Sour cream**
- **Lemon or lime wedges**

1. Combine potatoes, water, and salt in large saucepan. Cover and cook over medium-low heat, stirring occasionally, until paring knife inserted into potatoes meets no resistance, about 20 minutes.

2. Remove from heat. Using potato masher, mash potatoes until mostly smooth with some small chunks remaining. Let cool until no longer hot to touch, about 30 minutes. (Mashed sweet potatoes can be transferred to bowl, covered with plastic wrap, and refrigerated for up to 2 days.)

3. Set wire rack in rimmed baking sheet and line half of rack with triple layer of paper towels. Stir feta, flour, eggs, scallions, cilantro, dill, cumin, and pepper into potato mixture until fully combined.

4. Heat oil in 12-inch nonstick skillet over medium heat to 350 degrees (to take temperature, tilt skillet so oil pools on 1 side). Using greased ¼-cup dry measuring cup, place 6 portions of potato mixture in skillet. Press portions into approximate 3-inch disks with back of spoon.

5. Cook fritters until deep brown, 2 to 3 minutes per side, using 2 spatulas to carefully flip. Transfer fritters to paper towel–lined side of prepared rack, drain for 15 seconds on each side, then move to unlined side of rack. Return oil to 350 degrees and repeat with remaining potato mixture. Serve with sour cream and lemon wedges.

Tourte aux Pommes de Terre (French Potato Pie)

SERVES 6 TO 8

We strongly recommend measuring the flour for the pie crust by weight. The potatoes can be sliced on a mandoline. Serve as a main course with a salad or in small slices as a side dish.

CRUST

20 tablespoons (2½ sticks) unsalted butter, chilled, divided

2½ cups (12½ ounces) all-purpose flour, divided

1 teaspoon table salt

½ cup ice water, divided

FILLING

1 onion, halved and sliced thin

1½ teaspoons table salt

2 pounds Yukon Gold potatoes, peeled and sliced crosswise ⅛ inch thick

½ teaspoon baking soda

1¼ cups heavy cream

3 garlic cloves, minced

½ teaspoon pepper

¼ teaspoon ground nutmeg

2 tablespoons minced fresh parsley

1 egg, lightly beaten

1. FOR THE CRUST: Shred 4 tablespoons butter on large holes of box grater and place in freezer. Cut remaining 16 tablespoons butter into ½-inch cubes.

2. Pulse 1½ cups flour and salt in food processor until combined, 2 pulses. Add cubed butter and process until homogeneous paste forms, 40 to 50 seconds. Using your hands, carefully break paste into 2-inch chunks and redistribute evenly around processor blade. Add remaining 1 cup flour and pulse until mixture is broken into pieces no larger than 1 inch (most pieces will be much smaller), 4 to 5 pulses. Transfer mixture to medium bowl. Add shredded butter and toss until butter pieces are separated and coated with flour.

3. Sprinkle ¼ cup ice water over mixture. Toss with rubber spatula until mixture is evenly moistened. Sprinkle remaining ¼ cup ice water over mixture and toss to combine. Press dough with spatula until dough sticks together. Use spatula to divide dough into 2 portions. Transfer each portion to sheet of plastic wrap. Working with 1 portion at a time, draw edges of plastic over dough and press firmly on sides and top to form compact, fissure-free mass; wrap in plastic and form into 5-inch disk. Refrigerate dough for at least 2 hours or up to 2 days. Let chilled dough sit on counter until softened slightly, about 10 minutes, before rolling. (Wrapped dough can be frozen for up to 1 month. If frozen, let dough thaw completely on counter before rolling.)

4. FOR THE FILLING: One hour before baking pie, make filling. Toss onion and salt in bowl and set aside. Bring 4 quarts water to boil in Dutch oven over high heat. Add potatoes and baking soda. Return to boil and cook for 1 minute. Drain potatoes. Return potatoes to pot; add cream, garlic, pepper, nutmeg, and onion and any accumulated liquid; and bring to simmer over high heat. Adjust heat to maintain simmer and cook, stirring gently and frequently (it's OK if some slices break), until cream thickens and begins to coat potatoes, about 5 minutes. Let cool off heat for at least 30 minutes or up to 2 hours.

NOTES FROM THE TEST KITCHEN

HOW TO ACHIEVE A TENDER, INTACT FILLING

To ensure that the pie bakes up with a filling that's tender and can be cut into neat wedges, prep the ingredients as follows.

1. Salt onion to draw out excess moisture and soften it so it bakes up tender.

2. Boil potatoes with baking soda for 1 minute to break down their exteriors and release starch.

3. Simmer potatoes and onion with cream for 5 minutes. Starch from potatoes will thicken cream.

5. Roll 1 disk of dough into 12-inch round on well-floured counter. Loosely roll dough around rolling pin and gently unroll onto 9-inch pie plate, letting excess dough hang over edge. Ease dough into plate by gently lifting edge of dough with your hand while pressing into plate bottom with your other hand. Refrigerate until dough is firm, about 30 minutes. Roll second disk of dough into 12-inch round on well-floured counter, then transfer to parchment paper–lined baking sheet; refrigerate for 30 minutes. Adjust oven rack to lower-middle position and heat oven to 450 degrees.

6. Stir parsley into potato mixture, transfer mixture to dough-lined pie plate, and spread into even layer (it's OK if potato mixture is still slightly warm). Using paring knife or round cutter, cut ½-inch hole in center of second dough round. Loosely roll dough round around rolling pin and gently unroll it over filling, aligning hole with center of pie and leaving at least ½-inch overhang all around. Fold dough under itself so edge of fold is flush with outer rim of pie plate. Flute edges using your thumb and forefinger or press with tines of fork to seal. Place pie on parchment-lined rimmed baking sheet and brush with egg. Bake until top is light golden brown, 18 to 20 minutes.

7. Reduce oven temperature to 325 degrees and continue to bake until crust is deep golden brown and potatoes at vent hole are tender when pricked with paring knife, 30 to 40 minutes longer. If pie begins to get too brown before potatoes are softened, cover loosely with aluminum foil. Let pie cool on wire rack for at least 30 minutes. Serve warm or at room temperature.

CHEESY MASHED POTATO CASSEROLE

✔ **WHY THIS RECIPE WORKS** We wanted irresistibly cheesy mashed potatoes that could be made ahead. To achieve this, we sliced Yukon Gold potatoes and simmered them in seasoned water. Once they were tender, we drained and mashed them with lots of butter until they were smooth and lump-free. Then we stirred in 1½ cups of half-and-half for the right balance between milk and cream. Next, the cheese: We loved the nutty depth of Gruyère but also wanted something with a little more cheesiness, so we added mild mozzarella, which played well with the Gruyère and gave the potatoes a supple, stretchy texture. Just before baking, we topped the potatoes with buttery panko bread crumbs, which crisped up and provided a crunchy contrast.

Some Thanksgiving classics are untouchable, right? I wouldn't dare suggest you upend tradition by replacing the trusty turkey or stuffing, and I'm not about to propose you go without creamy, comforting mashed potatoes either. But maybe there's room for improvement, especially if it means crossing an item off your to-do list on the big day.

Typically, mashed potatoes are made and served right away, which can take up precious time on a holiday. But you can assemble a creamy, buttery mashed potato casserole ahead of time. While you're at it, why not up the flavor ante with almost too much cheese and a crispy, buttery topping to boot? Here's how.

To start, slice 4 pounds of Yukon Gold potatoes and simmer them in well-seasoned water. Once they are completely tender, drain and mash them with butter until they're smooth and lump-free. Adding two sticks of butter in this step prevents the potatoes from becoming gluey as you work them; plus, the residual heat from the potatoes melts the butter. Then stir in a hefty pour of half-and-half (heavy cream is just a tad too rich here, and milk is not quite rich enough)—the mixture should be loose enough to slump when scooped but not so loose that it pools.

Now the cheese. My tasters loved Gruyère's nutty depth but also wanted something that melted more readily. Mozzarella fit the bill: Its mild flavor allowed the Gruyère to sing, and it gave the potatoes a supple, stretchy texture that screamed "cheesy." Stir in a generous 1½ cups of each, plus ½ cup of minced chives.

At this point, you can go ahead and bake the casserole—the potatoes will be looser than they would be if they were made ahead, but they will still be delicious. Alternatively, you can refrigerate the casserole for up to three days, during which time the potatoes will firm up a tiny bit but will still be sumptuously creamy when baked. Either way, before baking, top the potatoes with cheesy, buttery panko bread crumbs, which will crisp up into the perfect crunchy foil for the luscious potatoes underneath.

And if you do want to mess with tradition a bit more, you can try one of the spruced-up variations.

—JESSICA RUDOLPH, *Cook's Country*

CHEESY MASHED POTATO CASSEROLE

Cheesy Mashed Potato Casserole

SERVES 10 TO 12

This recipe can be easily halved: Boil the potatoes in a large saucepan and bake them in an 8-inch square baking dish. If made ahead, the casserole will be slightly more firm and set than a freshly made one; we liked both versions.

POTATOES

4   pounds Yukon Gold potatoes, peeled and sliced ½ inch thick

1   teaspoon table salt, plus salt for cooking potatoes

16 tablespoons unsalted butter, cut into 16 pieces

1½ cups half-and-half

1   teaspoon pepper

6   ounces Gruyère cheese, shredded (1½ cups)

6   ounces whole-milk block mozzarella cheese, shredded (1½ cups)

½   cup minced fresh chives

TOPPING

¾   cup panko bread crumbs

2   ounces Gruyère cheese, shredded (½ cup)

2   tablespoons unsalted butter, melted

1. FOR THE POTATOES: Adjust oven rack to upper-middle position and heat oven to 400 degrees. Place potatoes and 2 tablespoons salt in Dutch oven, add water to cover by 1 inch, and bring to boil over high heat. Reduce heat to medium and simmer until potatoes are tender and can be easily pierced with paring knife, 18 to 20 minutes.

NOTES FROM THE TEST KITCHEN

WHY YUKON GOLDS?

We love all potatoes, but Yukon Golds are perfect here for their lovely flavor and supercreamy texture once cooked.

2. Drain potatoes and return them to pot. Add butter and mash with potato masher until smooth and no lumps remain. Stir in half-and-half, pepper, and salt until fully combined. Stir in Gruyère, mozzarella, and chives until incorporated. Transfer potato mixture to 13 by 9-inch baking dish and smooth top with spatula.

3. FOR THE TOPPING: Combine bread crumbs, Gruyère, and melted butter in bowl. Sprinkle topping evenly over potato mixture.

4. Bake until casserole is heated through and topping is crisp and golden brown, about 30 minutes. Let cool for 30 minutes. Serve.

TO MAKE AHEAD: At end of step 2, let potato mixture cool completely in dish, cover tightly with plastic wrap, and refrigerate for up to 3 days. When ready to bake, remove plastic, cover dish tightly with aluminum foil, and bake for 25 minutes. Remove foil and proceed with step 3.

VARIATIONS

Cheesy Mashed Potato Casserole with Blue Cheese, Bacon, and Rosemary

Substitute 1 cup crumbled blue cheese for Gruyère and 2 teaspoons minced fresh rosemary for chives in potatoes. Add 12 ounces crumbled cooked bacon with cheeses in step 2. Omit Gruyère from topping.

Cheesy Mashed Potato Casserole with Parmesan, Browned Butter, and Sage

Substitute 2 cups shredded Parmesan for Gruyère in potatoes. Omit Gruyère from topping. While potatoes boil, melt butter for potatoes in 10-inch skillet over medium-high heat. Cook, swirling skillet constantly, until milk solids in butter are color of milk chocolate and have toasted aroma, 3 to 5 minutes. Off heat, stir in 2 tablespoons minced fresh sage and 4 minced garlic cloves. Transfer to heatproof bowl. Add browned butter mixture to drained potatoes in pot before mashing. Omit chives.

TORN AND FRIED POTATOES

☑ **WHY THIS RECIPE WORKS** We wanted irresistible fried potatoes with a compelling mix of textures: soft, fluffy interiors and craggy, crispy-crunchy exteriors. To get there, we fully baked russet potatoes (starchy russets resulted in the best interior texture and the most delicious crispy skins), allowed them to cool completely, tore them into chunks, and fried them in 375-degree oil. Starting the oil quite hot and turning up the heat after adding the cold potatoes ensured crispy potatoes that cooked quickly enough to not dry out inside. Every bit as satisfying as the best french fries, these potatoes won't last long at your next dinner party.

Few ingredients are as adaptable and versatile as potatoes. You can boil, bake, mash, fry, or grill them—just about any method you can think of, you can use it on potatoes. But I'm extra-excited about a process I've been tinkering with a lot in my home kitchen: tearing and frying them.

By baking potatoes first and then letting them cool before tearing them into pieces and frying them, you get soft, fluffy interiors with crispy-crunchy exteriors, a compelling mix of textures.

Be prepared: This recipe takes a while. But most of that time is inactive—waiting for the potatoes to bake and then waiting for them to cool. Once that chunk of time is out of the way (the baking and cooling can be done a couple days ahead), all that's left is to fry and serve them.

It's essential that your frying oil is at the right temperature: 375 degrees. It takes a few minutes to get the oil that hot, but don't shortchange this step, because when you add the cold potatoes the oil temperature will drop dramatically. You'll need to increase the heat after adding the potatoes to bring the oil back up to temperature quickly. This ensures crispy potatoes and keeps them from drying out or cooking unevenly.

Russets work best here, not only because their starchy centers create just the right texture but also because their skins provide beautiful earthy flavors. The result is a mash-up of baked potatoes, potato skins, and french fries.

My top tip: Make sure that everyone is at the table and ready to eat when these potatoes come out of the oil. For the best experience, they must be eaten hot. To let them go cold would be a real disappointment. If you're serving these for a holiday dinner, have everything else ready to go as soon as you start frying. Your fellow celebrants can sit down, cool their heels, and prepare their forks for the moment when you set these gorgeous potatoes down in front of them. Talk about a reason to celebrate.

—BRYAN ROOF, *Cook's Country*

Torn and Fried Potatoes
SERVES 4

Since you eat the potato skins in this recipe, make sure to scrub them well before cooking. In addition to the salt, these potatoes can be seasoned with any variety of seasoning or herb blend; they're also great dipped in ketchup or aioli.

2½ pounds russet potatoes, unpeeled, scrubbed
 1 quart vegetable oil for frying
 1 teaspoon kosher salt

1. Adjust oven rack to middle position and heat oven to 400 degrees. Prick each potato 6 times with fork. Place potatoes on rack and bake until tip of paring knife can be easily inserted into potatoes, about 1 hour 20 minutes. Let potatoes cool completely and then refrigerate until cold throughout, at least 3 hours. (Potatoes can be refrigerated for up to 2 days.)

2. Keeping skins on potatoes, use your hands to break potatoes into approximate 1½-inch pieces; transfer to bowl. Line rimmed baking sheet with triple layer of paper towels.

3. Add oil to Dutch oven and heat over medium-high heat to 375 degrees. Carefully add potatoes to hot oil and increase heat to high to compensate for oil cooling. Cook, stirring occasionally with metal spoon and taking care to scrape bottom of pot to prevent sticking, until potatoes are consistently browned and crispy, 13 to 15 minutes. Using spider skimmer or slotted spoon, transfer potatoes to prepared sheet. Sprinkle with salt. Serve.

COCONUT RICE TWO WAYS

✓ **WHY THIS RECIPE WORKS** Coconut and rice pair well together, and there are many ways to combine them. After some testing, we decided to focus on two styles of coconut rice: hung kao mun gati (Thai coconut rice) and arroz con titoté (Colombian coconut rice). While these two dishes are both made primarily with rice, canned coconut milk, sugar, and salt, they're very different.

For hung kao mun gati, we found it best to rinse the grains before cooking to remove surface starch, so our rice turned out delicately clingy rather than sticky. Though many recipes call for a full can of coconut milk, we found that it made the rice too greasy; using 2 parts coconut milk to 3 parts water produced rice that was luxuriously rich and perfumed without being too heavy. Letting the rice sit for 10 minutes after cooking allowed the delicate grains to firm up a bit so that they didn't break when served, and gently stirring the rested rice redistributed any coconut oil that had risen to the top during cooking.

Arroz con titoté is similar to a classic pilaf, but it uses coconut oil rather than olive oil. We started ours by boiling pure coconut milk in a partially covered saucepan until the water evaporated, leaving the fat behind. After browning the particles of coconut that were suspended in the fat, we added the rice, which we had rinsed to remove excess surface starch that would otherwise make the finished product sticky. Adding just enough water to hydrate and gel the starches in the rice ensured that the cooked grains would be light and fluffy. We added a small amount of sugar and raisins, which are traditional ingredients, to enhance the natural sweetness of the coconut. Finishing with a spritz of lime juice brought all the sweet, salty, nutty flavors into focus.

The expression "What grows together goes together" is a cliché, but it's true: In temperate climates, strawberries go with rhubarb; where it's cold, preserved fish and rye bread are a dynamic duo; and near the equator, coconut gets cooked with rice.

But coconut rice varies from one tropical cuisine to another. The coconut component might be fresh or dried, or it might be canned milk or cream. Some versions are served plain or perhaps with a squeeze of lime; others are embellished with spices, alliums, chiles, tomatoes, meat, fish, or beans. But even the simple versions made with few ingredients can have surprisingly different flavors and textures. After cooking a handful of recipes from around the globe, I homed in on two styles that I loved for their ability to pair well with a range of dishes—and because, despite having nearly identical ingredients (rice, canned coconut milk, sugar, and salt), they were as different as could be.

The first was coconut rice from Thailand: hung kao mun gati. This simple, elegant dish always seems to take my meal up a notch when I order it in restaurants. It turns out that it may have an illustrious provenance: Sources suggest that it can be traced to the Persians in the court of King Narai of Thailand (1632–1688), who enjoyed rice dishes prepared with liquids other than water, including coconut milk.

Happily, this Thai classic is just as easy to make as plain white rice: All you do is simmer jasmine rice in a mixture of coconut milk, water, sugar, and salt until the liquid is absorbed. The simple simmer leaves the grains rich-tasting and subtly sweet, with a tender, slightly clingy texture. Serve the rice as is or top with garnishes such as fried shallots and peanuts.

One of the few variables I saw among recipes was the ratio of coconut milk to water used to cook the rice. While many incorporated a full 14-ounce can (plus water) for 1½ cups of rice, I found the rice too oily and perfumed. The sweet spot was 1½ cups of rice cooked in 1 cup of coconut milk and 1½ cups of water. I also found that it was necessary to treat the rice as I would in any other application, rinsing it well to rid it of excess starch that would otherwise make the grains gummy and letting it stand for 10 minutes after cooking to allow the moisture to distribute evenly. Unlike plain rice, a gentle stir was necessary before serving this version to blend in any coconut oil that had risen to the top.

Hung kao mun gati pairs as beautifully with traditional entrées such as stir-fries, curries, and satay as it does with everything from steamed vegetables to lean fish to rich grilled pork.

Now, spin the globe; we're going to the Caribbean.

Arroz con titoté, a tan-colored, brown-flecked coconut rice that is popular in beachside restaurants along the Caribbean coast of Colombia, is a knockout dish whose taste stunned me the first time I cooked it. Made with virtually the same ingredients as its Thai cousin, it featured a toasty aroma and rich, nutty flavor that I barely recognized as coconut—a result of the unique treatment of the coconut milk.

Here's how it works: Pour a whole can of coconut milk into a saucepan and boil it until all the water is gone, leaving only coconut oil and tiny particles of coconut solids. Then keep cooking until those coconut solids darken to a rich, toasty brown. Add the rice and coat it well with the fat before stirring in water, brown sugar, salt, and raisins.

When I first made this dish, which is often served with whole grilled or fried fish and patacones (double-fried smashed plantains), I expected it to be heavy and sweet, but it was neither. Coating the rice grains with fat before adding the liquid was a classic pilaf strategy that ensured that the grains cooked up separate and not gluey (here again, rinsing the rice was also critical). And the browned coconut, which along with the rendered fat is known as titoté, imparted very little coconut heft and creaminess and more of a rich, toasty depth instead. The raisins heightened the dish's slight sweetness without making it seem at all dessert-y. A spritz of lime, the traditional garnish, snapped all the flavors into focus.

This is not to say my arroz con titoté was completely without problems. Some brands of coconut milk had a tendency to splatter dramatically during the reducing step, which was messy and hazardous until I thought to partially cover the saucepan. And some cans of the stuff simply refused to separate into fat and solids due to the presence of emulsifiers, so I had to be careful to buy one that listed only coconut and water on the label. I also had to learn to be patient while the milk reduced and to trust that the oil would eventually separate out. Then I had to allow the coconut solids to get good and dark before I added the rice to ensure that the dish had just the right nutty flavor.

With those issues sorted, I had another coconut rice in my repertoire that also amply demonstrated how brilliantly these two ingredients work together.

—ANDREA GEARY, *Cook's Illustrated*

Hung Kao Mun Gati (Thai Coconut Rice)
SERVES 4 TO 6

Our favorite coconut milk is from Aroy-D; do not use low-fat coconut milk in this recipe. Many brands of coconut milk separate during storage; be sure to stir yours until it's smooth before measuring it. We like the delicately clingy texture of jasmine rice here, but regular long-grain white rice can be substituted. Avoid basmati; the grains will remain too separate. The rice can be cooked in a rice cooker instead of on the stovetop. Chopped toasted peanuts, toasted sesame seeds, fried shallots, and pickled chiles are great toppings for this rice. Serve with stir-fries or grilled meat or fish.

1½ cups jasmine rice
1 cup canned coconut milk
1 tablespoon sugar
¾ teaspoon table salt

1. Place rice in fine-mesh strainer set over bowl. Rinse under running water, swishing with your hands, until water runs clear. Drain thoroughly. Stir rice, 1½ cups water, coconut milk, sugar, and salt together in large saucepan. Bring to boil over high heat. Reduce heat to

maintain bare simmer. Cover and cook until all liquid is absorbed, 18 to 20 minutes.

2. Remove saucepan from heat and let sit, covered, for 10 minutes. Mix rice gently but thoroughly with rubber spatula, transfer to bowl or platter, and serve.

Arroz con Titoté (Colombian Coconut Rice)
SERVES 4

Our favorite coconut milk is from Aroy-D; do not use a product with additives or the milk won't cook properly. Do not use low-fat coconut milk here. The coconut solids may bond to the surface of your saucepan in step 2, but they will release as the rice cooks. Serve with grilled or broiled fish or meat. Don't omit the lime wedges; they bring all the flavors into focus.

1 (14-ounce) can coconut milk
1½ cups long-grain white rice
2¼ cups water, divided
⅓ cup raisins
2 tablespoons packed dark brown sugar
1 teaspoon table salt
Lime wedges

1. Pour coconut milk into large saucepan. Cover, leaving lid slightly ajar so steam can escape. Cook over medium-high heat, stirring occasionally, until coconut milk is reduced by about three-quarters and begins to sputter, 10 to 12 minutes. While coconut milk cooks, place rice in fine-mesh strainer set over bowl. Rinse under running water, swishing with your hands, until water runs clear. Drain thoroughly.

2. Reduce heat to medium. Uncover saucepan and cook, stirring frequently, until fat separates from coconut solids, about 2 minutes. Continue to cook, stirring frequently, until coconut solids turn deep brown (solids will stick to saucepan), about 3 minutes longer. Add rice and cook, stirring constantly, until grains are well coated with fat. Stir in ½ cup water (mixture may sputter) and scrape bottom and sides of saucepan with wooden spoon to loosen coconut solids. Stir in raisins, sugar, salt, and remaining 1¾ cups water. Bring mixture to boil. Adjust heat to maintain low simmer. Cover and cook until all liquid is absorbed, 18 to 20 minutes.

3. Remove saucepan from heat and let sit, covered, for 10 minutes. Mix rice gently but thoroughly and transfer to serving bowl. Serve with lime wedges.

HUNG KAO MUN GATI (THAI COCONUT RICE)

CRISPY FISH SANDWICHES WITH TARTAR SAUCE

CHAPTER 3

PASTA, PIZZA, SANDWICHES, AND MORE

SPAGHETTI CARBONARA

✔ **WHY THIS RECIPE WORKS** We wanted a bulletproof version of this much-beloved, simple Roman pasta dish of noodles draped in a luscious, porky, cheesy sauce. We began by rendering some guanciale (succulent and fatty cured pork jowl) until it was slightly crispy but still chewy and intensely porky. For the classic rich and creamy sauce base, we whisked the right number (obtained through careful testing) of egg yolks and whole eggs with a hefty amount of freshly ground pepper and tangy Pecorino Romano cheese. Once the spaghetti was cooked to a perfect al dente, we whisked some of the pasta cooking water into the egg and cheese mixture to begin tempering the eggs. To emulsify the sauce, we tossed the hot pasta with the guanciale, its rendered fat, and the egg mixture until the eggs cooked and tightened into a silky sauce.

When pasta carbonara—a Roman dish of pasta, cured pork, and sharp cheese—is done well, its bold flavors and creamy texture are a revelation. But it's also one of those seemingly simple dishes that can go wrong at several turns. The two most common failures are unbalanced flavor caused by the wrong ratios of ingredients and a gummy or runny texture from an improperly emulsified sauce.

As for the ingredients, sharp, bold Pecorino Romano is the traditional cheese. This cheese's pleasantly funky flavor is the key to a potent but well-rounded carbonara. You can make this dish with Parmesan and it will be great, but it won't be quite as assertive. With Pecorino, you generally get what you pay for, and this is the time to splurge on the good stuff if it's available to you.

The cured pork product we use is salty, meaty guanciale. We cut it into chunks and render some of the fat; this fat, in turn, serves as the backbone of the sauce. With ingredients this potent, balance proved to be key; through weeks of testing, we landed on just the right proportions of cheese and meat.

One last note on flavor: Use freshly ground black pepper if possible, as the dusty preground stuff is too mild to hold its own here. Freshly ground pepper makes a big difference.

The keys to ensuring that your carbonara has great texture are threefold: the eggs, the pasta water, and the tossing. We call for three whole eggs plus two yolks for added richness and creaminess; the raw eggs are tossed into the hot pasta and (just barely) cook from the heat of the noodles. Reserved pasta cooking water is integral here, as its starches help bind the sauce so that it coats and clings to every strand of spaghetti. And in order for that to happen, you have to vigorously toss the sauced pasta for a couple minutes (it's tiring!) right before serving.

We also recommend heating your serving bowls or plates right before you eat; this will help the carbonara stay warm and fluid.

—MARK HUXSOLL, *Cook's Country*

Spaghetti Carbonara

SERVES 4

It is important to immediately add the egg mixture to the hot pasta in step 5. The hot pasta cooks the eggs, which thickens them and creates a luscious, creamy sauce that coats the pasta. We call for Pecorino Romano here, but Parmesan can be used, if preferred. If you can't find guanciale, you can substitute pancetta; just be sure to buy a 4-ounce chunk and not presliced pancetta. It's best to use freshly ground black pepper here.

- 3 large eggs plus 2 large yolks
- 2½ ounces Pecorino Romano cheese, grated (1¼ cups), plus extra for serving
- 1 teaspoon pepper, plus extra for serving
- ¼ teaspoon table salt, plus salt for cooking pasta
- 4 ounces guanciale, cut into ½-inch chunks
- 2 tablespoons extra-virgin olive oil
- 1 pound spaghetti

NOTES FROM THE TEST KITCHEN

THE CHEEKIEST OF CURED MEATS

Guanciale is an Italian spiced, cured meat product made from pork jowls, or cheeks. "Guancia" is the Italian word for cheek. Guanciale has a richer pork flavor than pancetta does (but you can use pancetta in this recipe if you can't find guanciale). For this recipe, buy a 4-ounce piece and cut it into planks, then into strips, and then crosswise into chunks. Any extra guanciale can be wrapped tightly in plastic wrap and refrigerated for a few weeks; it also freezes well. Try it in bean soups, with sautéed greens, or tossed in with browning onions to start stews and braises. And remember: A little goes a long way.

SPAGHETTI CARBONARA

1. Bring 4 quarts water to boil in large Dutch oven.

2. Meanwhile, beat eggs and yolks, Pecorino, pepper, and salt together in bowl; set aside. Combine guanciale and oil in 12-inch nonstick skillet and cook over medium heat, stirring frequently, until guanciale begins to brown and is just shy of crispy, about 6 minutes. Remove skillet from heat.

3. Add pasta and 1 tablespoon salt to boiling water and cook, stirring often, until al dente.

4. Reserve ½ cup cooking water, then drain pasta and immediately return it to pot. Add guanciale and rendered fat from skillet and toss with tongs to coat pasta.

5. Working quickly, whisk ¼ cup reserved cooking water into egg mixture, then add egg mixture to pasta in pot. Toss pasta until sauce begins to thicken and looks creamy, 1 to 2 minutes. Adjust consistency with remaining reserved cooking water as needed. Serve immediately, passing extra Pecorino and pepper separately.

CHEESEBURGER MAC

✔ **WHY THIS RECIPE WORKS** We wanted to create the perfect marriage of a cheeseburger and mac and cheese in one pan. We started by soaking ground beef in a solution of salt, pepper, water, and baking soda for 15 minutes before searing it. This trick kept the beef tender, allowing us to emulate that beloved burger crust in the skillet without the side effect of dry, pebbly, overcooked meat. For the macaroni we cooked the pasta right in the skillet with just enough milk and water to cook it until it was al dente. We stirred in sharp cheddar and classic American cheese for maximum flavor and meltability. Finally, to drive home the cheeseburger flavor, we folded in all our favorite cheeseburger toppings: finely chopped raw onion, ketchup, mustard, chopped dill pickles, and a hefty dose of Worcestershire sauce to boost the dish's meatiness. We topped the dish with a little more cheese, finished it under the broiler, and served it sprinkled with more onion and pickles for sharpness.

When I was a kid, no meal ever made me as happy as macaroni and cheese did. As an adult, I still hold a place in my heart for mac and cheese alongside one of my other all-time favorites: cheeseburgers. I set out to combine the two in a one-pot meal.

I started by cooking ground beef in a 12-inch skillet. I added a pound of elbow macaroni and water and cooked it, covered, until the pasta was al dente, and then I folded in shredded cheese to melt it. Finally, I sprinkled over extra cheese and broiled it all for a brown top.

It was a bit of a mess. The skillet couldn't contain all that pasta, and the dish yielded too much food. To make it a little more manageable, I cut back to ½ pound of pasta. This was easier to maneuver and produced plenty for four to six diners. But the dish still suffered from pebbly beef and a shortage of cheeseburger flavor. I had ideas.

To close the flavor gap, I made sure to get a solid sear on the ground beef to emulate that beloved burger crust. One potential side effect of browning is pebbly meat, so I turned to a test kitchen trick and soaked the ground beef in a solution of salt, water, and baking soda for 15 minutes before searing it. This kept things tender. I also added onion to the skillet to soften before adding the pasta. After experimenting with several cheeses, I settled on American and sharp cheddar for flavor and meltability.

Half the fun of a good cheeseburger is the toppings, so I stirred in ketchup, mustard, and chopped dill pickles. Switching to raw onion instead of cooked gave me that familiar sharp flavor I love on burgers. Finally, a tablespoon of Worcestershire sauce bolstered the overall meatiness.

A younger version of myself would jump for joy—just like the current grown-up version.

—MARK HUXSOLL, *Cook's Country*

NOTES FROM THE TEST KITCHEN

BURGER FLAVORS
What makes our version of one-pan macaroni and cheese taste like cheeseburgers? Aside from the ground beef, it's this roster of savory burger toppings: chopped onion and pickles, ketchup, mustard, Worcestershire sauce, sharp cheddar, and melty-gooey American cheese.

Cheeseburger Mac

SERVES 4 TO 6

Tossing the beef with the baking soda solution in step 1 helps keep it tender.

1½ tablespoons plus 1½ cups water, divided
1 teaspoon table salt, divided
1 teaspoon pepper
½ teaspoon baking soda
1 pound 85 percent lean ground beef
1 tablespoon vegetable oil
8 ounces (2 cups) elbow macaroni
1 cup whole milk
8 ounces American cheese, chopped (2 cups), divided
8 ounces sharp cheddar cheese, shredded (2 cups), divided
½ cup finely chopped onion, plus extra for serving
¼ cup finely chopped dill pickles, plus extra for serving
2 tablespoons ketchup
2 tablespoons yellow mustard
1 tablespoon Worcestershire sauce

1. Stir 1½ tablespoons water, ½ teaspoon salt, pepper, and baking soda in medium bowl until baking soda and salt are dissolved. Add beef and mix until thoroughly combined. Let sit for 15 minutes.

2. Heat oil in 12-inch broiler-safe skillet over medium-high heat until just smoking. Add beef and cook, breaking up meat with wooden spoon, until well browned, 6 to 8 minutes.

3. Add macaroni, milk, and remaining 1½ cups water and bring to simmer. Cover; reduce heat to medium-low; and cook until macaroni is al dente, about 5 minutes, stirring halfway through cooking.

4. Adjust oven rack 6 inches from broiler element and heat broiler. Stir 1½ cups American cheese, 1½ cups cheddar, onion, pickles, ketchup, mustard, Worcestershire, and remaining ½ teaspoon salt into macaroni until fully combined and cheese is melted, about 2 minutes.

5. Off heat, sprinkle remaining ½ cup American cheese and remaining ½ cup cheddar over top of macaroni. Broil until spotty brown, about 2 minutes. Let cool for 5 minutes. Sprinkle with extra onion and pickles. Serve.

PASTA E PISELLI (PASTA AND PEAS)

✓ **WHY THIS RECIPE WORKS** Like its better-known cousins pasta e fagioli and pasta e ceci, the traditional Italian dish pasta e piselli combines a legume, peas, with small pasta to form a hearty soup. The soup comes together in one pot—we cooked the pasta in a broth flavored with sautéed onion and savory pancetta, simultaneously infusing the pasta with savoriness and thickening the rich, silky broth. Then we added the peas (we used frozen petite peas) and immediately took the pot off the heat to preserve their tenderness and color. Grated Pecorino Romano contributed richness and tangy depth. Last-minute additions of minced herbs (fresh parsley and mint) and extra-virgin olive oil punched up the aroma and flavors of the dish.

The earliest pasta dishes weren't the perfectly sauced plates that are common today. Rather, they were humble, brothy soups made by resourceful home cooks who combined water and noodle scraps with dried legumes, stale bread, bits of meat, and whatever else they happened to have on hand. According to Danielle Callegari, a historian of Italian food at Dartmouth College whom I consulted for a little bit of background on this centuries-old way of eating pasta, a family would make a batch of soup and keep the pot warm on the stove, enhancing it with more odds and ends as the days passed and sitting down together to eat a simple, nourishing meal at any time. It was "a dish of convenience, unquestionably," Callegari said.

Pasta e fagioli and pasta e ceci are two well-known examples of these soups, but I homed in on pasta e piselli. This dish is a less familiar style of the soup that trades the beans and chickpeas for peas. Like these other pasta and legume soups, the dish has evolved over the years to be a more carefully constructed preparation that is made with specific ingredients instead of whatever leftovers are available. It can take different forms—some versions have lost the liquid almost entirely, others have come to include tomatoes—but most modern versions feature sweet peas and small pasta, such as ditalini or tubetti, that won't overshadow the diminutive legumes. My favorite rendition is a little more substantial than the earliest soupy iterations, featuring a rich, savory broth bulked up with plenty of tender pasta and sweet peas.

PASTA E PISELLI (PASTA AND PEAS)

It came as no surprise to me that the broth is a make-or-break component of the dish—too subtle and the dish will be bland, too robust and the delicate sweetness of the peas will be lost. After a couple rounds of testing, I decided to build the broth on a base of onion and pancetta. Briefly sautéing these ingredients created a flavorful foundation, but when I added 5 cups of water, I found that the resulting broth tasted flat. The fix, fortunately, was simple: I replaced half the water with chicken broth. The chicken broth boosted the sweet, mellow taste of the onion as well as the porkiness of the pancetta but was still subtle enough to let the sweet peas shine.

Next, I worked on how much pasta to stir in to give the dish the right amount of bulk. I landed on 1½ cups of ditalini, which over the course of 8 to 10 minutes of cooking released starches that lent ample body to the broth, developing the dish's rich, silky texture. Meanwhile, the savory broth flavored the pasta.

Once the pasta was al dente, it was time to add the peas. Because the season for fresh peas is fleeting—and they lose sweetness from the moment they're harvested—using frozen peas was a much better bet. I chose petite peas, which we have found to have an even sweeter taste than larger peas. Peas of any kind can overcook in a flash, becoming starchy and mushy. To make sure that they retained their firmness and vibrant color, I stirred them frozen into the hot broth and immediately took the pot off the heat. The peas heated through right away, with nary a chance of turning Army green or overcooking.

I now had a solid rendition of pasta e piselli, but I wanted to add a little more depth and brightness. First, I swapped out the more milky and savory Parmesan that usually finishes the soup for Pecorino Romano. Made with sheep's milk, Pecorino brings a sharpness to the broth that enhances the sweetness of the peas. Then, I minced fresh parsley and mint and stirred in the herbs off the heat, giving my soup a boost of freshness. At the table, more grated Pecorino Romano and a drizzle of olive oil punched up the flavors even more.

Simple but satisfying and taking barely an hour to throw together, pasta e piselli might just be the gold standard of one-pot cooking.

—LAN LAM, *Cook's Illustrated*

Pasta e Piselli (Pasta and Peas)

SERVES 4

If you'd prefer to substitute small pasta such as tubetti, ditali, elbow macaroni, or small shells for the ditalini, do so by weight, not by volume. We prefer frozen petite peas (also labeled as petit pois or baby sweet peas) in this recipe because they are sweeter and less starchy than fresh peas or regular frozen peas. There's no need to defrost the peas before using them. For a vegetarian version, omit the pancetta, substitute vegetable broth for the chicken broth, and add an extra 2 tablespoons of grated cheese. Pecorino Romano adds a welcome sharpness; we do not recommend substituting Parmesan in this recipe.

- 2 tablespoons extra-virgin olive oil, plus extra for drizzling
- 1 onion, chopped fine
- 2 ounces pancetta, chopped fine
- ½ teaspoon table salt
- ½ teaspoon pepper
- 2½ cups chicken broth
- 2½ cups water
- 7½ ounces (1½ cups) ditalini
- 1½ cups frozen petite peas
- ⅓ cup minced fresh parsley
- ¼ cup grated Pecorino Romano cheese, plus extra for serving
- 2 tablespoons minced fresh mint

1. Heat oil in large saucepan over medium heat until shimmering. Add onion, pancetta, salt, and pepper and cook, stirring frequently, until onion is softened, 7 to 10 minutes.

2. Add broth and water and bring to boil over high heat. Stir in pasta and cook, stirring frequently, until liquid returns to boil. Reduce heat to maintain simmer; cover; and cook until pasta is al dente, 8 to 10 minutes.

3. Stir in peas and remove saucepan from heat. Stir in parsley, Pecorino, and mint. Season with salt and pepper to taste. Serve, drizzling with extra oil and passing extra Pecorino separately.

CASHEW E PEPE E FUNGHI

✔ **WHY THIS RECIPE WORKS** We had hoped to develop a vegan version of either pasta carbonara or pasta cacio e pepe, but as it turned out, tasters loved this oh-so-creamy dish that includes the best hallmarks of both these Italian favorites. Having done lots of work with cashews in the test kitchen, we knew that this nut would be able to provide a thick and creamy sauce base because of its uniquely low fiber and high starch content. We discovered that by breaking the cashews up in a blender (to increase their surface area), we could soak them for just 15 minutes in the flavorful sauce ingredients. We usually use raw cashews for their more neutral flavor, but since we used only ½ cup here, we opted for roasted cashews; they added nuanced warmth without imparting a nutty taste. Miso and nutritional yeast each contributed different aspects of umami to the sauce. Plenty of coarsely ground pepper added subtle heat. Oyster mushrooms were a revelation: Because they contain very little moisture (relative to other mushrooms), they quickly cooked into chewy, golden, almost bacony nuggets. Some parsley and a splash of lemon juice provided freshness and acidity.

Plant-based cooking has become increasingly popular in recent years as more people—not just vegans and vegetarians—have been incorporating more plant-focused meals into their diets, whether for ethical, environmental, or health reasons. So for our *Complete Plant-Based Cookbook*, we aimed to make favorite recipes into satisfying vegan dishes. When I set out to make a vegan cacio e pepe with a touch of pasta alla carbonara, I had my work cut out for me—traditional cacio e pepe ("cheese and pepper" in Italian) relies on very few ingredients to create a stunning dish. And two of those ingredients, the traditional Pecorino Romano or Parmesan and the butter or cream, would need replacing to make a vegan version. For my dish, I wanted to make an elevated, modern pasta that was a departure from heavier, cheesy comfort foods such as macaroni and cheese or an American-style fettuccine Alfredo. I also wanted it to be a complete meal in and of itself, with nuanced flavors and textures and a full-bodied but not overly rich sauce.

I started my recipe development by testing three recipes for modern vegan creamy pasta dishes. These recipes helped me see both what I wanted and what I didn't want. One recipe for vegan pasta alla carbonara was full of unexpected ingredients and overly complicated processes—it called for tofu and sauerkraut brine, both of which we hated. Tofu helped create a sauce with good texture, but the flavor was off. I knew I could find something that would make a sauce with the same texture but better flavor. One component of this recipe that we liked was the oyster mushroom "bacon," so I filed that away as a possible addition. Two of the recipes we tried called for miso and nutritional yeast, both of which are flavor powerhouses that can be valuable additions to plant-based recipes where you aren't getting any savory flavor from animal products. We liked these additions, as well as the cashew butter in one recipe. The cashew butter sauce, our favorite of the three recipes we tested, was creamy, supersimple, and perfectly balanced. After these tests, I decided to stick with cashews but go with plain cashews rather than hard-to-find cashew butter.

After testing these recipes, I had identified four key vegan superstars that I wanted to include in my recipe: miso, oyster mushrooms, nutritional yeast, and cashews. The first three all bring umami flavor. Umami is often associated with meats and cheeses and can be described as savory- or meaty-tasting, but it can be found in many plant-based ingredients that are high in glutamates (amino acids that are associated with umami flavor). In addition, some food preservation techniques such as fermentation and drying can increase an ingredient's umami flavor. The fermentation of soybeans for miso helps it give a hit of savoriness to dishes, which is why I included it here. Nutritional yeast is yeast that has been deactivated with heat to make a flaky yellow powder that tastes cheesy and nutty, perfect for replicating the flavor of Pecorino or Parmesan here. Oyster mushrooms are also high in glutamates, and their cell walls are made of a heat-stable substance called chitin, so instead of breaking down when cooked, they take on a chewy texture similar to that of meat. I chose to include them for their similarity to the bacon bits in carbonara and because of the interesting textural element they added. The key to the whole recipe was the cashews, which are indispensable in a plant-based kitchen for their ability to turn into creamy vegan cheeses and sauces.

After deciding on the inclusion of cashews, I had some experimenting to do to figure out the best way to turn them into the luscious sauce I was imagining. I tried roasted and plain cashews and found that they had a rounder, more nuanced flavor when roasted. Most recipes where cashews will be turned into a sauce call for soaking the cashews overnight, but I had an ace up my sleeve there. While making a creamless creamy dressing, my colleague Andrea Geary had discovered that briefly blending the cashews to make smaller pieces and then soaking them in the other dressing ingredients for just 15 minutes was just as effective as an overnight soak. My cashew sauce was a bit watery postblending, but once added to the hot pasta, the starches in the cashews soaked up any extra water and became a creamy sauce with a full-bodied consistency.

In the end, I had a complete meal with a silky sauce; lots of umami flavor; a satisfying mix of textures; and simple, straightforward prep. I had started out trying to make a vegan cacio e pepe, but I ended up with something that was more than that—an elevated pasta that combined the best qualities of cacio e pepe and carbonara but was a dish all its own, more than the sum of its parts. I had my perfect vegan pasta.

—JOSEPH GITTER, *America's Test Kitchen Books*

Cashew e Pepe e Funghi
SERVES 4 TO 6

You can substitute portobello mushrooms for the oyster mushrooms, but the mushroom "bacon" won't be nearly as crispy.

½ cup roasted cashews
¼ cup nutritional yeast
2 tablespoons white miso
½ teaspoon table salt, plus salt for cooking pasta
¼ cup extra-virgin olive oil
6 ounces oyster mushrooms, trimmed and chopped
5 garlic cloves, sliced thin
1 teaspoon coarsely ground pepper
1 pound spaghetti
2 tablespoons chopped fresh parsley
1 teaspoon lemon juice

1. Process cashews in blender on low speed until consistency of fine gravel mixed with sand, 10 to 15 seconds. Add 1½ cups water, nutritional yeast, miso, and salt and process on low speed until combined, about 5 seconds. Scrape down sides of blender jar and let mixture sit for 15 minutes.

2. Process on low speed until all ingredients are well blended, about 1 minute. Scrape down sides of blender jar, then process on high speed until sauce is completely smooth, 3 to 4 minutes.

3. Heat oil in 12-inch skillet over medium-high heat until shimmering. Add mushrooms and cook until deep golden brown and crispy, 7 to 10 minutes. Off heat, stir in garlic and pepper and cook using residual heat of skillet until fragrant, about 1 minute.

4. Meanwhile, bring 4 quarts water to boil in large pot. Add pasta and 1 tablespoon salt and cook, stirring often, until al dente. Reserve ½ cup cooking water, then drain pasta and return it to pot.

5. Add sauce, mushroom mixture, parsley, and lemon juice to pasta and toss until sauce is thickened slightly and pasta is well coated, about 1 minute. Before serving, adjust consistency with reserved cooking water as needed and season with salt and pepper to taste.

SPAGHETTI WITH TUNA AND CAPERS

✓ **WHY THIS RECIPE WORKS** We wanted a streamlined one-pot pantry pasta that featured meaty oil-packed tuna, briny capers, and savory Parmesan cheese. We started by slightly undercooking the pasta in 3 quarts of water to ensure that plenty of starch was in the cooking water. After reserving some cooking water and draining the pasta, we added a glug of olive oil and plenty of sliced garlic to the now-empty pot to cook over medium-low heat until the garlic was fragrant. We quickly added in some plump little capers, spicy red pepper flakes, and the cooked pasta along with 2 cups of the starchy cooking water. After bringing the liquid to a boil, we tossed the pasta constantly, not stopping until the water was nearly all absorbed and the pasta was al dente. This motion helped create something like an emulsion around the still-cooking pasta, a velvety sauce that was ready for a can or jar of flaked tuna, grated Parmesan, and chopped fresh parsley.

It's late afternoon on a Wednesday, and the sun has just sunk behind the horizon. I've spent the day at home, juggling work, kids (three), and a brand-new puppy. My stomach is rumbling, but my energy reserves are running short—the last thing I can imagine doing is going to the grocery store. Instead, I'll dive into the pantry.

SPAGHETTI WITH TUNA AND CAPERS

Good news. There's a can of tuna. There's a box of spaghetti, a jar of capers, a head of garlic, and some red pepper flakes. Oh, and in the refrigerator, there's half a bunch of parsley and a wedge of Parmesan cheese. "Good news, kids!" I shout. "It's pasta night!"

I'm a die-hard fan of simple pasta dishes such as aglio e olio, the streamlined Italian dish of noodles, olive oil, garlic, and red pepper flakes. For dinner tonight, I'll simply be layering in more flavor in the form of meaty oil-packed tuna, briny capers, and savory Parmesan cheese. And unlike most pasta recipes we've created in the past, this one will be cooked all in one pot. Fewer dishes to deal with.

I start by cooking the spaghetti. Experience tells me that undercooking the pasta up front is the way to go; I'll finish it off in the sauce so that it's al dente once it hits the table. Just 5 minutes in a pot of rapidly boiling water (a strict 3 quarts to ensure plenty of starch in the cooking water, which I'll use in the sauce) is enough for now. I drain the not-quite-cooked noodles, but not before reserving 3 cups of that starchy cooking water.

In the same pot, now empty, I add a glug of olive oil and plenty of sliced garlic (eight cloves, because I have no time for vampires) to cook over medium-low heat until the kitchen is filled with its aroma. It smells enticing, and I can feel the family starting to circle. Next come some plump little capers and spicy red pepper flakes, and, quickly now, the pasta and 2 cups of the reserved cooking water, which I bring to a boil.

I grab my tongs and start tossing. Toss, toss, toss—I don't stop. I keep going until the water's nearly all absorbed and the pasta is perfectly al dente, about 5 minutes. The motion helps create something like an emulsion around the still-cooking pasta, a velvety sauce that's ready for flaked tuna, a shower of grated Parmesan, and some chopped fresh parsley. I add just a little more cooking water to make sure that the consistency is saucy and smooth.

Everyone's at the table now. It's time to eat.

—BRYAN ROOF, *Cook's Country*

Spaghetti with Tuna and Capers

SERVES 4 TO 6

Make sure that you have all the ingredients prepped and ready to go when you start cooking. For the best results, you'll need to flow seamlessly through the recipe steps. Oil-packed tuna comes in a variety of can and jar sizes, hence the weight range in the ingredient list. Use a product you like that fits your budget.

- 1 **pound spaghetti**
- ¼ **teaspoon table salt, plus salt for cooking pasta**
- ⅓ **cup extra-virgin olive oil, plus extra for drizzling**
- 8 **garlic cloves, sliced thin**
- 2 **tablespoons capers, rinsed**
- ½ **teaspoon red pepper flakes, plus extra for serving**
- 1 **(5- to 7-ounce) can/jar olive oil–packed tuna, flaked with packing oil**
- 1 **ounce Parmesan cheese, grated (½ cup), plus extra for serving**
- ¼ **cup chopped fresh parsley**

1. Bring 3 quarts water to boil in large Dutch oven. Add pasta and 1 tablespoon salt and cook, stirring often, until strands are flexible but still very firm in center, about 5 minutes. Turn off heat, reserve 3 cups cooking water, then drain pasta.

2. In now-empty pot, heat oil and garlic over medium-low heat until fragrant and just shy of browning, 2 to 3 minutes. Stir in capers and pepper flakes and cook until fragrant, about 20 seconds.

3. Add pasta, 2 cups reserved cooking water, and salt and bring to boil over medium heat. Cook, stirring often with tongs and folding pasta over itself, until water is mostly absorbed but still pools slightly at bottom of pot, about 5 minutes.

4. Off heat, stir in tuna, Parmesan, parsley, and ½ cup reserved cooking water with tongs until all ingredients are well combined, about 1 minute. Adjust consistency with additional reserved cooking water as needed. Serve, sprinkled with extra Parmesan and pepper flakes and drizzled with extra oil.

NOTES FROM THE TEST KITCHEN

THE BEST OIL-PACKED TUNA
A recent test kitchen taste test of tuna packed in oil crowned co-winners: Tonnino Tuna Fillets in Olive Oil (shown here) and Ortiz Bonito del Norte Albacore White Tuna in Olive Oil. While both tunas are fantastic, the Tonnino is less expensive. Our tasters loved this yellowfin tuna for its "slightly silky," "firm but tender" texture and "clean," "bright" flavor.

DAN DAN MIAN (SICHUAN NOODLES WITH CHILI SAUCE AND PORK)

✓ **WHY THIS RECIPE WORKS** Sichuan's most popular street food consists of chewy noodles bathed in a spicy, fragrant chili sauce and topped with crispy, deeply savory bits of ground pork and plump, juicy lengths of baby bok choy. Gently heating Sichuan chili powder, ground Sichuan peppercorns, and cinnamon in vegetable oil for just 10 minutes yielded a flavorful chili oil base for the sauce. Whisking in soy sauce, Chinese black vinegar, sweet wheat paste, and Chinese sesame paste added earthy, faintly sweet depth and appropriately thickened the mixture. We smeared the ground pork into a thin layer across the wok with a rubber spatula, jabbing at it with the tool's edge to break it up into bits, and seared it hard to produce crispy bits that clung to the noodles. Stirring in minced garlic and grated ginger, plus a big scoop of the Sichuan pickle called ya cai, added unique tang and complexity. Blanching baby bok choy brightened its color and freed water from its cell walls, giving the vegetable its juicy, palate-cleansing effect. We trimmed the base of each bulb and halved the bulbs lengthwise to create bite-size pieces that softened at the same rate. Saving the blanching water to boil the noodles was efficient, and thoroughly rinsing them after they were cooked washed away surface starch that would have caused them to stick together.

If you love noodles and Sichuan food, you're probably well versed in dan dan mian and all its chewy, spicy, electric glory. The dish, named for the pole that vendors use to tote ingredients, is iconic street food within the province, where diners savor even the act of mixing together their own portion—a custom known as "ban." The ritual starts with four color-blocked elements neatly composed in a bowl: a pool of vivid red chili sauce, a mound of ivory wheat noodles, crispy browned bits of seasoned ground pork, and lengths of jade-green baby bok choy. Then, with the nudge of your chopsticks, all that color, heat, and savory tang washes over the noodles—and then your palate. Just as the numbing sensation and richness builds and nearly overwhelms your tastebuds, a juicy, cooling piece of bok choy swoops in and resets your system for the next bite. If there's a more dynamic noodle-eating experience out there, I don't know it.

And yet, I'd rarely made dan dan mian until recently. The hang-up wasn't about the cooking; even though there are four components, each one is fast and simple to prepare. It was about sourcing the handful of very particular ingredients that make dan dan mian so complex. Without a robust Sichuan pantry, I was missing many of them—and my impression had always been that this is not a dish where I could just hack it with substitutions and expect to get it right.

But when I ran a diagnostic breakdown of the dish, sussing out where I could and couldn't compromise, I learned that my assumption was only partially true. Yes, there were a few must-haves to seek out, but there was also a good bit of ingredient flexibility that helped bring dan dan mian within my grasp. Zeroing in so deeply also prompted me to polish up a few steps along the way so that the flavors and textures of the dish really popped. Now I knock out a version whenever I want, and you should, too. Because the only thing more satisfying than tucking into a bowl yourself will be hearing your friends and family clamor for seconds.

The noodles should soak up the sauce, capture the crumbly bits of pork, and deliver springy chew. Fresh, thin, egg-free Chinese wheat noodles are the standard for dan dan mian, but fresh lo mein and ramen check all those boxes, too. Even dried lo mein works, as long as you use half as much. Whichever kind you use, be sure to give the noodles a thorough rinse after cooking them to remove their sticky surface starch. Otherwise, they'll fuse into a doughy mass.

Sichuan chili oil is the base of the sauce that reddens, lubricates, and lights up the noodles with má ("numbing") là ("spicy") flavor. Making your own usually involves heating spices and sometimes aromatics in neutral oil and letting the mixture sit for several days to draw out maximum flavor. But I found that you can make a good version by gently heating Sichuan chili powder (you can substitute Korean gochugaru, which is a tad milder), ground Sichuan peppercorns (their numbing sensation is critical here), and cinnamon in oil for just 10 minutes.

Turning that oil into a deeply savory sauce is simply a matter of whisking in a handful of bottled condiments and pastes. Soy sauce is the easy one, and balsamic vinegar can mimic the fruity tang of Chinese black vinegar. Traditionally, it's a combination of Chinese sweet wheat and sesame pastes that adds earthy, faintly sweet depth and thickens the mixture, but hoisin and

DAN DAN MIAN (SICHUAN NOODLES WITH CHILI SAUCE AND PORK)

tahini make admirable stand-ins. Don't worry if the oil separates and pools as the sauce sits; it's normal—and quite pretty.

Tender, juicy meat is not the goal here. What you want is a crispy, umami-rich seasoning that clings to the noodles. To get it really fine-textured and brown, I smear the ground pork into a thin layer across the wok with a rubber spatula, jab at it with the tool's edge to break it up into bits, and sear it hard—really hard. The end result is fine bits of pork with crispy edges.

Then I stir in minced garlic and grated ginger, followed by a big scoop of the Sichuan pickle called ya cai. Made by fermenting the stalks of a Chinese mustard plant, it adds tangy, complex, subtly spicy funk. There's nothing quite like it (even in Sichuan, where fermented foods are a particular specialty), and since it's shelf-stable, you may as well stock up on it for future dan dan mian.

Blanching baby bok choy brightens its color and slightly softens its texture, but that softening does more than tenderize. It frees water from the cell walls, giving the vegetable its juicy, palate-cleansing effect. To create bite-size pieces that soften at the same rate, I trim the base of each bulb, which causes the larger outer leaves to separate, and then halve the bulb lengthwise. The pieces need only a minute-long dunk in the water before they're crisp-tender (save the water to boil the noodles!), and there's no need to fuss with shocking in an ice bath, since they will cool quickly once transferred to a plate.

—LAN LAM, *Cook's Illustrated*

Dan Dan Mian (Sichuan Noodles with Chili Sauce and Pork)

SERVES 4

If you can't find Sichuan chili powder, substitute Korean red pepper flakes (gochugaru). Sichuan peppercorns provide a tingly, numbing sensation that's important to this dish; find them in the spice aisle at Asian markets. We prefer the chewy texture of fresh, eggless Chinese wheat noodles here. If they aren't available, substitute fresh lo mein or ramen noodles or 8 ounces of dried lo mein noodles. Ya cai, Sichuan preserved mustard greens, gives these noodles a savory and pungent boost; you can buy it online or at an Asian market. If ya cai is unavailable, omit it and increase the soy sauce in step 2 to 2 teaspoons. This dish can be served warm or at room temperature.

SAUCE

¼ cup vegetable oil

1 tablespoon Sichuan chili powder

2 teaspoons Sichuan peppercorns, ground fine

¼ teaspoon ground cinnamon

2 tablespoons soy sauce

2 teaspoons Chinese black vinegar or balsamic vinegar

2 teaspoons sweet wheat paste or hoisin sauce

1½ teaspoons Chinese sesame paste or tahini

NOODLES

8 ounces ground pork

2 teaspoons Shaoxing wine or dry sherry

1 teaspoon soy sauce

2 small heads baby bok choy (about 3 ounces each)

1 tablespoon vegetable oil, divided

3 garlic cloves, minced

2 teaspoons grated fresh ginger

1 pound fresh Chinese wheat noodles

⅓ cup ya cai

2 scallions, sliced thin on bias

1. FOR THE SAUCE: Heat oil, chili powder, peppercorns, and cinnamon in 14-inch wok or 12-inch nonstick skillet over low heat for 10 minutes. Using heat-resistant rubber spatula, transfer oil mixture to bowl (do not wash wok). Whisk soy sauce, vinegar, wheat paste, and sesame paste into oil mixture. Divide evenly among 4 shallow bowls.

2. FOR THE NOODLES: Bring 4 quarts water to boil in large pot. While water comes to boil, combine pork, Shaoxing wine, and soy sauce in medium bowl and toss with your hands until well combined. Set aside. Working with 1 head bok choy at a time, trim base (larger leaves will fall off) and halve lengthwise through core. Rinse well.

3. Heat 2 teaspoons oil in now-empty wok over medium-high heat until shimmering. Add pork mixture and use rubber spatula to smear into thin layer across surface of wok. Break up meat into ¼-inch chunks with edge of spatula and cook, stirring frequently, until pork is firm and well browned, about 5 minutes. Push pork mixture to far side of wok and add garlic, ginger, and remaining 1 teaspoon oil to cleared space. Cook, stirring constantly, until garlic mixture begins to brown, about 1 minute. Stir to combine pork mixture with garlic mixture. Remove wok from heat.

4. Add bok choy to boiling water and cook until leaves are vibrant green and stems are crisp-tender, about 1 minute. Using slotted spoon or spider skimmer, transfer boy choy to plate; set aside. Add noodles to boiling water and cook, stirring often, until almost tender (center should still be firm with slightly opaque dot). Drain noodles. Rinse under hot running water, tossing with tongs, for 1 minute. Drain well.

5. Divide noodles evenly among prepared bowls. Return wok with pork to medium heat. Add ya cai and cook, stirring frequently, until warmed through, about 2 minutes. Spoon equal amounts of pork topping over noodles. Divide bok choy evenly among bowls, shaking to remove excess moisture as you portion. Top with scallions and serve, leaving each diner to stir components together before eating.

NOTES FROM THE TEST KITCHEN

HOW TO BUILD THE BOWL
Proper dan dan mian starts with carefully composing the four elements (chili sauce, noodles, pork topping, and blanched bok choy) in the bowl. Doing so allows diners to enjoy the visual contrast of each plated portion as well as the act of tossing everything together—a Sichuan custom known as "ban." Below is a breakdown of how to layer everything in the bowl.

BLANCHED BOK CHOY

PORK TOPPING

NOODLES

CHILI SAUCE

SPINACH AND RICOTTA GNUDI WITH TOMATO-BUTTER SAUCE

✓ WHY THIS RECIPE WORKS Pillowy, verdant, milky-rich gnudi are Italian dumplings cobbled together from ricotta and greens (usually fresh spinach or chard), delicately seasoned, and bound with egg and flour and/or bread crumbs. The trick to making them well is water management: Both the cheese and the greens are loaded with moisture, which needs to be removed or bound up. We found that "towel-drying" the ricotta on a paper towel–lined rimmed baking sheet efficiently drained the cheese in just 10 minutes. Instead of blanching fresh spinach to break down its cells and release its water, we used frozen spinach, which readily gives up its water when it thaws; all we had to do was squeeze it dry. Protein-rich egg whites, flour, and panko bread crumbs (which lightened the mixture because they broke up the structure and made it heterogeneous) bound the mixture into a light, tender dough that we scooped and rolled into balls and then gently poached in salted water. Taking inspiration from both traditional sauces—bright tomato sugo and rich browned butter—we made a hybrid accompaniment by toasting garlic in browning butter and adding halved fresh cherry tomatoes, which released their bright juice.

Italian cooks came by gnudi the way other cooks in that part of the world came by panzanella and pappa al pomodoro—by necessity more than by design. They patched together the cheese and greens (usually chard or spinach) that were abundant in pastoral pockets of Tuscany, binding them with egg, flour and/or bread crumbs, grated Parmesan or pecorino, and seasonings. When the dough was adequately cohesive, they molded portions into round or cylindrical dumplings; gently poached them in salty water; and sauced them simply, with tomato sugo or browned butter.

This was cucina povera at its best: a couple of naturally paired provisions deftly worked into something substantial and satisfying. And while the dish's name suggests a certain deficiency, the dumplings' appeal is arguably thanks to the absence of pasta dough. ("Gnudi" literally means "nudes," referring to the way they seem like ravioli filling without the wrapper.) In fact, Italian food scholars such as Oretta Zanini De Vita have traced praise for gnudi as far back as the 13th century. In her *Encyclopedia of Pasta* (2009), Zanini De Vita notes that the Franciscan friar and chronicler Salimbene da Parma ". . . tasted gnudi for the feast of Saint Clare and considered them a true delicacy."

At the same time, it must have taken practiced hands to turn out the tender, verdant dumplings that still make up the dish today. I stumbled through my first batches as I confronted the dish's universal challenge: water management. Both the ricotta and the greens are full of moisture, much of which must be removed lest the dough be too difficult to handle or require so much binder that the dumplings are leaden instead of light.

Michael Pagliarini, chef-owner of Giulia and Benedetto restaurants in Cambridge, Massachusetts, underscored the latter risk for me, noting that cooks must tread carefully when it comes to binders if they don't want dense results. Jody Adams, a Boston-area chef best known for her restaurants Porto, Trade, and (now-shuttered) Rialto, echoed that sentiment.

"[There's a] physical challenge to getting it right," she said of the dough. "[There should be] just enough firmness that it doesn't disintegrate . . . but [it should be] really airy."

To tackle the water issue, most recipes suggest draining the ricotta in a paper towel–lined strainer and blanching the greens (I was using fresh spinach) before squeezing out as much water as possible. I had no trouble with either technique, except efficiency. It took hours for the cheese to drain sufficiently and multiple batches of blanched spinach to yield enough for four servings of dough. Ultimately, I changed tack on both: I "towel-dried" the ricotta on a rimmed baking sheet for 10 minutes and used frozen spinach, which simply needed to be thawed and dried in a single batch.

From there, I chopped the spinach in a food processor and transferred it to a bowl with the drained ricotta. Then I seasoned the mixture with Parmesan, salt and pepper, and lemon zest and started experimenting with binders. I needed just the right balance of eggs and starch: Egg proteins hold the dough together as it cooks, but eggs also add water; starch from flour and/ or bread crumbs absorbs water, firming the dough and making it easy to manipulate, but too much can lead to dense results.

Case in point: I made a beautifully workable dough with a pair of egg whites (more valuable than yolks for their preponderance of binding proteins) and a little more than ½ cup of flour. I rolled it into tidy ropes and cut the ropes into small pieces as I would gnocchi—the shaping approach I'd seen in several recipes. But the cooked dumplings were dense and tight.

I could have kept fiddling with the ratios, but instead I solicited ideas from Lydia Reichert, a friend of mine who is the former chef at Sycamore in Newton, Massachusetts. She offered a clutch suggestion: Instead of making a dough that's firm enough to roll, make one that's just cohesive enough to scoop and roll into rounds.

To do that, I had to cut back on some of the flour without removing so much starch that the dough became sticky. That was a perfect job for the bread crumbs I'd seen in some gnudi recipes: Just 1 tablespoon of conventional crumbs in place of an equal amount of flour produced a light but cohesive dough and noticeably airier gnudi. The results were better with panko; these coarser crumbs are more absorbent and made the dough easier to handle.

Bright tomato sugo and rich browned butter are classic gnudi sauces, but I was intrigued by the thoughtful, less traditional riffs I'd seen and ended up making something of a hybrid. I melted some butter, toasting thinly sliced garlic in it as I swirled the pan, and then added halved cherry tomatoes along with a splash of cider vinegar. I cut the heat and covered the pan so that the tomatoes collapsed and spilled their bright juice into the butter—almost like tomato confit. Fresh basil and grated Parmesan made the whole ensemble pop and placed my take on this dish just where I wanted it: comfortably wedged between traditional and personal.

—LAN LAM, *Cook's Illustrated*

Spinach and Ricotta Gnudi with Tomato-Butter Sauce

SERVES 4

Ricotta without stabilizers such as locust bean, guar, and xanthan gums drains more readily. You can substitute part-skim ricotta for the whole-milk ricotta. Frozen whole-leaf spinach is easiest to squeeze dry, but frozen chopped spinach will work. Squeezing the spinach should remove ½ to ⅔ cup of liquid; you should have ⅔ cup of finely chopped spinach. Our tomato-butter sauce isn't strictly canonical; if you'd prefer a more traditional accompaniment, substitute browned butter and fresh sage. Serve with a simple salad.

GNUDI

- 12 ounces (1½ cups) whole-milk ricotta cheese
- ½ cup all-purpose flour
- 1 ounce Parmesan cheese, grated (½ cup), plus extra for garnishing
- 1 tablespoon panko bread crumbs
- ¾ teaspoon table salt, plus salt for cooking gnudi
- ½ teaspoon pepper
- ¼ teaspoon grated lemon zest
- 10 ounces frozen whole-leaf spinach, thawed and squeezed dry
- 2 large egg whites, lightly beaten

SAUCE

- 4 tablespoons unsalted butter
- 3 garlic cloves, sliced thin
- 12 ounces cherry or grape tomatoes, halved
- 2 teaspoons cider vinegar
- ¼ teaspoon table salt
- ¼ teaspoon pepper
- 2 tablespoons shredded fresh basil

1. FOR THE GNUDI: Line rimmed baking sheet with double layer of paper towels. Spread ricotta in even layer over towels; set aside and let sit for 10 minutes. Place flour, Parmesan, panko, salt, pepper, and lemon zest in large bowl and stir to combine. Process spinach in food processor until finely chopped, about 30 seconds, scraping down sides of bowl as needed. Transfer spinach to bowl with flour mixture. Grasp paper towels and fold ricotta in half; peel back towels. Rotate sheet 90 degrees and repeat folding and peeling 2 more times to consolidate ricotta into smaller mass. Using paper towels as sling, transfer ricotta to bowl with spinach mixture. Discard paper towels but do not wash sheet. Add egg whites to bowl and mix gently until well combined.

2. Transfer heaping teaspoons of dough to now-empty sheet (you should have 45 to 50 portions). Using your dry hands, gently roll each portion into 1-inch ball.

3. FOR THE SAUCE: Melt butter in small saucepan over medium heat. Add garlic and cook, swirling saucepan occasionally, until butter is very foamy and garlic is pale golden brown, 2 to 3 minutes. Off heat, add tomatoes and vinegar; cover and set aside.

4. Bring 1 quart water to boil in Dutch oven. Add 1½ teaspoons salt. Using spider skimmer or slotted spoon, transfer all gnudi to water. Return water to

gentle simmer. Cook, adjusting heat to maintain gentle simmer, for 5 minutes, starting timer once water has returned to simmer (to confirm doneness, cut 1 dumpling in half; center should be firm).

5. While gnudi simmer, add salt and pepper to sauce and cook over medium-high heat, stirring occasionally, until tomatoes are warmed through and slightly softened, about 2 minutes. Divide sauce evenly among 4 bowls. Using spider skimmer or slotted spoon, remove gnudi from pot, drain well, and transfer to bowls with sauce. Garnish with basil and extra Parmesan. Serve immediately.

STUFFED PIZZA

✓ **WHY THIS RECIPE WORKS** We wanted to re-create the impressive stuffed pizza served at Michelangelo's Pizzeria and Italian Restaurant in Sarasota, Florida. For an at-home take, we started with store-bought dough to simplify the process. We rolled out one ball of dough on a sheet of floured parchment paper and topped it with a mixture of mozzarella, hot Italian sausage, ham, pepperoni, and salami. We then rolled out a second ball of dough and carefully placed it over the stuffing, using a rolling pin to maneuver the dough. We pressed down on the pizza to force out any air and compact the ingredients, ensuring that the filling would hold itself together when sliced. Finishing the baked pizza with garlic butter and dried oregano gave it a beautiful sheen and crowning touch. Finally, we let the pizza cool so it held its shape when sliced, and we served it with sauce.

The stuffed pizza at Michelangelo's in Sarasota, Florida, a behemoth packed with meat and cheese, is truly special. But is it a reasonable dish to make at home? I was determined to find out.

The concept is simple enough: two layers of pizza dough with "toppings" in between. But I suspected that the pizza's tricky architecture could lead to spillage. I wondered if baking the pizza in a cake pan would help, so I tested a basic recipe on a rimmed baking sheet and in a 9-inch cake pan. The pan helped with structure, but the pie didn't develop a deep golden color.

When I tried building the pizza directly on the baking sheet, however, the rim impeded my ability to seal it tightly. I built the next pie on a lightly floured piece of parchment paper, and then, once it was sealed, I used

STUFFED PIZZA

the parchment to transfer it to the sheet. After some experimenting, I found that baking the pizza on the lowest oven rack produced even browning.

Stuffing the pizza generously but carefully and sealing it tightly are the keys to a sliceable pie that won't explode. Also essential: letting the pizza cool for at least 45 minutes to allow the cheese to set up so that the slices stay intact. A short stint in a hot oven rewarms the pie for serving.

In a series of tests, I found that store-bought pizza dough worked just as well as homemade; once you brush the hot pizza with melted garlic butter and dried oregano, either type of dough is transformed into something utterly irresistible.

—MARK HUXSOLL, *Cook's Country*

Stuffed Pizza

SERVES 8

Once baked, the pizza needs to rest for at least 45 minutes so that it can be sliced cleanly without the filling oozing out. Do not use canned pizza dough such as Pillsbury Pizza Crust here. When using store-bought pizza dough, it is helpful to let it come to room temperature to make it easier to roll out and shape. Buy a 4-ounce chunk of salami rather than sliced salami from the deli.

PIZZA

- 4 ounces hot Italian sausage, casings removed
- 4 ounces thinly sliced pepperoni, quartered
- 4 ounces thinly sliced Black Forest deli ham, cut into ½-inch pieces
- 4 ounces salami, cut into ¼-inch cubes
- ¾ teaspoon dried oregano, divided
- 2 (1-pound) balls pizza dough, room temperature
- 1 pound whole-milk block mozzarella cheese, shredded (4 cups), divided
- 2 tablespoons unsalted butter, cut into 2 pieces
- 1 garlic clove, minced

SAUCE

- 1 (14.5-ounce) can whole peeled tomatoes, drained
- 1½ teaspoons extra-virgin olive oil
- 1 small garlic clove, minced
- ½ teaspoon red wine vinegar
- ½ teaspoon table salt
- ½ teaspoon dried oregano

1. FOR THE PIZZA: Adjust oven rack to lowest position and heat oven to 425 degrees. Cook sausage in 8-inch nonstick skillet over medium heat, breaking up meat with wooden spoon, until no longer pink, 5 to 7 minutes. Transfer to medium bowl and let cool completely, about 20 minutes. Add pepperoni, ham, salami, and ½ teaspoon oregano to bowl with sausage and toss to combine.

2. Turn out 1 dough ball onto lightly floured 16 by 12-inch sheet of parchment paper. Using your hands, flatten into 8-inch disk. Using rolling pin, roll dough into 12-inch circle, dusting lightly with flour as needed.

3. Sprinkle 1 cup mozzarella evenly over dough, leaving ½-inch border. Sprinkle one-third of sausage mixture (about 1 heaping cup) over cheese. Repeat layering until cheese and meat mixture are used up (top layer should be cheese).

4. Roll remaining dough ball into 12-inch circle on lightly floured counter, dusting lightly with flour as needed. Brush edges of dough on parchment with water. Loosely roll dough on counter around rolling pin and gently unroll it directly over dough on parchment and filling. Press dough edges together firmly to seal. Using pizza cutter, trim and discard dough just beyond sealed edge of pizza, about ¼ inch from filling.

5. Using paring knife, cut 1-inch hole in top center of pizza. Lifting parchment, transfer pizza to rimmed baking sheet. Using your hands, press down on top of pizza to compress filling into even layer. Bake until deep golden brown, 20 to 25 minutes.

6. Slide pizza from sheet onto wire rack. Microwave butter and garlic in small bowl until butter is melted and mixture is fragrant, about 1 minute. Brush top of hot pizza with garlic butter, then sprinkle with remaining ¼ teaspoon oregano. Let pizza cool on rack for at least 45 minutes. (Cooled pizza can be covered loosely with aluminum foil and refrigerated for up to 2 days.)

7. FOR THE SAUCE: Meanwhile, process all ingredients in food processor until smooth, about 30 seconds. Transfer to serving dish. (Sauce can be refrigerated for up to 3 days or frozen for up to 1 month.)

8. To serve, adjust oven rack to lowest position and heat oven to 425 degrees. Slice pizza into 8 wedges and place on parchment-lined rimmed baking sheet. Bake pizza slices until hot throughout, about 10 minutes. Microwave sauce until hot, about 2 minutes, stirring occasionally. Serve pizza with sauce.

LAHMAJUN (ARMENIAN FLATBREAD)

✓ **WHY THIS RECIPE WORKS** To make the dough for our lahmajun, an Armenian meat-and-vegetable-topped flatbread, we started with a higher-protein all-purpose flour to create an ample amount of gluten that gave the dough both crispness and tenderness. Using ice water and very little yeast and letting the dough ferment slowly in the refrigerator minimized the formation of gas bubbles and allowed the gluten to fully relax so that the dough didn't resist rolling. Garlic, allspice, paprika, cumin, cayenne, and biber salçası (Turkish red pepper paste) added earthy warmth, sweetness, and heat to a savory lamb topping. To control moisture that would make the crust soggy, we minimized watery onions and peppers and replaced juicy fresh or canned tomatoes with tomato paste. Placing plastic wrap over the topping afforded us the dexterity of spreading it with our fingers but avoided any messy direct contact with the meat and vegetable paste. We set a baking stone on the upper-middle rack of the oven and heated it at 500 degrees for an hour: That way, there was intense heat both underneath the flatbreads and reflecting onto them from above, guaranteeing crispness and browning in the few minutes it took the flatbreads to bake, with just enough headspace to usher them into and out of the oven.

I'm Armenian, which means I've been eating lahmajun ("lah-mah-joon") my whole life. My aunties would make it for us when we'd visit, rolling the yeasted dough into paper-thin rounds, spreading the rounds with spiced ground lamb, and baking them until they were crispy and browned. And my mother often brought home the flatbreads from local Armenian bakeries, keeping them stacked face-to-face between sheets of parchment paper until it was time to reheat them. We'd spray the flatbreads with lemon juice and eat them like pizza (lahmajun predates—and is sometimes considered a precursor to—pizza) or turn them into sandwiches by rolling them around a vegetable salad.

My love for the dish had always been more than just habitual, but it wasn't until a few years ago that I ate lahmajun so good that it upped my standards for the dish as both an Armenian and a baker. Cooked in a blazing wood-fired oven, the bread had a delicate and crispy paper-thin crust, yet it was still tender within. And the lamb paste—fragrant with garlic and onion; red pepper; tomato; parsley; and earthy, warm spices—tasted rich and vibrant. Part of the difference was the hearth, which made for exceptional browning and rusticity. But the crumb of these flatbreads boasted more flavor and textural contrast between the exterior and interior than premade bakery versions. In fact, they were more akin to good pizza—sorting out a great recipe was right in my wheelhouse.

The dough for my Thin-Crust Pizza actually seemed like a logical place to start, since it shares many of the assets I had in mind for lahmajun. It's a cold-fermented dough made in the food processor with bread flour, ice water, a fraction of the amount of yeast you'd normally put into a bread, salt, and a little oil and shaped into a ball that gets refrigerated for at least a day. When mixed with water, the bread flour builds up lots of gluten that generates both interior chew and exterior crunch (the gluten sheets that form on the crust's exterior shatter when you bite into them). And the combination of the cold temperature, minimal yeast, and time ensures that the dough ferments gently and gradually, minimizing the formation of large gas bubbles that would make the dough difficult to roll and giving the yeast time to digest sugars in the dough and build up maximum flavor. The lengthy rest also allows the gluten to relax so that the dough is extensible for stretching thin.

But my pizza formula wasn't perfect for lahmajun. For one thing, there was still too much yeast, which made the flatbreads puffy, not flat. They also baked up tough: Lahmajun should be thinner than a typical thin-crust pizza, and the only way to get the dough really thin was to roll (instead of stretch) it, which overworked the gluten. Upping the dough's hydration (the amount of water in relation to the amount of flour) might have increased tenderness but would also have made it stickier—and, frankly, the dough was already sticking to the counter, so I was planning to cut back on the water.

For the next few tests, I adjusted the formula until the dough was supple but not sticky and baked up flat. My revised formula contained a mere ⅛ teaspoon of yeast, a little less water, and—in its best, crispiest iteration—King Arthur All-Purpose Flour, which contains more gluten-forming protein than most other all-purpose flours but not as much as bread flour.

After cold-fermenting for 16 hours and resting at room temperature for about 1 hour, the dough was easy to press into 5-inch disks with the heel of my hand. But rolling the disks into paper-thin 12-inch rounds was trickier and still required so much manipulation with the rolling pin that the dough became overworked and snapped back by a couple inches when I transferred it from the counter to the baking peel. The solution was to skip flouring the counter and use the dough's now-subtle tackiness to anchor it to the counter while I rolled; that way, I didn't have to use as much force to produce thin rounds, and they shrank only a little when I transferred them to the baking peel.

The lamb topping for lahmajun is more like a meaty veneer than a sauce. It should be moist but not wet; heady from garlic, spices, and Turkish pepper paste; and concentrated so that each bite tastes vibrant despite the topping being spread so thin. But those are tricky goals when many of the topping's core components bring along lots of water.

Some recipes control that water by calling for coarsely chopping the vegetables so that they shed minimal liquid, but I prefer toppings that are finely ground. Blitzing the lamb, vegetables, and seasonings in the food processor guarantees that the topping's texture and flavor will be uniform. And I found that the trick to keeping the liquid at bay was going easy on the watery onion, bell pepper, and tomatoes. In fact, I used tomato paste in place of fresh or canned tomatoes.

The real challenge was applying the mixture to the dough, since it's too thick to spread with a spoon or spatula. Lahmajun pros use their hands—arguably the most effective tools for the job—but I came up with a mess-free method: After placing one portion of the topping in the center of a dough round, I covered it with a sheet of plastic wrap. The thin barrier afforded me the dexterity of using my hands but helped me avoid the mess of touching the topping directly. Bonus: I reused the plastic wrap for topping all four dough rounds.

To mimic the wood-fired oven's blazing heat, I set my baking stone on the oven's upper-middle rack and ran the oven at 500 degrees for an hour: That way, there would be intense heat both underneath the flatbreads and reflecting onto them from above, with just enough headspace to usher them into and out of the oven. Each round baked up crispy, browned, and fragrant in about 5 minutes, so baking all four of them didn't take any longer than baking a couple of my thin-crust pizzas. I made sure to have lemon wedges ready and waiting, as well as a minty cucumber-tomato salad for rolling up sandwiches. Now I can join the ranks of lahmajun makers in my family.

—ANDREW JANJIGIAN, *Cook's Illustrated*

HOW TO ROLL AND TOP LAHMAJUN

1. Using heel of your hand, press dough ball into 5-inch disk.

2. Using rolling pin, gently roll into 12-inch round.

3. Dust top with flour. Peel dough from counter and flip, floured side down, onto floured baking peel.

4. Place ½ cup topping in center of dough. Cover with 12-inch square sheet of plastic wrap.

5. Using your fingertips, gently spread filling evenly across dough, leaving ⅛-inch border.

6. Peel back plastic and remove (save plastic for use with remaining dough).

Lahmajun (Armenian Flatbread)

SERVES 4 TO 6

You'll need a baking peel; if you don't have one, use an overturned rimmed baking sheet. King Arthur All-Purpose Flour gives these flatbreads the perfect balance of crispness and tenderness, but if it's unavailable, substitute any major brand of all-purpose flour. We strongly recommend weighing the flour and water. Biber salçası (Turkish red pepper paste) can be found in Middle Eastern grocery stores or online. Be sure to use the mild variety; if it's unavailable, increase the tomato paste to 2 tablespoons and the paprika to 4 teaspoons. Eighty-five percent lean ground beef can be substituted for the lamb. Eat the lahmajun out of hand, either whole, cut into halves or quarters, folded in half, or rolled into a cylinder. If desired, omit the lemon wedges and serve with Cucumber-Tomato Salad (recipe follows). If serving with the salad, use a slotted spoon to distribute 1 cup of salad evenly along the center third of each lahmajun. Fold the outer thirds of the lahmajun over the filling, one side at a time. Turn the rolled lahmajun seam side down and cut in half crosswise.

DOUGH

- 3¼ cups (16¼ ounces) King Arthur All-Purpose Flour
- ⅛ teaspoon instant or rapid-rise yeast
- 1¼ cups (10 ounces) ice water
- 1 tablespoon vegetable oil
- 1½ teaspoons table salt
  Vegetable oil spray

TOPPING

- 1 red bell pepper, stemmed, seeded, and cut into 1-inch pieces
- ¼ small onion
- ¼ cup fresh parsley leaves and tender stems
- 2 tablespoons mild biber salçası
- 1 tablespoon tomato paste
- 1 garlic clove, peeled
- 1 teaspoon ground allspice
- 1 teaspoon paprika
- ½ teaspoon ground cumin
- ½ teaspoon table salt
- ⅛ teaspoon pepper
- ⅛ teaspoon cayenne pepper
- 6 ounces ground lamb, broken into small pieces

  Lemon wedges

1. FOR THE DOUGH: Process flour and yeast in food processor until combined, about 2 seconds. With processor running, slowly add ice water; process until dough is just combined and no dry flour remains, about 10 seconds. Let dough rest for 10 minutes.

2. Add oil and salt and process until dough forms shaggy ball, 30 to 60 seconds. Transfer dough to lightly oiled counter and knead until uniform, about 1 minute (texture will remain slightly rough). Divide dough into 4 equal pieces, about 6⅔ ounces each. Shape dough pieces into tight balls and transfer, seam side down, to rimmed baking sheet coated with oil spray. Spray tops of balls lightly with oil spray. Cover tightly with plastic wrap and refrigerate for at least 16 hours or up to 2 days.

3. FOR THE TOPPING: In now-empty processor, process bell pepper, onion, parsley, biber salçası, tomato paste, garlic, allspice, paprika, cumin, salt, pepper, and cayenne until smooth, scraping down sides of bowl as needed, about 15 seconds. Add lamb and pulse to combine, 8 to 10 pulses. Transfer to container, cover, and refrigerate until needed (topping can be refrigerated for up to 24 hours).

4. One hour before baking lahmajun, remove dough from refrigerator and let stand at room temperature until slightly puffy and no longer cool to touch. Meanwhile, adjust oven rack to upper-middle position (rack should be 4 to 5 inches from broiler element), set baking stone on rack, and heat oven to 500 degrees.

5. Place 1 dough ball on unfloured counter and dust top lightly with flour. Using heel of your hand, press dough ball into 5-inch disk. Using rolling pin, gently roll into 12-inch round of even thickness. (Use tackiness of dough on counter to aid with rolling; if dough becomes misshapen, periodically peel round from counter, reposition, and continue to roll.) Dust top of round lightly but evenly with flour and, starting at 1 edge, peel dough off counter and flip, floured side down, onto floured baking peel (dough will spring back to about 11 inches in diameter). Place one-quarter of topping (about ½ cup) in center of dough. Cover dough with 12 by 12-inch sheet of plastic and, using your fingertips and knuckles, gently spread filling evenly across dough, leaving ⅛-inch border. Starting at 1 edge, peel away plastic, leaving topping in place (reserve plastic for topping remaining lahmajun).

6. Carefully slide lahmajun onto stone and bake until bottom crust is browned, edges are lightly browned, and topping is steaming, 4 to 6 minutes. While lahmajun bakes, begin rolling next dough ball.

LAHMAJUN (ARMENIAN FLATBREAD)

7. Transfer baked lahmajun to wire rack. Repeat rolling, topping, and baking remaining 3 dough balls.

8. Serve with lemon wedges.

Cucumber-Tomato Salad

SERVES 4 TO 6

Use the ripest in-season tomatoes you can find. This salad is best eaten within 1 hour of being dressed. Be sure to drain excess liquid before placing the salad on the lahmajun.

1	English cucumber, quartered lengthwise and cut into ¼-inch pieces
2	tomatoes, cored and cut into ¼-inch pieces
¾	teaspoon table salt
½	cup pitted green olives, chopped coarse
¼	cup fresh mint leaves, shredded
2	tablespoons extra-virgin olive oil
2	tablespoons lemon juice
½	teaspoon pepper

Toss cucumber, tomatoes, and salt together in colander set over bowl. Let drain for 15 minutes, then discard liquid. Transfer cucumber-tomato mixture to medium bowl. Add olives, mint, oil, lemon juice, and pepper and toss to combine.

SMASHED BURGERS

✔ **WHY THIS RECIPE WORKS** A smashed burger's big selling point is an ultrabrown, crispy crust. We used commercial ground beef instead of grinding our own because the former is finer and thus exposes more myosin, a sticky meat protein that helps the patties hold together when they are smashed. Using a small saucepan to press down on the meat ensured that it spread and stuck uniformly to the skillet, which helped guarantee deep browning. We made two smaller patties at a time instead of one larger one because they fit nicely inside a burger bun. Sandwiching an ultramelty slice of Kraft American cheese between the patties helped the cheese melt thoroughly and seep into the meat almost like a rich, salty cheese sauce would. Our creamy, tangy burger sauce added more richness and moisture; lettuce and thinly sliced tomato provided freshness and acidity; and the soft bun offered tenderness.

If the edge-versus-center debate were about burgers instead of brownies, my allegiances would fall squarely with Team Edge—or, in this case, Team Crust. Because as much as I appreciate the beefy, medium-rare middle of a plump, juicy burger, the savory depth of well-browned beef is simply unrivaled.

That's why I love smashed burgers. These diner icons share the same thin, verging-on-well-done profile as typical fast-food burgers, as well as their all-American array of fixings: gooey American cheese; creamy, tangy burger sauce; crisp lettuce; thinly sliced tomato; and a soft bun. But with a smashed burger, extra-special attention is paid to making the brownest, crispiest, most savory crust.

Maximizing that Maillard browning is where technique comes in, but as I discovered, there's more to it than simply searing the patty hard on each side. Furthermore, you have to get the toppings just right, because smashed burgers—more than any other style of burger—rely on the condiments to deliver the moisture and tenderness that are sacrificed in pursuit of the ultimate crust. It's a smart, sum-of-its-parts approach to burgers, and when the elements are pitch-perfect and properly assembled, each bite is absolute nirvana.

Smashed burgers are fast and easy to make. Since the patty is thoroughly cooked and the crust delivers so much flavor, there's no need to be choosy about the cut of beef or to grind your own meat. In fact, commercially ground beef (we prefer 80 percent lean) makes better smashed burgers than home-ground chuck does because the commercially ground beef is more finely ground and thus stays more cohesive when it's flattened.

The first step is to form the meat into balls no larger than 4 ounces each (any bigger and the flattened patties will comically overhang the edges of the bun). Then you place one of the balls of meat in a smoking-hot cast-iron skillet and—literally, as the name suggests—smash it so that the meat spreads out as much as possible and creates loads of surface area for seasoning and browning. It takes only a minute or two for the crust to form, at which point you flip the patty, cook it just a few seconds longer so that the meat cooks through, slide it onto the bun, and top it with cheese. Since the whole operation goes fast, it's easy to make more. Just scrape out the residual browned bits from the skillet and repeat.

At least, that's how it should work, but my results have always been inconsistent. Sometimes the burgers have stayed thin and flat against the metal, searing and crisping deeply; other times they've shriveled and cooked up with spotty, disappointing browning—and a smashed burger without its signature crust is just a disk of gray, overcooked meat.

The problem, I realized after closely observing a failed attempt, was sticking—or lack thereof. Meat contracts as it cooks, and unless the patties were uniformly stuck to the metal, they shrank as they seared, going from pancake thin to too thick in seconds. I then understood why many recipes call for brushing no more than a few drops of oil onto the skillet's surface and why the best burgers I'd made were the ones that I'd had to scrape loose from the pan.

Clearly I needed to refine my smashing tactics so that the meat stuck more. I started by reconsidering my smashing instrument. When I went at the beef with a metal spatula (the best tool for loosening and flipping the patties), its offset handle made it difficult to press with even force. I rummaged around the kitchen for a better device and eventually found an unlikely alternative: a small saucepan. By gripping the sides of the pan, I was well positioned to press straight down on the ball of meat so that it spread into a round that made stronger, more uniform contact with the skillet. The raw meat left a bit of a mess on the bottom of the saucepan, but I fixed that by wrapping the pan in a large piece of aluminum foil, which made cleanup a cinch.

Knowing that the meat needed to be really anchored to the skillet, I also put even more mustard behind my pressing motion than I had been, which had the added benefit of maximizing the patty's brownable surface area. The downside was that the burger now overhung the bun by a good inch or two, which looked silly and made the whole package awkward to eat. So I decided to divide and conquer: Instead of making two 4-ounce patties, I split the beef into four 2-ounce balls. Even when flattened as much as possible, two of these smaller patties fit in the skillet together, and each one extended just past the edge of the bun, accentuating the effect of their jagged, supercrisp edges in a way that I hadn't even anticipated.

The other benefit of double-stacked patties was that they helped the cheese between them melt. By the time I topped the patties with lettuce and tomato and capped them with the buns (which I toasted and spread with a creamy mayonnaise, shallot, ketchup, and pickle sauce ahead of time to make assembly easy), the slice of cheese was starting to seep into the meat, acting almost like a rich, salty cheese sauce. It was precisely the right effect for this application, and to hammer it home, I made sure to use ultramelty Kraft Singles.

With that, I had ironed out every detail for my ultimate smashed burger and could get back to campaigning for Team Crust. Who's with me?

—LAN LAM, *Cook's Illustrated*

NOTES FROM THE TEST KITCHEN

CHOOSING THE RIGHT TOOL

Flattening a ball of ground beef into a thin disk is as simple as it sounds, but the tool you use affects the force you exert on the meat and, consequently, how uniformly flat the patties will be. Avoid a spatula; its offset handle makes it difficult to press the meat evenly. Instead, choose an object that allows you to press the meat from the top down, such as a small saucepan (grip the sides of the pan), burger press, or 28-ounce can. And don't worry about oversmashing the meat: Even if you press really hard, the small amount of meat won't spread much beyond the diameter of the bun.

SPATULA
Indirect pressure

SAUCEPAN
Direct pressure

SMASHED BURGERS

Smashed Burgers

SERVES 2

Do not use a stainless-steel or nonstick skillet here. You can use 85 percent lean ground beef, but 90 percent lean will produce a dry burger. Open a window or turn on your exhaust fan before cooking. Be assertive when pressing the patties. We strongly prefer Kraft Singles here for their meltability. To serve four, double the ingredients for the sauce and burgers and use the same amount of oil; once the burgers are cooked, transfer them to a wire rack set in a rimmed baking sheet, adding cheese to the first four burgers, and keep warm in a 200-degree oven. Place on buns right before serving.

SAUCE

- 2 tablespoons mayonnaise
- 1 tablespoon minced shallot
- 1½ teaspoons finely chopped dill pickle plus
  ½ teaspoon brine
- 1½ teaspoons ketchup
- ⅛ teaspoon sugar
- ⅛ teaspoon pepper

BURGERS

- 2 hamburger buns, toasted if desired
- 8 ounces 80 percent lean ground beef
- ¼ teaspoon vegetable oil
- ¼ teaspoon kosher salt, divided

- 2 slices American cheese (2 ounces)
  Bibb lettuce leaves
  Thinly sliced tomato

1. FOR THE SAUCE: Stir all ingredients together in bowl.

2. FOR THE BURGERS: Spread 1 tablespoon sauce on cut side of each bun top. Divide beef into 4 equal pieces (2 ounces each); form into loose, rough balls (do not compress). Place oil in 12-inch cast-iron or carbon-steel skillet. Use paper towel to rub oil into bottom of skillet (reserve paper towel). Heat over medium-low heat for 5 minutes. While skillet heats, wrap bottom and sides of small saucepan with large sheet of aluminum foil, anchoring foil on rim, and place large plate next to stovetop.

3. Increase heat to high. When skillet begins to smoke, place 2 balls about 3 inches apart in skillet. Use bottom of prepared saucepan to firmly smash each ball until 4 to 4½ inches in diameter. Place saucepan on plate next to stovetop. Sprinkle patties with ⅛ teaspoon salt and season with pepper. Cook until at least three-quarters of each patty is no longer pink on top, about 2 minutes (patties will stick to skillet). Use thin metal spatula to loosen patties from skillet. Flip patties and cook for 15 seconds. Remove skillet from heat. Transfer 1 burger to each bun bottom and top each with 1 slice American cheese. Gently scrape any browned bits from skillet, use tongs to wipe with reserved paper towel, and return skillet to heat. Repeat with remaining 2 balls and place burgers on top of cheese. Top with lettuce and tomato. Cap with prepared bun tops. Serve immediately.

CRISPY FISH SANDWICHES WITH TARTAR SAUCE

✓ **WHY THIS RECIPE WORKS** In New England, a fish sandwich usually includes a generous piece of fried haddock, halibut, or cod topped with lettuce and creamy tartar sauce. We started by coating the fish in a batter of beer, flour, cornstarch, and baking powder. The proteins in the flour helped the batter fuse to the fish and also brown deeply; the cornstarch crisped up nicely. Baking powder and the carbonation in the beer helped produce airiness. We fried the fish in 375-degree peanut oil until the coating was golden brown on both sides and the fish had steamed to perfection within. A toasted brioche bun, creamy tartar sauce, and Bibb lettuce completed this quintessential New England sandwich.

New England seafood shacks sure know how to make the most of the white fish caught in the cold, deep waters of the North Atlantic. They dunk the fillets in a thick batter, deep-fry them until they're crispy and golden brown, and load them onto a toasted bun with tender lettuce and a smear of tartar sauce. It's a quintessential coastal sandwich that's all about the succulent fish and its shatteringly crispy coating.

The fish is so good because the batter creates a physical barrier that protects the delicate fillets (haddock, cod, and halibut are popular choices for their large, sturdy flakes) from the hot oil and mitigates moisture loss. As the batter crisps and browns, the fish inside gently steams to moist, tender perfection.

After reviewing our existing recipes for deep-fried fish, I narrowed the ingredient list for my batter to equal parts all-purpose flour and cornstarch, beer (for its carbonation and malty sweetness), baking powder, and salt. The flour and cornstarch would play complementary roles: The proteins in the flour would help the batter fuse to the fish and also brown deeply, and the cornstarch, which doesn't cling or brown as well as flour, would help the batter crisp up nicely. Cornstarch also can't form gluten, so it doesn't turn tough. The baking powder would assist in developing a light, airy crust, as would the beer.

After letting the batter rest for 20 minutes so that the starch could fully hydrate, I dunked four haddock fillets into the mixture and fried them in 375-degree oil (our preferred temperature for frying fish) for about 4 minutes per side. As the pieces sizzled in the oil, carbon dioxide from the beer and baking powder started to escape, followed by steam from the beer, leaving hundreds of tiny pockets in their wake and creating a sturdy, lacy structure that became pleasingly crispy as it hardened.

To complement the crispy fish, I whipped up a tangy tartar sauce with capers, shallot, and sweet pickle relish mixed into mayonnaise and spiked with Worcestershire sauce. I spread the sauce onto a toasted brioche bun and topped it with the fish and some tender lettuce. This was a mighty fine representation of a mighty fine sandwich.

—CAMILA CHAPARRO, *America's Test Kitchen Books*

Crispy Fish Sandwiches with Tartar Sauce

SERVES 4

Cod or halibut can be substituted for the haddock; you can substitute plain seltzer for the beer. Do not use a dark beer in this recipe. Use a Dutch oven that holds 6 quarts or more here.

TARTAR SAUCE

- ¾ cup mayonnaise
- 2 tablespoons capers, rinsed and minced
- 2 tablespoons sweet pickle relish
- 1½ teaspoons minced shallot
- 1½ teaspoons distilled white vinegar
- ½ teaspoon Worcestershire sauce

FISH

- ½ cup all-purpose flour
- ½ cup cornstarch
- ½ teaspoon table salt
- ½ teaspoon baking powder
- ¾ cup beer
- 2 quarts peanut or vegetable oil for frying
- 4 (4- to 6-ounce) skinless haddock fillets, 1 inch thick
- 4 brioche buns, toasted
- 4 leaves Bibb lettuce
  Lemon wedges

1. FOR THE TARTAR SAUCE: Combine all ingredients in bowl, let sit for 15 minutes, and season with salt and pepper to taste.

2. FOR THE FISH: Whisk flour, cornstarch, salt, and baking powder together in large bowl. Whisk in beer until smooth. Cover and refrigerate for 20 minutes.

3. Set wire rack in rimmed baking sheet. Add oil to large Dutch oven until it measures about 1½ inches deep and heat over medium-high heat to 375 degrees. Pat haddock dry with paper towels and transfer to batter, tossing gently to coat. Using fork, remove haddock from batter, 1 piece at a time, allowing excess batter to drip back into bowl; add to hot oil, briefly dragging haddock along surface of oil to set batter before gently dropping into oil. Adjust burner, if necessary, to maintain oil temperature between 350 and 375 degrees.

4. Cook, stirring gently to prevent pieces from sticking together, until deep golden brown and crispy, about 4 minutes per side. Using spider skimmer or slotted spoon, transfer haddock to prepared rack. Divide tartar sauce evenly among bun bottoms, followed by haddock and lettuce. Cover with bun tops. Serve with lemon wedges.

NOTES FROM THE TEST KITCHEN

HOW TO PREVENT STICKING

To keep the pieces of haddock from sticking together in the hot oil, spear each piece of battered fish with a fork, let the excess batter drip off, and then drag the fish along the oil's surface before releasing it. This gives the batter a chance to set up and harden so that it won't adhere to other pieces it touches in the oil.

MUMBAI FRANKIE WRAPS

✓ **WHY THIS RECIPE WORKS** In Mumbai, India's largest city, easy-to-eat street foods such as these wraps are hugely popular. Frankies take many forms but tend to share a few key characteristics. A warm, tender, whole-wheat flatbread (called chapati or roti) is filled with meat, vegetables, eggs, or cheese and topped with condiments such as chutneys, sauces, and pickles before being rolled up. For our take on the Frankie, we wanted to develop a wrap where each element on its own was simple and delicious but together formed a veritable cornucopia of well-balanced flavors and textures. We started with Yukon Gold potatoes, which we mashed with an aromatic mixture of shallot, ginger, garlic, turmeric, and coriander and enriched with creamy coconut milk. We spread the mixture over our wrap, sprinkled it with a combo of mildly spiced roasted cauliflower and chickpeas, and topped it with sweet-spicy pickled onion and a bright herbal chutney before rolling it into a cone shape.

India is home to an impressive array of street foods. From soft and creamy pav bhaji to crispy, sweet-and-sour pani puri, these flavorful handheld dishes fuel Indians on the go. One of the most popular street foods in Mumbai is the Frankie, which consists of a warm chapati wrapped around vegetables, eggs, meat, or cheese; chopped onion; chutneys; and pickled chiles. I wanted to create a wrap for our vegan cookbook *The Complete Plant-Based Cookbook*, and I knew that a vegetable Frankie would be a great one to showcase all that plant-based eating has to offer.

Although the fillings can vary, one element of the Frankie remains a constant: the chapati. I figured I'd start there. Made from a whole-wheat dough, chapatis are rolled into thin disks and cooked on a hot surface until they're slightly puffed and blistered. The result is a mildly nutty flatbread that's soft and pliable yet sturdy enough to wrap around hearty fillings. Chapatis reminded me of whole-wheat tortillas, so I bought a package of store-bought tortillas in the hopes that I could streamline my recipe. One bite and my hopes were dashed: The tortillas tasted like cardboard. I'd have to make the chapatis myself.

I started with a test kitchen recipe for flour tortillas made in a cast-iron skillet. The method was similar to those of the chapati recipes I'd found, and the cast iron was the closest I could get to the superhot griddle

(called a tawa) used by Frankie vendors. But when I swapped out the all-purpose flour for whole-wheat flour, the chapatis cooked up dense and inflexible. That's because chapatis are traditionally made from atta flour, which is derived from a harder wheat and thus goes through more rounds of milling. The extra milling damages the starches in the flour, which allows it to absorb more water than American whole-wheat flour does. This, along with extensive kneading, makes atta-flour chapatis tender and elastic. To achieve that texture, I decided to use equal parts all-purpose flour and whole-wheat flour in my dough. I swapped the vegetable shortening in the tortilla recipe with vegetable oil, and my chapatis cooked up tender and slightly chewy—perfect for stretching around fillings.

Of the many Frankie fillings I found in my research (anything from stewed lamb or grilled chicken to chickpeas or eggs), the one that intrigued me the most was a creamy potato mixture. Flavored with aromatics and spices, the mixture is mashed and either spread on the chapati or formed into patties. I went with a spread, which would help my other fillings stick to the chapati. I simmered chunks of Yukon Gold potatoes in a saucepan until they were tender and then drained the potatoes and built the aromatic base in the same saucepan. Minced shallot and garlic brought savory allium flavors, while grated fresh ginger, ground coriander, and cayenne added brightness and warmth. A teaspoon of ground turmeric accented the potatoes' earthy notes and turned the mixture a beautiful golden color. And, while not traditional, I stirred in canned coconut milk to create a rich, creamy mash with a subtle sweetness.

I love the hearty combination of cauliflower and chickpeas, especially in a meatless meal, and I thought their flavors would complement the potatoes nicely. I chopped the cauliflower into bite-size florets and roasted it at high heat to bring out its sweetness. For the chickpeas, I envisioned a stew-like mixture that would add a saucy component to the filling. But with a saucepan for the potatoes, a skillet for the chapatis, and a baking sheet for the cauliflower, I didn't want to add another dirty dish to my sink. I decided to roast the chickpeas and the cauliflower together with a bit of garam masala. Roasting the chickpeas enhanced their nuttiness, and their crisp exteriors provided a textural contrast to the creamy potato.

With the vegetables settled, I turned to the condiments. Frankies are usually sprinkled with chopped raw onions and pickled chiles; I merged the two by quickly pickling a sliced red onion with jalapeños. For the chutney, I opted for a vibrant cilantro-mint mixture, which came together in the food processor in less than 30 seconds.

To assemble the wraps, I spread the potato mixture over one half of each chapati, covered it with the cauliflower and chickpeas, and sprinkled the chutney and pickled onion on top. I then rolled each loaded chapati into a cone. With a mixture of textures, colors, and flavors, these Frankie-style wraps made a standout vegan lunch. And given that each component, from the chapatis to the chutney, can be prepared ahead of time, they'll be my lunchtime staple—just as Frankies are for people in Mumbai.

—NICOLE KONSTANTINAKOS,
America's Test Kitchen Books

Mumbai Frankie Wraps

SERVES 4

We prefer to make our own chapatis, but you can substitute store-bought chapatis or rotis. We do not recommend naan or other (thicker) flatbreads. For the easiest assembly, we recommend making the pickled onions, chutney, and chapatis ahead.

12 ounces cauliflower florets, cut into 1-inch pieces
 1 (15-ounce) can chickpeas, rinsed
 2 tablespoons vegetable oil, divided
 ¾ teaspoon garam masala
 ¾ teaspoon table salt, divided
 1 pound Yukon Gold potatoes, peeled and cut into 1-inch pieces
 1 shallot, minced
 3 garlic cloves, minced
 1 tablespoon grated fresh ginger
 1 teaspoon ground turmeric
 ⅛ teaspoon ground coriander
   Pinch cayenne pepper
 ½ cup canned coconut milk
 1 recipe Chapatis (Whole-Wheat Wraps) (recipe follows), warmed
 ½ cup Cilantro-Mint Chutney (recipe follows)
 ½ cup Quick Sweet-and-Spicy Pickled Red Onions (recipe follows)

1. Adjust oven rack to lowest position and heat oven to 500 degrees. Line rimmed baking sheet with aluminum foil. Toss cauliflower, chickpeas, 1 tablespoon oil, garam masala, and ¼ teaspoon salt together in bowl. Spread cauliflower mixture in even layer on prepared sheet and roast, stirring halfway through roasting, until cauliflower is spotty brown and tender, about 10 minutes; set aside. (Cauliflower mixture can be refrigerated for up to 24 hours; let come to room temperature before serving.)

2. Place potatoes and remaining ½ teaspoon salt in large saucepan, add cold water to cover by 1 inch, and bring to boil over high heat. Reduce heat to medium and simmer until potatoes are tender, about 12 minutes; drain well.

3. Heat remaining 1 tablespoon oil in now-empty saucepan over medium heat until shimmering. Add shallot and cook until softened and lightly browned, 3 to 5 minutes. Stir in garlic, ginger, turmeric, coriander, and cayenne and cook until fragrant, about 30 seconds. Stir in coconut milk, scraping up any browned bits, and bring to simmer. Stir in potatoes, then remove from heat and mash with potato masher until mostly smooth, about 2 minutes. Season with salt to taste; set aside. (Potato mixture can be refrigerated for up to 24 hours; microwave, covered, before serving.)

4. Divide potato mixture evenly among chapatis, then spread in even layer over half of each chapati. Divide cauliflower mixture evenly over top, then top each with 2 tablespoons chutney and 2 tablespoons pickled onions. Roll into cone shape and serve.

Chapatis (Whole-Wheat Wraps)

SERVES 4 (MAKES 4 WRAPS)

We like King Arthur Premium Whole Wheat Flour.

 ¾ cup (4⅛ ounces) whole-wheat flour
 ¾ cup (3¾ ounces) all-purpose flour
 1 teaspoon table salt
 ½ cup warm water (110 degrees)
 3 tablespoons plus 2 teaspoons vegetable oil, divided

1. Whisk whole-wheat flour, all-purpose flour, and salt together in bowl. Stir in warm water and 3 tablespoons oil until cohesive dough forms. Transfer dough to lightly floured counter and knead by hand to form smooth ball, 1 minute.

MUMBAI FRANKIE WRAPS

2. Divide dough into 4 pieces and cover with plastic wrap. Working with 1 piece at a time (keep remaining pieces covered), form into ball by stretching dough around your thumbs and pinching edges together so top is smooth. Place ball seam side down on clean counter and shape into smooth, taut ball. Place on plate seam side down, cover with plastic wrap, and let sit for 30 minutes. (Dough balls can be refrigerated for up to 3 days.)

3. Line rimmed baking sheet with parchment paper. Roll 1 dough ball into 9-inch round on lightly floured counter (keep remaining pieces covered). Transfer to prepared sheet and top with additional sheet of parchment. Repeat with remaining dough balls.

4. Heat 12-inch cast-iron or nonstick skillet over medium heat for 3 minutes. Add ½ teaspoon oil to skillet, then use paper towels to carefully wipe out skillet, leaving thin film of oil on bottom; skillet should be just smoking. (If using 12-inch nonstick skillet, heat ½ teaspoon oil over medium heat in skillet until shimmering, then wipe out skillet.)

5. Place 1 dough round in hot skillet and cook until dough is bubbly and bottom is browned in spots, about 2 minutes. Flip dough and cook until puffed and second side is spotty brown, 1 to 2 minutes. Transfer to clean plate and cover with dish towel to keep warm. Repeat with remaining oil and dough rounds. Serve. (Cooked chapatis can be refrigerated for up to 3 days or frozen for up to 3 months. To freeze, layer chapatis between parchment paper and store in zipper-lock bag. To serve, stack chapatis on plate, cover with damp dish towel, and microwave until warm, 1 to 1½ minutes.)

Cilantro-Mint Chutney
MAKES ABOUT 1 CUP

This herb-based chutney comes together in a flash in the food processor, with no need to chop the herbs in advance. If using dairy yogurt, we prefer whole-milk yogurt.

- 2 cups fresh cilantro leaves
- 1 cup fresh mint leaves
- ⅓ cup plain plant-based yogurt or dairy yogurt
- ¼ cup finely chopped onion
- 1 tablespoon lime juice
- 1½ teaspoons sugar
- ½ teaspoon ground cumin
- ¼ teaspoon table salt

Process all ingredients in food processor until smooth, about 20 seconds, scraping down sides of bowl as needed. (Chutney can be refrigerated for up to 2 days.)

Quick Sweet-and-Spicy Pickled Red Onions
MAKES ABOUT 1 CUP

The drained pickled onions can be refrigerated for up to one week.

- 1 red onion, halved through root end and sliced thin
- 1 cup red wine vinegar
- ⅓ cup sugar
- 2 jalapeño chiles, stemmed, seeded, and cut into thin rings
- ¼ teaspoon table salt

Place onion in bowl. Bring vinegar, sugar, jalapeños, and salt to simmer in saucepan over medium-high heat, stirring occasionally, until sugar dissolves. Pour hot vinegar mixture over onion; cover; and let cool completely, about 1 hour. Drain cooled vegetables in colander.

TACOS AL PASTOR

✓ **WHY THIS RECIPE WORKS** This traditional and historical taco has both Mexican and Lebanese roots. Toasting and soaking the deeply red and smoky guajillo and ancho chiles brought out their natural flavors and color. We blended these chiles with pungent raw garlic, sweet pineapple juice, some acidic cider vinegar, and plenty of dried oregano to create a potent paste to marinate our pork. Traditionally, thin slices of marinated pork are layered on a rotating spit and roasted in front of an open flame. For a home cook–friendly recipe, we opted to cook our marinated slabs of pork butt roast on the grill. First, we cooked the pork through slowly, ensuring moist and tender meat, and then we gave the steaks a quick sear over a hot fire to char the marinated edges. Slicing the meat thin made it look just as it would coming right off the spit and into a warm, fresh corn tortilla.

Tacos al pastor contain an irresistible combination of flavorful components: deeply seasoned pork, charred fresh pineapple, warm corn tortillas, and a bounty of lively toppings.

Traditional versions are made by slicing fatty pork (usually shoulder) thin and then marinating it in what is essentially an adobo sauce of dried chiles, spices, and often citrus or vinegar. The marinated slices are then stacked high on a vertical spit and cooked slowly—as they spin around and around—until they're tender. When it's time to make the tacos, the heat is cranked up so that the outer layer of meat on the spit gets lightly charred; the cook slices the charred pork off the rotating spit right onto warm tortillas and then adds toppings before handing the tacos over to waiting taco fiends. So . . . how could I make this process work at home on a simple backyard grill?

After researching and reading through dozens of recipes, I started my testing with the marinade, eventually landing on a combination of (toasted and rehydrated) guajillo and ancho chiles, garlic, dried oregano, cider vinegar, and some pineapple juice, all liquefied together in a blender.

I tested several cuts of meat but ended up back at the beginning, with a boneless pork butt roast. Since the meat wouldn't be stacked on a spit, there was no need to slice it thin; instead, I cut the roast into steaks that had enough surface area to drink up lots of marinade and would cook through relatively quickly.

I found that grilling the marinated pork steaks over indirect heat for about an hour was the best route to tender meat. Then, for the pork's signature char, I brushed the steaks with some of the reserved marinade and moved them over the hot coals to crackle and brown. Since the pineapple just needed to soften a bit and warm through, this was the time to toss it on the grill.

All that was left to do was to let the meat rest, slice it thin, warm the tortillas, and set out the toppings. And to my delight, my leftover pork was just as good the next day.

—ALLI BERKEY, *Cook's Country*

Tacos al Pastor

SERVES 8 TO 10

Pork butt roast is often labeled as Boston butt in the supermarket. Note that 1½ ounces of guajillos is about six chiles and 1 ounce of anchos is about two chiles. The pineapple doesn't need to be charred in step 8. Any leftover pork can be used to make sandwiches, stir-fries, or more tacos.

TACOS AL PASTOR, STEP BY STEP
Here's how to make our version of tacos al pastor.

1. Dry-toast dried chile pieces in skillet.

2. Transfer chiles to bowl and rehydrate with hot water.

3. Transfer chiles to blender jar and blend with other marinade ingredients.

4. Reserve ¼ cup marinade for grilling.

5. Marinate pork steaks for at least 1 hour or up to 24 hours in refrigerator.

6. Grill steaks to internal temperature of 150 degrees.

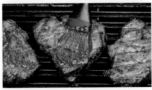

7. Brush both sides of steaks with reserved marinade and grill over coals.

8. Lightly grill pineapple quarter, then slice thin.

TACOS AL PASTOR

1½ ounces dried guajillo chiles, stemmed

1 ounce dried ancho chiles, stemmed

½ cup cider vinegar

½ cup pineapple juice

4 garlic cloves, peeled

1 tablespoon table salt

1 tablespoon dried oregano

2 teaspoons ground cumin

1½ teaspoons pepper

½ teaspoon ground cinnamon

1 (2½-pound) boneless pork butt roast, trimmed

1 pineapple

24 (6-inch) corn tortillas, warmed

   Finely chopped onion

   Fresh cilantro leaves

   Lime wedges

1. Using kitchen shears, cut guajillos and anchos in half lengthwise and discard seeds. Cut guajillos and anchos into 1-inch pieces. Place guajillos and anchos in 12-inch skillet and cook over medium heat, stirring often, until fragrant and darkened slightly, about 6 minutes. Immediately transfer guajillos and anchos to bowl and cover with hot water. Let sit until soft, about 5 minutes.

2. Using slotted spoon, lift guajillos and anchos from water and transfer to blender; discard soaking water. Add vinegar, pineapple juice, garlic, salt, oregano, cumin, pepper, and cinnamon and process until smooth, about 1 minute, scraping down sides of blender jar as needed. Set aside ¼ cup marinade.

3. Cut pork crosswise into approximate 1½-inch-thick steaks. Transfer pork to 1-gallon zipper-lock bag. Add remaining marinade to bag with pork. Seal bag and turn to distribute marinade evenly. Refrigerate for at least 1 hour or up to 24 hours.

4. Using sharp chef's knife, cut top and bottom from pineapple, then peel. Quarter pineapple lengthwise through core. Reserve 3 quarters for another use. Remove and discard core from remaining pineapple quarter; set aside.

5A. FOR A CHARCOAL GRILL: Open bottom vent completely. Light large chimney starter filled with charcoal briquettes (6 quarts). When top coals are partially covered with ash, pour evenly over half of grill. Set cooking grate in place, cover, and open lid vent completely. Heat grill until hot, about 5 minutes.

5B. FOR A GAS GRILL: Turn all burners to high; cover; and heat grill until hot, about 15 minutes. Turn primary burner to medium-high and turn off other burners. (Adjust burner as needed to maintain grill temperature of 350 degrees.)

6. Clean and oil cooking grate. Remove pork from marinade and place on cooler side of grill. Cover and cook until pork registers 150 degrees, about 50 minutes for charcoal or 1 hour 5 minutes to 1 hour 10 minutes for gas.

7. Brush tops of steaks with 2 tablespoons reserved marinade. Flip steaks marinade side down onto hotter side of grill. Brush second side of steaks with remaining 2 tablespoons reserved marinade. Place pineapple on hotter side of grill next to steaks.

8. Cook, uncovered for charcoal and covered for gas, until pork is well charred and registers 175 degrees, 6 to 8 minutes per side for charcoal or 12 to 15 minutes per side for gas. Cook pineapple until warmed through, about 10 minutes. Transfer pork and pineapple to wire rack set in rimmed baking sheet, tent with aluminum foil, and let rest for 15 minutes.

9. Transfer pork and pineapple to carving board and slice thin. Season with salt to taste. Fill tortillas with few slices of pork and pineapple. Top tacos with onion and cilantro. Serve with lime wedges.

TUNA TOSTADAS

✔ **WHY THIS RECIPE WORKS** We love fish tacos—from the traditional to the unique—and we think they work for nearly any type of fish. But to give tuna the tortilla treatment, we turned to the taco's open-faced cousin, the tostada; we loved the contrast of the fish's buttery texture with the crispy shell, and its pretty pink color provided visual appeal on top. A sesame crust added extra crunch and served as a jumping-off point for a tostada with East Asian–inspired ingredients. We rested slices of the seared tuna on a bed of delicate napa cabbage shreds, which we tossed in a soy sauce, fresh ginger, and sesame oil vinaigrette. For a side slaw we often salt our cabbage in advance, but since tostadas are eaten right away, we tossed the cabbage with the dressing just before assembling the tostadas to easily avoid waterlogged slaw. A spicy, creamy, tangy component came in the form of a sriracha mayo. A sprinkling of thinly sliced scallions finished the dish with bright-green color.

I'm a big believer in the old adage "you eat with your eyes first," so it's no wonder that I love seared tuna. The moist, translucent-red interior of a rare tuna steak stands out on any plate, and when the fish is cooked to perfection, the striking center is neatly framed by a thin, delectable crust—it's like an edible work of art. So when I was tasked with developing a recipe that featured seared tuna for our cookbook *Foolproof Fish*, I knew I wanted a dish that would let the impressive steaks take center stage.

Enter: tostadas. The crispy, crunchy, open-faced relatives of the soft-shelled taco, tostadas would serve as the perfect canvas for artfully arranged slices of seared tuna nestled among a bevy of flavorful, visually appealing garnishes. But before I could begin composing the perfect palette of supporting ingredients, I'd need to get the tuna just right. Because I was aiming for both a rare interior and a substantial sear, I knew that nailing down the perfect timing, temperature, and technique for cooking my tuna steaks could be tricky. I was in a race against the clock: I needed enough time to achieve a deeply seared exterior, but I also needed to act quickly enough to spare the centers of the tuna steaks from overcooking. (Our preferred doneness temperature for tuna is just 110 degrees; while that temperature may seem low, the tuna continues to rise in temperature from residual heat as it's taken off the stove.) Fortunately, my colleague had recently developed a foolproof recipe for seared tuna steaks to include in our "Everyday Essentials" chapter, so I was well on my way to a delicious result. Here's why their method worked for me.

Using relatively thick tuna steaks, those that were 1 inch thick, gave me sufficient time to achieve ample browning on the exteriors of the steaks while their centers remained protected from the brunt of the skillet's heat. (A very hot skillet, left over medium-high heat until the oil was just smoking, allowed me to achieve the quickest sear and a superior crust.) And flipping the steaks every 1 to 2 minutes as they seared sped up the process, further ensuring that the exteriors of the steaks cooked quickly while their interiors remained perfectly rosy and rare. Why? A hot skillet cooks food from the bottom up, and when a protein is flipped, the seared side remains quite hot. Some of its heat dissipates into the air, but some of it cooks the protein from the top down. Therefore, the more often a protein is flipped, the more it will cook from both the bottom up and the top down, resulting in an even, quick cook.

Using that foolproof method, I could reliably produce meaty, rare steaks with a moist, translucent-red center and a thin border of nicely seared tuna. All that was left was a bit of fine-tuning. I wanted a more substantial crust to complement the tender interior of the fish, so I added a sesame seed coating for the visual appeal, a pleasantly toasty flavor, and a bit of crunch. Rubbing the fish with some vegetable oil before pressing the steaks into the seeds helped them adhere in an even layer and stay put during searing.

With my tuna looking (and tasting) picture-perfect, I could move on to prepping the rest of my tostada components. Cabbage is a common component of fish tacos, and a cool, tangy slaw seemed apt here to complement the warm seared fish. So I shredded half a head of napa cabbage and tossed it with a stir-together dressing that echoed the East Asian flavor profile of the sesame-crusted tuna. I simply combined sesame oil and a bit of soy sauce with fresh, spicy grated ginger and a little sugar for balanced sweetness, tossing the dressing with the shredded cabbage just before serving. Looking for a rich, creamy element that would unite the rest of the components and provide some welcome heat, I also whipped up a simple sriracha mayo to drizzle over the tostadas. Though I experimented with a slew of typical taco garnishes such as sour cream, sliced avocado, and cilantro, I found that their flavors and textures clashed with the tangy slaw and rich mayo, so a sprinkle of scallions wound up being all I needed to tie my tostadas together. After I had all my elements prepared and assembled, I stepped back to admire the final product: crispy rounds piled with generous mounds of crunchy slaw and pristine slices of rosy-red tuna. The tostadas were pretty as a picture, but I was ready to take a bite.

—CAMILA CHAPARRO, *America's Test Kitchen Books*

Tuna Tostadas

SERVES 6

We found that 1½ pounds of tuna was ideal for 12 tostadas. The test kitchen's favorite toasted sesame oil is Ottogi Premium Roasted Sesame Oil, and our favorite soy sauce is Kikkoman Soy Sauce. For the tostada shells, we like Mission Tostadas Estilo Casero.

SRIRACHA SAUCE

⅓ cup mayonnaise

1 tablespoon sriracha

SLAW

2 tablespoons toasted sesame oil

2 tablespoons unseasoned rice vinegar

2 tablespoons soy sauce

2¼ teaspoons sugar

1½ teaspoons grated fresh ginger

½ head napa cabbage, shredded (about 5½ cups)

TUNA

¾ cup sesame seeds

4 (6-ounce) skinless tuna steaks, 1 inch thick

2 tablespoons vegetable oil, divided

½ teaspoon table salt

¼ teaspoon pepper

12 (6-inch) corn tostada shells

2 scallions, sliced thin on bias

1. FOR THE SRIRACHA SAUCE: Whisk mayonnaise and sriracha together in small bowl. Refrigerate until ready to serve.

2. FOR THE SLAW: Whisk oil, vinegar, soy sauce, sugar, and ginger together in large bowl. Set dressing aside until ready to serve.

3. FOR THE TUNA: Spread sesame seeds in shallow dish. Pat tuna dry with paper towels, then rub steaks all over with 1 tablespoon oil and sprinkle with salt and pepper. Press both sides of each steak in sesame seeds to coat.

4. Heat remaining 1 tablespoon oil in 12-inch nonstick skillet over medium-high heat until just smoking. Place steaks in skillet and cook, flipping every 1 to 2 minutes, until center is translucent red when checked with tip of paring knife and registers 110 degrees (for rare), 2 to 4 minutes. Transfer steaks to cutting board and slice ¼ inch thick.

5. Add cabbage to dressing in large bowl and toss to coat. Divide slaw, tuna, and sriracha sauce evenly among tostada shells. Sprinkle tostadas with scallions and serve.

CORN RISOTTO

✓ **WHY THIS RECIPE WORKS** To make risotto that featured truly vibrant corn flavor, we started by blending 3 cups of fresh corn kernels with a little water and the pulpy, flavorful "milk" we scraped from the cobs to yield a supersweet, bright-tasting puree to stir into the rice. Adding the corn puree near the end of cooking preserved its freshness. The puree also contributed extra liquid as well as naturally occurring cornstarch: The liquid loosened up the risotto to an appropriately fluid consistency (called "all'onda" in Italian), and the cornstarch gelled and acted like a sauce, making the dish especially creamy. Instead of adding the traditional white wine, which overwhelmed the corn's flavor, we stirred in crème fraîche. The cultured dairy added much subtler acidity, and its flavor and richness underscored the risotto's creamy, luxurious profile.

I was deep into recipe development for corn risotto when I started to wonder if the dish might be fundamentally flawed. There were hurdles to saturating the creamy rice with corn flavor that also seemed integral to risotto cookery. First, heat drives off many of the compounds we associate with the vegetable's fresh, sweet taste. Second, chicken broth and wine obscure the flavor further. When I tried to overcome these challenges by adding handfuls of snappy peak-season kernels to the pot and infusing the rice with a concentrated broth I'd made by simmering the spent cobs, I failed to capture the vibrant, sweet corn flavor that is the raison d'être of the whole dish.

Happily, it all worked out in the end, and even better than I thought it would. Because along with figuring out how to make risotto that's suffused with the bright, grassy, buttery flavors of high-season corn, I discovered that corn itself—when treated just right—can transform your average pot of risotto into one that's exceptionally lush and velvety.

My framework was our unique risotto method, which produces rice as creamy as a conventional approach does but requires a fraction of the hands-on work. The key differences are that after sautéing the aromatics and Arborio rice and deglazing the pot with wine, we add almost all the cooking liquid (4 to 5 cups of warm chicken broth cut with water) up front and simmer the mixture in a covered pot for the better part of 20 minutes rather than gradually ladle the liquid into the rice while stirring constantly. Both methods cause the rice grains to slough off starch into the cooking liquid and form a viscous gel, giving risotto its signature creaminess, but our method lets agitation from the simmering liquid do most of the work so that we need to stir the pot just twice during that first phase. Only during the last few minutes of cooking do we add a bit more liquid and stir constantly to enhance the risotto's thick, creamy body.

Replacing the chicken-y cooking liquid with home-made corn broth and stirring kernels into the rice were two of the most common—and unsuccessful—approaches I found in my research. But no matter how long I simmered the cobs in water for broth, the liquid tasted dilute because the bare cobs had almost nothing valuable left to offer. And while there was loads of bright corn flavor inside the kernels, it was confined to sporadic pops, not distributed throughout the dish.

So I took a more radical approach and buzzed the kernels (3 cups), along with the pulpy, flavor-packed "milk" I scraped from their cobs, in the blender, adding just enough water to engage the blades. The result was a sunny puree bursting with fresh corn flavor—an elixir of sorts that I hoped would transform my workaday risotto into corn-saturated gold.

Before putting it to work, I strained the puree to remove the tough bits of skin, which left me with about 2 cups of gleaming liquid. Then I picked up with my risotto method, simmering the rice in a combination of the strained puree and water, the latter of which I swapped in for the chicken broth so that the vegetable's flavor would stand out as much as possible.

The sun-colored rice certainly looked awash in corn. And thanks to the natural cornstarch in the puree, which gelled and acted like a silky sauce, the risotto was exceptionally lush and glossy. But after simmering for nearly 20 minutes, the puree had a flat and, well, cooked flavor.

That test turned out to be my crash course in corn flavor compounds: Many of these compounds develop only after some cooking; others, including the grassy, fresh-tasting ones that I was going for, are volatile and vanish when heated. If I wanted to preserve fresh corn flavor, I had to wait until the rice was nearly done before adding the puree. This change altered the whole dish, saturating the risotto with the corn's bright flavor.

In a last-ditch effort to maximize the corn's presence, I circled back to adding kernels. A cup of them contributed just enough snap, sweetness, and color.

Then I took a closer look at the wine, which is almost as common in risotto as the rice itself but tasted harsh

NOTES FROM THE TEST KITCHEN

LIQUID GOLD

Truly vibrant corn flavor is hard to capture in risotto. Kernels add only sporadic pops of sweetness, and broth made from boiled cobs tastes insipid.

So instead of merely accenting the rice with corn, we made it an integral part of the dish by stirring in a puree made from kernels and the "milk" that we scraped from the cobs. That liquid not only saturated every bite with corn flavor but also added naturally occurring starch from the corn, which, when heated, thickened to a sauce-like consistency that gave the risotto exceptionally silky body.

RAW PUREE
Thin and loose

COOKED PUREE
Viscous and glossy

CORN PUREE
Adding it toward the end of cooking preserves the corn's fresh flavor.

CORN RISOTTO

against the vegetable's delicate sweetness. It had to go, but I needed to add something in its place that would further brighten up the rice. The unconventional answer turned out to be crème fraîche, a source of much subtler acidity as well as fat and rich dairy flavor that complemented the corn and enhanced the risotto's already refined, luxurious consistency.

I stirred in a generous scoop before serving, along with grated Parmesan, chopped chives, and a splash of lemon juice just to tease out the cultured dairy's tang a bit more. The result was startlingly good—a next-level kind of risotto, distinct and flavorful enough to stand on its own but restrained enough to accompany almost anything. My inauspicious start was a distant memory, and this dish was shaping up to be the raison d'être of many summer dinners to come.

—ANNIE PETITO, *Cook's Illustrated*

Corn Risotto

SERVES 6 TO 8

Serve this risotto with a side salad as a light main course, or serve it as an accompaniment to seared scallops or shrimp or grilled meat. Our favorite Arborio rice is RiceSelect Arborio Rice, and our favorite Parmesan cheese is Boar's Head Parmigiano-Reggiano. If crème fraîche is unavailable, you can substitute sour cream. A large ear of corn should yield 1 cup of kernels, but if the ears you find are smaller, buy at least six.

4–6	ears corn, kernels cut from cobs (4 cups), divided, cobs reserved
5½	cups hot water, divided
2	tablespoons unsalted butter
1	shallot, minced
2	teaspoons table salt
1	garlic clove, minced
½	teaspoon pepper
1½	cups Arborio rice
3	sprigs fresh thyme
1	ounce Parmesan cheese, grated (½ cup)
¼	cup crème fraîche
2	tablespoons chopped fresh chives
½	teaspoon lemon juice

1. Stand 1 reserved corn cob on end on cutting board and firmly scrape downward with back of butter knife to remove any pulp remaining on cob. Repeat with remaining reserved cobs. Transfer pulp to blender. Add 3 cups corn kernels.

2. Process corn and pulp on low speed until thick puree forms, about 30 seconds. With blender running, add ½ cup hot water. Increase speed to high and continue to process until smooth, about 3 minutes longer. Pour puree into fine-mesh strainer set over large liquid measuring cup or bowl. Using back of ladle or rubber spatula, push puree through strainer, extracting as much liquid as possible (you should have about 2 cups corn liquid). Discard solids.

3. Melt butter in large Dutch oven over medium heat. Add shallot, salt, garlic, and pepper and cook, stirring frequently, until softened but not browned, about 1 minute. Add rice and thyme sprigs and cook, stirring frequently, until grains are translucent around edges, 2 to 3 minutes.

4. Stir in 4½ cups hot water. Reduce heat to medium-low; cover; and simmer until liquid is slightly thickened and rice is just al dente, 16 to 19 minutes, stirring twice during cooking.

5. Add corn liquid and continue to cook, stirring gently and constantly, until risotto is creamy and thickened but not sticky, about 3 minutes longer (risotto will continue to thicken as it sits). Stir in Parmesan and remaining 1 cup corn kernels. Cover pot and let stand off heat for 5 minutes. Stir in crème fraîche, chives, and lemon juice. Discard thyme sprigs and season with salt and pepper to taste. Adjust consistency with remaining ½ cup hot water as needed. Serve immediately.

KIMCHI BOKKEUMBAP (KIMCHI FRIED RICE)

✓ **WHY THIS RECIPE WORKS** Iconic, quick-cooking Korean comfort food, kimchi bokkeumbap is typically made with leftover cooked short-grain rice and gently spicy, well-fermented kimchi, but from there seasonings and additions to bulk it up vary widely from cook to cook. We started by stir-frying some aromatics (chopped onion and sliced scallions) with chopped ham—a popular addition that we liked for its smoky flavor and pleasantly springy texture. Then we added lots of chopped cabbage kimchi along with some of its savory, punchy juice and a little water and seasoned it with soy sauce, toasted sesame oil, and gochujang to add savoriness, rich nuttiness, and a little more heat. We simmered the cabbage leaves so that they softened a bit; stirred in the rice and cooked the mixture until the liquid had been absorbed; and topped the rice with small strips of gim, sesame seeds, and scallion greens.

Like all forms of fried rice, kimchi bokkeumbap is straight-up home cooking: cozy, unfussy sustenance that's rooted in the spirit of making do with what you have. At its core is leftover cooked rice stir-fried with the ruddy, gently spicy fermented napa cabbage that most Korean cooks keep on hand. But from there it can—and usually does—get personal, since that rib-sticking, umami-charged base is just the thing to capture all sorts of odds and ends. In any given kitchen, you'll find the rice bulked up with ham, Spam, sausage, or seafood (fresh, tinned, or smoked); seasoned with gochujang, plum extract, or oyster sauce; dolloped with mayonnaise; topped with crumbled gim (dried seaweed); bundled in a gauzy omelet; cradling a runny fried egg; or teeming with gooey cheese.

"Every family has their own twist," said Sun-Jung Yum. The daughter of South Korean immigrants, she grew up eating kimchi bokkeumbap with her family in Cambridge, Massachusetts. Yum's family personalizes their kimchi fried rice with bacon, sausage, and pieces of tteokbokki (chewy Korean rice cakes). "This is how my family has grown to love it," said Yum.

Its unscripted nature says a lot about why kimchi bokkeumbap is so widely cooked among Koreans. But there's an even simpler explanation that goes back to the common framework running through every batch: Rice and kimchi are fixtures of Korean cuisine, and they form a perfect merger. The chew of the stubby grains; the crunch of the hot-and-sour cabbage; and the way that each bite glows in your mouth, insisting that you take another bite and another, becomes a powerful learned craving.

Craving is a sentiment that comes up a lot when talking about kimchi bokkeumbap and its two main components. Regarding kimchi, Yum refused to go to sleepaway camp because she couldn't go a day without it. For Jeisook Thayer, who makes and sells kimchi on Martha's Vineyard under the label MV Kimchi, the craving begins at breakfast.

"It's better than having cold cereal in the morning," Thayer said. "A hot bowl of rice with a little bit of smoked fish and kimchi, and you're good to go."

Thayer started making kimchi shortly after she emigrated from Seoul. "I missed my food," she said, recalling that few people knew what kimchi was when she moved to the United States in 1964. She relied on memory and improvisation at first: "I cooked remembering how it should taste: a little salty, a little spicy . . . with its own umami from the fermentation."

In well-fermented kimchi, "you no longer bite into a piece of garlic and say, 'I just got a piece of garlic' or 'Oh, I got ginger,'" Thayer explained. "All those flavors blend, and it creates its own umami . . . There's nothing like it."

It's hard to overemphasize the importance of rice in the Korean diet. For example, in an essay on food52.com, writer Eric Kim describes how his dad would routinely dip a spoon into the rice cooker after returning home from a steakhouse dinner, as if needing a rice fix to feel "fully satiated."

Yum added: "There are rare occasions where someone opens the rice cooker and there's no rice left—and everyone is just kind of at a loss."

That sentiment is documented in the Korean language, since "bap," the Korean word for cooked rice and other grains, is also the word for "food." And the importance of rice persisted against great odds, since for most of the 20th century, rice was out of reach for most Koreans. During the Japanese occupation of Korea (1910–1945), the Japanese government exported Korean-grown rice to Japan, forcing locals to subsist on other grains. Rice scarcity lasted long after Japanese occupation ended, prompting the South Korean government to implement initiatives such as "No Rice Days" and to exhort its citizens to mix rice with legumes and alternative grains.

"My mother mixed barley and sometimes even beans with rice every time," said Kyung-Jin Rhee, Yum's mother, who emigrated from Seoul in 1992 and recalls the rice shortages from her childhood in Korea. "I went to elementary school in 1976 and clearly remember teachers checking our homemade lunches every day," she said, alluding to the government-mandated searches for rice-based foods.

Eventually food supplies and the economy stabilized and rice regained its role as a linchpin of the Korean diet. Now, in her Cambridge household, Rhee makes a point of keeping cooked rice on hand.

KIMCHI BOKKEUMBAP (KIMCHI FRIED RICE)

"The moment we run out, we just make another batch."

When there is leftover rice, kimchi bokkeumbap is one of the best ways to use it. The starch molecules in stale rice have crystallized, or retrograded, so the rice grains are hard and dry—able to be stir-fried without turning mushy. That firm texture is especially valuable in a dish such as kimchi bokkeumbap, where the rice soaks up a good bit of the kimchi's pungent liquid. In fact, kimchi makes this dish come together easily because it does most of the flavor work.

"Kimchi bokkeumbap is really tasty and easy to make, which makes it such a staple for lots of Koreans," said Rhee. "That's why recipes for kimchi bokkeumbap never have anything (besides kimchi and rice) that is necessary to the dish—everything can be substituted with what you have on hand."

In other words, think of that framework as a well-seasoned blank slate. Andrew Janjigian's formula starts with stir-fried onion and scallions and smoky, springy chopped ham, which pair well with the dish's crunch and tang. Then he adds lots of chopped cabbage kimchi along with some of its pungent juice and, depending on the texture of the cabbage, a little water (if your kimchi is relatively crunchy, add it; if not, omit it). To amp up the umami and heat, he works in soy sauce, toasted sesame oil, and gochujang. Then he simmers the kimchi so that the leaves soften a bit; stirs in the rice; cooks until the liquid is absorbed; and tops it with strips of gim, toasted sesame seeds, and scallion greens.

—ELIZABETH BOMZE AND ANDREW JANJIGIAN, *Cook's Illustrated*

Kimchi Bokkeumbap (Kimchi Fried Rice)

SERVES 4 TO 6

This recipe works best with day-old rice; alternatively, cook your rice 2 hours ahead, spread it on a rimmed baking sheet, and let it cool completely before chilling it for 30 minutes. Plain pretoasted seaweed snacks can be substituted for the gim (seaweed paper); omit the toasting in step 1. You'll need at least a 16-ounce jar of kimchi; if it doesn't yield ¼ cup of juice, make up the difference with water. If using soft, well-aged kimchi, omit the water and reduce the cooking time at the end of step 2 to 2 minutes. We developed this recipe with a 12-inch nonstick skillet, but you can use a well-seasoned carbon-steel skillet or 14-inch flat-bottomed wok instead. If desired, top each portion of rice with a fried egg.

1 (8-inch square) sheet gim
2 tablespoons vegetable oil, divided
2 (¼-inch-thick) slices deli ham, cut into ¼-inch pieces (about 4 ounces)
1 large onion, chopped
6 scallions, white and green parts separated and sliced thin on bias
1¼ cups cabbage kimchi, drained with ¼ cup juice reserved, cut into ¼-inch strips
¼ cup water
4 teaspoons soy sauce
4 teaspoons gochujang paste
½ teaspoon pepper
3 cups cooked short-grain white rice
4 teaspoons toasted sesame oil
1 tablespoon sesame seeds, toasted

1. Grip gim with tongs and hold 2 inches above low flame on gas burner. Toast gim, turning every 3 to 5 seconds, until gim is aromatic and shrinks slightly, about 20 seconds. (If you do not have a gas stove, toast gim on rimmed baking sheet in 275-degree oven until gim is aromatic and shrinks slightly, 20 to 25 minutes, flipping gim halfway through toasting.) Using kitchen shears, cut gim into four 2-inch-wide strips. Stack strips and cut crosswise into thin strips.

2. Heat 1 tablespoon vegetable oil in 12-inch nonstick skillet over medium-high heat until shimmering. Add ham, onion, and scallion whites and cook, stirring frequently, until onion is softened and ham is beginning to brown at edges, 6 to 8 minutes. Stir in kimchi and reserved juice, water, soy sauce, gochujang, and pepper. Cook, stirring occasionally, until kimchi turns soft and translucent, 4 to 6 minutes.

3. Add rice; reduce heat to medium-low; and cook, stirring and folding constantly until mixture is evenly coated, about 3 minutes. Stir in sesame oil and remaining 1 tablespoon vegetable oil. Increase heat to medium-high and cook, stirring occasionally, until mixture begins to stick to skillet, about 4 minutes. Transfer to serving bowl. Sprinkle with sesame seeds, gim, and scallion greens and serve.

CHANA MASALA

✓ **WHY THIS RECIPE WORKS** Chana masala can be a quick and easy dish, but it doesn't have to taste like it was thrown together. We started by using the food processor to grind the aromatic paste that formed the base of our dish. We opted for canned chickpeas because their flavor and texture were nearly indistinguishable from those of chickpeas that are cooked from dried, and we didn't drain them because the canning liquid added body and savory depth to the dish. The canned chickpeas still retained a bit of snap, so we simmered them in the sauce until they turned soft. Adding stronger foundational spices such as cumin, turmeric, and fennel seeds at the beginning of cooking ensured that they permeated the dish, and reserving the sweet, delicate garam masala until near the end preserved its aroma. A generous garnish of chopped onion, sliced chile, and cilantro added so much vibrancy, texture, and freshness that you'd never guess that most of the ingredients in the recipe were from the pantry.

The allure of chana masala, arguably one of the most popular vegetarian dishes in India, is multifaceted. First, the visuals: Golden chickpeas glimmer in an orangey-red tomato sauce, with a small side salad providing a pop of green. Then, the fragrance: The aromas of spices, ginger, and garlic perfume the dish. Finally, the taste: The yielding, almost creamy chickpeas and feisty sauce are balanced by the freshness and crunch of onion, chile, and cilantro.

It's also a practical dish, since it comes together easily and it calls for inexpensive, readily available ingredients.

To come up with my own version, I reviewed several recipes. Some started with dried chickpeas that required soaking, along with fresh tomatoes that had to be peeled and chopped, while others called for canned products. But once the ingredients were prepped, the method was similar: Fry a paste of onion, ginger, and garlic in oil. Stir in spices such as cumin, garam masala, and a mild chile powder (Kashmiri chile powder is traditional, but paprika is a common sub), and then add the tomatoes, chickpeas, and some water. Simmer until the chickpeas are soft and the sauce has thickened; then serve with rice, naan (or bhature), and the salad.

But none of these versions matched the stellar examples I'd eaten in the past. Several seemed lean and austere, the kind of thing devout carnivores expect vegetarian food to be. In some, the chickpeas were so soft that they were escaping their skins; in others, they remained too snappy. And the dishes lacked the nuanced spice flavor and heady aroma that are the hallmarks of chana masala.

My first round of testing had yielded one happy discovery: There was no advantage in starting with dried chickpeas and fresh tomatoes. Canned chickpeas were not only nicely seasoned but also 90 percent of the way to the ideal tender but intact texture. And canned tomatoes were sweet and tangy—far better than the fresh ones available at the supermarket 10 months out of the year. I wanted a smooth sauce, so for my next batch I decided to puree canned whole tomatoes, which have a fresh flavor and break down readily in the food processor.

I moved on to the onion, ginger, and garlic. For this dish (and many other Indian dishes) these aromatics are ground to a paste to produce big flavor without a distracting texture. In many Indian homes, an appliance called a mixer grinder is used to do this job, but I used a food processor. While I was at it, I added the stems of the cilantro sprigs I had set aside for the salad, along with a serrano chile.

I fried the paste in a tablespoon of oil until it was soft and brown and then added my spice mixture, which I had bolstered with fennel seeds and sweet, earthy turmeric for more depth. I added the drained chickpeas, the tomato puree, and 1 cup of water before letting it all simmer for 15 minutes.

I was making progress, but I wasn't there yet. The turmeric and fennel had added depth, but I wanted more; plus, the dish was too lean. Increasing the oil from 1 to 3 tablespoons solved both problems: Besides adding richness, the extra fat emboldened the spices (fat carries flavor, especially the fat-soluble flavors in spices). It also contributed much-needed body to the sauce, though not enough.

The next time around, instead of draining and rinsing the cans of chickpeas, I added their contents—liquid and all—to the pan and omitted the additional water. Admittedly, it's not canonical, but that liquid is full of proteins and carbohydrates, which boosted the savoriness and consistency of the sauce nicely.

Still, the flavor wasn't complex enough. It jumped straight from the earthy, foundational flavors of turmeric, cumin, and beans to the overt grassiness of the cilantro, chile, and onion, with nothing bridging the gap. A friend with a deep knowledge of Indian cooking guessed my misstep: "No garam masala?"

I'd been adding it all along; the problem was that I'd been adding it too early. In Indian cuisine, the coriander, cinnamon, cardamom, and other sweet spices that make up the blend are valued for their vibrant flavors, so they're often added at the end of cooking and sometimes even sprinkled atop a dish right before serving. Adding the spices late means that fewer volatile compounds are driven off, so their taste is more prominent. Indeed, holding the garam masala until near the end of the simmering time worked brilliantly, producing layered flavors. Speaking of layers, instead of serving the dish with a salad, I used the chiles, onion, and cilantro as a topping so that each bite would benefit. Once I'd set out a small bowl of lime wedges for additional tang, it was time to eat.

Because this dish comes together quickly, it is ideal for busy nights. But if you have the time, I recommend that you make the most delicious and traditional accompaniment: the puffed fried breads known as bhature.

—ANDREA GEARY, *Cook's Illustrated*

Chana Masala

SERVES 4 TO 6

Because the sodium contents of canned chickpeas and tomatoes vary, we include only a small amount of salt in this recipe; season with additional salt at the end of cooking if needed. If you prefer a spicier dish, leave the seeds in the serrano chiles. This dish is often paired with bhature, deep-fried breads that puff up as they cook; alternatively, serve it with rice or naan.

NOTES FROM THE TEST KITCHEN

FOR MULTIDIMENSIONAL FLAVOR, STAGGER SPICES

 The European tradition generally calls for adding spices to dishes early on so that their flavors have time to diffuse throughout the food. But in Indian cooking, the approach is more nuanced. Though there aren't any hard-and-fast rules, generally, the spices that are meant to permeate and offer background flavor—here, paprika, cumin, turmeric, and fennel—are added early. Spices that are meant to provide vibrant top notes—garam masala in this case—are added toward the end, as prolonged cooking drives off some volatile compounds.

---

1   **small red onion, quartered, divided**

10 **sprigs fresh cilantro, stems and leaves separated**

1   **(1½-inch) piece ginger, peeled and chopped coarse**

2   **garlic cloves, chopped coarse**

2   **serrano chiles, stemmed, halved, seeded, and sliced thin crosswise, divided**

3   **tablespoons vegetable oil**

1   **(14.5-ounce) can whole peeled tomatoes**

1   **teaspoon paprika**

1   **teaspoon ground cumin**

½ **teaspoon ground turmeric**

½ **teaspoon fennel seeds**

2   **(15-ounce) cans chickpeas, undrained**

1½ **teaspoons garam masala**

½ **teaspoon table salt**

    Lime wedges

1. Chop three-quarters of onion coarse; reserve remaining quarter for garnish. Cut cilantro stems into 1-inch lengths. Process chopped onion, cilantro stems, ginger, garlic, and half of serranos in food processor until finely chopped, scraping down sides of bowl as necessary, about 20 seconds. Combine onion mixture and oil in large saucepan. Cook over medium-high heat, stirring frequently, until onion is fully softened and beginning to stick to saucepan, 5 to 7 minutes.

2. While onion mixture cooks, process tomatoes and their juice in now-empty processor until smooth, about 30 seconds.

3. Add paprika, cumin, turmeric, and fennel seeds to onion mixture and cook, stirring constantly, until fragrant, about 1 minute. Stir in chickpeas and their liquid and processed tomatoes and bring to boil. Adjust heat to maintain simmer, then cover and simmer for 15 minutes. While mixture cooks, chop reserved onion fine.

4. Stir garam masala and salt into chickpea mixture and continue to cook, uncovered and stirring occasionally, until chickpeas are softened and sauce is thickened, 8 to 12 minutes longer. Season with salt to taste. Transfer to wide, shallow serving bowl. Sprinkle with chopped onion, remaining serranos, and cilantro leaves and serve, passing lime wedges separately.

Bhature

SERVES 4

If you'd like to make the bhature to serve with our Chana Masala (page 111), first prepare the bhature dough, following step 1 here, and then prepare the chana masala through step 2. Next, portion, shape, and fry the bhature, following steps 2 and 3 in the recipe below. Finally, finish preparing the chana masala. To get the right dough texture for the bhature, we recommend weighing the flour and stirring the yogurt well before measuring it. Do not substitute Greek yogurt for the plain yogurt in this recipe. The test kitchen's favorite plain yogurt is Brown Cow Cream Top Plain Yogurt. Be sure to use a Dutch oven that holds 6 quarts or more for frying. Each bhatura takes less than a minute to cook, so make sure that you have everything in place before you start to fry. Our favorite vegetable oil is Crisco Blends.

½ cup plain yogurt

¼ cup water

3 tablespoons vegetable oil, plus extra for shaping

2 cups (10 ounces) all-purpose flour

1 teaspoon sugar

¾ teaspoon table salt

¾ teaspoon baking powder

¼ teaspoon baking soda

2 quarts vegetable oil for frying

1. Whisk yogurt, water, and 3 tablespoons oil in small bowl until smooth. Pulse flour, sugar, salt, baking powder, and baking soda in food processor until combined, about 2 pulses. With processor running, add yogurt mixture and process until mixture forms smooth ball, about 30 seconds. Using your lightly oiled hands, transfer dough to lightly oiled counter. Knead until dough is smooth and springy, about 5 minutes. Form dough into ball and transfer to lightly greased bowl. Place plastic wrap or damp dish towel on surface of dough and let rest for at least 1 hour or up to 3 hours.

2. Add 2 quarts oil to large Dutch oven until it measures about 1½ inches deep and heat over medium-high heat to 390 degrees. Set wire rack in rimmed baking sheet and line with double layer of paper towels. Divide dough into 8 equal portions and shape into tight, round

FRYING BHATURE

As the bread begins to puff on one side, gently press the unpuffed side into the oil until the bread is evenly inflated, about 20 seconds. Continue to cook until the bottom is light golden brown, about 10 seconds longer, and then flip the bread and cook on the second side, lightly pressing each side into the oil to ensure even browning, about 20 seconds.

balls. Place balls seam side down on counter, coat lightly with extra oil, and cover with plastic. Use heel of your hand to press 1 dough ball into 3-inch round. Using rolling pin, gently roll into 6-inch round of even thickness, adding extra oil to counter as necessary to prevent sticking. Roll slowly and gently to prevent creasing. Cover with plastic or damp dish towel. Repeat with remaining dough balls.

3. Carefully place 1 dough round in hot oil. Press gently with back of spider skimmer to keep dough submerged until it begins to puff. As bread begins to puff on 1 side, gently press unpuffed side into oil until bread is evenly inflated, about 20 seconds. Continue to cook until bottom is light golden brown, about 10 seconds longer. Flip bread and cook on second side, lightly pressing both sides into oil to ensure even browning, about 20 seconds. Lift bhatura with spider skimmer and let drain briefly over pot before transferring to prepared rack. Repeat with remaining dough rounds, adjusting burner, if necessary, to maintain oil temperature between 380 and 400 degrees. Serve.

CHANA MASALA AND BHATURE

KEEMA ALOO (GARAM MASALA–SPICED GROUND BEEF WITH POTATOES)

MEAT

EASIER PRIME RIB

✓ WHY THIS RECIPE WORKS We set out to establish a new, foolproof method for cooking an occasion-worthy prime rib—one that would allow us to do the prep work, start the roast, and then essentially leave it alone while we took care of preparing the rest of the meal. Choosing a boneless roast was the first good move, as boneless roasts are much easier to carve and serve. To ensure that the roast would have a flavorful and well-seasoned exterior, we brushed it with Dijon mustard, which we chose for its sharp flavor and crust-enhancing qualities, and then we sprinkled the roast liberally with salt and pepper. A little research turned up an interesting trick for a hands-off, foolproof way to cook the roast to the perfect temperature. We started the roast in a 500-degree oven for a predetermined amount of time based on its weight, and then we shut off the oven and let the roast climb slowly to medium-rare over the course of the next 2 hours using just the oven's residual heat. This method left us with perfect, rosy medium-rare slices.

A beautiful prime rib roast is usually a special-occasion centerpiece, one that's surrounded by equally special side dishes. All that makes for a busy day in the kitchen, and when you add in the worry of an overcooked roast, it can be overwhelming.

I set out to establish a new method that would allow me to do the prep work, get the roast started, and then leave it alone and, more important, not worry about it overcooking while I attended to the rest of the meal. That way, I could focus on finishing up all my stovetop side dishes.

I selected a boneless roast for ease of carving. To ensure a well-seasoned exterior, I brushed it with Dijon mustard, which I chose for its sharp flavor and crust-enhancing qualities, and sprinkled the roast with salt and pepper.

From there I knew that I had a few options. I could sear the roast on the stovetop first and then finish it in the oven, but maneuvering a roast of that size in a skillet is an unwieldy endeavor. Or I could bring the roast up to temperature slowly in a relatively low oven and then blast it at the end, but that would mean I'd have to constantly monitor its temperature as it came up.

A little research turned up an interesting hack: Start the roast in a hot oven for a predetermined amount of time based on its weight, and then shut off the oven and let the roast climb slowly to medium-rare over the course of the next 2 hours in the oven's residual heat. The promise was that with a little elementary math, this method would work for any size roast. And since it's seared in the oven rather than on the stovetop, the process is far less messy.

The recipe I found online called for cooking a bone-in prime rib for 5 minutes per pound at 500 degrees. In that scenario, the bone offers some protection against the meat overcooking, so for a boneless roast I would have to adjust the active oven time.

I tinkered with the equation and ended up with 3 minutes of "on" time per pound for a boneless roast. For a 3½-pound roast this walk-away method requires cooking the roast for 11 minutes at 500 degrees before turning off the oven completely and leaving the roast alone for 2 hours.

After a 20-minute rest out of the oven, the roast yielded perfectly juicy, medium-rare slices. What's more, I had 2 hands-free, worry-free hours to prepare all the side dishes I wanted to go with it. Happy holidays, indeed.

—BRYAN ROOF, *Cook's Country*

NOTES FROM THE TEST KITCHEN

COOKING TIME CHEAT SHEET FOR MEDIUM-RARE MEAT
Weigh your roast and round up to the nearest ½ pound. Triple that number and, if necessary, round up again to the nearest whole number. This is your oven-on roasting time (in minutes). Place the roast into a 500-degree oven and set your timer to the time you calculated. When the time's up, turn off the oven and leave the roast alone for 2 hours. Perfect.

EXAMPLE FORMULA
Your roast is 3.3 pounds. Round that to 3.5 pounds. Triple the rounded weight to 10.5, and then round this up to 11. There's your oven-on roasting time: 11 minutes.

roast weight	oven-on roasting time	walk-away time
2.6–3.0 pounds	9 minutes	2 hours
3.1–3.5 pounds	11 minutes	2 hours
3.6–4.0 pounds	12 minutes	2 hours
4.1–4.5 pounds	14 minutes	2 hours
4.6–5.0 pounds	15 minutes	2 hours

Easier Prime Rib

SERVES 6 TO 8

It is critical that you not open the oven door at all while the roast is cooking. If you do, the heat will escape from the oven and the calculated cooking time will be ineffective. It's good to use an oven thermometer to ensure that your oven truly reaches 500 degrees before starting. This technique works for roasts outside of the weight range given here; see "Cooking Time Cheat Sheet for Medium-Rare Meat" to calculate the correct oven time for roasts of different weights. Our recipe for prepared horseradish follows, but you can also use store-bought.

1½ tablespoons kosher salt
1½ tablespoons pepper
 1 (3- to 3½-pound) boneless prime rib roast
 2 tablespoons Dijon mustard
    Prepared horseradish

1. Adjust oven rack to middle position and heat oven to 500 degrees. Line rimmed baking sheet with aluminum foil and set wire rack in sheet; spray rack with vegetable oil spray. Combine salt and pepper in bowl.

2. Using scale, weigh prime rib. Round weight up to nearest ½ pound. Multiply rounded weight by 3, then round that number up to nearest whole number. Record that number; this will be your oven-on roasting time (in minutes).

3. Pat prime rib dry with paper towels. Brush all over with mustard. Sprinkle salt and pepper mixture evenly on all sides. Transfer to prepared rack, fat side up.

4. Transfer sheet with prime rib to oven and roast for time recorded in step 2. Without opening oven door, turn off oven and leave roast in oven, undisturbed, for 2 hours. Do not open oven during this time.

5. Remove sheet from oven and let prime rib rest on rack for 20 minutes. Transfer prime rib to carving board. Slice ¼ to ½ inch thick. Serve with horseradish.

Prepared Horseradish

SERVES 8 TO 10 (MAKES ABOUT 2 CUPS)

We call for canning and pickling salt here, which is often called preserving salt. Noniodized table salt can be used in an equal amount. To substitute Morton Kosher Salt for the canning and pickling salt, increase the amount to 1½ teaspoons; to use Diamond Crystal Kosher Salt, increase the amount to 2 teaspoons.

10 ounces fresh horseradish root, peeled and cut into 1-inch pieces (2 cups)
 1 teaspoon canning and pickling salt
 1 cup cider vinegar

1. Pulse horseradish and salt in food processor until coarsely chopped, about 15 pulses, scraping down sides of bowl as needed. With processor running, slowly add vinegar until incorporated and mixture has pulp-like consistency, about 1 minute, scraping down sides of bowl as necessary.

2. Spoon horseradish into two 1-cup jars; seal jars. (Horseradish can be refrigerated for up to 3 weeks; flavor will deepen over time.)

SPICE-CRUSTED SIRLOIN STEAK WITH ASPARAGUS AND LEMON-SHALLOT BUTTER

✔ **WHY THIS RECIPE WORKS** Our favorite steakhouse combo is a juicy steak with vibrant asparagus. We set out to replicate it using only one small baking sheet and our toaster oven. While steaks are rarely baked, we knew that we could achieve a hands-off version of a flawless medium-rare steak by getting creative. We tried various approaches to deliver the crust we desired with an ideal interior. Only a spice rub gave us an attractive crust without overcooking the interior to a gray slab. To fine-tune the middle of our steak, we baked it directly on a sheet and flipped it halfway through cooking to produce a perfectly pink, medium-rare interior. On the same baking sheet, we roasted the asparagus in the time it took to cook and rest the steak. A lemon-shallot butter complemented each component. The final product was a steakhouse dinner from the toaster oven: a medium-rare sirloin, an elevated butter, and beautifully cooked asparagus.

There are many paths to the perfect steak. In the test kitchen, for example, we've developed steak recipes for gas and charcoal grills and cast-iron and traditional skillets. We've mastered methods that call for a sous-vide water bath or a stint in the oven followed by a quick, hot sear over the stove. And we've even made succulent, juicy steaks in an air fryer. So when I was tasked with

SPICE-CRUSTED SIRLOIN STEAK WITH ASPARAGUS AND LEMON-SHALLOT BUTTER

the challenge of developing a steak recipe for our cookbook *Toaster Oven Perfection*, I knew that a foolproof technique was out there—I just needed to discover it.

To bring the classic steakhouse experience to my kitchen table, I wanted a recipe that would yield a substantial steak dinner (steak, side, and sauce) for two. And for efficiency and ease of cleanup, I wanted to cook the whole thing in a single pan. For the side, asparagus was an easy choice—the vegetable is a classic restaurant pairing with steak, and I knew from experience that it would take very well to oven roasting. The sauce would be simple, too—I'd whip up a quick compound butter that would melt lusciously over the hot steak and vegetables, adding richness and a bright pop of flavor.

The steak itself, however, would be a little more complicated to pin down. No matter the method, there are two main benchmarks for a perfectly cooked medium-rare steak: a consistently pink, juicy interior and a dark-brown, flavorful, crusty exterior. If I could achieve both of those elements in a toaster oven, everything else would come together in a snap.

For my first test, I trimmed 12 ounces of asparagus (this amount filled about half of the baking sheet that came with my toaster oven) and spread the stalks out next to a halved top sirloin steak—a relatively inexpensive but flavorful and well-marbled cut. I popped the sheet into a 450-degree oven, hoping the high temperature would yield some attractive browning on my steak as the asparagus roasted, and then I waited—and waited, and waited—for that browning to appear.

After about 10 minutes, my asparagus looked bright green and just about ready to eat, and the interiors of the steaks had already come up to temperature (120 to 125 degrees for medium-rare doneness), but their exteriors had taken on a decidedly unappetizing gray cast, and there was no browning in sight. To make matters worse, the steaks' juices had bubbled up and pooled around their bottom edges—creating a moist environment in which the steaks had essentially steamed rather than seared. This was a far cry from the browned, crusty sirloin I'd been aiming for.

I sliced into one of my sad-looking steaks with a sigh, fully expecting to reveal a tough slab of well-done meat. But I was greeted by a pleasant surprise: a nicely pink interior that was juicy and tender. This was far closer to the steakhouse standard I was after—I'd just have to focus my energy on achieving that substantial exterior crust.

I turned to the broiler, hoping its intense heat would give me a better shot at browning; the broiled steaks did pick up some sporadic browning, mostly in the few fatty areas on the surface, but I still wasn't satisfied. If the highest heat available to me couldn't produce a proper crust, I'd need to find a way to bring it to the steak myself. After experimenting with a few other techniques and coming up short, I finally found my answer.

Adding a simple spice rub to the exterior of the steaks provided the color, texture, and flavor I needed with barely any fuss. Though I played with a few variations, my favorite was a steakhouse blend of coriander, pepper, garlic, and dried dill, which I could pack on generously for good texture and substantial browning without overshadowing the pure, meaty flavor of the steak. Baked at 450 degrees for about 10 minutes, and flipped halfway through for even cooking, these spice-rubbed steaks emerged with a delicious, worthy crust and a juicy center that was perfectly pink from edge to edge.

With the steak method settled, I finally cooked my steakhouse spread all the way through. I whipped up a compound butter with bright lemon and minced shallot, both of which would nicely complement the heavier flavors of the savory, spiced steak, and then I popped the coated steaks into the toaster oven along with the asparagus. Once the steaks were done, I pulled them out and let the asparagus keep roasting until it was perfectly crisp-tender, bright green, and spottily browned. By that time, the tender steaks were rested and juicy, and I was ready to slice and serve. Order up!

—JOSEPH GITTER, *America's Test Kitchen Books*

Spice-Crusted Sirloin Steak with Asparagus and Lemon-Shallot Butter

SERVES 2

The test kitchen's favorite unsalted butter is Challenge Unsalted Butter.

- 1   small shallot, minced
- 2   tablespoons unsalted butter, softened
- ¼   teaspoon grated lemon zest plus ½ teaspoon juice
- 1   (12- to 16-ounce) boneless top sirloin, strip, or rib-eye steak, 1 inch thick, trimmed
- 1   tablespoon extra-virgin olive oil, divided
- 4   teaspoons spice blend (recipes follow)
- ¼   teaspoon plus ⅛ teaspoon table salt, divided
- ⅛   teaspoon pepper
- 12 ounces asparagus, trimmed

1. Adjust toaster oven rack to lowest position and heat oven to 450 degrees. Combine shallot, softened butter, and lemon zest and juice in bowl; set aside for serving.

2. Cut steak crosswise to yield two 1-inch-thick steaks. Pat steaks dry with paper towels, rub evenly with 1 teaspoon oil, and sprinkle with spice blend and ¼ teaspoon salt, pressing to adhere. Arrange steaks on 1 half of small rimmed baking sheet. Toss asparagus with remaining 2 teaspoons oil, remaining ⅛ teaspoon salt, and pepper in bowl and arrange in even layer on empty side of sheet. Roast until steaks register 120 to 125 degrees (for medium-rare) or 130 to 135 degrees (for medium), 10 to 15 minutes, flipping steaks halfway through roasting.

3. Remove sheet from oven. Transfer steaks to cutting board and let rest for 5 minutes. Meanwhile, return sheet to oven and continue to roast asparagus until crisp-tender, 2 to 4 minutes longer. Slice steaks thin, top with butter, and serve with asparagus.

Steakhouse Spice Blend
MAKES 8 TEASPOONS

The spice rub can be stored in an airtight container for up to three months.

- 4 teaspoons ground coriander
- 2 teaspoons pepper
- 1 teaspoon garlic powder
- 1 teaspoon dried dill weed or parsley

Combine all ingredients in small bowl.

Tex-Mex Spice Blend
MAKES 8 TEASPOONS

The spice rub can be stored in an airtight container for up to three months.

- 1 tablespoon paprika
- 2 teaspoons ground coriander
- 1½ teaspoons ground cumin
- 1½ teaspoons garlic powder

Combine all ingredients in small bowl.

GRILLED BONELESS BEEF SHORT RIBS

✓ **WHY THIS RECIPE WORKS** A couple simple steps ensured that our grilled beef short ribs were as satisfying as steaks that are twice as expensive. We chose boneless short ribs (a cut from the chuck, or shoulder, of the animal) because they have well-distributed fat that's packed with compounds that break down as the meat cooks, imbuing it with rich, beefy flavor. Some of their abundant collagen also breaks down, enhancing the juiciness of the rendered fat. Instead of flavoring just the surface of the ribs with a marinade, we salted them for an hour to ensure that they were seasoned throughout. We grilled the ribs over high heat to allow the drippings to flare up, creating great grill flavor. Frequent flipping cooked the meat evenly and gently, since each time the meat was turned, the side not facing the heat cooked with residual heat. Finally, we sliced the ribs against the grain so that they were as tender as possible.

The best steaks for searing over hot coals are those that have enough fat and beefy flavor to support the smoky, charred aromas that the meat acquires during grilling. Meaty rib eyes and strip steaks fit the bill—but they are a real splurge. So what if I told you that there is an equally flavorful cut that will run you only about half as much? Boneless beef short ribs are ribboned with fat and grill up as juicy as can be, with a satisfying chew similar to that of flank or skirt steak.

The seams of fat that run through beef short ribs are responsible for the incredible flavor that they can achieve on a grill. As with any well-marbled steak, as the beef cooks, fatty acids form aromatic compounds. It's these compounds that enhance the meat's rich, beefy taste. Meanwhile, the proteins on the surface of the ribs brown and contribute roasty flavors. Finally, the fat-laden juices drip onto the coals, creating flare-ups that impart charred savoriness to the meat.

To get my bearings, I reviewed several existing recipes. Many start with a marinade, which I rejected out of hand, since a marinade flavors only the surface of the meat and would be barely noticeable in a cut this thick. But I decided to give the grilling approach used by most recipes a test run. It's the same technique that is often suggested for a rib-eye or strip steak: Sprinkle with salt and sear over hot coals until the meat reaches a rosy medium-rare, flipping it halfway through searing. But although boneless short ribs grilled this way had a deeply beefy taste, the meat was unevenly seasoned and rather chewy. What's more, the short ribs' blocky shape and roughly 1½-inch thickness meant that by the time their centers were up to temperature, their exteriors were burnt. I knew that I could do a lot better.

I started by ensuring that the meat would be thoroughly seasoned, sprinkling 2½ teaspoons of kosher salt onto 2 pounds of boneless ribs that I'd cut into 3- to 4-inch lengths. I let the ribs sit for an hour—plenty of time for the sodium ions to penetrate deep into the muscle fibers. While they sat, I considered the best way to grill them.

I decided to try a method that we've used on the stovetop for other thick cuts of beef, pork chops, and even swordfish. It calls for repeatedly flipping the protein over high heat until it comes up to temperature. (Boneless short ribs are so thick and chunky that I'd need to grill them on all four sides, not just the top and bottom.) The upshot is that the interior warms evenly and gently, since each time the meat is flipped, the side not touching the pan (or the cooking grate in this case) cooks via residual heat, producing rosiness from edge to edge. Meanwhile, a rich, dark crust builds up gradually.

NOTES FROM THE TEST KITCHEN

SLICING AGAINST THE GRAIN

Meat is made up of bundles of muscle fibers that run parallel to one another. The fibers form a pattern that is referred to as the "grain"; it looks similar to wood grain. Slicing against the grain means cutting the fibers into shorter pieces. This makes tougher cuts such as boneless short ribs more pleasant to eat because shorter lengths of muscle fibers are easier to chew. It's easy to cut boneless short ribs against the grain because the muscle fibers tend to run diagonally. That means that as long as you slice the meat lengthwise, you'll be cutting against the grain.

To produce a concentrated area of heat, I spread hot coals over just one side of the grill. I then seared the ribs on each of their four sides for 2 to 3 minutes per side. But I soon realized that I wasn't flipping them often enough. Boneless short ribs are not uniformly sized and some are tapered at one end, so a few were done after just three of their sides were browned. It was better to flip them every minute until they were well seared on all sides and had come up to temperature, checking the smaller ones early and often.

Speaking of temperature, to determine how high to take the ribs, I cooked half a batch to medium-rare and the remainder to medium. A few years ago while working on a grilled skirt steak recipe, I learned that cooking tougher cuts to medium instead of medium-rare causes the muscle fibers to shrink and separate, making the meat more tender—and in a well-marbled cut, the rendered fat makes up for any loss of juices. I suspected that short ribs would also benefit from this treatment.

Inside, after letting the ribs rest for 10 minutes, I sliced them thin against the grain to shorten the meat fibers—another trick to ensure that each bite is tender. Both samples were juicy and beefy, with deeply browned crusts, and just as I had suspected, the 130-degree ribs were more tender.

I love these steaks with nothing more than a sprinkle of flake sea salt and a spritz of tart lemon juice to balance their richness, but they're also terrific with a bold, bright sauce: I whipped up two that get their backbones from fermented products. The first features kimchi combined with a hit of fresh scallions; the second marries citrus and nuts in the form of tangy, floral preserved lemon and crunchy toasted almonds. No matter how you serve these steaks, I guarantee that you'll be getting more than your money's worth.

—LAN LAM, *Cook's Illustrated*

Grilled Boneless Beef Short Ribs
SERVES 4 TO 6

This recipe was developed using Diamond Crystal Kosher Salt. If you're using Morton Kosher Salt, which is denser, use only 1¾ teaspoons of salt. We like these ribs cooked to about 130 degrees (medium). If you prefer them medium-rare, remove the ribs from the grill when they register 125 degrees. Serve with lemon wedges and flake sea salt or with one of our sauces (recipes follow).

2 pounds boneless beef short ribs, trimmed

2½ teaspoons kosher salt

1 teaspoon pepper

1. Cut ribs into 3- to 4-inch lengths. Sprinkle all sides with salt and pepper. Let sit at room temperature for 1 hour.

2A. FOR A CHARCOAL GRILL: Open bottom vent completely. Light large chimney starter mounded with charcoal briquettes (7 quarts). When top coals are partially covered with ash, pour evenly over half of grill. Set cooking grate in place, cover, and open lid vent completely. Heat grill until hot, about 5 minutes.

2B. FOR A GAS GRILL: Turn all burners to high; cover; and heat grill until hot, about 15 minutes. Turn off 1 burner (if using grill with more than 2 burners, turn off burner farthest from primary burner) and leave other burner(s) on high.

3. Clean and oil cooking grate. Arrange ribs on hotter side of grill. Cook (covered if using gas), flipping ribs every minute, until meat is well browned on all sides and registers about 130 degrees at thickest part, 8 to 14 minutes. (Ribs will be very pale after first flip but will continue to brown as they cook. This cut can quickly overcook; start checking temperature of smaller ribs after 8 minutes.)

4. Transfer ribs to cutting board, tent with aluminum foil, and let rest for 10 minutes. Slice ribs as thin as possible against grain. (Grain runs diagonally, so as long as you slice lengthwise, you will be cutting against grain.) Serve.

Kimchi-Scallion Sauce
SERVES 6 (MAKES ABOUT 1 CUP)

Cider vinegar or seasoned rice vinegar can be substituted for the unseasoned rice vinegar.

6 scallions, sliced thin

⅓ cup finely chopped cabbage kimchi

¼ cup vegetable oil

4 teaspoons soy sauce

4 teaspoons unseasoned rice vinegar

¼ teaspoon sugar

Stir all ingredients together in bowl. Let sit for 15 minutes. Stir well before using. (Sauce can be refrigerated for up to 24 hours. Let sit at room temperature for 15 minutes before serving.)

Preserved Lemon–Almond Sauce
SERVES 6 (MAKES ABOUT 1 CUP)

Sliced almonds provide a delicate crunch; do not substitute slivered or whole almonds.

5 tablespoons extra-virgin olive oil, divided

¼ cup sliced almonds, chopped

½ cup minced fresh parsley

2 tablespoons finely chopped preserved lemon plus 2 tablespoons brine

2 tablespoons lemon juice

¼ teaspoon sugar

Combine 1 tablespoon oil and almonds in 8-inch skillet; toast over medium-high heat, stirring constantly, until almonds are golden brown, 1 to 2 minutes. Immediately transfer to bowl. Stir in parsley, preserved lemon and brine, lemon juice, sugar, and remaining ¼ cup oil. Let sit for 15 minutes. Stir well before using. (Sauce can be refrigerated for up to 24 hours. Let sit at room temperature for 15 minutes before serving.)

GLAZED MEATLOAF FOR ONE

☑ **WHY THIS RECIPE WORKS** Meatloaf brings to mind diner-style fare for a family, but we wanted down-home goodness in a smaller package (without the assistance of cutesy, single-use mini equipment). To mix up the classic flavor profile, we used ground pork and incorporated Asian-inspired ingredients for a meatloaf that reminded us of the filling of our favorite dumplings. To avoid the sometimes dense bounciness of dumpling filling, we added some panko and an egg yolk to the ground pork, which kept our meatloaf supermoist and tender. We pressed the meat mixture into a free-form loaf, browned it in a skillet, flipped it, and finished it in the oven in the same skillet (bonus points for less cleanup!). We glazed the loaf with a mixture of fruity, umami-packed hoisin sauce and a splash of tangy rice vinegar.

I don't think I'm alone when I say that I'm not a fan of meatloaf. I've always found the texture monotonously soft and the ketchup glaze artificially sweet. So when I was tasked with creating a single-serving meatloaf for our cookbook *Cooking for One*, I wasn't thrilled. But soon I realized that I had the opportunity to make a

GLAZED MEATLOAF FOR ONE

meatloaf I actually liked: one that had more flavor and better texture and—because it was a single serving—was quicker and easier to make.

The average meatloaf is made with ground beef or meatloaf mix, which is a combination of beef, pork, and veal. But I wasn't interested in the average meatloaf: I thought it would be fun to go with an all-pork meatloaf that evoked the flavors of my favorite Chinese pork dumplings. Just 6 ounces of ground pork was plenty for a single portion.

Pork dumplings feature a pleasantly bouncy filling that's cohesive enough to keep the ingredients from tumbling out of the wrapper when you bite in. This texture is the result of a vigorous mixing method that releases a sticky protein (called myosin) from the meat. The protein binds up the ingredients, ensuring a cohesive filling. I wanted a meatloaf that stayed together, but a bouncy texture wasn't desirable here. I needed to find a way to bind the mixture without overworking it.

Enter: the panade. Most meatloaf and meatball recipes include a panade, a combination of milk and some form of bread (torn bread, bread crumbs, or saltines) that's mixed until it forms a paste. This paste helps bind the other ingredients and lubricates the meat, keeping it tender. Milk felt out of place in my meatloaf, so I tried swapping the milk with a splash of soy sauce. Combined with a single egg yolk (a full egg introduced too much moisture), it adequately moistened the bread and bound the meatloaf mixture but kept the final texture light. For the bread, I turned to the test kitchen's favorite bread crumbs: panko. A few tablespoons absorbed the liquid from the soy sauce and egg yolk and helped open up the dense ground pork.

Many meatloaf recipes call for sautéing aromatics and vegetables in a skillet and letting them cool before stirring them into the meat mixture. This not only adds flavor but also breaks up the meatloaf's texture. I certainly wanted to improve the dish's flavor and texture, but the sautéing and cooling steps seemed too fussy for such a small loaf. Instead, I added 1½ teaspoons of grated fresh ginger, one minced garlic clove, and a thinly sliced scallion directly to the meat mixture. The aromatics contributed deeply fragrant flavor but didn't taste "raw" in the finished meatloaf.

Once I mixed the pork with the panade and aromatics, I shaped the mixture into a 5 by 3-inch loaf and contemplated my cooking method. I had been following a test kitchen recipe that called for transferring the loaf to a baking sheet, broiling it to develop a crust, glazing it, and then baking it until it was cooked through. This was too much of a process for a single-serving meatloaf, so I looked for ways to streamline. Rather than broiling the tiny loaf (which would risk overcooking it), I seared it on one side in a skillet, flipped it, and then transferred the skillet to the oven. There the loaf would develop a crust on its exposed side. This would prevent the meat juices from leaking out of the loaf, which would make it too slippery for the glaze to stick.

I knew that I wanted to avoid ketchup in my glaze, so I scanned my pantry for alternatives. My eyes landed on hoisin sauce, a mahogany paste often used in Cantonese cuisine that's made with soybeans, spices, garlic, and chiles. Hoisin is viscous like ketchup, so it would easily cling to the meatloaf, and the soybeans and spices would complement the soy sauce and aromatics in the pork mixture. I stirred the hoisin with rice vinegar to cut through some of its sweetness and thin its texture slightly. Hoisin's high sugar content caused it to burn in the oven when I applied it at the start of cooking; I had better luck brushing it on halfway through.

I let the cooked meatloaf rest for 5 minutes before sprinkling on sliced scallion greens and digging in. This was the meatloaf I had envisioned: moist, tender pork seasoned with flavorful aromatics and covered in a sweet and savory glaze. It was an exciting spin on a tired dish, and it was all for me. Who said I didn't like meatloaf?

—NICOLE KONSTANTINAKOS,
America's Test Kitchen Books

Glazed Meatloaf for One

SERVES 1

We love this meatloaf paired with green beans or mashed potatoes for a classic combo or turned into a sandwich with melted cheese and extra hoisin for dunking. You can substitute meatloaf mix or ground beef for the pork.

- **2 tablespoons hoisin sauce**
- **1 tablespoon unseasoned rice vinegar**
- **3 tablespoons panko bread crumbs**
- **2 scallions, sliced thin, divided**
- **1 tablespoon soy sauce**

1 large egg yolk

1½ teaspoons grated fresh ginger or ¼ teaspoon
ground ginger

1 garlic clove, minced, or ⅛ teaspoon garlic powder

6 ounces ground pork

½ teaspoon vegetable oil

1. Adjust oven rack to middle position and heat oven to 350 degrees. Whisk hoisin and vinegar together in small bowl; set aside.

2. Combine panko, half of scallions, soy sauce, egg yolk, ginger, and garlic in medium bowl. Add pork and gently knead with your hands until just combined. Shape mixture into rough 5 by 3-inch loaf of even thickness.

3. Heat oil in 8- or 10-inch ovensafe nonstick skillet over medium heat until just smoking. Gently add meatloaf and cook on first side until well browned, 2 to 3 minutes. Carefully flip meatloaf, neatening edges as needed, and transfer skillet to oven. Bake for 10 minutes.

4. Remove skillet from oven. Being careful of hot skillet handle, brush top and sides of meatloaf with hoisin mixture. Return skillet to oven and continue to bake until meatloaf registers 160 degrees, 5 to 10 minutes longer. Transfer meatloaf to plate and let rest for 5 minutes. Sprinkle with remaining scallions and serve.

PALOMILLA STEAK

✓ **WHY THIS RECIPE WORKS** For a spin on this classic Cuban steak dish, we swapped out thin, tough cuts of beef for tender skirt steak that could be cooked to medium-rare. We cooked the onions until they just started to turn golden brown, imparting a savory sweetness that paired well with the beef flavor and the brightness of fresh lime juice and garlic. Cilantro added a welcome pop of green and a wonderful herbaceous undertone, driving home the dish's Cuban identity.

The promise of bistec de palomilla (which translates as "butterfly steak," indicating the way in which the steaks are sliced and/or pounded to resemble a butterfly) is meat deeply infused with vibrant garlic and citrus flavors and smothered in gently sweet, golden-brown onions. It's a celebrated Cuban tradition in thousands of American and Caribbean homes.

Many of the recipes I found called for marinating less expensive steaks with garlic and lime juice to help tenderize the meat and introduce flavor. But my experiments consistently yielded steaks with muted flavor and uneven texture—a result of the meat sitting in the acidic lime juice. Did I need to marinate the steaks at all, or could I introduce these flavors in a different way to keep them vibrant and fresh?

After trying various cuts of steak, I settled on skirt steak for its wonderfully intense beef flavor. Plus, there was no need to marinate or pound the meat to improve its texture, since skirt steak, when sliced thin against the grain, has just a slight pleasant chew.

To streamline the process and dirty just one pan, I tried searing the steaks and then cooking the onions in the pan while the steaks rested, but by the time the onions were the right texture, the steaks weren't just rested—they were cold. I found that cooking the onions first, setting them aside while I cooked the meat, and then reheating them while the meat rested was the easiest approach. I added the garlic 2 minutes before the onions were done to release its flavor.

By using a nonstick skillet I could simply (but carefully) wipe the pan clean after the onions finished and cook the steaks. Then, as the meat rested, I quickly reheated the onions in the warm pan off the heat. It took a little back and forth, but the process wasn't complicated and it was all done in one pan for easy cleanup.

Some chopped cilantro and a squeeze of lime juice added freshness and acidity, producing a dish with deep savory-sweet flavor and a vibrant punch. My palomilla steak was flavorful, satisfying, and simple.

—MARK HUXSOLL, *Cook's Country*

Palomilla Steak

SERVES 4

You'll need about three medium onions for this recipe. Try to find skirt steaks with an even thickness throughout to allow for more even cooking. It is difficult to take an accurate temperature on skirt steaks because they are so thin; if you have trouble getting a reading, rely on the times in the recipe. Depending on the length of your whole skirt steaks, you will get anywhere from five to eight portions once the steaks are cut into 3-inch sections. Fresh lime juice is essential here. You'll need a 12-inch nonstick skillet with a lid for this recipe.

PALOMILLA STEAK

2 tablespoons unsalted butter

3 cups (¼-inch-thick) sliced onions

1¼ teaspoons table salt, divided

3 garlic cloves, minced

1½ pounds skirt steak, trimmed and cut with grain into 3-inch portions

1 teaspoon pepper

2 tablespoons vegetable oil

2 tablespoons chopped fresh cilantro

1 tablespoon lime juice

1. Melt butter in 12-inch nonstick skillet over medium heat. Add onions and ½ teaspoon salt. Cover and cook, stirring occasionally, until onions have softened, about 10 minutes. Uncover and continue to cook until onions begin to brown, about 2 minutes longer. Add garlic and cook until fragrant, about 2 minutes. Transfer to bowl and tent with aluminum foil. Wipe skillet clean with paper towels.

2. Pat steaks dry with paper towels and sprinkle with pepper and remaining ¾ teaspoon salt. Heat oil in now-empty skillet over high heat until just smoking. Add steaks and cook, without moving them, until well browned on first side, about 3 minutes.

3. Flip steaks and cook, without moving them, until browned on second side and registering 130 to 135 degrees, about 2 minutes. Transfer steaks to carving board, tent with foil, and let rest for 10 minutes. Pour off fat from skillet. Add onion mixture to now-empty skillet, cover, and let sit off heat to rewarm while steaks rest.

4. Stir cilantro and lime juice into onion mixture. Slice steaks thin against grain and transfer to platter. Spoon onion mixture over top. Serve.

BEEF WELLINGTON

✔ **WHY THIS RECIPE WORKS** For beef Wellington that's packed with flavor, we salted beef tenderloin overnight and then slathered it with piquant Dijon mustard before wrapping it in umami-rich prosciutto spread with super-concentrated duxelles. We traded the traditional puff pastry for sturdier, easier-to-work-with pâte brisée, which produces a firm yet flaky and tender crust that slices neatly when serving. Finally, we tackled the biggest challenge of making a Wellington: producing both a perfectly baked crust and uniformly medium-rare beef. To accomplish this, we roasted the Wellington in a 450-degree oven and removed it when the beef registered a mere 85 degrees. Carryover cooking did the rest of the work, as the meat's temperature gradually rose to 130 degrees (medium-rare). We created a Creamy Green Peppercorn Sauce and a Madeira Sauce, which gave us two options for finishing the decadent dish.

Of all the recipes I've developed, none has made me as proud as beef Wellington. That's not to say I wasn't intimidated at first: The ingredients are expensive, there are multiple components to consider, and success is notoriously elusive. But over time, I figured out how to orchestrate the steps into a foolproof process to produce a stunningly beautiful—and delicious—dish.

Most beef Wellington recipes come together like this: Coat a well-seared beef tenderloin in duxelles (finely chopped sautéed mushrooms), wrap it in crepes or thinly sliced prosciutto, top it with smears of liver pâté or slabs of foie gras, and encase everything in fancifully decorated pastry. Then slide it into the oven, keeping your fingers crossed that the beef emerges juicy and pink inside a crisp, golden crust.

I spent three days (and a staggering $600) evaluating five such recipes, and none fully justified the time or expense. However, there were bright spots: One Wellington featured deeply savory duxelles; another boasted medium-rare, juicy beef; and yet another had a beautifully crisp, golden crust.

Coming up with my own version was a tall mountain to climb, so I tackled the easy stuff first. I salted the beef overnight to enhance its flavor, and I ditched the dull crepes in favor of umami-rich prosciutto. I fortified the duxelles with shallots and a splash of Madeira and cooked the mixture long enough to drive off moisture from the mushrooms, concentrating their earthiness. Finally, I jettisoned the pâté, since its liver-y taste competed with rather than complemented the beef, and instead brushed the beef with Dijon mustard to add a complex kick. In the end, the package was so improved that I found I could skip the usual step of searing the meat.

Next, the pastry. Most modern Wellington recipes call for store-bought puff pastry, but the frozen dough often emerged from its package cracked where it had been folded and, as it warmed, was easy to tear. Once cooked, it slumped in spots and never fully crisped.

However, one recipe from the innovators at ChefSteps promised success with pâte brisée, an all-butter dough often used for tarts. Sure enough, this dough was easy to work with, even as I decorated the top of the Wellington with slender dough strips arranged on an elegant diagonal. Unlike the doughs of many other recipes I tried, which crumbled when sliced, this buttery, flaky crust was just sturdy enough to pass the slicing test.

My last challenge was simple to understand but hard to solve. Here's the deal: Pastry requires high heat to set its shape, crisp, and brown. A beef roast, on the other hand, benefits from a low-and-slow approach to produce medium-rare meat from edge to center. A sample that I cooked in a 425-degree oven yielded a crisp, golden crust but overdone beef; a 325-degree oven produced a Wellington with rosy beef but slack, pale pastry.

It wasn't until I called a side-by-side tasting that I had a breakthrough. I served the first roast while the other one waited nearby, and a lengthy discussion kept me from promptly returning to the second roast. When I finally sliced into it, the meat was gray, not pink. I had expected a certain amount of carryover cooking, but I was surprised at how significant the effect was here: This meat had been pushed to 150 degrees, well beyond my 130-degree target.

So why not make carryover cooking work for me instead of against me? Thus began a series of tests in which I pulled the Wellington from the oven at progressively lower temperatures. In the end, I landed on a technique in which I blasted the Wellington in a 450-degree oven for 45 minutes until the crust was crisp, flaky, and golden and then removed it when the meat registered a mere 85 degrees. During a 45-minute rest on the counter, the temperature of the roast steadily climbed to 130 degrees.

It was Wellington perfection: When sliced, the roast exuded hardly any juice, and the well-seasoned, medium-rare tenderloin encased in savory duxelles, salty prosciutto, and crisp pastry was a sight to behold. I beamed as I served it with a luxe sauce of heavy cream, brandy, and piquant green peppercorns, knowing that it had been well worth the effort.

—STEVE DUNN, *Cook's Illustrated*

Beef Wellington

SERVES 8 TO 10

We recommend using a probe thermometer for this recipe. Center-cut beef tenderloin roasts are sometimes sold as Châteaubriand. Request a Châteaubriand from the thicker end of the tenderloin; some butchers refer to this as the "cannon cut." Dry sherry can be substituted for the Madeira. Use packaged prosciutto rather than freshly sliced deli prosciutto, as the slices will be easier to handle. Although the timing for many of the components is flexible, we recommending making the Wellington over a three-day period: Prepare the components on the first day, assemble it on the second day (remember to reserve your leftover egg wash so that you can give the pastry a final coat before roasting it), and bake and serve it on the third day. Serve with Creamy Green Peppercorn Sauce or Madeira Sauce.

BEEF

- 1 center-cut beef tenderloin roast, 3 pounds trimmed weight, 12 to 13 inches long and 4 to 4½ inches in diameter
- 1 tablespoon kosher salt
- 1 tablespoon Dijon mustard
- 1 teaspoon pepper

PASTRY

- 3¼ cups (17¾ ounces) bread flour
- 22 tablespoons (2¾ sticks) unsalted butter, cut into ½-inch cubes and chilled
- 1 teaspoon table salt
- ½ cup plus 1 tablespoon ice water

DUXELLES

- 8 shallots, chopped
- 4 garlic cloves, peeled
- 2 pounds cremini mushrooms, trimmed and quartered, divided
- 8 tablespoons unsalted butter
- ¼ teaspoon pepper
- ⅛ teaspoon table salt
- 1 tablespoon Madeira
- 2 teaspoons minced fresh thyme

ASSEMBLY

- 12 thin slices prosciutto (6 ounces)
- 1 large egg plus 1 large yolk

BEEF WELLINGTON

DAY ONE: PREP COMPONENTS

1. FOR THE BEEF: Sprinkle all sides of beef evenly with salt. Wrap in plastic wrap and refrigerate for at least 12 hours or up to 3 days.

2. FOR THE PASTRY: Using stand mixer fitted with paddle, mix flour, butter, and salt on medium-low speed until mixture is crumbly and pieces of butter are no larger than peas, 4 to 5 minutes. With mixer running, add ice water in steady stream. Increase speed to medium and continue to mix until smooth dough comes together around paddle, 1 to 3 minutes longer. Transfer dough to lightly floured counter. Remove one-quarter (about 8 ounces) of dough and shape into 6-inch square. Shape remaining dough into 6-inch square. Wrap both pieces in plastic and refrigerate for at least 8 hours or up to 2 days.

3. FOR THE DUXELLES: Process shallots and garlic in food processor until very finely chopped, about 30 seconds, scraping down sides of bowl as needed. Transfer to small bowl. Pulse half of mushrooms until mushrooms resemble couscous, about 10 pulses, scraping down sides of bowl halfway through processing (do not overprocess). Transfer to large bowl and repeat with remaining mushrooms.

4. Melt butter in 12-inch nonstick skillet over medium-low heat. Add shallot mixture and cook,

---

NOTES FROM THE TEST KITCHEN

ON-THE-COUNTER COOKING

When you're making an elaborate dish such as beef Wellington, the stakes are high: Anything less than juicy, rosy meat and a crisp, golden crust signals a disappointing waste of time and money. The conundrum is that well-browned pastry requires high heat, whereas medium-rare meat is generally produced via a low-and-slow approach.

Our solution was to cook the Wellington in a 450-degree oven just until the pastry was well browned, at which point the meat was a mere 85 degrees. As the roast rested, the temperature at its center climbed 45 degrees, reaching a perfect 130-degree medium-rare in about 45 minutes.

The fix relies on the phenomenon known as "carryover cooking," wherein meat continues to cook even after it is removed from a heat source. This happens for two reasons: First, the exterior of a large roast gets hot much more quickly than the interior. Second, because heat always moves from a hotter to a cooler area, as long as there is a difference in temperature between the two regions, heat will keep moving from the surface to the center. In our Wellington, the pastry also insulates the meat, so heat on its surface tends to travel toward the center rather than dissipate into the air during the carryover period.

---

stirring frequently, until softened, 3 to 5 minutes. Stir in mushrooms, pepper, and salt and cook, stirring occasionally, until liquid given off by mushrooms has evaporated and mushrooms begin to sizzle, about 45 minutes. Add Madeira to mushroom mixture and cook, stirring constantly, until evaporated, about 2 minutes. Off heat, stir in thyme. (If making duxelles ahead, let cool completely and refrigerate in airtight container for up to 3 days.)

DAY TWO: ASSEMBLE

5. TO ASSEMBLE: Overlap 2 to 3 pieces of plastic on counter to form 30 by 30-inch square (it's OK if up to 2 inches of plastic hangs off edge of counter). Shingle prosciutto in center of plastic in 2 rows of 6 slices, slightly overlapping to form 14 by 15-inch rectangle, with shorter side parallel to edge of counter. Transfer duxelles to prosciutto and use offset spatula to spread in even layer, leaving 1-inch border of prosciutto on all sides (if duxelles is cold, microwave for 1 minute to soften before spreading).

6. Unwrap beef and pat dry with paper towels. Brush all sides of beef with mustard and sprinkle with pepper. Arrange roast parallel to edge of counter, about one-third of way up duxelles. Using both hands, lift bottom edge of plastic to begin wrapping roast. Continue to roll roast, leaving plastic behind, until roast is completely wrapped in prosciutto. Tuck overhanging slices of prosciutto over each end of roast.

7. Tightly roll roast in plastic and twist plastic tightly at each end to seal. Continue to twist ends of plastic and roll roast on counter until formed into snug cylinder. Refrigerate for at least 30 minutes or up to 2 days before cooking.

8. Line 2 rimmed baking sheets with parchment paper. Roll out larger piece of dough on generously floured counter into 18 by 16-inch rectangle. Drape dough over rolling pin, transfer to 1 prepared sheet, and refrigerate for 15 minutes. Roll smaller piece of dough into 16 by 7-inch rectangle. Transfer to second prepared sheet and refrigerate.

9. Whisk together egg and yolk. Lay larger pastry sheet directly on counter with long side parallel to edge of counter. Brush entire surface with egg wash; set aside remaining egg wash. Unwrap beef and place on pastry, arranging it parallel to edge of counter and 2 inches from pastry edge closest to you. Wrap edge of pastry closest to you over beef. Holding edge in place, slowly roll roast away from you, keeping pastry snug to meat, until roast is covered.

10. Allow pastry to overlap by 1 inch and trim away excess. Roll roast so seam is on top. Gently press and pinch overlapping dough to seal. Roll roast so seam is on bottom.

11. To seal ends of roast, tuck sides of pastry tightly against meat as though you are wrapping a present, then fold top of pastry down, pressing snugly.

12. Using rolling pin, roll excess dough at end of roast against counter to make it thinner and longer. Trim rolled end to 2-inch length and tuck under roast. Repeat process on other end of roast. Transfer roast seam side down to lightly greased rimmed baking sheet and refrigerate for at least 15 minutes or up to overnight (if refrigerating longer than 1 hour, wrap in plastic).

13. Transfer smaller pastry sheet, still on parchment, to counter, with short side parallel to edge of counter. Using ruler and sharp knife or pizza cutter, cut pastry lengthwise into ¼-inch-wide strips.

14. Brush top, sides, and ends of roast with some of reserved egg wash; set aside remaining egg wash. Lay pastry strips diagonally across top of roast, leaving ¼ to ½ inch between strips. Gently press strips to adhere to roast and trim excess at each end to ¼ inch. Using bench scraper, tuck ends of strips under roast. Refrigerate roast for at least 10 minutes. (Roast can be loosely covered with plastic and refrigerated for up to 24 hours.)

DAY THREE: BAKE AND SERVE

15. Adjust oven rack to lower-middle position and heat oven to 450 degrees. Brush roast thoroughly with reserved egg wash. Place thermometer probe, if using, through 1 end of roast so tip of probe is positioned at center of roast. Roast until beef registers 85 degrees and crust is well browned and crisp, 40 to 45 minutes. Transfer sheet to wire rack, leaving probe in place to monitor temperature. Let rest, uncovered, until internal temperature reaches 130 degrees, 40 to 45 minutes.

16. TO SERVE: Slide large metal spatula under roast to loosen from sheet. Use both hands to transfer roast to carving board. Using serrated knife, cut roast into 1-inch-thick slices (to keep pastry intact, score through decorative strips before cutting each slice) and serve.

Creamy Green Peppercorn Sauce

SERVES 8 TO 10

The sauce can be made as the roast is resting; alternatively, prepare it up to three days ahead and warm it right before serving.

2	tablespoons unsalted butter
¼	cup jarred green peppercorns
2	tablespoons minced shallot
1	tablespoon all-purpose flour
1½	cups beef broth
¼	cup brandy
2	tablespoons soy sauce
1	cup heavy cream

1. Melt butter in medium saucepan over medium-low heat. Add peppercorns and shallot and cook, stirring frequently, until shallot is softened, 3 to 5 minutes. Add flour and cook, stirring constantly, for 2 minutes. Increase heat to medium and whisk in broth, brandy, and soy sauce. Bring to boil. Cook, whisking occasionally, until mixture is reduced to 1½ cups, 12 to 15 minutes.

2. Add cream and cook, whisking occasionally, until reduced to 2 cups, about 10 minutes. Season with salt and pepper to taste.

Madeira Sauce

SERVES 8 TO 10

The test kitchen's favorite beef broth is Better Than Bouillon Roasted Beef Base.

6	tablespoons unsalted butter
1	shallot, minced
2	sprigs fresh thyme
3	tablespoons all-purpose flour
2	teaspoons chopped dried porcini mushrooms
1	teaspoon tomato paste
2	cups beef broth
½	cup Madeira
¼	cup ruby port

Melt butter in medium saucepan over medium-low heat. Add shallot and thyme sprigs and cook, stirring occasionally, until shallot is golden, about 5 minutes. Add flour and cook, stirring frequently, for 2 minutes. Add mushrooms and tomato paste and cook until fragrant,

1 minute. Stir in broth, Madeira, and port. Increase heat to medium-high and bring to boil. Cook until reduced to 2 cups, about 15 minutes. Season with salt and pepper to taste. Strain sauce through fine-mesh strainer set over bowl; discard solids in strainer. Return sauce to saucepan and cover to keep warm. (Sauce can be refrigerated for up to 3 days; warm gently before serving.)

BRACIOLE

✅ **WHY THIS RECIPE WORKS** For our take on these stuffed beef rolls, we chose flank steak rather than top or bottom round (the other common choices) because its loose grain made it easier to pound thin and its higher fat content meant that it emerged from the oven tender and moist. Our filling was on the bold side, with the inclusion of umami-rich ingredients such as prosciutto; anchovies; and fontina, a good melter that also brought much-needed fat to the dish. In addition, a gremolata-inspired mix added to the filling provided a jolt of flavor and freshness. Finally, we added beef broth to the tomato sauce to integrate the beef and the sauce into a unified whole.

My nonna is no longer with us, but if I close my eyes, I can still hear the thwack-thwack of her meat mallet as she pounded pieces of beef thin for her weekly batch of braciole. She rolled the meat around a simple bread crumb, cheese, and herb filling; pinned the parcels with toothpicks; seared them; and slowly simmered them in a rich tomato sauce. The braciole was often just one element of her Sunday gravy, which could also include savory meatballs and rich sausages to serve at a family gathering with guests numbering in the teens. But the meaty bundles were always what really captivated me, and I figured it was time I learned to make them myself.

First, an acknowledgment that "braciole" means different things to different people: In much of mainland Italy, including Piedmont, where my nonna grew up, it refers to the dish I just described, prepared with beef, pork, or veal and assembled into either one large roll to be sliced into pinwheels for serving or smaller individual ones, like my nonna preferred. However, in the far north of the country, along the Austrian border, "braciole" refers to a grilled bone-in pork or veal chop. In the deep Sicilian south, it's the name for tiny skewered and grilled stuffed beef rolls. Calabrian braciole features pounded pork shoulder and is spicy with the region's chiles, whereas Neapolitan versions are typically made with beef and stuffed with pine nuts, raisins, cured meat, and/or hard-cooked eggs.

I wanted to stick with the style of braciole that my nonna made, in keeping with the deep traditions established by her mother and grandmother. As a kid, I never thought to inquire about the type of meat she used, so I took a guess and picked up some top round steak from my butcher—it, along with bottom round and flank steak, is one of the most commonly used cuts for the dish.

Pounding the steak to ¼-inch thickness was tough going, as top round has a tight grain. But I persevered, and once the meat was sufficiently thin, I cut it into roughly 6-inch squares that I topped with the thrifty ingredients I could remember from my nonna's kitchen: dried bread crumbs, Parmesan cheese, and dried oregano. I tied the rolls with twine (more secure than toothpicks) and browned them before oven-braising them in a simple sauce for a couple hours.

I took a taste, waiting for a flood of cozy childhood memories to wash over me. It never came. The meat was somewhat dry, the filling lacked presence, and the sauce was thin and weak. I made a few more batches, braising each one for a successively longer period of time, but even after 4 hours the top round remained parched.

Flank steak has about twice as much fat as top or bottom round and exhibits a much looser grain, so I tried it next. It was easy to whack the meat ¼ inch thick before dividing it into eight squares to stuff and roll. Sticking with my basic filling and sauce for now, I braised a batch for 2½ hours and was thrilled to find that the flank steak braciole cooked up beautifully moist and fork-tender.

With the meat settled, I addressed the filling. I wanted to turn the austere mixture into something more luxurious, as I think that Nonna would have done if she had had the means and wasn't cooking for more than a dozen people, week in and week out. I hoped that the finished product would have made her proud, not only of my interpretation but also of how her cooking inspired me.

First, I switched to Pecorino Romano instead of Parmesan for its gamier, saltier profile. Next, I added minced anchovies—the tiny fillets worked their usual magic of adding umami depth. To give the mixture some richness and help it hold together, I stirred in a

BRACIOLE

STEP BY STEP: ASSEMBLING BRACIOLE

1. Lay 1 steak on cutting board with grain running parallel to counter edge. Slice horizontally to create 2 thin pieces. Repeat with second steak.

2. Cover 1 piece with plastic wrap and pound into rough rectangle measuring about ¼ inch thick. Repeat with remaining 3 pieces.

3. Cut each piece in half, with grain, to create total of 8 pieces.

4. Arrange 4 pieces so grain runs parallel to counter edge. Distribute filling over each piece and top with prosciutto slice.

5. Keeping filling in place, roll each piece away from you to form tight log.

6. Tie each roll with 2 pieces kitchen twine to secure. Repeat process with remaining steak pieces, filling, and prosciutto.

handful of nutty shredded fontina (a great melter) and a swirl of extra-virgin olive oil. To incorporate bright notes, I turned to one of my favorite Italian seasonings: gremolata. Made with heady minced garlic, fresh parsley, and fragrant lemon zest (I added some fresh basil, too), this vibrant blend contributed a burst of freshness. Finally, for a salty, porky component, I draped thin slices of silky prosciutto atop the filling before rolling, tying, and searing the tidy bundles.

Sauces for braciole tend to be rather straightforward, but mine was hardly more than a can of crushed tomatoes fortified with sautéed onion, minced garlic, and a pinch of red pepper flakes. It needed more body and deeper tomato flavor, and a generous scoop of tomato paste provided both. A pour of hearty red wine was a smart complexity-building addition as well.

I was now quite pleased with the consistency and taste of the sauce, but it didn't seem to meld well with the beef rolls. A colleague suggested that I swap out some of the crushed tomatoes for beef broth. It was a brilliant idea: Now the sauce had beefy depth that pulled the whole affair together into a unified whole.

As I spooned the rolls onto a platter of spaghetti, I took stock: The beef was tender and moist; the vibrant filling enhanced the meat without overwhelming it; and the beefy, tomatoey sauce made the whole dish sing. I wish Nonna could taste it.

—STEVE DUNN, *Cook's Illustrated*

Braciole

SERVES 6 TO 8

Cut sixteen 10-inch lengths of kitchen twine before starting the recipe. You can substitute sharp provolone for the fontina, if desired. For the most tender braciole, be sure to roll the meat so that the grain runs parallel to the length of the roll. Serve the braciole and sauce together, with pasta or polenta, or separately, as a pasta course with the sauce followed by the meat.

- 7 **tablespoons extra-virgin olive oil, divided**
- 10 **garlic cloves, minced, divided**
- 2 **teaspoons grated lemon zest**
- 3 **anchovy fillets, rinsed and minced**
- ⅓ **cup plus 2 tablespoons chopped fresh basil, divided**
- ⅓ **cup minced fresh parsley**
- ⅓ **cup grated Pecorino Romano cheese, plus extra for serving**

⅓ cup plain dried bread crumbs

3 ounces fontina cheese, shredded (¾ cup)

1 (2- to 2½-pound) flank steak, trimmed

8 thin slices prosciutto (4 ounces)

1 teaspoon kosher salt

½ teaspoon pepper

1 large onion, chopped fine

¼ teaspoon red pepper flakes

¼ cup tomato paste

¾ cup dry red wine

1 (28-ounce) can crushed tomatoes

2 cups beef broth

1. Adjust oven rack to lower-middle position and heat oven to 325 degrees. Stir 3 tablespoons oil, half of garlic, lemon zest, and anchovies together in medium bowl. Add ⅓ cup basil, parsley, Pecorino, and bread crumbs and stir to incorporate. Stir in fontina until evenly distributed and set aside filling.

2. Halve steak against grain to create 2 smaller steaks. Lay 1 steak on cutting board with grain running parallel to counter edge. Holding blade of chef's knife parallel to counter, halve steak horizontally to create 2 thin pieces. Repeat with remaining steak. Cover 1 piece with plastic wrap and, using meat pounder, flatten into rough rectangle measuring no more than ¼ inch thick. Repeat pounding with remaining 3 pieces. Cut each piece in half, with grain, to create total of 8 pieces.

3. Lay 4 pieces on cutting board with grain running parallel to counter edge (if 1 side is shorter than the other, place shorter side closer to you). Distribute half of filling evenly over pieces. Top filling on each piece with 1 slice of prosciutto, folding to fit, and press firmly. Keeping filling in place, roll each piece away from you to form tight log. Tie each roll with 2 pieces kitchen twine to secure. Repeat process with remaining steak pieces, filling, and prosciutto. Sprinkle rolls on both sides with salt and pepper.

4. Heat remaining ¼ cup oil in large Dutch oven over medium-high heat until shimmering. Brown rolls on 2 sides, 8 to 10 minutes. Using tongs, transfer rolls to plate. Add onion to pot and cook, stirring occasionally, until softened and lightly browned, 5 to 7 minutes. Stir in pepper flakes and remaining garlic; cook until fragrant, about 30 seconds. Stir in tomato paste and cook until slightly darkened, 3 to 4 minutes. Add wine and cook, scraping up any browned bits. Stir in tomatoes and broth. Return rolls to pot; bring to simmer. Cover and transfer

to oven. Braise until meat is fork-tender, 2½ to 3 hours, using tongs to flip rolls halfway through braising.

5. Transfer braciole to serving dish and discard twine. Stir remaining 2 tablespoons basil into tomato sauce and season with salt and pepper to taste. Pour sauce over braciole and serve, passing extra Pecorino separately.

KEEMA (GARAM MASALA-SPICED GROUND BEEF)

✔ **WHY THIS RECIPE WORKS** Keema is a rich and savory spiced ground meat dish that's been a staple of South Asian cuisine for centuries, even gracing the tables of the Turkic sultans and Mughal emperors of the 15th and 16th centuries. Whether it's made with ground goat, lamb, beef, or poultry, the meat is broken into small bits and coated with a complexly spiced, velvety sauce that's rich and savory. Our version features a garam masala, or warming spice mix, comprising a whole cinnamon stick; black and green cardamom pods; and ground coriander, cumin, turmeric, and Kashmiri chile powder. We bloomed the whole spices early to coax out their oil-soluble compounds. Then we carefully browned red onion to deepen its flavor before spiking the mixture with garlic and ginger pastes. Next we added 90 percent lean ground beef, and when it sizzled and browned, we stirred in the ground spices in the masala. As soon as these were fragrant, in went tomatoes and whole-milk yogurt. The tomatoes broke down as the keema cooked, and the yogurt added subtle richness. Together they created a clingy sauce that flavored every bite of beef.

There are a few good reasons the ground meat dish called keema has been beloved on the Indian subcontinent since at least the 15th century, when it even graced the tables of Turkic sultans and, later, Mughal emperors. First, it's a preparation that warms you from the inside out: Spices such as cinnamon, cumin, and cardamom mingle with the meat's juices, creating a fragrant sauce that coats the supple bits and lightly pools in their nooks and crannies. It's also quick to make and highly versatile: Serve it alongside rice, rolled into rotis, or stuffed into vegetables. Spread it between two halves of a plush roll and you've got keema pav, sold in Irani cafes all over the subcontinent. No wonder that keema shows up in so many seminal works on classic Indian cookery, including those penned by Madhur Jaffrey and Julie Sahni, or that *New York Times* restaurant critic Tejal Rao recently put it on her list of recipes that exemplify Indian home cooking.

It's also a dish that changes depending on who's doing the cooking. "If you say 'keema,' everyone will have a recipe, and every recipe will be different," noted my friend Saarah Taher, who grew up eating keema in central India and makes the preparation regularly for her husband and children in Southern California. Within families, those differences sometimes play out like a game of telephone. "I cobbled together my recipe based on what I saw my grandma make and what I saw my mom make," my colleague Rachel Schowalter, whose family is from Mangalore, told me. "I have my uncle's recipe, too. We all do different things."

My first decision for my own keema was the type of meat ("keema" comes from the Turkic word for "minced" and can refer to any meat that gets this treatment). Goat tends to be the default on the subcontinent (where it's called "mutton," whether from a kid or an older animal), but beef is popular abroad, and I chose that for its wider availability. Though cooks in India often buy meat freshly ground to order from a butcher, good-quality preground is perfectly acceptable. But how fatty should it be? While traditionalists want a slick of red-tinted grease to cling to the mince, I liked the lushness of versions that add yogurt. Since the dairy would provide plenty of richness, I followed the advice of such recipes and settled on 90 percent lean ground beef.

As with much of Indian cooking, spices are the soul of keema—and in a meat dish with roots in Persian cooking such as this one, that often means garam masala. This iconic blend can vary in the number and proportion of spices, but they tend to be drawn from the same 10 or so warm varieties ("garam" translates as "warming" in Hindi). I was excited to assemble my own roster of spices from among the most commonly used ones and then figure out how best to incorporate them. Both these things can make a dish that "distinctly special creation of the individual cook," as Sahni puts it so nicely in *Classic Indian Cooking* (1980).

First on the list was black cardamom. This spice is a powerhouse of smoky flavor, and I loved the depth it brought to keemas that included it. I also singled out green cardamom for its menthol notes, cinnamon for sweetness, and black pepper for piney heat, along with earthy cumin and lemony coriander. Plus, I rounded up two other spices typically found in keema: nutty turmeric and mildly spicy Kashmiri chile powder, both of which lend color to the dish.

In many recipes, ground spices are added to the meat late in the process to preserve more of their volatile compounds. But in the keemas that tasted notably more complex—including Taher's, which she kindly shared with me—a few whole spices also get bloomed in oil at the start of cooking, which allows their oil-soluble compounds to infuse the fat and permeate both the meat and the sauce. "You don't have to use both [whole and ground]," Taher noted, "but using them together . . . brings out the spice profile more intensely."

I singled out the most potent spices—the peppercorns, a cinnamon stick, and both types of cardamom pods—to use whole, and I gently bloomed them in a little vegetable oil in a medium saucepan. When they began to smell fragrant, I added thinly sliced red onion. Now I made sure to follow another critical piece of advice from the best recipes in my research: I took my time with the onions, cooking them slowly until they turned golden brown and softened but still retained a little bite—unlike with caramelizing onions, you don't want them to collapse completely and turn jammy and sweet. Once I got them to this point, which took about 10 minutes, I stirred in same-size dabs of grated garlic and ginger, fried these briefly, and then added the ground beef and salt. After another 10 minutes, much of the moisture from the meat had evaporated and enough of it had browned to deepen the dish's savory flavor. I then sprinkled in my ground spices—the cumin, coriander, turmeric, and chile powder.

I was at another crossroads. Should I add tomatoes to lend the mixture a little brightness? Recipes that say yes don't often incorporate yogurt at the same time. I decided to try using both anyway, stirring in two chopped tomatoes with ¼ cup of yogurt and a halved green chile for some fresh grassy heat. And I was glad I had: The tomatoes broke down and mingled with the dairy to create a velvety sauce with a nice hint of tang. For a consistency just moist enough for naan or roti swooping across a plate to get a good grip on the mince, I simmered the dish for about 15 minutes.

And just like that, my keema was everything I'd hoped it would be: ultratender, lush with sauce, and infused with all the warm spices that I'd so carefully chosen. I was inspired to create two common variations—keema aloo (with potatoes) and keema matar (with peas)—which took barely any extra time and gave me two more good reasons to make this supremely satisfying dish.

—LAN LAM, *Cook's Illustrated*

Keema (Garam Masala–Spiced Ground Beef)

SERVES 4 TO 6

Have your ingredients in place before you begin to cook. Look for black and green cardamom pods, Kashmiri chile powder, and 4- to 5-inch long green chiles at Indian or Pakistani markets. If you can't find Kashmiri chile powder, toast and grind one large guajillo chile and use 2 teaspoons; if a long green chile is unavailable, substitute a serrano. For a milder keema, omit the fresh chile or use only half of it. A rasp-style grater makes it easy to turn garlic and ginger into pastes. Serve with roti, naan, or basmati rice.

- 2 tablespoons vegetable oil
- 6 black peppercorns
- 4 green cardamom pods
- 2 black cardamom pods
- 1 cinnamon stick
- 1 red onion, halved and sliced thin crosswise
- 1 teaspoon grated garlic
- 1 teaspoon grated fresh ginger
- 1 pound 90 percent lean ground beef
- ¾ teaspoon table salt
- 2 teaspoons ground coriander
- 2 teaspoons Kashmiri chile powder
- ½ teaspoon ground turmeric
- ½ teaspoon ground cumin

NOTES FROM THE TEST KITCHEN

BROWN YOUR ONIONS JUST SO

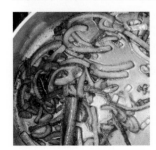

Browned onions add to keema's complexity, but stop cooking while they still have some texture and before they get jammy, so their flavors will be more savory than sweet. Browning the meat isn't as important—the spices and onions do most of the work in this highly seasoned dish.

- 2 (6-ounce) vine-ripened tomatoes, cored and chopped
- ¼ cup plain whole-milk yogurt
- 1 long green chile, halved lengthwise (optional)
- ¼ cup chopped fresh cilantro, plus extra for garnish

1. Heat oil in medium saucepan over medium heat until shimmering. Add peppercorns, green and black cardamom pods, and cinnamon stick and cook, stirring occasionally, until fragrant, about 30 seconds. Add onion and cook, stirring occasionally, until onion is browned, 7 to 10 minutes.

2. Add garlic and ginger and cook, stirring constantly, until fragrant, about 30 seconds. Add beef and salt. Increase heat to medium-high and cook, stirring to break up meat into very small pieces and scraping up any browned bits. Continue to cook, stirring occasionally, until mixture sizzles and bottom of saucepan appears dry, 7 to 12 minutes longer.

3. Add coriander, chile powder, turmeric, and cumin and cook, stirring constantly, until spices are well distributed and fragrant, about 1 minute. Add tomatoes; yogurt; and chile, if using, and cook, stirring frequently, until tomatoes release their juice and mixture begins to simmer, about 2 minutes. Adjust heat to maintain gentle simmer. Cover and cook, stirring occasionally, until tomatoes have broken down and wooden spoon scraped across bottom of saucepan leaves clear trail, 12 to 18 minutes. Stir in cilantro and season with salt and pepper to taste. If desired, remove cinnamon stick and cardamom pods. Transfer to serving bowl, garnish with extra cilantro, and serve.

VARIATIONS

Keema Aloo (Garam Masala–Spiced Ground Beef with Potatoes)

Add 1 Yukon Gold potato, peeled and cut into ½-inch pieces, and 2 tablespoons water with tomatoes and yogurt. Cook until potatoes are tender, 12 to 18 minutes, before adding cilantro.

Keema Matar (Garam Masala–Spiced Ground Beef with Peas)

Add 1 cup frozen peas after tomatoes have broken down. Cook for 2 minutes before adding cilantro.

FRESH BULK SAUSAGE

FRESH BULK SAUSAGE

✓ **WHY THIS RECIPE WORKS** Fresh bulk sausage is nothing more than salted and seasoned meat that you grind and vigorously mix, and making a good batch is simple if you adhere to a few principles and use a reliable formula. We started by weighing the trimmed pork (well-marbled shoulder) in grams; this allowed us to calculate the precise amount of salt to add (1.5 percent of the weight of the trimmed meat), making the recipe easy to scale up or down. Curing the meat with the salt (and seasonings) for at least 8 hours before grinding ensured proper salinity and juiciness; plus, the salt dissolved the meat proteins (myosin), which acted as a glue that bound up the meat mixture and gave the sausage its snap. Kneading the ground pork mixture further developed its myosin. Briefly freezing the cured pork before grinding firmed it up so that the ground pork contained distinct pieces of meat and fat. This prevented the pork fat from overheating and melting away from the protein during grinding and from leaking out when the sausage was cooked, which would leave it dry and crumbly. Once made, the sausage could be used right away or refrigerated or frozen for later use.

Resourceful hunters, butchers, and cooks have been piecing together and preserving scraps of meat and fat as sausage for thousands of years. The process, which has roots in almost every cuisine around the world, came about as a simple and effective way to stretch valuable protein, and the transformation of those ingredients into a juicy, deeply seasoned product is pure culinary alchemy.

These days, most sausage production is done by professionals who have the expertise and equipment to stuff, dry, smoke, and/or ferment the meat. But fresh bulk sausage is much simpler: It's nothing more than salted, seasoned meat that you grind and vigorously mix, and anyone with a food processor, a solid grasp of the fundamentals, and a reliable formula can churn out a great batch. Once you've mastered the core technique, you can flavor sausage any way you like, and since it's easy to portion into small batches and freezes well, you can keep it on hand for countless applications: breakfast patties; frittatas; ragus; and pastas such as my all-time favorite, orecchiette con rapini e salsiccia (orecchiette with broccoli rabe and Italian sausage).

The fundamentals and a reliable formula are what I wanted to nail down here, and most sources suggest the same basic process: Start with a cut of pork that boasts plenty of fat, and cut it into small pieces; cure the meat for several hours with a precise amount of salt and any other seasonings you want to add; briefly freeze the meat so that it's firm but not frozen; finely grind it in a meat grinder (or a food processor); and finally, knead the ground meat vigorously by hand so that it becomes cohesive and sticky.

"Sausage is like meat, perfected," said J. Kenji López-Alt, a chef and former *Cook's Illustrated* test cook who cofounded Wursthall in San Mateo, California, where house-made links headline the menu. Unlike a perfect steak, which requires sourcing a cut with the ideal ratio of meat to fat and working hard to keep its juices intact when you cook it, with sausage "you build all that stuff in," he said.

Read on, and I'll detail how these steps lead to the juicy, snappy texture that defines great fresh sausage plus walk you through my formula that can be flavored with spice blends or used as a base for your own seasonings.

Start by using meat with plenty of fat. Fresh sausage typically contains from 20 to 30 percent fat. That amount makes the mixture appropriately rich and succulent and carries the seasonings' vibrant flavors to your palate.

Most pork butt naturally contains this meat-to-fat ratio, and it is the standard choice for fresh sausage. Look for a well-marbled roast with a defined fat cap, and don't be tempted to trim any fat. Do, however, remove any connective tissue and sinew, which can clog the grinding mechanism.

Salt—the root of the word "sausage"—is arguably the most critical variable in the mix. Besides seasoning the meat, it fends off harmful microbes; restructures proteins in the meat so that they retain flavorful juices during cooking; and dissolves meat proteins (myosin), which act as a glue that binds up the meat and gives sausage its snap.

"Sausage made without [adequate] salt is not just underseasoned," said López-Alt. "It won't actually bind properly."

There are two keys to using salt effectively. The first is calculating the salinity relative to the weight of the pork. Most sources recommend using from 1.5 to 2 percent of the weight of the meat, and after comparing batches made with 1.5, 1.75, and 2 percent salt, I settled on 1.5 for my own formula. With this amount, the seasoning and texture were spot-on.

The second is salting the meat for several hours, if not days, since the more time the salt has to migrate into the meat, the snappier, juicier, and more evenly seasoned the results will be. My own tests confirmed this: The batch ground from meat chunks that I had salted overnight (I also added the seasonings with the salt) cooked up noticeably springier and juicier than the one ground from meat I had salted moments before grinding.

One of the biggest sausage production mistakes you can make is not chilling the meat mixture before you grind it. Chilling compensates for the significant heat created by the friction of the grinding process—and if you skip that step, the relatively warm fat will melt during grinding, separate (or "break") from the protein, and then leak out when the sausage is cooked, leaving behind dry, crumbly meat.

"Heat is the enemy of fat," said Brian Polcyn, chef and coauthor of *Charcuterie: The Craft of Salting, Smoking, and Curing* (2005). Polcyn said that commercial sausage production is always done under refrigeration.

When I compared sausage ground from pork chunks that I'd frozen for 45 minutes before grinding (long enough to firm up the meat but not freeze it solid) to a batch made from fridge-cold meat, I could literally see the difference. The freezer-chilled pork broke down into defined bits of meat and solid fat, while the fat in the fridge-cold pork smeared into the meat like a paste.

"That one little step, that one little extra effort," Polcyn stressed about chilling, "will have dramatic results to the end product."

Salting and grinding the meat encourages some of its sticky myosin proteins to cross-link and bind into a strong network, but for properly cohesive, springy sausage, you need to encourage even more of that cross-linking by briefly but vigorously kneading the ground meat mixture. Conceptually, it's a lot like kneading bread dough to develop gluten: The more you work the meat, the more myosin cross-links, and the snappier the sausage will be. All it takes is a couple minutes of working the meat by hand in a mixing bowl; you'll know it's done when the meat becomes tacky on its surface.

—STEVE DUNN, *Cook's Illustrated*

Fresh Bulk Sausage

MAKES ABOUT 2 POUNDS SAUSAGE

Because sausage requires a precise ratio of salt to trimmed meat, you'll need a scale that measures in grams, and you'll need to do some simple math. This recipe requires at least 8 hours of salting. Because you'll be measuring the salt by weight instead of volume, you can use either table salt or kosher salt. Pork butt roast is often labeled Boston butt. For the best texture, buy a well-marbled roast that has a defined fat cap. This recipe can easily be halved or doubled and freezes well.

2   **pounds boneless pork butt roast with at least ¼-inch-thick fat cap**

    Salt

1   **recipe sausage seasoning (recipes follow)**

1. Leaving fat cap intact, cut pork into ¾-inch pieces, trimming and discarding all sinew and connective tissue. Weigh trimmed pork and note weight in grams. Multiply weight of pork by 0.015 to determine salt amount (round to nearest gram). Weigh out salt.

2. Toss pork, salt, and seasoning in bowl until well combined. Cover and refrigerate for at least 8 hours or up to 2 days.

3. Transfer pork to rimmed baking sheet and spread in single layer, leaving space around each piece. Freeze until pork is very firm and starting to harden around edges but still pliable, 35 to 55 minutes.

4A. FOR A GRINDER: Place meat grinder attachments, including coarse die (³⁄₁₆ or ¼ inch), in freezer and chill for at least 1 hour before using. Set medium bowl in large bowl filled with ice. Grind pork at medium speed into prepared medium bowl.

4B. FOR A FOOD PROCESSOR: Place one-quarter of pork in food processor and pulse until ground into ⅛- to ¹⁄₁₆-inch pieces, 14 to 16 pulses, stopping to redistribute pork around bowl as necessary to ensure meat is evenly ground. Transfer ground pork to large bowl. Repeat with remaining 3 batches of pork.

5. Inspect ground pork carefully, discarding any strands of gristle or silverskin. Using your hands or stiff rubber spatula, knead pork vigorously, smearing against sides and bottom of bowl, until pork begins to tighten, feels tacky, and sticks to bottom of bowl and palm of your hand, 1½ to 2 minutes. Use immediately or wrap bowl tightly in plastic wrap and refrigerate for up to 24 hours (or transfer sausage to zipper-lock bag and freeze for up to 1 month).

TO MAKE PATTIES: Using your damp hands, divide meat into 16 pieces (about 2 ounces each) and form into 2½-inch patties about ½ inch thick. Heat 2 teaspoons vegetable oil in 12-inch nonstick skillet over medium heat. Cook half of patties until well browned on both sides and meat registers 145 to 150 degrees, 3 to 5 minutes per side. Transfer to serving platter and tent with aluminum foil. Repeat with remaining patties. Serve. (Raw sausage patties can be refrigerated, covered, for up to 24 hours or frozen for up to 1 month. Cook frozen patties for 7 to 9 minutes per side.)

Breakfast Seasoning
MAKES ABOUT 3 TABLESPOONS

- 1 tablespoon packed light brown sugar
- 2 teaspoons rubbed sage
- 1 teaspoon pepper
- ¼ teaspoon cayenne pepper

Combine all ingredients in small bowl.

Fresh Garlic Seasoning
MAKES ABOUT 2 TABLESPOONS

- 1 tablespoon minced garlic
- 1 teaspoon paprika
- 1 teaspoon pepper
- ½ teaspoon ground coriander

Combine all ingredients in small bowl.

Italian Seasoning
MAKES ABOUT 3 TABLESPOONS

We like the flavor of the sausage made with both whole and ground fennel, but you don't have to buy both forms; simply use a spice grinder or mortar and pestle to finely grind the whole seeds. For "hot" Italian sausage, add 1 tablespoon of red pepper flakes and ¼ teaspoon of cayenne pepper.

- 4 teaspoons fennel seeds
- 2 teaspoons sugar
- 2 teaspoons paprika
- 1 teaspoon pepper
- ¼ teaspoon ground fennel
- ¼ teaspoon garlic powder

Combine all ingredients in small bowl.

CAST IRON PORK FAJITAS

✓ WHY THIS RECIPE WORKS Making multipart dishes is not hard at restaurants that have a team of cooks, but we wanted a weeknight version that would involve just one cook and one pan: the cast-iron skillet. Chicken, steak, and shrimp are typically used for fajitas because they're tender and cook quickly. We wanted to try another popular quick-cooking, tender cut: pork tenderloin. Seasoned properly with a generous amount of a complex, boldly flavored spice mixture, we knew it would be a hit. To fit two tenderloins side by side in a 12-inch cast-iron skillet, we cut the tenderloins in half crosswise. Pounding the cylindrical tenderloins into ¾-inch-thick steaks increased their surface area and helped ensure even browning. Searing the pork first and then cooking the vegetables while the pork rested was an easy call to make; because the skillet was already hot, the peppers and onion blistered, softened, and browned very quickly. And in a happy twist, we found that the bits of delicious spice rub left behind after removing the meat adhered easily to the vegetables, distributing more flavor throughout the dish.

Every time I visit my local Tex-Mex restaurant, I contemplate ordering several different dishes, but inevitably I hear the familiar, mesmerizing sizzle of fajitas being delivered to a neighboring table. I smell the tantalizing aromas from the searing-hot grilled meat and charred vegetables, and I am overcome with what I like to call "Fajita FOMO" (fear of missing out). I order the fajitas.

Restaurants have an advantage with multipart dishes such as fajitas—a team of cooks. There may be a cook at the meat station, a cook overseeing vegetables, and still another responsible for tortillas. But I wanted a weeknight version at home, where it's just me doing the cooking, and I wanted to use only one pan: my trusty cast-iron skillet.

The most challenging part of fajitas is the meat. Chicken, steak, and shrimp are the usual suspects because they're tender and cook quickly. I wanted to branch out with another popular quick-cooking, tender cut: pork tenderloin. With a flavorful spice rub (mine would include pepper, cumin, chili powder, granulated garlic, dried oregano, allspice, and plenty of salt), it would be a hit.

To make enough for four to six people, I needed to use two tenderloins. I cut them in half crosswise to create pieces that would fit side by side in my cast-iron

CAST IRON PORK FAJITAS

pan. But I still wasn't achieving the even browning I wanted with the cylindrical pieces. Pounding them into ¾-inch-thick steaks helped achieve more browning; plus, it increased their surface area, so the pork held more of the spice rub.

The next thing to figure out was how to make the rest of the dish in the same pan. First searing the pork and then cooking the vegetables while the pork rested was an easy call to make; because the skillet is already hot, the peppers and onion blister, soften, and brown very quickly. And in a happy twist, I found that the bits of delicious spice rub left behind after removing the meat adhered easily to the vegetables, distributing more flavor throughout the dish.

A smoky kitchen is a real pitfall when it comes to fajitas, especially when cooking at high heat. Restaurants have ventilation systems to handle this, but I needed to find a way to avoid setting off the smoke alarm. After a few tests, I realized that cast iron, with its strong heat retention, would allow me to cook everything just right even if I lowered my heat to medium—no need for an industrial Vent-A-Hood.

After slicing the succulent pork into fajita-size strips, I pushed the vegetables to one side of the skillet to make room for the pork and brought the cast-iron pan straight to the table to serve.

—AMANDA LUCHTEL, *Cook's Country*

NOTES FROM THE TEST KITCHEN

A SERIOUS PAN

This recipe calls for a 12-inch cast-iron skillet (you can also use a nonstick skillet); cast iron retains heat well and thus is a good option for browning foods. When properly maintained, a cast-iron pan develops a nonstick surface. We use these heavy pans—our winning 12-inch model weighs more than 7 pounds—for shallow frying; baking cornbread; searing steaks and chops; and, yes, making fajitas.

LODGE CLASSIC CAST IRON SKILLET, 12"
Our testing winner

Cast Iron Pork Fajitas
SERVES 4 TO 6

Serve the fajitas with pico de gallo, avocado or guacamole, sour cream, your favorite hot sauce, and lime wedges. A nonstick skillet can also be used here; in step 3, add 2 tablespoons of oil to the skillet, swirl to coat, and heat until the oil is just smoking.

2½ teaspoons kosher salt, divided
1½ teaspoons pepper, divided
 1 teaspoon ground cumin
 1 teaspoon chili powder
 1 teaspoon granulated garlic
 1 teaspoon dried oregano
 ⅛ teaspoon ground allspice
 2 (12- to 16-ounce) pork tenderloins, trimmed
 3 tablespoons vegetable oil, divided
 2 yellow, red, orange, or green bell peppers, stemmed, seeded, and cut into ¼-inch-wide strips
 1 onion, halved and sliced ¼ inch thick
 2 garlic cloves, minced
 ¼ cup chopped fresh cilantro
 1 tablespoon lime juice
 12 (6-inch) flour tortillas, warmed

1. Combine 2 teaspoons salt, 1 teaspoon pepper, cumin, chili powder, granulated garlic, oregano, and allspice in bowl.

2. Cut tenderloins in half crosswise. Working with 1 piece at a time, cover pork with plastic wrap and, using meat pounder, pound to even ¾-inch thickness. Pat pork dry with paper towels and sprinkle with spice mixture.

3. Heat 12-inch cast-iron skillet over medium heat for 3 minutes. Add 2 tablespoons oil to skillet and swirl to coat. Place pork in skillet and cook until meat is well browned on both sides and registers 135 to 140 degrees, 5 to 7 minutes per side. Transfer to carving board, tent with aluminum foil, and let rest while preparing pepper mixture.

4. Add remaining 1 tablespoon oil and bell peppers to now-empty skillet and cook for 3 minutes. Stir in onion, remaining ½ teaspoon salt, and remaining ½ teaspoon pepper and cook until vegetables are just softened, 3 to 5 minutes. Stir in garlic and cook until fragrant, about 30 seconds. Off heat, stir in cilantro and lime juice.

5. Slice pork thin crosswise. Stir any accumulated pork juices from carving board into vegetables. Push vegetables to 1 side of skillet and place pork on empty side. Serve pork and vegetables with tortillas.

RANCH FRIED PORK CHOPS

✓ **WHY THIS RECIPE WORKS** We set off to infuse crisp, meaty fried pork chops with the flavors of ranch dressing: tangy buttermilk, chives, cilantro, dill, garlic, and black pepper. Selecting bone-in pork blade chops and marinating them in a mixture of buttermilk and salt kept the meat juicy while frying. Using thin chops ensured a high ratio of crunchy coating to meat. Baking powder helped keep the crust light and crisp. Letting the coating rest on the meat for 30 minutes before frying ensured that it stuck well to each chop through the cooking process. Fresh chives, cilantro, and dill mixed into both the marinade and the breading flour gave a double dose of bold herb flavor. Cayenne, black pepper, and garlic brought the ranch flavor home.

For me, reading the word "ranch" in a recipe title creates instant intrigue. And if you put that magic word in front of "fried pork chops?" I'm all in. As a firm believer that most savory foods can be improved with the addition of ranch dressing, I was excited at the prospect of finding a new way—without using the actual dressing—to infuse crisp, meaty fried pork chops with the classic ranch flavors of tangy buttermilk, chives, cilantro, dill, garlic, and black pepper.

I started with four bone-in pork blade chops, which are mostly dark meat and therefore prone to staying juicy during high-heat cooking such as frying. I opted for thin (½-inch) chops to achieve a high ratio of crunchy coating to meat.

My favorite recipe for fried chicken calls for brining the raw chicken in a mixture of buttermilk and salt to season the meat. So I followed that path and soaked the raw chops in salted buttermilk for 30 minutes. Next, I tossed them in flour heavily seasoned with garlic powder; plenty of pepper; and chives, cilantro, and dill before shallow-frying them two chops at a time. The meat was tender and well seasoned, but the coating was a little thin and falling off the chops. Plus, it seemed like the intense heat from frying muted the fresh herb flavor.

To compensate, I added the herbs to the buttermilk brine, too, and increased the amount of minced fresh herbs in the flour mixture. I also augmented the flour mixture with cayenne pepper and baking powder—the former for a pop of heat, and the latter to help keep the crust light and crisp.

Next, I turned to a test kitchen technique and rubbed several tablespoons of buttermilk into the seasoned flour to create little nubs of moistened flour that resulted in a thicker, shaggier fried coating. And I let that shaggy coating rest on the meat for 30 minutes before frying so that it could set up and stick well to each chop through the frying process.

These crunchy, juicy, delicious pork chops are so full of bold herby flavor, they make me wonder what else I can ranch-ify. Ranch wings? Ranch pork roast? Maybe even ranch birthday cake . . . ?

—MORGAN BOLLING, *Cook's Country*

Ranch Fried Pork Chops

SERVES 4

We prefer pork blade chops here, but you can use pork rib chops, if desired. If using rib chops, use kitchen shears to snip through the fat surrounding the loin muscle of each chop in two places, about 2 inches apart, before marinating to prevent the chops from buckling while frying.

PORK

- 2 cups buttermilk
- 2 tablespoons minced fresh dill
- 2 tablespoons minced fresh chives
- 2 tablespoons minced fresh cilantro
- 1 tablespoon table salt
- 4 (5- to 8-ounce) bone-in pork blade chops, ½ inch thick, trimmed
- 1 cup peanut or vegetable oil for frying

NOTES FROM THE TEST KITCHEN

A CRAGGY, CRUNCHY COATING

Use your fingers to rub the seasoned buttermilk (from the brine) into the flour coating.

COATING

- 2 cups all-purpose flour
- ¼ cup minced fresh dill
- ¼ cup minced fresh chives
- ¼ cup minced fresh cilantro
- 2 teaspoons baking powder
- 2 teaspoons garlic powder
- 1½ teaspoons pepper
- ½ teaspoon table salt
- ½ teaspoon cayenne pepper

1. FOR THE PORK: Whisk buttermilk, dill, chives, cilantro, and salt in large bowl until salt is dissolved. Measure out 3 tablespoons buttermilk brine and set aside. Add pork to remaining brine and turn to coat. Cover with plastic wrap and refrigerate for at least 30 minutes or up to 24 hours.

2. FOR THE COATING: Combine all ingredients in large bowl. Add reserved 3 tablespoons brine and, using your fingers, rub flour mixture and brine together until craggy bits form throughout.

3. Working with 1 chop at a time, remove from brine, allowing excess to drip off, then coat with flour mixture, pressing to adhere. Transfer to rimmed baking sheet. Refrigerate pork, uncovered, for at least 30 minutes or up to 2 hours.

4. Set wire rack in second rimmed baking sheet. Heat oil in 12-inch nonstick skillet over medium-high heat to 375 degrees (to take temperature, tilt skillet so oil pools to 1 side). Carefully add 2 chops and cook until golden brown and registering 140 degrees, 2 to 4 minutes per side.

5. Transfer chops to prepared rack. Return oil to 375 degrees and repeat with remaining chops. Serve.

CHOUCROUTE GARNIE

✔ WHY THIS RECIPE WORKS The trick with choucroute garnie, a meat-centered, country-style dish that has roots in the Alsace region of France, is to create a dish that's rich and meaty but also tempered with just enough acidity (from wine and sauerkraut) and contrasting texture (also from sauerkraut) to keep things in balance. Everything is tied together with accents such as thyme, garlic, and caraway. The specific meats and sausages used in the dish can change from kitchen to kitchen and are often very local. We found that a combination of garlicky kielbasa, sweet and herbal bratwurst, smoky ham hock, and rich pork belly provided the range of flavors we sought. After experimenting with sauerkraut right from the jar, drained sauerkraut, and rinsed sauerkraut, we chose rinsed, which we squeezed dry. This provided just the right texture and moisture level for the dish and kept its brininess in check.

At its simplest, choucroute garnie is a rustic, rib-sticking, country-style dish that puts the focus on the meat. You might not guess it from the name: "Choucroute" means "sauerkraut" in French (the dish has roots in the Alsace region of France). And while there's plenty of sauerkraut in this dish, it's not exactly the first thing you see on your plate. Look at those sausage links! Look at that pork!

The trick with choucroute garnie is to create a dish that is rich and meaty but not overwhelming. You want clear and present pork flavor, tempered with just enough acidity (from wine and sauerkraut) to keep things in balance. And you want to tie all these flavors together with accents such as thyme, garlic, and caraway.

The specific meats and sausages used in choucroute garnie can change from kitchen to kitchen and are often very local (in Alsace, for example, you may find Strasbourg sausages or blood sausages), but I found that a combination of garlicky kielbasa, sweet and herbal bratwurst, smoky ham hock, and rich pork belly provided the range of flavors I sought. It sounds like a lot of meat, and it is. But that's what this dish is all about.

If you have lard on hand, this is a great place to use it (the recipe calls for only 2 tablespoons) to give the choucroute garnie a little extra something. But the dish is great with extra-virgin olive oil, too. Do seek out pork belly for this recipe; ask for it at the butcher counter if you don't see it in the case. But if you just can't find it, you can substitute pork blade chops, pork butt, or slab bacon.

After experimenting with sauerkraut straight from the jar, drained sauerkraut, and rinsed sauerkraut, I chose rinsed sauerkraut, which I squeezed dry. This provided just the right texture and moisture level for the dish and kept its brininess in check.

This recipe serves eight, but keep in mind that it makes excellent leftovers, to be enjoyed cold or gently warmed up. I've even used the leftovers for sandwiches, much to the delight of my kids.

—BRYAN ROOF, *Cook's Country*

Choucroute Garnie

SERVES 8

Note that we call for fully cooked bratwurst here. We developed this recipe with 12 ounces of bratwurst and 14 ounces of kielbasa, but if you can find only slightly larger packages of these sausages, it's OK to use the whole package. You can substitute two 8- to 10-ounce bone-in blade-cut pork chops; 1 pound of boneless pork butt, cut in half; or 1 pound of slab bacon for the pork belly. Serve with boiled potatoes, if desired.

  2 tablespoons lard, bacon fat, or extra-virgin olive oil

  1 onion, sliced thin

  1 teaspoon kosher salt, divided

  1 (12-ounce) smoked ham hock

  1 cup dry white wine

  5 garlic cloves, smashed and peeled

  6 sprigs fresh thyme

  1 pound skinless pork belly, cut into 2 equal pieces, fat cap trimmed to ¼ inch

  ½ teaspoon pepper

  2 pounds sauerkraut, rinsed and squeezed dry

  1 teaspoon caraway seeds

 14 ounces kielbasa sausage, cut into 6 equal pieces (about 3-inch segments)

 12 ounces cooked bratwurst, each sausage halved crosswise

     Whole-grain mustard

1. Adjust oven rack to middle position and heat oven to 325 degrees. Heat lard in Dutch oven over medium heat until shimmering. Add onion and ¼ teaspoon salt and cook until just softened, about 6 minutes. Remove pot from heat.

2. Add ham hock, wine, garlic, and thyme sprigs to pot. Sprinkle pork belly with pepper and remaining ¾ teaspoon salt, then add to pot. Cover contents of pot with sauerkraut, then sprinkle with caraway seeds. Cover pot, transfer to oven, and cook for 1½ hours.

3. Remove pot from oven and nestle kielbasa and bratwurst into sauerkraut. Cover; return to oven; and continue to cook until sausages are hot throughout and pork belly is tender when pierced with paring knife, about 45 minutes longer. Remove pot from oven and let rest, covered, for 20 minutes.

4. Transfer sauerkraut to shallow platter; place sausages on top. Discard thyme sprigs. Slice pork belly thin crosswise and add to platter. Remove meat from ham hock, slice thin, and add to platter; discard bone. Serve with mustard.

KANSAS CITY–STYLE BARBECUE RIBS

✔ **WHY THIS RECIPE WORKS** For assertively spiced, well-lacquered, tender ribs, we leaned on a charcoal snake, a C-shaped arrangement of charcoal briquettes that burns slowly for 4 hours without interruption. The dry rub, which consisted only of salt, pepper, and granulated garlic, provided ample bark while the ribs smoked, and the sauce was a simple blend of ketchup; brown sugar; spices; and a touch of corn syrup, which gave the ribs a glazed appearance. We applied the sauce at the halfway point so that it could tighten on the ribs as they cooked and then again when the ribs came off the grill for an extra flavor boost.

Kansas City is known for its great barbecue. And though many Kansas Citians are united in the belief that the so-called "Paris of the Plains" is the barbecue capital of the world, a hallmark of the regional style is actually the diversity and sheer variety of cuts and meats served. Pork, beef, lamb, and chicken are all in play, and individual cuts abound for each meat. That said, one common element unites most plates in the city: a generous coating of a sweet, sticky, smoky, tomato-based barbecue sauce. Burnt ends are bathed with the stuff, brisket is slathered, and ribs are glazed. The result is balanced flavor with peaks and valleys of spice and smoke.

As part of my research for an On the Road feature in *Cook's Country*, I spent four days eating my way through the Kansas City barbecue scene. As diverse as the menus across the region were, I came away from my trip inspired to make ribs similar to those I found at Harp Barbecue in Raytown, Missouri. Though Tyler Harp uses a mammoth 375-gallon offset smoker to make his professional barbecue, I wanted my recipe to be tailored to a backyard grill, and I wanted the ribs to emerge, like Tyler's, lacquered in a glazy sauce, tender to the bone, and assertively spiced.

KANSAS CITY–STYLE BARBECUE RIBS

Well-marbled whole spareribs produce moist, tender barbecue ribs, but some racks are so large that they barely fit on a backyard grill. So I opted for a smaller cut known as "St. Louis" ribs—narrower, rectangular racks that offer all the flavor and succulent bite of whole spareribs but without the fuss. Taking a cue from Tyler, I applied a simple rub of salt, pepper, and granulated garlic onto both sides of the racks; this would not only evenly season the meat but also encourage the formation of that signature dark, flavorful exterior crust known as bark.

A delicious cut of meat and some simple seasonings can go a long way, but I knew I'd get nowhere without the proper grilling technique. Part of the challenge of low-and-slow smoking, which is essential for achieving fully tender meat with a substantial bark, is keeping the heat consistent for hours on end. But I didn't want to babysit my ribs, and repeatedly adding fresh charcoal to the grill would mean opening the grill lid, a step that makes it hard to maintain a steady temperature. Luckily, we at *Cook's Country* are no strangers to home barbecuing, so I looked back at some of our recent recipes to find a foolproof solution.

I found my answer when I came to Morgan Bolling's backyard take on Texas-style smoked brisket, which calls for something known as a charcoal snake. The C-shaped array of briquettes slowly burns from one end to the other, providing hours of smoky heat without the need to open the grill or refuel. A disposable aluminum pan filled with water, placed in the center of the snake, helps moderate the grill temperature even further. Knowing that my ribs wouldn't need quite as long on the grill as Morgan's brisket, I tinkered with her setup until I found one that would burn consistently for at least 4 hours. I arranged 80 briquettes neatly around the perimeter of my grill, topped the snake with wood chunks for good smoky flavor, and poured a pile of lit coals at one end to start the low, slow burn.

My first few tests produced tender ribs with dark, crusty bark—not too bad for a backyard barbecue. But the edges of the racks were a little too charred for my liking. Orienting the racks lengthwise, into the arc of the charcoal snake, kept them more protected from the direct heat of the coals, and rotating the racks about halfway through cooking ensured that no exposed edges passed the threshold from bark to burnt.

With my ribs cooking up tender and crusty, it was finally time to take on that signature Kansas City sauce.

To a ketchup base, I added corn syrup (an ingredient I borrowed from Tyler's recipe) for glazy shine, brown sugar for molasses notes, cider vinegar for tang, savory Worcestershire sauce, and a generous array of spices. Slathered over the ribs, this sauce hit many of the flavor notes I was hoping for, but the racks weren't quite as lacquered and shiny as the ones I'd tried at Harp. Adding just 1 more tablespoon of corn syrup did the trick without compromising the sauce's sweet-savory profile. I slathered half the sauce onto the ribs halfway through cooking them to let the flavors meld; added the rest when the ribs came off the grill; and, after letting them rest briefly, rolled up my sleeves and got ready to take a bite. Kansas City, here I come.

—BRYAN ROOF, *Cook's Country*

Kansas City–Style Barbecue Ribs

SERVES 6 TO 8

The corn syrup helps give the sauce a nice shine when applied to the ribs. You can omit it if you like.

RIBS

- 2 tablespoons kosher salt
- 2 tablespoons pepper
- 1 tablespoon granulated garlic
- 2 (2½- to 3-pound) racks St. Louis ribs
- 1 (13 by 9-inch) disposable aluminum pan
- 5 (3-inch) wood chunks

SAUCE

- ¼ cup ketchup
- ¼ cup brown sugar
- 2 tablespoons cider vinegar
- 2 tablespoons light corn syrup
- 1 teaspoon Worcestershire sauce
- 1 teaspoon pepper
- ½ teaspoon table salt
- ½ teaspoon granulated garlic
- ¼ teaspoon ground cumin

1. FOR THE RIBS: Combine salt, pepper, and granulated garlic in bowl. Place ribs on rimmed baking sheet and pat dry with paper towels. Flip ribs meaty side down. Season bone side of ribs with about one-third of spice mixture. Flip ribs and season meaty side with remaining two-thirds spice mixture.

2. Open bottom vent of charcoal grill completely. Arrange 40 charcoal briquettes, 2 briquettes wide, around half of perimeter of grill, overlapping slightly so briquettes are touching, to form "C" shape. Place second layer of 40 briquettes, also 2 briquettes wide, on top of first. (Completed arrangement should be 2 briquettes wide by 2 briquettes high.)

3. Starting 2 inches from 1 end of charcoal "C," place wood chunks on top of charcoal 2 inches apart. Place disposable pan in center of grill, running lengthwise into arc of charcoal "C." Pour 6 cups water into pan.

4. Light chimney starter filled with 10 briquettes (pile briquettes on 1 side of chimney so they catch). When coals are partially covered with ash, use tongs to place them at end of "C" where you started wood chunks.

5. Place grate on grill, then clean and oil grate. Place ribs side by side on grill, with meaty side up, lengthwise over water pan. Cover grill, position lid vent over ribs, and open lid vent completely. Cook, without opening grill, for 2 hours.

6. FOR THE SAUCE: Meanwhile, whisk all ingredients together in small saucepan and cook over medium heat until sugar is dissolved. (Sauce does not need to come to boil.) Set aside off heat.

7. Open grill and rotate ribs 180 degrees. Brush meaty side of ribs with about half of sauce. Cover grill, positioning lid vent over ribs. Continue to cook, without opening grill, for 2 hours longer.

8. Transfer ribs to rimmed baking sheet, meaty side up. Brush meaty side of ribs with remaining half of sauce. Cover sheet tightly with aluminum foil and let rest for 30 minutes. Cut ribs between bones. Serve.

HERBED LEG OF LAMB WITH FINGERLING POTATOES AND ASPARAGUS

✔ **WHY THIS RECIPE WORKS** A roasted boneless leg of lamb is impressive enough for a holiday celebration, but could we make a nonholiday version that required less prep and cleanup? Starting with a butterflied leg of lamb was a good first step, and pounding it to an even thickness made it even easier to work with. We spread a potent herb paste of parsley, mint, and garlic over the lamb before rolling and tying the roast so that the lamb would be infused with flavor from the inside out. After a quick sear on the stovetop right in the roasting pan, we positioned the lamb fat side down on a bed of potatoes before moving it to the oven, where the fat slowly rendered, seasoning the potatoes below. We flipped the lamb halfway through cooking to allow the fat to crisp. While the lamb rested, we tossed asparagus in the pan drippings and let the vegetables roast until they were tender.

Lamb is often a special-occasion dish, but for *The Complete One Pot* cookbook, I was inspired to make a lamb dish that could be perfect for any day. I wanted a lamb recipe with minimal prep and cleanup that would still serve a crowd and deliver nuanced flavors. Since my aim was to minimize dirty dishes, I went with one pan—a roasting pan. I ended up with an impressive-looking dish that wasn't overly difficult to make and didn't leave a mountain of pans to clean.

To make this dish, I incorporated a few techniques that my colleagues and I found especially useful when developing other recipes for *The Complete One Pot*, namely stacking ingredients and staggering cooking times. We found stacking ingredients helpful in many recipes, and we found it especially effective to position vegetables with a protein on top of them. This both helps the meat cook evenly and allows the drippings from the meat to flavor the vegetables. Here, I could put the lamb with the fat side down on top of the potatoes so that as the fat rendered, the drippings would flavor the potatoes.

One of the biggest challenges with one-pot cooking is making sure that each component is properly cooked, because no one wants to have cold meat or overcooked vegetables. To that end, we've discovered that staggering cooking times and cooking ingredients in stages are indispensable techniques. For this recipe, I started by getting a good sear on the lamb before removing it from the pan, placing the potatoes on the bottom, and then putting the lamb back on top and moving it to the oven. I reserved the quicker-cooking asparagus to add to the pan while the lamb rested and kept the longer-cooking potatoes in the pan the whole time so that they would cook through properly.

While developing this recipe, I had to clear a few hurdles as I tried to get my ideal lamb dish. One of my first ideas, a bread crumb coating, was a total bust. It was impossible to sear the lamb with the crust on it, and the bread crumbs either overbrowned in the oven or got soggy while I was resting the lamb after roasting.

In the end, I nixed that and went with a vibrant herb paste that brought bright, clean flavor to the dish. I spread the herb paste on the lamb before rolling and tying the roast so that I had vibrant flavor that permeated the dish. I also reserved some of the herb mixture, plus some lemon zest, to toss with the potatoes after cooking for another layer of flavor and to tie together the different elements of the dish.

One key technique that changed throughout testing was the positioning of the lamb while it cooked in the oven. Early in the recipe development process, I was starting with the lamb fat side up and then flipping it halfway through cooking. That left the fat flabby rather than crispy and didn't allow the rendered fat to flavor the potatoes as much as I would have liked, so I tried it the other way around and found success. Starting the lamb fat side down gave me flavorful potatoes permeated by the delicious rendered lamb fat, and finishing it fat side up helped crisp the fat layer. Since this is a pretty straightforward dish, rendering those drippings onto the potatoes provides vital seasoning.

With a relatively short ingredient list, each ingredient adds something crucial to the dish. In my opinion, lamb is a vastly underused protein, so I was excited to spotlight it here. Using a butterflied leg of lamb makes for a dish that feeds a crowd, and it's easy to prep. I liked that I could just sear the lamb right in the roasting pan to start the dish. The potatoes were good for bulking up the dish to make it a complete meal, and the asparagus rounded out the meal and added some additional color. The herb paste with the mint and parsley was springy and helped liven up the dish and tie everything together. It did double duty, giving the lamb flavor from the inside out and helping give the potatoes some additional seasoning at the end. The lemon zest that we tossed the potatoes with at the end added a bright, floral note to the dish. I had a complete meal with protein, vegetable, and starch, and it was all made in one pan with minimal prep and cleanup. Finally, I had an impressive-looking lamb dish that I didn't need to wait for a holiday to make.

—SARAH EWALD, *America's Test Kitchen Books*

Herbed Leg of Lamb with Fingerling Potatoes and Asparagus

SERVES 6 TO 8

We prefer the subtler flavor of lamb labeled "domestic" or "American" for this recipe. Look for potatoes that are about 2 inches long and 1 inch in diameter. Small red potatoes measuring 1 to 2 inches in diameter can be substituted for the fingerling potatoes. Make sure to use asparagus spears between ¼ and ½ inch in diameter at the base.

½	cup fresh mint leaves
½	cup fresh parsley leaves
3	tablespoons extra-virgin olive oil, divided
3	garlic cloves, peeled
1	(3½- to 4-pound) butterflied leg of lamb
1¼	teaspoons table salt, divided
1¼	teaspoons pepper, divided
2	pounds fingerling potatoes, unpeeled
2	pounds asparagus, trimmed
1	tablespoon grated lemon zest

1. Adjust oven rack to lower-middle position and heat oven to 375 degrees. Process mint, parsley, 1 teaspoon oil, and garlic in food processor until finely chopped, scraping down sides of bowl as needed, about 1 minute; transfer to bowl.

2. Place lamb on cutting board with fat cap facing up. Using sharp knife, trim fat to between ⅛- and ¼-inch thickness. Flip lamb and trim any pockets of fat and connective tissue. Cover with sheet of plastic

NOTES FROM THE TEST KITCHEN

PREPARING BONELESS LEG OF LAMB

1. Place lamb on cutting board with fat cap facing up. Using sharp knife, trim fat cap to between ⅛- and ¼-inch thickness.

2. Flip lamb and trim any pockets of fat and connective tissue from underside of lamb. Pound roast to even 1-inch thickness.

wrap and pound to even 1-inch thickness. Rub interior with 2 teaspoons oil and sprinkle with ½ teaspoon salt and ½ teaspoon pepper. Spread 1½ tablespoons herb mixture evenly over lamb, leaving 1-inch border around edge. Roll roast tightly and tie with kitchen twine at 1½-inch intervals. Rub exterior of roast with 1 tablespoon oil and sprinkle with ½ teaspoon salt and ½ teaspoon pepper.

3. Heat remaining 1 tablespoon oil in 16 by 12-inch roasting pan over medium-high heat until just smoking. Brown roast well on all sides, 8 to 10 minutes; transfer to large plate.

4. Off heat, toss potatoes in fat left in pan, then spread into even layer. Place roast fat side down on top of potatoes. Transfer pan to oven and roast until lamb registers 120 to 125 degrees (for medium-rare), 45 minutes to 1 hour, flipping lamb halfway through roasting. Transfer roast to carving board, tent with aluminum foil, and let rest while finishing vegetables.

5. Increase oven temperature to 450 degrees. Push potatoes to 1 side of pan. Add asparagus to clearing and toss with remaining ¼ teaspoon salt, remaining ¼ teaspoon pepper, and any accumulated pan juices. Spread asparagus into even layer and roast vegetables until asparagus is crisp-tender, 10 to 12 minutes.

6. Transfer asparagus to serving platter. Toss potatoes with lemon zest and remaining herb mixture in pan and season with salt and pepper to taste; transfer to platter with asparagus. Remove twine from roast and slice ½ inch thick. Serve lamb with potatoes and asparagus.

BRAISED LAMB SHANKS

✓ **WHY THIS RECIPE WORKS** For this recipe we rubbed lamb shanks with a mixture of salt, pepper, ground cumin for warmth, citrusy coriander, and red pepper flakes for a small spark of heat. We browned the shanks in a little oil in a Dutch oven to bloom the spices and develop fond (those flavorful browned bits) on the bottom of the pot. Then we removed the shanks to make room for the garlic and onion to soften. Next, we tossed in diced carrots for earthy sweetness, green olives for pungency, thyme, lemon zest, dried oregano, and a tablespoon of soy sauce for an umami boost along with chicken broth for the base of our braising liquid. We nestled the shanks back into the pot, brought the liquid to a boil, and then covered the pot and

slid it into a relatively low (325-degree) oven for a few hours. We flipped the lamb shanks halfway through braising. Once the shanks were cooked and tender, we transferred them to a plate, skimmed the fat from the braising liquid, and stirred in some fresh cilantro and lemon juice to wake everything up. These lamb shanks are best enjoyed accompanied by anything that absorbs the flavorful braising liquid—such as a mound of polenta or nest of rice—along with a glass of wine.

Few things are more satisfying than the heady, promising aroma of lamb shanks slowly braising in a rich broth. As it fills the kitchen, the scent foretells a cozy, satisfying supper that's perfect for a cold winter evening.

It's not difficult to achieve this in your own home. But it does involve a focused shopping trip to a butcher that carries lamb shanks. If you don't have a specialty butcher nearby who can supply you with high-quality cuts, try the butcher counter at your local supermarket. Lamb shanks aren't always kept in the case of prewrapped meats, but they're often stocked for customers like you.

If you've braised meats before, the process for braising lamb shanks will feel familiar. For this recipe, which features a wide range of Mediterranean flavors, you'll rub the shanks with a mixture of salt, pepper, ground cumin and coriander, and red pepper flakes for a lively spark of heat. You'll lightly sear the shanks in a little oil in your Dutch oven to bloom the spices in the rub, give the shanks a bit of browning, and enrich the braising liquid with flavorful fond (those browned bits that form on the pan floor as food colors). Then you'll remove the shanks to make room for garlic and onion to soften.

Next, you'll add green olives for pungency, carrots for earthy sweetness, thyme, lemon zest, dried oregano, soy sauce for an umami boost, and chicken broth—or, if there's none at hand, water. You'll nestle the lamb shanks into this braising liquid; bring the liquid to a boil; and then cover the pot and slide it into a relatively low (325-degree) oven for a few hours, flipping the shanks halfway through braising.

Once cooked, your lamb shanks will be absurdly tender—and your kitchen will smell incredible. You'll transfer the shanks to a plate, skim the fat from your braising liquid (don't worry about getting all of it), stir in some fresh cilantro and lemon juice to wake everything up, and spoon the sauce over the shanks.

BRAISED LAMB SHANKS

Finally, you'll nestle those succulent shanks into a puddle of polenta or bed of rice; pour a glass of wine; and eat slowly, allowing the rich meat and mesmerizing flavors in the sauce to shore you up for a good night's rest. You'll wake up the next day still thinking about this dish, and if you have leftovers, lucky you—day-after braised lamb makes excellent sandwiches.

—BRYAN ROOF, *Cook's Country*

Braised Lamb Shanks

SERVES 4

Use a vegetable peeler to remove the zest from the lemon. If you're using table salt, cut the amount in half. If you don't have chicken broth, you can substitute water in this recipe, but you may have to add a little more salt at the end. This dish is great served over polenta, white beans, rice, or boiled potatoes—anything that will absorb the flavorful braising liquid. The test kitchen's favorite soy sauce is Kikkoman Soy Sauce.

NOTES FROM THE TEST KITCHEN

ALL ABOUT LAMB SHANKS

Lamb shanks are one of our favorite cuts for braising; they're relatively inexpensive, deeply flavorful, and—with long, moist cooking—supremely tender. Shanks are the lower leg of the animal, and most lamb shanks you'll find are from the larger rear legs. Note that you don't see the bones protruding from raw shanks, but, like spareribs, the meat shrinks from the bone when they're cooked.

Markets sell domestic and imported lamb; domestic cuts are often larger, and the meat is milder in flavor than most imported lamb. That's because most domestic lamb is pasture raised but finished on grain; the grain impacts the composition of the animal's fat, which is where most of its uniquely gamy flavor resides. Look for lamb with a dark-red hue and bright fat.

2 teaspoons kosher salt

2 teaspoons ground cumin

2 teaspoons ground coriander

1 teaspoon pepper

½ teaspoon red pepper flakes

4 (12- to 16-ounce) lamb shanks

3 tablespoons extra-virgin olive oil, divided

1 onion, chopped

8 garlic cloves, smashed and peeled

2 cups chicken broth

1 cup pimento-stuffed green olives

2 carrots, peeled and cut into ½-inch dice (½ cup)

2 tablespoons coarsely chopped fresh thyme

5 (3-inch) strips lemon zest plus 1 tablespoon juice

1 tablespoon soy sauce

1 teaspoon dried oregano

¼ cup coarsely chopped fresh cilantro leaves and stems

1. Adjust oven rack to middle position and heat oven to 325 degrees. Combine salt, cumin, coriander, pepper, and pepper flakes in bowl. Pat lamb shanks dry with paper towels and sprinkle all over with 2 tablespoons spice mixture.

2. Heat 2 tablespoons oil in Dutch oven over medium heat until shimmering. Add 2 lamb shanks and cook until lightly browned on both flat sides of each shank, about 2 minutes per side. (Searing here is more about toasting spices on lamb than about getting deep browning.) Transfer to plate and repeat with remaining 2 lamb shanks.

3. Add remaining 1 tablespoon oil, onion, and garlic to now-empty pot and cook until onion just begins to soften, about 2 minutes. Add broth, olives, carrots, thyme, lemon zest, soy sauce, oregano, lamb shanks, and remaining 1½ teaspoons spice mixture and bring to boil.

4. Cover pot, transfer to oven, and cook for 1½ hours. Remove pot from oven and flip lamb shanks. Cover pot and return to oven. Continue to cook until meat easily falls off bone when prodded with fork, about 1½ hours longer.

5. Transfer lamb shanks to shallow platter, tent with aluminum foil, and let rest for 10 minutes. Skim fat from braising liquid with large spoon. Stir cilantro and lemon juice into braising liquid. Season with salt and pepper to taste. Spoon sauce over lamb shanks and serve.

ORANGE CHICKEN

BROILED CHICKEN WITH GRAVY

✓ **WHY THIS RECIPE WORKS** We found that the key to getting a whole chicken on the table in a reasonable amount of time was broiling, not roasting. Spatchcocking the chicken kept it flat so that it cooked evenly under the intense direct heat, and it also helped speed up cooking. To get the white meat to finish at the same time as the dark meat, we preheated a skillet to jump-start the cooking of the leg quarters, and we started the chicken under a cold broiler to slow down the cooking of the breast. Because the broiler's heat is more intense than the oven's, carryover cooking has a bigger impact. To account for this, we pulled the chicken from the oven when the breast meat registered 155 degrees instead of 160 degrees. For a gravy that really tasted like the bird, we began by making a full-flavored chicken stock from the backbone, giblets, and excess skin and fat from the chicken—powerhouses of chicken flavor. We started the stock by simmering the backbone, giblets, and trimmings in chicken broth to efficiently extract juices and fat from the parts, which browned and formed a rich fond once the liquid evaporated. We then sautéed aromatics, deglazed the saucepan with white wine, added more broth, reduced it, and strained it. Then, to turn the stock into a gravy, we toasted flour in melted butter and whisked in the reduced stock.

When I roast a whole chicken, the accompaniment I always yearn for is a generous pour of gravy. You know, the rich, deeply flavorful kind that gives off the soul-soothing vibes of a Thanksgiving feast. Yet what often stops me is that great gravy typically begins with pan drippings, which means that you need to wait until the bird is finished roasting to make it. The best gravy also requires homemade stock, a time-consuming production unto itself.

If I could find a way to prepare juicy, crispy-skinned chicken and savory gravy in tandem, I'd have my dream dinner without too much fuss. I suspected that a mash-up of two classics from my colleague Lan Lam—One-Hour Broiled Chicken and Pan Sauce and Our Favorite Turkey Gravy—would deliver.

The chicken recipe starts with removing the backbone of the bird so that it lies flat in the skillet, helping it cook evenly and quickly under the broiler. (I figured that the backbone would make an excellent stand-in for the turkey neck called for in the gravy.)

To help the chicken fat render and to create escape routes for steam that would otherwise cause the skin to bubble up and burn, Lan nicks the skin with a paring knife. Preheating the skillet on the stovetop jump-starts the cooking of the leg quarters, and placing the skillet under a cold broiler and then turning on the broiler slows down the cooking of the breast meat. After about 45 minutes, the skin is browned and crispy, and both the white and dark meat are as juicy as can be.

Now, the gravy. Her ingenious method would be ideal here because it primarily relies on trimmings. It starts with simmering the turkey neck, giblets, and excess fat and skin in a small amount of store-bought chicken broth, which extracts the juices and fat much more thoroughly than searing would. The mixture is left to bubble away until all the liquid evaporates and the parts sizzle, leaving the pot coated with a gorgeous brown layer of fond, which signals that the proteins and sugars have undergone the Maillard reaction and transformed into hundreds of new flavor compounds.

Aromatics are added to the pot to soften before everything is deglazed with wine. Then in goes more broth before the mixture is covered and left to simmer for an hour. After straining the deeply savory stock and thickening it with a roux that's been cooked to just the right shade of golden brown, you end up with a truly outstanding gravy.

To merge the recipes, I started by preparing the chicken, reserving the giblets, backbone, and trimmings (also save the neck if it is included with your chicken). Once the bird was under the broiler, I turned to the gravy, scaling it down to serve four.

After just 15 minutes of simmering the scraps in 1 cup of broth, the liquid had evaporated and the bottom of the saucepan was coated with a substantial fond. In went onion, carrot, celery, garlic, parsley, and thyme; once the onion was translucent, I added a splash of dry white wine, poured in 3 more cups of broth, and cranked the heat to high. To speed things up, I left the lid off so that the mixture could rapidly concentrate.

A mere 20 minutes later, the stock had reduced by half, so I strained it and thickened it with a toasty golden-brown roux. Meanwhile, I removed the bird from the broiler and let it rest. I defatted the ultrachicken-y drippings to give a final boost to what was already a deep, dark, seriously flavorful gravy.

This supercomforting twofer dish was ready to serve.

—STEVE DUNN, *Cook's Illustrated*

BROILED CHICKEN WITH GRAVY

Broiled Chicken with Gravy

SERVES 4

If your broiler has multiple settings, choose the highest one. This recipe won't work with a drawer-style broiler. You will need a broiler-safe 12-inch skillet. We like to use the giblets and neck for the gravy here, but you can omit them if you prefer; the backbone and trimmings provide plenty of flavor on their own. Feel free to substitute dry vermouth for the white wine. In step 2, if the skin is dark golden brown but the breast has not yet reached 155 degrees, cover the chicken with foil and continue to broil. Monitor the temperature of the chicken carefully during the final 10 minutes of cooking, because it can quickly overcook.

1 (4-pound) whole chicken, giblets and neck reserved
1½ teaspoons vegetable oil, divided
1½ teaspoons kosher salt, divided
½ teaspoon pepper
4 cups chicken broth, divided
½ onion, chopped fine
1 carrot, peeled and chopped fine
1 celery rib, chopped fine
4 sprigs fresh parsley
2 sprigs fresh thyme
1 garlic clove, crushed and peeled
¼ cup dry white wine
2 tablespoons unsalted butter
2½ tablespoons all-purpose flour

1. Adjust oven rack 12 to 13 inches from broiler element (do not heat broiler). Place chicken breast side down on cutting board. Using kitchen shears, cut through bones on either side of backbone. Cut backbone into 1-inch pieces and reserve. Trim excess fat and skin from chicken and reserve with backbone. Flip chicken and use heel of your hand to press on breastbone to flatten. Using tip of paring knife, poke holes through skin over entire surface of chicken, spacing them approximately ¾ inch apart.

2. Rub ½ teaspoon oil over skin and sprinkle with 1 teaspoon salt and pepper. Flip chicken and sprinkle bone side with remaining ½ teaspoon salt. Flip chicken skin side up, tie legs together with kitchen twine, and tuck wings under breasts. Heat remaining 1 teaspoon oil in broiler-safe 12-inch skillet over high heat until just smoking. Place chicken in skillet, skin side up, and transfer to oven, positioning skillet as close to center of oven as handle allows (turn handle so it points toward one of oven's front corners). Turn on broiler and broil chicken for 25 minutes. Rotate skillet by moving handle to opposite front corner of oven and continue to broil until skin is dark golden brown and thickest part of breast registers 155 degrees, 20 to 30 minutes longer. While chicken broils, make gravy.

3. Bring 1 cup broth and reserved giblets, neck, backbone, and trimmings to simmer in large saucepan over high heat. Cook, adjusting heat to maintain vigorous simmer and stirring occasionally, until all liquid evaporates and trimmings begin to sizzle, about 12 minutes. Continue to cook, stirring frequently, until dark fond forms on bottom of saucepan, 2 to 4 minutes longer. Reduce heat to medium. Add onion, carrot, celery, parsley sprigs, thyme sprigs, and garlic to saucepan and cook, stirring frequently, until onion is translucent, 7 to 8 minutes. Stir in wine and bring to simmer, scraping up any browned bits. Add remaining 3 cups broth and bring to simmer over high heat. Adjust heat to maintain simmer and continue to cook, stirring occasionally, until stock (liquid only) is reduced by half, about 20 minutes longer.

NOTES FROM THE TEST KITCHEN

TIMELINE FOR BROILED CHICKEN WITH GRAVY
Our recipe is designed so that the chicken and gravy cook concurrently for about an hour.

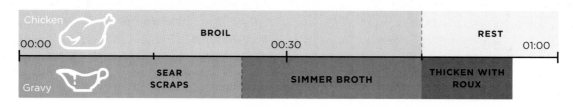

4. Strain stock through fine-mesh strainer set over bowl, pressing on solids to extract as much liquid as possible. Melt butter in now-empty saucepan over medium heat. Add flour and cook, stirring constantly, until mixture is deep golden brown, 5 to 8 minutes. Slowly whisk in stock. Increase heat to medium-high and bring to simmer. Simmer until thickened, about 5 minutes.

5. Transfer chicken to carving board and let rest, uncovered, for 15 minutes. While chicken rests, transfer fat and drippings in skillet to small bowl and let sit for 5 minutes. Spoon off fat and discard. Whisk drippings into gravy. Season gravy with salt and pepper to taste. Carve chicken and serve, passing gravy separately.

POULET AU VINAIGRE (CHICKEN WITH VINEGAR)

✔ **WHY THIS RECIPE WORKS** Our recipe for this classic French dish calls for using just chicken thighs rather than the usual mix of light and dark meat to ensure that all the meat cooks at the same rate. We browned the chicken to develop flavor and then braised it in a flavorful mix of chicken broth, white wine, and red wine vinegar until it reached 195 degrees and was meltingly tender and juicy. To finish the sauce, we fortified the braising liquid with tomato paste and reduced it to a luxurious, lightly thickened consistency before adding minced fresh tarragon. The sauce is typically finished with heavy cream, but we preferred to whisk in a couple tablespoons of butter instead, as we found that cream dulled the vibrant sauce.

When I was a culinary student in France, my most enduring food memories were made in the rustic bouchons of Lyon. That's where I experienced poulet au vinaigre, a dish that exemplifies the simple and stellar everyday French cooking known as "la cuisine traditionnelle française."

As you might guess, the sauce for poulet au vinaigre features vinegar—the bright, tangy red wine type—but it also includes white wine, chicken broth, fresh tomato, anise-y tarragon, and a bit of heavy cream. White wine is used so as not to impart too much color to the chicken; the red wine vinegar adds tannic intensity and sharpness to the creamy, satisfying sauce.

The dish comes together easily. Bone-in, skin-on chicken pieces are first browned in a skillet, and then one of two avenues is taken: The chicken is either pan-roasted before being removed so that the sauce can be built in the empty skillet, or the liquid ingredients are added to the browned chicken and used as a braising medium that is later reduced to a luxurious sauce.

For my version, braising was the way to go. It was more convenient, and it essentially created a ready-made sauce as the dish simmered. I also opted to use only thighs, as dark meat would turn luscious and tender during braising.

I started by arranging the thighs skin side down in a hot, oiled skillet. Once the fat was rendered and the skin was deeply browned, I flipped the chicken and browned the other side before removing it. In went minced shallot and sliced garlic, followed by chicken broth. Most recipes call for a 2:1 ratio of wine to vinegar, so I added 1 cup of wine and ½ cup of vinegar with the broth. I nestled the chicken into the liquid skin side up and slid the pan into a 325-degree oven to braise gently. After about 40 minutes, the chicken hit 195 degrees. The dark meat was silky and succulent because its collagen had turned to supple gelatin.

I kept the thighs covered while I reduced the braising liquid, which was now reinforced with chicken juices. When the sauce was nicely thickened, I finished it with fresh tarragon; a peeled, seeded, and diced tomato; and a drizzle of cream.

The chicken was incredibly moist and tender, but the sauce was too sharp. An extra pour of cream mellowed the tanginess but made the sauce overly rich. I dropped the vinegar to ⅓ cup. And I finished the sauce with a couple pats of butter instead of cream to enrich it without the dulling effects of excess water and dairy.

The dish now embodied la cuisine traditionnelle française: It was full of flavor, uncomplicated, and unfussy. Well, there was one minor annoyance: having to peel, seed, and dice a tomato. To eliminate that step, I turned to one of my favorite flavor enhancers, tomato paste. Just a tablespoon whisked into the reducing sauce was a fuss-free way to add sweet-tart umami notes without having to mess with a tomato.

As I poured the vibrant, savory sauce around a platter of bronzed, juicy chicken, I smiled, knowing that I now had the means to enjoy one of my favorite French dishes whenever the mood struck.

—STEVE DUNN, *Cook's Illustrated*

POULET AU VINAIGRE (CHICKEN WITH VINEGAR)

Poulet au Vinaigre (Chicken with Vinegar)

SERVES 4 TO 6

Use an inexpensive dry white wine here. Fresh tarragon is traditional for poulet au vinaigre, but parsley can be substituted. Likewise, dry vermouth can stand in for the wine. Leftovers reheat well, but the recipe can also be halved: Use a 10-inch skillet and keep the cooking times the same.

8 (5- to 7-ounce) bone-in chicken thighs, trimmed
1¼ teaspoons table salt
¾ teaspoon pepper
1 tablespoon vegetable oil
1 large shallot, minced
2 garlic cloves, sliced thin
1 cup chicken broth
1 cup dry white wine
⅓ cup red wine vinegar, plus extra for seasoning
1 tablespoon tomato paste
2 tablespoons unsalted butter, chilled
1 tablespoon minced fresh tarragon

1. Adjust oven rack to lower-middle position and heat oven to 325 degrees. Pat chicken dry with paper towels and sprinkle both sides with salt and pepper. Heat oil in 12-inch ovensafe skillet over medium heat until shimmering. Add chicken, skin side down, and cook, without moving it, until well browned, about 8 minutes. Using tongs, flip chicken and brown on second side, about 3 minutes. Transfer chicken to large plate.

2. Pour off all but 2 tablespoons fat from skillet. Add shallot and garlic and cook, stirring frequently, until garlic is golden brown, about 1½ minutes. Add broth, wine, and vinegar; bring to simmer, scraping up any browned bits. Return chicken to skillet, skin side up (skin will be above surface of liquid). Transfer skillet to oven and bake, uncovered, until chicken registers 195 degrees, 35 to 40 minutes.

3. Using tongs, transfer chicken to clean serving platter and tent with aluminum foil. Place skillet over high heat. Whisk tomato paste into liquid and bring to boil. Cook, occasionally scraping side of skillet to incorporate fond, until sauce is thickened and reduced to 1¼ cups, 5 to 7 minutes. Off heat, whisk in butter and tarragon. Season with salt, pepper, and up to 1 teaspoon extra vinegar (added ¼ teaspoon at a time) to taste. Pour sauce around chicken and serve.

KHAO MAN GAI (THAI-STYLE CHICKEN AND RICE)

✓ **WHY THIS RECIPE WORKS** We wanted to create a recipe for home cooks for the famous chicken and rice at Nong's Khao Man Gai in Portland, Oregon. We started by poaching the chicken whole with garlic and ginger, as the cooks do at Nong's. Poaching resulted in perfectly juicy meat and flavorful chicken broth. We let the chicken rest and then sliced and shredded it. For an accompaniment to the chicken, we made use of the poaching liquid to cook jasmine rice. To re-create Nong's bright, savory, spicy sauce, we whisked together a mixture of white vinegar, soy sauce, Thai soybean paste, garlic, ginger, and Thai chiles. The ultracomforting chicken and rice could stand on their own, but the sauce elevated them to a truly exceptional dinner.

After our executive food editor returned from feasting on the deservedly famous chicken and rice at Nong's Khao Man Gai in Portland, Oregon, he requested that I create a recipe for this dish for home cooks. Following what he had learned from the cooks at Nong's, I began by poaching the chicken whole with smashed garlic and sliced ginger, simultaneously creating perfectly juicy meat and flavorful chicken broth. Then, while the bird rested, I cooked fragrant jasmine rice, plus more garlic and ginger and a finely chopped shallot, in the poaching liquid to make a rich, poultry-infused rice to serve alongside the chicken.

The ultracomforting, subtly flavored chicken and rice could stand on their own, but at Nong's it's the bright, savory, spicy sauce that wakes it all up and keeps customers coming back for more. The sauce is a combo of soy sauce, vinegar, ginger, fresh Thai chiles, Thai pickled garlic, and fermented soybeans.

With some testing, I was able to make my own vibrant sauce and to work out some substitutions for ingredients that may be hard to find in your area. I call for fresh Thai chiles to give the sauce an unapologetic kick of heat. But if you can't find them, my testing revealed that Asian chili-garlic sauce makes a good substitute. Also note that while the recipe calls for Thai soybean paste (sometimes labeled as yellow bean sauce or soybean sauce) for a deeply savory flavor, you can substitute Japanese red miso for similar results.

And just a couple things to keep in mind: When grating ginger on a rasp-style grater, be sure to scrape up the flavorful juice that is exuded onto your work surface after grating and include it in your measurement. And don't forget to wash your hands after mincing the Thai chiles. They are hot!

—MATTHEW FAIRMAN, *Cook's Country*

Khao Man Gai (Thai-Style Chicken and Rice)
SERVES 4 TO 6

One tablespoon of Asian chili-garlic sauce can be substituted for the Thai chiles, if desired. Use a Dutch oven with at least a 7-quart capacity to comfortably fit the chicken. Thai soybean paste is sometimes labeled as yellow bean sauce or soybean sauce. If this ingredient is unavailable, you can substitute Japanese red miso. The test kitchen's favorite jasmine rice is Dynasty Jasmine Rice.

CHICKEN AND BROTH

- 12 cups water
- 1 (2-inch) piece ginger, peeled and sliced into ¼-inch-thick rounds
- 2 tablespoons table salt
- 6 garlic cloves, smashed and peeled
- 1 (3½- to 4-pound) whole chicken, giblets discarded

RICE

- 1 tablespoon vegetable oil
- 1 shallot, chopped fine
- 1 (2-inch) piece ginger, peeled and cut in half lengthwise
- 2 garlic cloves, minced
- ¼ teaspoon table salt
- 2 cups jasmine rice, rinsed
- 1 cup fresh cilantro leaves and stems
- ½ English cucumber, sliced into thin rounds

SAUCE

- ¼ cup Thai soybean paste
- ¼ cup soy sauce
- ¼ cup distilled white vinegar
- 2 tablespoons sugar
- 3 garlic cloves, minced
- 2 Thai chiles, stemmed and minced
- 1 teaspoon grated fresh ginger

- 2 scallions, sliced thin

1. FOR THE CHICKEN AND BROTH: Combine water, ginger, salt, and garlic in large Dutch oven. Add chicken to pot, breast side up, and bring to simmer over high heat. Place large sheet of aluminum foil over pot, then cover with lid. Reduce heat to low and simmer until breast registers 160 degrees and thighs register at least 175 degrees, 25 to 35 minutes.

2. Transfer chicken to bowl, tent with foil, and let rest while making rice. Using slotted spoon, skim foamy residue from surface of chicken broth. Set aside 3 cups broth for cooking rice. Cover remaining broth.

3. FOR THE RICE: Heat oil in large saucepan over medium heat until shimmering. Add shallot, ginger, garlic, and salt and cook until shallot is softened, about 2 minutes. Add rice and cook, stirring frequently, until edges begin to turn translucent, about 2 minutes.

4. Stir in reserved 3 cups broth and bring to boil over medium-high heat. Stir once more, then cover and reduce heat to low. Cook for 20 minutes. Without removing lid, remove saucepan from heat and let sit, covered, for 10 minutes.

5. FOR THE SAUCE: Whisk all ingredients in bowl until sugar is dissolved, about 1 minute. (Sauce can be refrigerated for up to 2 days.)

6. Rewarm remaining broth over medium heat. Using boning knife, remove breast meat from chicken carcass; discard skin. Remove chicken leg quarters by dislocating thigh joint from carcass. Using 2 forks, shred leg quarter meat into bite-size pieces; discard skin and bones. Slice breasts crosswise ½ inch thick.

7. Transfer rice to large serving platter. Arrange shredded chicken on top of rice. Arrange sliced breast meat on top of shredded chicken. Place cilantro in pile in 1 corner of platter and shingle cucumber along side of platter.

8. Portion four to six 1-cup servings of remaining hot broth into individual soup bowls and sprinkle with scallions (you will have more than 6 cups broth; reserve extra broth for another use). Serve chicken and rice with sauce and portions of broth.

TO MAKE AHEAD: Follow recipe through step 2 and let chicken and broth cool completely. Remove breasts and leg quarters from chicken carcass (as in step 6), but do not slice breasts or shred meat from leg quarters. Refrigerate broth and chicken for up to 24 hours. To serve, proceed with step 3. Reheat chicken in broth before shredding and slicing.

KHAO MAN GAI (THAI-STYLE CHICKEN AND RICE)

KOMBDI, JIRA GHALUN (CUMIN-SCENTED CHICKEN)

KOMBDI, JIRA GHALUN (CUMIN-SCENTED CHICKEN)

✔ **WHY THIS RECIPE WORKS** Kombdi, Jira Ghalun, or cumin-scented chicken, is a dish from Maharashtra, a state on India's west coast. It is a simple, aromatic recipe adapted by us from Kaumudi Marathé's *The Essential Marathi Cookbook* (2009) and shared with Kaumudi by her friend, Anuradha Samant, a member of the warrior (Maratha) community. The Marathas are known for elaborate, flavorful meat dishes, but this recipe is neither elaborate nor time-consuming. The chicken is first marinated in yogurt, garlic, and ginger. Then it is braised in a tomato-onion sauce until tender and cooked through to produce deeply nuanced flavor. Rather than relying on warm spices, such as cinnamon, cardamom, and cloves, as in north Indian recipes, this dish calls for only cumin. The cumin is added just before serving, rather than before braising, so it adds fresh smokiness to both the chicken and the sauce.

As a child, I had no interest in cooking. My head was always in a book; I dreamed of being a writer, and I later trained to be a journalist. But food was circling in the air above me. After all, I had grown up with great cooks who were always throwing parties and discussing food.

My parents came from India, from a generation that made everything from scratch. Mom was the speediest, most inventive cook I knew. If she lacked equipment or ingredients, she found innovative solutions. Her food was experimental but delicious. Her mother, Aji, by contrast, was precise and deliberate. Aji's recipes tasted the same every time: familiar, fabulous, and comforting. When I was working as a reporter in Bombay, Aji generously taught me to cook many of my favorite recipes; cooking alongside her and documenting those recipes sparked my career as a food writer.

Kombdi, Jira Ghalun (Cumin-Scented Chicken) is a recipe from my second cookbook, *The Essential Marathi Cookbook* (2009), which features food from Maharashtra, the state on India's west coast, where I was born. I researched and wrote the book because the region's cuisines had not previously been widely represented in English-language cookbooks. In fact, until the late 2000s, regional Indian food was not much talked about, and I wanted to change the status quo. Saag paneer, chicken tikka, naan, and samosas were delicious and well-known dishes in India and abroad, but they did not represent a huge swath of the country.

My idea was to showcase Maharashtra's rich culinary heritage, some of which I knew about from personal experience. I also wanted to document it for my daughter and others like her who were growing up far from family and roots, with no opportunity to learn from an older generation. And finally, I wanted this book to highlight the vast variety of people in the state, not just my family, whom my previous cookbook had featured.

So I gathered recipes from a long list of contributors—people who represented different Hindu castes (priests, warriors, merchants, and the working class) and those of other religions such as Islam and Christianity, since each community cooks their own versions of Marathi food, influenced by religious dietary laws (I regret that I could not include Marathi Jewish cooking nor tribal food, but those are on my list for the next book). I interviewed my contributors to learn more about the recipes they shared and also researched Maharashtra's cultural and culinary history.

Kombdi, jira ghalun is a simple, aromatic recipe shared by my friend Anuradha Samant. Anuradha is a native of Kolhapur, 145 miles south of Pune, where I was born. Anuradha belongs to the warrior (Maratha) community, which eats meat (not all castes do). The Marathas are known for elaborately created, deeply flavored meat dishes. This recipe is an exception in that it is not elaborate and can easily be made on a weeknight. But it proves the rule that braising meats produces deeply nuanced flavors. The chicken is first marinated in yogurt, garlic, and ginger, and then it is braised in a tomato-onion sauce until it's tender and cooked through.

Unlike north Indian recipes, which often rely on warm spices such as cinnamon, cardamom, and cloves to add aromatic flavor, this dish calls for only cumin. But the chicken is not braised with the ground spice. Cumin is added just before serving so that its smokiness adds fresh top notes to both the chicken and the sauce. Cook drumsticks for a quick, fragrant, oh-so-satisfying dinner, served with rice or Indian bread. If you use chicken breasts and cut them into bite-size pieces, this recipe makes a great cocktail snack. Onion raita is an easy, cooling accompaniment.

—KAUMUDI MARATHÉ, *America's Test Kitchen Books*

Kombdi, Jira Ghalun (Cumin-Scented Chicken)
SERVES 4 TO 6

We strongly prefer toasting and grinding our own whole cumin seeds for this recipe, but you can substitute 7 teaspoons of ground cumin if you like. If you're using ground cumin, toast it in an 8-inch skillet over medium heat until it's fragrant, about 1½ minutes. This recipe can also be made with 2¾ pounds of boneless, skinless chicken breasts instead of the drumsticks, if preferred. If you're using chicken breasts, cook them until the meat registers 160 degrees in step 6 (18 to 25 minutes). If you enjoy spicy food, use the full 1½ teaspoons of cayenne. For a milder version, reduce the amount of cayenne to ½ teaspoon. Serve with rice or Indian bread and extra yogurt or our Onion Raita (recipe follows).

3⅓ cups water, divided
 ¼ cup plain whole-milk yogurt, plus extra for serving
 8 garlic cloves, smashed and peeled
 1 (2-inch) piece ginger, peeled and chopped coarse
1½ tablespoons paprika
 1 tablespoon table salt, divided
1½ teaspoons cayenne pepper
 2 tomatoes, cored and chopped coarse
2¾ pounds chicken drumsticks (about 8 large drumsticks)
 3 tablespoons cumin seeds
 ¼ cup vegetable oil
 1 large onion, chopped fine
 ½ cup fresh cilantro leaves

1. Process ⅓ cup water, yogurt, garlic, ginger, paprika, 2 teaspoons salt, and cayenne in blender until smooth, about 2 minutes, scraping down sides of blender jar as needed. Transfer yogurt marinade to bowl.

2. Process tomatoes in now-empty blender until coarsely pureed, about 5 seconds. Transfer to second bowl.

3. Add chicken to bowl with yogurt marinade and toss to coat, rubbing marinade into chicken. Cover and refrigerate for at least 1 hour or up to 24 hours (if marinating longer than 1 hour, cover and refrigerate tomatoes as well).

4. Heat cumin seeds in 8-inch skillet over medium heat, stirring frequently, until fragrant, about 3 minutes. Transfer to spice grinder or mortar and pestle and grind to powder; set aside.

5. Heat oil in large Dutch oven over medium-high heat until just smoking. Add onion and remaining 1 teaspoon salt and cook until onion is softened, 5 to 7 minutes. Add tomatoes; increase heat to high; and cook until mixture darkens slightly and begins to stick to bottom of pot, 5 to 7 minutes.

6. Add chicken, along with any marinade left in bowl, and remaining 3 cups water and bring to boil. Cover; reduce heat to medium-low; and simmer, stirring occasionally, until chicken registers at least 175 degrees, 25 to 30 minutes.

7. Using tongs, transfer chicken to large plate. Increase heat to high and cook, uncovered and stirring occasionally, until sauce is thickened and reduced to about 2¾ cups, 12 to 15 minutes. Stir cumin into sauce. Add chicken back to pot and stir to coat with sauce. Serve, sprinkled with cilantro and passing extra yogurt.

Onion Raita
SERVES 4 TO 6 (MAKES ABOUT 1¼ CUPS)

This recipe is best with plain, whole-milk yogurt. Do not use low-fat, nonfat, or Greek yogurt in this raita.

 1 cup plain whole-milk yogurt
 ¾ teaspoon ground cumin
 ½ teaspoon sugar
 ½ teaspoon table salt
 ⅓ cup finely chopped onion
 1 tablespoon chopped fresh cilantro

Whisk yogurt, cumin, sugar, and salt in bowl until thoroughly combined. Stir in onion and cilantro. Season with salt to taste.

GRILLED CHICKEN SATAY

✓ **WHY THIS RECIPE WORKS** Malaysian chicken satay (satay ayam) features pieces of chicken coated in a deeply fragrant paste, skewered, and charred on the grill. We used fatty, collagen-rich chicken thighs because they cooked up juicier and more tender than white meat and could stay on the grill longer to pick up flavorful charring without drying out. Cutting the chicken into wide strips (instead of chunks) and stretching them between two skewers created more surface area for coating with the paste and for charring. Loads of lemongrass, ginger, and galangal, plus garlic, shallots, pepper flakes, spices, and a touch of sugar made for a complex, aromatic paste that developed savory character when charred. Briefly microwaving the paste deactivated the enzyme in ginger that makes meat mushy. We used a portion of the paste as the base for our dipping sauce, browning it deeply to soften the aromatics' raw edge and fibrous texture and to develop savory depth. We then simmered it with ground peanuts, water, tamarind, and sugar to create a subtle sweet-tangy undertone that added complexity; simmering also thickened the mixture.

Imagine the most flavorful bite of grilled chicken you've ever had: robustly seasoned, gorgeously charred, and crisp at the edges. That's what you get with every bite of satay, one of the world's proudest examples of meat on a stick and quintessential street-food fare all over Southeast Asia. The proteins and flavors vary from region to region, but the gist is more or less the same across the board: Small pieces of chicken, pork, beef, goat, or various types of seafood are coated in a flavorful

NOTES FROM THE TEST KITCHEN

STREAMLINING MALAYSIAN SATAY

The aromatics and spices that give Malaysian satay its distinctly fresh, herbal, and savory profile set it apart from other satay styles. Many of these ingredients are used in both the paste that coats the meat and the peanut-based dipping sauce that accompanies it, so we simplified the prep work by grinding a big batch of the paste in the food processor (or in a mortar and pestle) and using a portion of it as a fragrant foundation for the dipping sauce.

PASTE INGREDIENTS
Lemongrass, shallots, garlic, ginger, galangal, red pepper flakes, coriander, turmeric, cumin, brown sugar

PEANUT SAUCE INGREDIENTS
Tamarind paste, peanuts, brown sugar

liquid or paste; threaded onto skewers; and grilled hot and fast and very close to the coals so that almost every inch of their surfaces singes and picks up savory, smoky grill flavor. As soon as the food comes off the fire, it's embellished with a condiment—often a potent dipping sauce—that ups its already strong appeal.

Two of the most familiar versions of chicken satay are native to Thailand and Malaysia, but they're notably different. Whereas Thai satay tends to be relatively sweet and rich thanks to coconut milk and sugar both in the paste that coats the meat and in the peanut-based dipping sauce, the Malaysian version skews more herbal and savory. Its paste typically includes loads of fragrant lemongrass, ginger, galangal, garlic, and shallots; dried chiles; and spices such as turmeric, coriander, and cumin. And while the dipping sauce is also peanut-based, it's usually leaner and less sweet.

That vibrant, herb-forward profile is precisely what I find so appealing about the Malaysian kind (called satay ayam), especially the savory depth that develops when the aromatics char. But as with any grilled meat, it can be tricky to deeply brown the exterior before the interior dries out. I wanted to look carefully at that challenge and at the prep work: Pounding the large volume of aromatics and spices into a paste in a mortar and pestle requires multiple batches, and many recipes call for marinating the meat in the paste for hours. Maybe there were ways to shortcut those steps and make this dish.

Satay ayam can be made with either white or dark meat, but I pivoted directly to boneless, skinless thighs. Their abundant collagen and fat would keep the meat succulent over the fire while the surface browned and crisped.

I cut 2 pounds of thighs into chunks, coated them in a paste that I'd pounded together, and let the meat marinate for a few hours. Then I skewered the chicken and set it over a hot fire so that the meat would char quickly. And it did—but only in the few spots where it made direct contact with the grate. The chunks didn't offer much surface area, and they spun around when I flipped the kebabs.

Going forward, I cut each thigh into wide strips that created loads of surface area for coating with the paste and charring. Then I threaded the strips onto double skewers so that the meat stretched over the grate and stayed secure. I also brushed both sides of the meat with oil to prevent the paste from sticking to the grate. Within 10 minutes, the chicken was nicely browned with deep char marks—but its surface was downright mushy.

GRILLED CHICKEN SATAY

After some thought, I recognized the culprit: An enzyme in the ginger called zingibain had broken down the meat's surface proteins. My first instinct was to eliminate the marinating time, since we know that marinades don't penetrate much beyond the surface of meat anyway. But the mushy texture persisted even when I coated the meat just before grilling it, so I took a more radical approach and microwaved the paste for 1½ minutes before applying it. The heat deactivated the enzyme, meaning I could coat every inch of the chicken with the paste without compromising its texture. In fact, deactivating that enzyme allowed me to apply the paste ahead of time and store the chicken in the refrigerator until I was ready to grill.

A mortar and pestle is my go-to tool for pounding aromatics into a uniform paste, but given the large volume required for this recipe, it was easier to use the food processor. I minced the lemongrass and galangal and sliced the ginger into coins before grinding them in the food processor with shallots, garlic, and red pepper flakes (they mimicked the heat of whole dried chiles but didn't require stemming and seeding). Adding a few tablespoons of water and a little oil to the mix helped the paste come together.

Next I studied up on the peanut sauce. In addition to being leaner and less sweet than Thai satay sauce, this style is coarser and more rustic; underscored by a fruity, sour tang from tamarind; packed with many of the same aromatics that are in the paste; and often briefly simmered to mellow any sharp flavors and reduce the mixture to a thick consistency.

That overlap between the paste and sauce ingredients seemed like an obvious place to further streamline my method, so going forward I simply made a bigger batch of the paste and set aside ⅓ cup of it for the sauce. The first step was to brown it in a little oil, and after a few tries I discovered that getting it good and dark—essentially creating a rich fond—gave the final sauce nice savory depth. Then I added an equal amount of peanuts (dry-roasted) that I'd coarsely ground in the food processor, along with water and a tablespoon each of tamarind paste and brown sugar, and gently simmered the mixture until it thickened. I seasoned it with salt and had a taste: Fragrant, nutty, and bright, it was the ideal complement to the smoky, savory chicken, and it was so well-balanced that I was tempted to eat it by the spoonful.

In fact, the whole package is so flavor-packed, flexible to prepare, and fast to cook that it's become one of my default grilled chicken dishes. No doubt, it will become the same for you.

—STEVE DUNN, *Cook's Illustrated*

Grilled Chicken Satay

SERVES 4 TO 6

You will need eight 12-inch metal skewers for this recipe. If galangal is unavailable, increase the ginger to one 1½-inch piece. The aromatic paste can also be prepared using a mortar and pestle. For a spicier dish, use the larger amount of red pepper flakes. Lime juice can be substituted for the tamarind paste.

AROMATIC PASTE

- 2 lemongrass stalks, trimmed to bottom 6 inches
- 3 shallots, chopped (⅔ cup)
- 3 tablespoons water
- 1 tablespoon vegetable oil
- 1 tablespoon packed brown sugar
- 3 garlic cloves, chopped
- 1 (1-inch) piece galangal, peeled and minced
- 1 (1-inch) piece ginger, peeled and sliced into ⅛-inch-thick coins
- 2 teaspoons table salt
- 1 teaspoon ground turmeric
- ½–¾ teaspoon red pepper flakes
- ½ teaspoon ground coriander
- ½ teaspoon ground cumin

PEANUT SAUCE

- ⅓ cup dry-roasted peanuts
- 2 tablespoons vegetable oil
- ¾ cup water, plus extra as needed
- 1 tablespoon tamarind paste
- 1 tablespoon packed brown sugar

CHICKEN

- 2 pounds boneless, skinless chicken thighs, trimmed and cut crosswise into 1- to 1½-inch-wide strips
- 2 tablespoons vegetable oil

1. FOR THE AROMATIC PASTE: Halve lemongrass lengthwise and, using meat pounder, lightly crush on cutting board to soften. Mince lemongrass and transfer to food processor. Add shallots, water, oil, sugar, garlic, galangal, ginger, salt, turmeric, and pepper flakes and process until uniform paste forms, about 2 minutes, scraping down sides of bowl as necessary. Measure out ⅓ cup paste and set aside. Transfer remaining paste to bowl and stir in coriander and cumin. Cover bowl and microwave paste for 1½ minutes, stirring halfway through microwaving. Transfer bowl to refrigerator and let paste cool while preparing sauce.

2. FOR THE PEANUT SAUCE: Place peanuts in now-empty processor and process until coarsely ground, about 15 seconds. Heat oil and reserved ⅓ cup paste in medium saucepan over medium-low heat until fond begins to form on bottom of saucepan and paste starts to darken, about 5 minutes. Stir in water, tamarind, sugar, and peanuts and bring to boil, scraping up any browned bits. Reduce heat to maintain gentle simmer and cook, stirring occasionally, until sauce is reduced to about 1 cup, 8 to 10 minutes. Season with salt to taste, cover, and set aside.

3. FOR THE CHICKEN: Add chicken to cooled paste and toss to combine. Thread chicken onto 4 sets of two 12-inch metal skewers. (Hold 2 skewers 1 inch apart and thread chicken onto both skewers at once so strips of chicken are perpendicular to skewers.) Do not crowd skewers; each set of skewers should hold 7 to 8 pieces of chicken. Transfer kebabs to large plate and refrigerate while preparing grill. (Kebabs can be refrigerated for up to 4 hours.)

4A. FOR A CHARCOAL GRILL: Open bottom vent completely. Light large chimney starter mounded with charcoal briquettes (7 quarts). When top coals are partially covered with ash, pour evenly over grill. Set cooking grate in place, cover, and open lid vent completely. Heat grill until hot, about 5 minutes.

4B. FOR A GAS GRILL: Turn all burners to high; cover; and heat grill until hot, about 15 minutes. Turn all burners to medium.

5. Clean and oil cooking grate. Brush both sides of kebabs with oil. Place kebabs on grill and cook (covered if using gas) until browned and char marks appear on first side, about 5 minutes. Using large metal spatula, gently release chicken from grill; flip; and continue to cook until chicken registers 175 to 180 degrees, 3 to 5 minutes longer. Transfer to large platter. Gently reheat peanut sauce, thinning with extra water, 1 tablespoon at a time, to desired consistency. Serve chicken, passing peanut sauce separately.

LARD-FRIED CHICKEN

✔ **WHY THIS RECIPE WORKS** In Indiana kitchens, chicken pieces are seasoned with salt and plenty of black pepper, dunked in a light coating of flour, and then cooked in bubbling lard. The result is fried chicken that is crisp (not craggy) in texture on the outside, superjuicy on the inside, and uniquely savory. To make our own version with a light yet substantially crisp crust, we dipped the chicken pieces in flour, then water, and then back in flour. For fast frying, we cooked the chicken all in one batch. Keeping the lard between 300 and 325 degrees ensured that the coating on the chicken became golden brown all over without developing any off-flavors (which can happen when lard is heated to higher temperatures). Draining the fried chicken on paper towels wicked off any excess lard to make for juicy, not greasy, chicken.

Frying chicken pieces in lard, aka rendered pork fat, is hardly a newfangled idea. Back in 1836, Mary Rudolph's cookbook, *The Virginia Housewife*, included a recipe for "Fried Chickens" that starts: "Cut [the chickens] up as for the fricassee, dredge them well with flour, sprinkle them with salt, put them into a good quantity of boiling lard, and fry them a light brown . . . "

Rudolph wasn't the only one calling for frying chicken in lard. At the time, lard was more readily available to cooks in many regions of the country than other fats. And even with the advent of more commonly available frying mediums, cooks across the United States—including a personal hero of mine, chef and cookbook author Edna Lewis—stuck to lard for the rich flavor and consistent results it produced.

But you don't see lard called for as a frying medium much in contemporary cookbooks. Over the course of the 20th century, the fat fell out of fashion. This happened in large part as a result of health reports—many of which have since been discredited—that denounced animal fats.

But in many kitchens, in the South and Midwest especially, this old-school method has survived. Our inspiration here comes from Indiana.

In this recipe, chicken pieces are seasoned with salt and plenty of freshly ground black pepper before being dunked in a very light coating of flour—unlike what's called for in typical batter-fried chicken recipes, this coating is a bit more delicate and restrained.

LARD-FRIED CHICKEN

After the pieces are cooked in a pot full of bubbling lard, they emerge supremely flavorful, with tender, juicy interiors and crispy, supersavory exteriors. While the lard doesn't make it taste overtly porky, it adds a big, bold savory flavor that makes this one of our favorite fried chicken recipes ever.

Even better: It all cooks in a single batch, which means supper is on the table even faster. Just give it a few minutes to cool down, so you don't burn your tongue.

—MORGAN BOLLING, *Cook's Country*

Lard-Fried Chicken

SERVES 4

Use a Dutch oven that holds 6 quarts or more for this recipe. We developed this recipe using John Morrell Snow Cap Lard. You can substitute 1 quart of peanut or vegetable oil, if desired, although the taste will be different. If you're breaking down a whole chicken for this dish, a 4½-pound chicken would yield the necessary pieces. If you're using table salt, reduce the amount by half. Before taking the temperature of the chicken pieces, take them out of the oil and place them on a plate; this is the safest way and provides the most accurate reading.

3 pounds bone-in chicken pieces (2 split breasts cut in half crosswise, 2 drumsticks, and 2 thighs), trimmed
5 teaspoons kosher salt, divided
1 tablespoon pepper
1½ cups all-purpose flour
1½ teaspoons baking powder
4 cups water
2 pounds lard

1. Sprinkle chicken all over with 2 teaspoons salt and pepper. Whisk flour, baking powder, and remaining 1 tablespoon salt in large bowl until combined. Pour water into medium bowl.

2. Working with 1 piece of chicken at a time, dredge chicken in flour mixture, shaking off excess; dunk in water, letting excess drip off; then dredge again in flour mixture, pressing to adhere. Transfer to large plate and refrigerate for at least 30 minutes or up to 2 hours.

3. Set wire rack in rimmed baking sheet and line half of rack with triple layer of paper towels. Melt lard in large Dutch oven and heat over medium-high heat to 350 degrees.

4. Add all chicken to lard, skin side down, in single layer (some slight overlap is OK) so pieces are mostly submerged. Fry for 10 minutes, rotating pot 180 degrees after 5 minutes. Adjust burner, if necessary, to maintain oil temperature between 300 and 325 degrees.

5. Carefully flip chicken and continue to fry until golden brown and breasts register 160 degrees and drumsticks/thighs register 175 degrees, 5 to 9 minutes longer. Transfer chicken to paper towel–lined side of prepared rack and drain for about 10 seconds per side, then move to unlined side of rack. Let cool for 10 minutes. Serve.

ORANGE CHICKEN

WHY THIS RECIPE WORKS We wanted crispy, juicy boneless chicken tossed in a sweet-sour orange sauce, but we didn't want to work all night and dirty up every dish in the house to get there. So we looked for ways to streamline the recipe. Lots of recipes out there call for marinating the chicken pieces before breading and frying them, but we found that we could skip the marinade and rely on the potent, sticky orange sauce to deliver flavor instead. Looking for a way to bread the chicken pieces that didn't involve using several bowls and covering the kitchen in cornstarch, we turned to a mess-free technique we've used in the past: shaking the chicken pieces with the dredge ingredients in a large paper bag. After experimenting, we found that we needed only 1 quart of oil for the perfect results.

For me, the appeal of orange chicken is undeniable. Crispy fried bits of juicy boneless chicken tossed in a vibrant, sweet-sour, slightly spicy orange sauce—what's not to like? According to Panda Express cofounder Andrew Cherng, orange chicken was invented by chef Andy Kao in Hawaii in 1987. The layers of flavor that permeated the satisfying dish have made it a favorite ever since.

On a recent evening in my tiny kitchen, I looked around halfway through cooking a batch of orange chicken and found that I'd used nearly every mixing bowl in my cupboard and covered the entirety of my limited counter space with prep equipment and cornstarch—and I hadn't even begun to fry.

The end product—savory pieces of chicken tossed in a beautifully complex citrus sauce—tasted really good, but I wondered if I could find a way to make it without my wife (and my cat) looking askance at the mess.

I examined my working recipe and started asking some hard questions and doing a bit more testing to find out the answers. I'd been marinating the chicken and then patting it dry before coating and frying it, but after making a batch without the marinating step, I didn't miss it in the final dish. I would rely on the sauce to deliver the flavor.

What I really wanted was a way to coat the chicken with a mixture that would fry up crispy and crunchy but that didn't involve my dirtying several bowls and covering my kitchen in cornstarch. I turned to a technique we've used in the past for coating small pieces of chicken: shaking them together with the dredge ingredients in a large paper shopping bag.

After experimenting with different amounts of oil, from a couple cups to a couple quarts, I found that just 1 quart of oil (which measured about ¾ inch deep in my Dutch oven) worked perfectly. What's more, the frying oil could be strained and reused several times.

This orange chicken is a winner. The orange juice and zest make the sticky, sweet-and-sour sauce sing; the hot, freshly fried chicken stays crunchy until the end of the meal; and a side of rice soaks up all that lovely sauce, so every bite is vibrant.

—MATTHEW FAIRMAN, *Cook's Country*

Orange Chicken
SERVES 4

If your oranges are small, you may need more than two to yield ¾ cup of juice. The chicken will be somewhat pale when it's fried in step 5; it will get more color when you toss it in the sauce. Serve with rice and steamed broccoli.

SAUCE
- 2 oranges, divided
- ¾ cup chicken broth
- ⅓ cup distilled white vinegar
- ⅓ cup packed brown sugar
- ¼ cup soy sauce
- 2 tablespoons cornstarch
- 3 garlic cloves, minced
- 1 tablespoon grated fresh ginger
- 1 tablespoon sriracha
- 1 tablespoon toasted sesame oil

CHICKEN
- 1½ pounds boneless, skinless chicken thighs, trimmed and cut into 1-inch pieces
- 2 large egg whites
- ½ teaspoon table salt
- 1½ cups cornstarch
- ½ cup all-purpose flour
- 1 teaspoon baking powder
- 1 quart peanut or vegetable oil for frying
- 2 scallions, sliced thin on bias

1. FOR THE SAUCE: Using vegetable peeler, remove eight 2-inch strips of zest from 1 orange. Using rasp-style grater, grate 1½ teaspoons zest from remaining orange. Halve both oranges and squeeze to get ¾ cup juice. Combine orange zest (strips and grated) and juice, broth, vinegar, sugar, soy sauce, cornstarch, garlic, ginger, sriracha, and oil in medium saucepan and whisk to dissolve cornstarch.

2. Bring sauce to simmer over medium-high heat, stirring frequently. Cook until dark brown and thickened, about 2 minutes. Cover and set aside.

3. Combine chicken, egg whites, and salt in bowl. Place cornstarch, flour, and baking powder in double-bagged large paper shopping bag. Roll top of bag to seal and shake gently to combine. Add chicken mixture to cornstarch mixture in bag, roll top of bag to seal, and shake vigorously to thoroughly coat chicken; set aside.

4. Line rimmed baking sheet with triple layer of paper towels. Add oil to large Dutch oven and heat over medium-high heat to 350 degrees.

5. Shake chicken in bag once more. Add half of chicken to hot oil and fry until cooked through (chicken will still be somewhat pale), 4 to 6 minutes, stirring frequently. Adjust burner, if necessary, to maintain oil temperature between 300 and 350 degrees. Using slotted spoon or spider skimmer, transfer fried chicken to prepared sheet. Return oil to 350 degrees and repeat with remaining chicken.

6. Warm sauce over medium heat until simmering, about 1 minute. Toss sauce and chicken in large bowl until chicken is evenly coated. Serve, sprinkling individual portions with scallions.

CAST IRON CHICKEN AND VEGETABLES

✔ WHY THIS RECIPE WORKS We wanted golden, juicy roast chicken and hearty vegetables cooked all in one pan to limit cleanup. First we butterflied a whole chicken, and then we rubbed the skin generously with olive oil. A seasoning mixture of salt, thyme, granulated garlic, and smoked paprika produced a hit of complex flavor with a subtle smokiness. For the side dish, we sprinkled potatoes, fennel, onion, and carrots with the same spice mixture that went on the chicken. We then added them to a hot cast-iron skillet with more olive oil and set the chicken on top. Starting in a preheated cast-iron skillet yielded browned rather than braised vegetables (because the juices from the bird cooked off faster), while butterflying the chicken meant that the white and dark meat cooked through at the same time. Laying the chicken out flat also meant that all the skin was exposed to the hot air in the oven. In just an hour, the chicken was cooked perfectly, and all the skin was golden and crispy. For a final touch, we stirred together a bright sauce while the chicken roasted.

What could be simpler or more comforting than a golden, crispy-skinned, juicy chicken perched atop a heap of hearty, schmaltzy roasted vegetables? When I started to develop this recipe, I expected it to be a snap. But for such a seemingly straightforward idea, it's surprising how fast it can go sideways on you. I first threw together a mixture of salt, pepper, and fresh thyme; rubbed a whole chicken generously with olive oil (to help the spice mixture stick and the skin crisp); and then tossed my favorite vegetables for roasting—potatoes, fennel, onion, and carrots—with the rest of the spice mixture and a bit more oil. I added the vegetables to an ovensafe skillet; plopped the bird on top; and put it all into the oven to roast, eager to taste the delicious results.

The results were, well, underwhelming. My chicken needed more flavor, and more important, by the time the dark meat had cooked fully, the temperature of the white meat had rocketed well past 160 degrees, turning it dry and chalky. And rather than the well-browned roasted vegetables I had hoped for, I ended up with something more like a soupy vegetable braise. Adding to my disappointment, the skin on the chicken thighs—which had been partially covered by some of the vegetables—came out pale and soggy. The nicest thing I could say about that meal was that, with only one pan, at least the cleanup was easy.

I started making adjustments. I figured that nestling my chicken into a pile of cold vegetables on top of a cold heavy-bottomed skillet was a big reason that my chicken took so long to cook (nearly an hour and 45 minutes) and that the juices never had time to cook off.

So for my next test, I used a preheated cast-iron skillet instead and decided to butterfly my bird. This was a huge improvement. Starting in the hot skillet yielded browned rather than braised vegetables (because the chicken juices cooked off), and laying the chicken out flat meant that the dark meat cooked through faster and that all the skin was exposed to the hot air in the oven. In just an hour, the breast meat registered 160 degrees, all the skin was golden and crispy, and the dark meat was fully cooked and tender.

All I needed for the final touches were a more interesting spice mixture and a vibrant fresh sauce to contrast the savory roasted chicken and vegetables. Adding granulated garlic and smoked paprika to the spice mix on the chicken produced an instant hit of complex flavor with a subtle smokiness. For the sauce, a bright parsley, lemon, and garlic dressing was easy enough to stir together while the chicken roasted, and it proved to be just the thing to make this comforting dinner truly memorable.

—MATTHEW FAIRMAN, *Cook's Country*

CAST IRON CHICKEN AND VEGETABLES

Cast Iron Chicken and Vegetables

SERVES 4

You can make this recipe in a traditional stainless-steel or ovensafe nonstick skillet, but it will take the potatoes longer to brown in step 7. Be sure to buy potatoes measuring 1 to 2 inches in diameter. If you're using table salt, cut the amounts in half and distribute the spice mixture accordingly. If you can't find a 1-pound bulb of fennel, buy several smaller ones. The weight of the trimmed fennel going into the skillet should be about 8 ounces.

SPICE MIXTURE
- 4 teaspoons kosher salt
- 1 tablespoon chopped fresh thyme
- 1 teaspoon granulated garlic
- 1 teaspoon pepper
- ½ teaspoon smoked paprika

CHICKEN AND VEGETABLES
- 1 (3½- to 4-pound) whole chicken, giblets discarded
- 2 tablespoons extra-virgin olive oil, divided
- 1 pound small Yukon Gold potatoes, unpeeled, halved
- 1 (1-pound) fennel bulb, stalks discarded, bulb halved through root end and cut into 1-inch wedges
- 1 red onion, cut through root end into 1-inch wedges
- 2 carrots, peeled, halved lengthwise, then halved crosswise

SAUCE
- 3 tablespoons extra-virgin olive oil
- 2 tablespoons chopped fresh parsley
- 1½ tablespoons lemon juice
- 1 garlic clove, minced
- 1 teaspoon chopped fresh thyme
- 1 teaspoon kosher salt
- ¼ teaspoon pepper
- ¼ teaspoon smoked paprika

1. FOR THE SPICE MIXTURE: Combine all ingredients in bowl and set aside.

2. FOR THE CHICKEN AND VEGETABLES: Adjust oven rack to middle position and heat oven to 425 degrees. With chicken breast side down on cutting board, use kitchen shears to cut through bones on either side of backbone; discard backbone or reserve for another use. Flip chicken and press on breastbone to flatten. Tuck wingtips underneath breast. Pat chicken dry with paper towels. Cut ½-inch-deep slit into drumstick-thigh joint on each side of chicken.

3. Sprinkle underside of chicken with 1 tablespoon spice mixture. Flip chicken and rub skin with 1 tablespoon oil. Sprinkle chicken skin with 5 teaspoons spice mixture.

4. Heat 12-inch cast-iron skillet over medium heat for 5 minutes. Add remaining 1 tablespoon oil to skillet and heat until just smoking. Add potatoes to skillet, cut side down. Add fennel, onion, and carrots to skillet, allowing them to come into contact with bottom of skillet as much as space permits; some vegetables will have to sit on top of potatoes. Sprinkle vegetables with remaining spice mixture.

5. Place chicken on top of vegetables, skin side up. Transfer skillet to oven and roast until breast registers 160 degrees and drumsticks/thighs register at least 175 degrees, about 1 hour.

6. FOR THE SAUCE: Meanwhile, whisk all ingredients together in bowl; set aside.

7. Transfer chicken to carving board. Return skillet with vegetables to oven and roast until potatoes are browned on bottom, about 15 minutes.

8. Carve chicken, spoon sauce over top, and serve with vegetables.

NOTES FROM THE TEST KITCHEN

CHICKEN PREP: BUTTERFLY AND SMASH

1. With chicken breast side down on cutting board, use kitchen shears to cut through bones on either side of backbone; remove backbone and save for stock.

2. Flip chicken, then use your palm to forcibly press down on breastbone to flatten.

3. Tuck wingtips underneath breast, pat chicken dry, and cut ½-inch-deep slit into joint between thigh and drumstick on each side.

ONE-PAN TURKEY BREAST AND STUFFING WITH POMEGRANATE-PARSLEY SAUCE

✓ **WHY THIS RECIPE WORKS** We were after a holiday-worthy one-pan turkey and stuffing, not just to cut down on dirty dishes but also to create a stuffing packed with savory poultry flavor. Using a 6-pound turkey breast (instead of a whole bird) made for easier carving and eliminated one of the hardest parts of cooking turkey: trying to sync the cooking times for white and dark meat. For an homage to classic Thanksgiving stuffing, we used a combination of sage, thyme, onion, wine, and chicken broth; hot Italian sausage added deep meaty savoriness. Instead of small cubes of sandwich bread, we opted for larger chunks of ciabatta; the bigger pieces retained some chew even as they soaked up the flavors from the turkey and sausage. We roasted the breast on top of the stuffing and, when it was done, removed it and returned just the stuffing to the oven to create a crisp top that nicely contrasted with the chewy chunks of bread below. For a final holiday flourish, we stirred together a vibrant, bright, and gorgeous sauce with pomegranate seeds and parsley.

Thanksgiving is my favorite holiday. But even as a professional chef, I've had my fair share of near meltdowns trying to juggle the cooking, hosting, and—let's face it—guests who don't always get along. So I'm all for any recipe that streamlines my efforts. This led me to my goal this year: a holiday-worthy turkey and stuffing cooked together in one pan. Not only would this save me from cleaning extra dishes, but the turkey would slowly render its fat into the stuffing below and infuse it with savory poultry flavor.

I opted to use a bone-in turkey breast rather than a whole turkey. A 6-pound breast is easier to carve than a whole bird and is plenty to feed about eight to 10 diners—or just four with lots of leftovers for sandwiches.

Plus, by using a breast, I didn't have to deal with one of the hardest parts of cooking turkey: trying to sync the cooking times for white and dark meat. And opting for a bone-in breast, as opposed to boneless, made for more-flavorful drippings for the stuffing below.

Given my already nontraditional approach, I wanted to tweak the stuffing by making it both more rustic and more flavorful. The combination of sage, thyme, onion,

wine, and chicken broth was an homage to classic Thanksgiving flavors and a perfect jumping-off point. Hot Italian sausage added deep meaty savoriness and a bit of heat (which I augmented with red pepper flakes). And instead of small cubes of sandwich bread, I opted for large chunks of ciabatta; the bigger pieces retained some chew even as they soaked up the flavors from the turkey and sausage.

I roasted the turkey breast on top of the stuffing and, when the breast was done, I removed it and returned just the stuffing to the oven to create a crisp top that nicely contrasted with the chewy chunks of bread below.

For a final holiday flourish, I stirred together a vibrant, bright, and gorgeous sauce with pomegranate seeds and parsley. (Don't worry, I'll still serve gravy on the side.)

—MORGAN BOLLING, *Cook's Country*

One-Pan Turkey Breast and Stuffing with Pomegranate-Parsley Sauce
SERVES 8 TO 10

The salted turkey needs to be refrigerated for at least 2 hours before it's cooked. If you can't find a loaf of ciabatta, you can substitute 2 pounds of another rustic, mild-tasting white bread. Do not use sourdough here; its flavor is too assertive.

TURKEY
- 1½ tablespoons kosher salt
- 1 tablespoon pepper
- 1 tablespoon minced fresh thyme
- 1 (5- to 7-pound) bone-in turkey breast, trimmed

STUFFING
- ½ cup extra-virgin olive oil
- 3 cups chopped onion
- 1¾ teaspoons kosher salt, divided
- 6 garlic cloves, minced
- 3 cups chicken broth
- ⅓ cup dry white wine
- 2 tablespoons minced fresh sage
- 1 tablespoon minced fresh thyme
- ¼ teaspoon red pepper flakes
- 2 pounds ciabatta, cut into 1-inch cubes (about 20 cups)
- 1 pound hot Italian sausage, casings removed
- 1½ cups coarsely chopped fresh parsley

ONE-PAN TURKEY BREAST AND STUFFING WITH POMEGRANATE-PARSLEY SAUCE

SAUCE

¾ cup chopped fresh parsley

¾ cup pomegranate seeds

½ cup extra-virgin olive oil

1 shallot, minced

2 tablespoons lemon juice

2 garlic cloves, minced

¾ teaspoon kosher salt

1. FOR THE TURKEY: Combine salt, pepper, and thyme in bowl. Place turkey on large plate and pat dry with paper towels. Sprinkle all over with salt mixture. Refrigerate, uncovered, for at least 2 hours or up to 24 hours.

2. FOR THE STUFFING: Adjust oven rack to lower-middle position and heat oven to 325 degrees. Spray large heavy-duty roasting pan with vegetable oil spray, then add oil to pan. Heat oil in roasting pan over medium heat until shimmering. Add onion and ¼ teaspoon salt and cook until onion is golden brown, about 10 minutes. Add garlic and cook until fragrant, about 30 seconds.

3. Off heat, stir in broth, wine, sage, thyme, pepper flakes, and remaining 1½ teaspoons salt, scraping up any browned bits. Add bread and, using tongs or your hands, toss until bread is evenly coated. Break sausage into ¾-inch chunks and toss with bread mixture to combine.

4. Nestle turkey, skin side up, into stuffing in center of roasting pan. Roast until thickest part of turkey registers 160 degrees, 2¼ to 2¾ hours.

5. FOR THE SAUCE: Meanwhile, combine all ingredients in bowl; set aside.

6. Transfer turkey to carving board, skin side up, and let rest, uncovered, for at least 30 minutes or up to 1 hour.

7. Meanwhile, stir stuffing in roasting pan. Return pan to oven and cook until top of stuffing looks golden brown and is evenly dry, 10 to 15 minutes.

8. Remove breast meat from bone and slice thin crosswise. Toss parsley with stuffing in roasting pan. Arrange turkey over stuffing in pan. Drizzle with sauce. Serve, passing remaining sauce separately.

TO USE A DISPOSABLE ROASTING PAN: Heat oil in 12-inch skillet over medium heat until shimmering. Add onion and ¼ teaspoon salt and cook until onion is golden brown, about 10 minutes. Add garlic and cook until fragrant, about 30 seconds. Off heat, stir in broth, wine, sage, thyme, pepper flakes, and remaining 1½ teaspoons salt, scraping up any browned bits. Transfer mixture to 16 by 12-inch disposable aluminum roasting pan. Add bread and sausage as described in step 3. Place disposable pan on rimmed baking sheet before roasting for added stability. Increase roasting time for turkey in step 4 to 2½ to 3 hours. Increase cooking time for stuffing in step 7 to 30 to 35 minutes.

TURKEY THIGH CONFIT WITH CITRUS-MUSTARD SAUCE

✓ **WHY THIS RECIPE WORKS** Before refrigeration, confit was used as a simple and effective way to prolong the shelf life of foods, including duck or goose parts. The poultry was cured in salt and then gently poached in its own fat before being buried beneath the fat and stored in an airtight crock. At serving time, all that was needed was a blast of heat to crisp the skin. Today, all types of dark-meat poultry, pork, and game are given the treatment (tender white meat breaks down too much with this method), though regardless of the protein, duck fat is the traditional choice for the poaching step. For silky, supple, evenly seasoned, full-flavored turkey confit, we started by processing onion, salt, pepper, sugar, and thyme in a food processor. Next, we coated the turkey thighs in this paste and let them cure for at least four days. As the thighs sat, the salt, sugar, and some water-soluble compounds in the aromatics gave the turkey a deeply savory flavor. We rinsed away the cure and oven-poached the thighs in duck fat until they were tender. The thighs could then be refrigerated for up to six days or immediately browned and served with our bright and tangy citrus-mustard sauce.

I know a lot about turkey—I've roasted hundreds of birds while developing two previous recipes for *Cook's Illustrated*. I'm adept at keeping the delicate breast meat moist while ensuring that the longer-cooking legs and thighs turn tender. I have tricks for seasoning the flesh all the way to the bone, producing crackling brown skin, and maximizing the flavors of herbs and spices. But if I really wanted to wow you with a single unadorned bite—no drizzle of gravy, no sprinkle of flake salt, no dollop of cranberry sauce—I wouldn't bother with any of those techniques. I'd make turkey confit.

The term "confit" is derived from the French verb "confire," which means "to preserve." Before refrigeration, confit was used as a simple and effective way to prolong the shelf life of foods, including duck or goose parts. The poultry was cured in salt and then gently poached in its own fat before being buried beneath the fat and stored in an airtight crock. At serving time, all that was needed was a blast of heat to crisp the skin. Today, all types of dark-meat poultry, pork, and game are given the treatment (tender white meat breaks down too much with this method), though regardless of the protein, duck fat is a classic choice for the poaching step.

But the most important thing you need to know about confit is that its benefits go far beyond preservation. In fact, the method is a near miracle for turkey, producing satisfyingly dense, silky meat and concentrated savory flavor with very little effort. In other words, Thanksgiving dinner just got a lot better.

I decided to work with bone-in, skin-on turkey thighs, since turkey drumsticks have multiple tendons that can be unwieldy to navigate during carving. Curing the thighs would be similar to brining or salting; it would just involve more time and a higher concentration of salt. But there's no standard approach: In my research, I came across a wide variety of times and salt amounts.

After several experiments, I landed on a four-day cure using 5 teaspoons of table salt for 4 pounds of thighs. Shorter cures didn't give the salt enough time to fully penetrate, producing thighs that were salty at the exterior and underseasoned near the bone.

When the curing time was up, I rinsed the salt from the thighs, patted them dry, and slowly oven-poached them in 6 cups of duck fat along with bay leaves and a head of garlic. (A 250-degree oven was preferable to the stovetop since it didn't require babysitting. Sous vide cooking is also a great option.) After an hour, the thighs were hovering in the 140-degree range, which allowed their collagen to break down into gelatin. At the 3½-hour mark, the thighs were tender, so I transferred them to a foil-lined baking sheet, cranked the oven up to 500 degrees, and slid them in. Fifteen minutes later, the thighs were beautifully browned and the meat was evenly and deeply seasoned, with a firm, dense texture.

Seasonings were my next consideration. When salting or brining meat, we don't normally add extra flavorings, because they take too long to penetrate the flesh. But with a cure, water-soluble ingredients actually

have time to travel deep inside, so many recipes recommend mixing some combination of fresh herbs (parsley or thyme), spices (black pepper, allspice, or juniper berries), and alliums (onion, garlic, or shallots) with the salt.

To help everything stick to the thighs and to ensure even distribution, I processed the salt with chopped onion, fresh thyme leaves, and black pepper, plus a touch of sugar for complexity. I increased the salt to 2½ tablespoons because the onions would capture some of it, preventing it from seasoning the turkey's interior. I spread a portion of the green-and-black-flecked mixture in a baking dish, arranged the thighs in the dish, and packed the remaining mixture on top before refrigerating the assembly for four days. (After a few more tests, I concluded that for the sake of convenience, the thighs could sit for up to six days.)

When I cooked the thighs, I was delighted to find that the aromatics had worked their way into the turkey, giving it a rich, deeply savory taste; the sugar rounded out the flavors. This was far better than the salt-only turkey. In fact, it was the finest turkey I'd ever eaten. A colleague described it best, proclaiming, "It tastes like turkey, gravy, and stuffing all in one delicious bite!"

The turkey's flavor was top-notch, but I couldn't help wishing that the meat were a little more moist. I had

NOTES FROM THE TEST KITCHEN

WHY YOU SHOULD INVEST IN DUCK FAT

Some confit recipes call for vegetable oil or chicken fat instead of duck fat, and we found that all three fats produce confits that brown beautifully and taste similar—even though the fats taste very different on their own. That's because the meat doesn't absorb fat during the confit process; it emerges with just a bare coating on its surface. But I still recommend using duck fat (chicken is my second choice) if you can swing it. The fat absorbs flavors from the meat as it cooks, making it even more complex-tasting, and I find duck fat to be particularly delicious. The upshot is that you end up with a fantastic by-product that can be reused in a variety of ways. Strain the leftover fat; freeze it; and then use it as the fat for gravy or to make more confit, sauté vegetables, or drizzle over a simple soup for depth.

TURKEY THIGH CONFIT WITH CITRUS-MUSTARD SAUCE

noticed a thin stream of bubbles rising through the poaching fat from the thighs as they cooked, indicating that moisture was escaping the meat. Would the turkey be juicier if I dropped the oven temperature?

Sure enough, when I reduced the oven to 200 degrees, the bubbles disappeared. Actually, it didn't look like anything was happening at all. But 5 hours later, the results were well worth the wait. This was the moistest turkey yet, because the ultralow-and-slow approach forced less water out of the meat.

Finally, many recipes call for transferring the protein to a clean container; separating the fat from the perishable juices; and refrigerating the meat, submerged in the fat, for a "ripening" period. I didn't want to bother separating the fat from the jus, so I tried six days of refrigeration (the longest I could go without the jus turning sour) directly in the pot of fat and jus. Ultimately, this waiting time had no effect on flavor or texture. That said, it was great to know that I had such a wide window for making the confit in advance.

Gravy, of course, is traditional with Thanksgiving turkey. But this turkey was anything but traditional, and a meaty sauce would only mimic the rich, decadent flavor of the meat. For a bold, fresh accompaniment, I combined citrus and mustard in the form of sweet orange marmalade, tart lime, and whole-grain mustard. A few spoonfuls of the concentrated turkey juices provided a savory backbone, and a pinch of cayenne added subtle warmth. It was bright and cheery—which is exactly how I felt when I served this turkey.

—LAN LAM, *Cook's Illustrated*

Turkey Thigh Confit with Citrus-Mustard Sauce

SERVES 6 TO 8

Start this recipe at least five days or up to 12 days before serving (almost all the time is hands-off). The proper measurement of salt is crucial here. Be sure to use table salt, not kosher salt, and to measure it carefully. To ensure proper seasoning, make sure that the total weight of the turkey is within 2 ounces of the 4-pound target weight; do not use enhanced or kosher turkey thighs. Though duck fat is traditional, we found that chicken fat or even vegetable oil will work nicely. Reserve the duck fat or chicken fat and remaining stock in step 5 for further use; used vegetable oil should be discarded. It is convenient to split up the cooking over

several days, but if you prefer to do all the cooking in one day, go straight from step 2 to step 5 without letting the turkey cool.

3	large onions, chopped coarse (4¾ cups)
12	sprigs fresh thyme
2½	tablespoons table salt for curing
4½	teaspoons sugar
1½	teaspoons pepper
4	pounds bone-in turkey thighs
6	cups duck fat, chicken fat, or vegetable oil for confit
1	garlic head, halved crosswise
2	bay leaves
½	cup orange marmalade
2	tablespoons whole-grain mustard
¾	teaspoon grated lime zest plus 2 tablespoons juice
¼	teaspoon table salt
⅛	teaspoon cayenne pepper

1. TO CURE: Process onions, thyme sprigs, 2½ tablespoons salt, sugar, and pepper in food processor until finely chopped, about 20 seconds, scraping down sides of bowl as needed. Spread one-third of mixture evenly in bottom of 13 by 9-inch baking dish. Arrange turkey thighs, skin side up, in single layer in dish. Spread remaining onion mixture evenly over thighs. Wrap dish tightly with plastic wrap and refrigerate for 4 to 6 days (whatever is most convenient).

2. TO COOK: Adjust oven rack to lower-middle position and heat oven to 200 degrees. Remove thighs from onion mixture and rinse well (if you don't have a garbage disposal, do not allow onion pieces to go down drain). Pat thighs dry with paper towels. Heat fat in large Dutch oven over medium heat to 165 degrees. Off heat, add turkey thighs, skin side down and in single layer, making sure thighs are completely submerged. Add garlic and bay leaves. Transfer to oven, uncovered, and cook until metal skewer inserted straight down into thickest part of largest thigh can be easily removed without lifting thigh, 4 to 5 hours. (To ensure that oven temperature remains steady, wait at least 20 minutes before retesting if turkey is not done.) Remove from oven.

3. TO MAKE AHEAD: Let turkey cool completely in pot, about 2 hours; cover pot; and refrigerate for up to 6 days.

4. Uncover pot. Heat pot over medium-low heat until fat is melted, about 25 minutes. Increase heat to medium, maintaining bare simmer, and continue to cook until thickest part of largest thigh registers 135 to 140 degrees, about 30 minutes longer. (If turkey has been cooked in vegetable oil, heat pot over medium heat, maintaining bare simmer, until thickest part of largest thigh registers 135 to 140 degrees, about 30 minutes.)

5. TO SERVE: Adjust oven rack to lower-middle position and heat oven to 500 degrees. While oven heats, crumple 20-inch length of aluminum foil into loose ball. Uncrumple foil, place in rimmed baking sheet, and top with wire rack. Using tongs, gently transfer thighs, skin side up, to prepared wire rack, being careful not to tear delicate skin. Set aside. Strain liquid through fine-mesh strainer into large bowl. Working in batches, pour liquid into fat separator, letting liquid settle for 5 minutes before separating fat from turkey stock. (Alternatively, use bulb baster to extract turkey stock from beneath fat.) Transfer 4 teaspoons turkey stock to small bowl; add marmalade; and microwave until mixture is fluid, about 30 seconds. Stir in mustard, lime zest and juice, ¼ teaspoon salt, and cayenne. Transfer to serving bowl.

6. Transfer thighs to oven and roast until well browned, 12 to 15 minutes. Transfer thighs to cutting board, skin side up, and let rest until just cool enough to handle, about 15 minutes.

7. Flip 1 thigh skin side down. Using tip of paring knife, cut along sides of thighbone, exposing bone. Carefully remove bone and any stray bits of cartilage. Flip thigh skin side up. Using sharp chef's knife, slice thigh crosswise ¾ inch thick. Transfer to serving platter, skin side up. Repeat with remaining thighs. Serve, passing sauce separately.

MOROCCAN FISH TAGINE

✔ **WHY THIS RECIPE WORKS** For a bright, flavorful fish tagine, we started by salting chunks of cod to season the flesh and help it retain moisture. We coated the fish in chermoula, a flavorful herb-spice paste of cilantro, garlic, cumin, paprika, cayenne, lemon juice, and olive oil, just before cooking to season its exterior. Softening bell pepper, onion, and carrot before adding the tomatoes and fish ensured that the vegetables would be soft and tender by the time the fish was cooked through. Preserved lemon and olives added acidity, complexity, and salty punch to the broth. To produce moist, flaky cod, we turned off the heat once the broth was bubbling at the bottom of the pot and allowed the fish to cook in the residual heat.

A tagine is a North African earthenware pot with a tall, cone-shaped lid; it's also the name for the wonderfully aromatic and complex fish, meat, or vegetable stews that are cooked inside it. But you don't need to own this specialty vessel to enjoy the dish, because these days the next best thing—a Dutch oven with a tight-fitting lid—is also commonly used. I set out to create a light, fresh-tasting fish tagine.

The type of fish used in a tagine depends on the region and its available seafood, though white-fleshed fillets are common in Morocco. Regardless of the type of fish, the fillets are typically marinated in chermoula, an extraordinarily flavorful mixture of fresh herbs, garlic, and heady spices that's loosened with olive oil and lemon juice.

To prepare a fish tagine, the bottom of the pot is lined with vegetables—often bell peppers, onions, carrots, and tomatoes—and the chermoula-coated fish is arranged on top before the lid is added and the assembly is moved to the stovetop or oven. At some point in the process, two signature Moroccan flavorings—pungent, floral preserved lemon and tangy green olives—are incorporated. (Preserved lemon can be hard to find and making it yourself can take weeks, but luckily, my colleague Andrew Janjigian developed a preserved lemon recipe that takes only 24 hours to make.) Without any additional liquid in the steamy pot, the fish and vegetables slowly turn soft and tender, and their juices meld to create a tangy, garlicky, herbal broth. It's just the thing to serve with warm flatbread or spoon atop a pile of fluffy couscous.

I chose cod for my tagine for its firm yet delicate meatiness and its wide availability. I divided the fillets into chunks to make serving easy and then proceeded with my chermoula, buzzing fresh cilantro, garlic, and lemon juice with cumin, paprika, and cayenne in the food processor. Finally, I stirred in a couple tablespoons of extra-virgin olive oil by hand since processing can make the oil taste bitter. Gently tossing the fish in the paste gave it a gorgeous orange-red, herb-flecked coat that would permeate the dish with its flavors.

Next I turned to the vegetables. I decided to give them a head start since they would take longer to cook than the delicate fish. To facilitate staggered cooking, I opted to work on the stovetop. I glossed a Dutch oven with olive oil and then sautéed a colorful mix of sliced grassy green bell pepper, savory onion, and sweet carrot. Once the vegetables were just softened, I poured in a can of diced tomatoes and layered the fish on top. I resisted adding more liquid since I knew that the fish and vegetables would eventually give up some of their juices. After about 10 minutes of covered cooking, I lifted the lid, delighted to find that my restraint had paid off: A shallow layer of richly scented broth bubbled at the bottom of the pot. I sprinkled a handful of quartered green olives and a couple tablespoons of finely chopped preserved lemon over the top and served the tagine.

It was a decent start: The carrot, onion, and pepper were soft and flavorful, but the cod, well seasoned on the outside, was bland within since marinades don't penetrate far beyond the surface. It was also overcooked. What's more, reserving the olives and lemon until the end was a mistake. Without time for their flavors to meld with the other ingredients, they seemed like an afterthought.

I made a few tweaks. First, before coating the cod in the chermoula, I tossed it with salt and let it sit while I prepped the rest of the ingredients. The salt would season the flesh and help keep it moist. The other change: adding the olives and preserved lemon earlier so that they could soften and mingle in the broth.

Both were good moves. The lemon and olives were now more integrated, as evidenced by the lively, tangy broth. The fish was well seasoned and held on to more moisture. And yet, it was still tough. I needed to cook it more gently.

I've had good luck in the past with other seafood recipes with heating the cooking liquid; adding seafood; covering the pot; and removing it from the burner, allowing residual heat to gently cook the flesh through. But at the point when I was adding the fish, the pot was essentially dry, so there wouldn't be enough steam. How about a hybrid approach?

For my next batch, I added the cod and cooked the pot as before, but once the cod had released enough liquid to be actively simmering, I took the pot off the heat. Within 5 minutes, the pieces of cod were just opaque, tender, and flaky. After a final sprinkling of fresh cilantro, this beauty of a dish—with its layered, complex flavors—was complete.

—ANNIE PETITO AND ANDREW JANJIGIAN,
Cook's Illustrated

Moroccan Fish Tagine

SERVES 4

You can substitute red snapper or haddock for the cod as long as the fillets are 1 to 1½ inches thick. Picholine or Cerignola olives work well in this recipe. If you can't find preserved lemon, you can make your own (our 24-hour recipe follows). Serve this dish with flatbread, couscous, or rice.

- 1½ pounds skinless cod fillets (1 to 1½ inches thick), cut into 1½- to 2-inch pieces
- ¾ teaspoon table salt, divided
- ½ cup fresh cilantro leaves, plus ¼ cup chopped
- 4 garlic cloves, peeled
- 1¼ teaspoons ground cumin
- 1¼ teaspoons paprika
- ¼ teaspoon cayenne pepper
- 1½ tablespoons lemon juice
- 6 tablespoons extra-virgin olive oil, divided
- 1 onion, halved through root end and sliced ¼ inch thick
- 1 green bell pepper, stemmed, seeded, and cut into ¼-inch strips
- 1 carrot, peeled and sliced on bias ¼ inch thick
- 1 (14.5-ounce) can diced tomatoes
- ⅓ cup pitted green olives, quartered lengthwise
- 2 tablespoons finely chopped preserved lemon

NOTES FROM THE TEST KITCHEN

POWER COUPLE: OLIVES AND PRESERVED LEMONS
Our tagine gets its fresh herb and heady spice flavors from the chermoula that coats the fish, but its bright top notes are provided by the heavy-hitting combination of preserved lemon and green olives. Preserved lemons are a stalwart of North African cuisines, made by curing the fruit with salt to soften the rind and imbue it with an intensely citrusy, floral, and pungent flavor through fermentation. The lemons are sliced or chopped and added to recipes, rind and all. Green olives, such as the picholine variety that is commonly used in Morocco, complement the lemon with briny tang and a meaty bite.

MOROCCAN FISH TAGINE

1. Place cod in bowl and toss with ½ teaspoon salt. Set aside.

2. Pulse cilantro leaves, garlic, cumin, paprika, and cayenne in food processor until cilantro and garlic are finely chopped, about 12 pulses. Add lemon juice and pulse briefly to combine. Transfer mixture to small bowl and stir in 2 tablespoons oil. Set aside.

3. Heat remaining ¼ cup oil in large Dutch oven over medium heat until shimmering. Add onion, bell pepper, carrot, and remaining ¼ teaspoon salt and cook, stirring frequently, until softened, 5 to 7 minutes. Stir in tomatoes and their juice, olives, and preserved lemon. Spread mixture in even layer on bottom of pot.

4. Toss cod with cilantro mixture until evenly coated, then arrange cod over vegetables in single layer. Cover and cook until cod starts to turn opaque and juices released from cod are simmering vigorously, 3 to 5 minutes. Remove pot from heat and let stand, covered, until cod is opaque and just cooked through (cod should register 140 degrees), 3 to 5 minutes. Sprinkle with chopped cilantro and serve.

24-Hour Preserved Lemons

MAKES 1 CUP

It's important to slice the lemons thin. Sugar offsets the acidity and bitterness of the fruit, and olive oil helps soften the pith.

    3 lemons, rinsed
    3 tablespoons sugar
    3 tablespoons table salt
    ¾ cup extra-virgin olive oil

1. Slice lemons thin crosswise.

2. Toss lemons with sugar and salt in bowl. Stir in oil.

3. Transfer lemons to bowl or pack into jar, cover, and refrigerate for at least 24 hours or up to 2 weeks.

4. To use, chop or mince lemon as desired.

BROILED SPICE-RUBBED SNAPPER

✔ **WHY THIS RECIPE WORKS** For an easy way to cook fish that we could use in tacos or serve with a simple vegetable side, we brushed a spice mixture on snapper fillets and cooked them under the broiler. To maximize the flavor of the spices, we hydrated ancho chile powder, ground coriander, granulated garlic, dried oregano, and cayenne and black peppers in a couple tablespoons of boiling water to bring out their water-soluble flavors. Then we added oil, which, when heated under the broiler, brought out the oil-soluble flavors.

Spice rubs and pastes are great for adding complexity to proteins such as chicken, pork, or beef, but they can also enhance fish. In fact, brushing a few fillets with a potent paste and sliding them under the broiler is one of the best strategies I know for quickly putting a light, fresh dinner on the table.

To choose the best type of fish for this application, I cast a wide net, finding that moderately fatty, slightly sweet snapper worked beautifully with vibrant seasonings; tilapia and sea bass were also excellent choices. I started by salting the fillets to season the flesh and help keep it moist. Next, I smeared the fish with a simple paste of pantry ingredients: raisiny-sweet ancho chile powder, citrusy ground coriander, dried oregano, black and cayenne peppers, minced fresh garlic, and a couple tablespoons of extra-virgin olive oil. After arranging the fillets on a greased, foil-lined baking sheet, I slid the assembly under the broiler. In just 10 minutes, the fish was starting to flake and had reached 135 degrees; carryover cooking would bring it to 140 degrees, the test kitchen's preferred temperature for white fish. What's more, the fillets had developed a deeply caramelized surface with edges that were crispy and beginning to blacken.

It was a good start, but the garlic had burned a bit and the paste was somewhat flat-tasting and gritty. The next time around, I switched to granulated garlic and tried to eke out flavor and soften the spices via a quick sizzle in hot oil. The taste improved somewhat, but not enough. (Plus, the entire paste now threatened to scorch because it was being cooked twice: first on the stovetop and again under the broiler.)

The oil was drawing out fat-soluble flavors, but spices have water-soluble flavors, too, so I tried drizzling 2 tablespoons of boiling water onto a fresh batch of spices. Once the mixture had thickened—a signal that the ingredients were well hydrated—I stirred in the oil. After brushing the fillets with the water-oil-spice paste, I broiled them as before.

Sure enough, the flavors were fuller and more pronounced, and the consistency of the paste had smoothed out, too. Finished with tart lime juice to balance the robust spices, here was a superflavorful—and superfast—midweek dinner.

—DAVID PAZMIÑO, *Cook's Illustrated*

Broiled Spice-Rubbed Snapper

SERVES 4

We developed this recipe using Diamond Crystal kosher salt. If using Morton's, which is finer, use ¾ teaspoon for the fish and ⅜ teaspoon for the spice paste. Sea bass or tilapia can be substituted for the snapper, if desired. If using tilapia, which is thinner, start checking for doneness at 8 minutes. We use granulated garlic in this recipe because fresh garlic burns under the broiler; feel free to substitute garlic powder. For an accurate measurement of boiling water, bring a kettle of water to a boil and then measure out the desired amount. If you prefer a spicier dish, add the full ½ teaspoon of cayenne pepper. Serve the fish with steamed white rice or roasted potatoes and a vegetable; as a taco filling with cilantro leaves, avocado slices, and pickled red onions; or with a green salad and crusty bread.

       3 (8-ounce) skinless snapper fillets, ¾ to 1 inch thick
    1½ teaspoons kosher salt, divided
       1 tablespoon ancho chile powder
       1 teaspoon ground coriander
       1 teaspoon granulated garlic
      ½ teaspoon dried oregano
      ½ teaspoon pepper
  ¼–½ teaspoon cayenne pepper
       2 tablespoons boiling water
       2 tablespoons extra-virgin olive oil
       1 tablespoon lime juice, plus lime wedges for serving

1. Sprinkle both sides of snapper evenly with 1 teaspoon salt. Refrigerate for 15 to 30 minutes.

2. While snapper chills, combine chile powder, coriander, granulated garlic, oregano, pepper, cayenne, and remaining ½ teaspoon salt in small bowl. Stir in boiling water and let sit until thickened, 2 to 3 minutes. Mix in oil to make smooth paste.

3. Adjust oven rack 6 inches from broiler element and heat broiler. Line rimmed baking sheet with aluminum foil and spray with vegetable oil spray. Place snapper, skinned side down, on prepared sheet and brush with spice mixture. Broil until top of fish is evenly browned and fish registers 135 degrees, 10 to 12 minutes. Transfer snapper to platter and drizzle with lime juice. Using spatula or large spoon, break snapper into portions. Serve with lime wedges.

SMOKED WHOLE SIDE OF SALMON

✔ WHY THIS RECIPE WORKS We love the sweet, salty flavor and silky yet firm texture of hot-smoked salmon, but we're not as fond of its price: $40 per pound. Making our own—a full side—cut the price by about three-quarters. We started by blanketing our salmon with a mixture of sugar and salt, which not only seasoned the fish but also drew out some moisture and firmed up the texture. After 4 hours, we rinsed off the cure and let the salmon dry in the refrigerator until a tacky film formed on the surface. We placed the side of salmon on a foil sling for maneuverability and cooked the fish over indirect heat with plenty of hardwood smoke until it was fully cooked yet moist and succulent, ready to be eaten right away as an entrée, flaked over a salad, or folded into a buttery kedgeree. Cut into portions and wrapped tightly, this salmon freezes well.

I cooked professionally in Scotland from 2000 to 2008, and I still miss the relationships I formed there, with friends, with coworkers, and with hot-smoked salmon. The last one might sound melodramatic, but that fish, produced by a smokehouse on the island of South Uist, was special: silky, tender, and well seasoned inside, with a smoky, lightly sweetened, and delicately chewy exterior providing subtle textural contrast. As the breakfast cook at a posh hotel, I flaked it into softly scrambled eggs. At another restaurant, I stirred it into buttery rice for a dish called kedgeree.

When I came back to the United States, however, my relationship with my favorite fish ended. Hot-smoked salmon is expensive here—about $10 for a 4-ounce vacuum-sealed piece—and I couldn't justify the splurge. But recently it occurred to me that if I were to make my own, I'd have few expenses beyond that of the fish. In fact, forget those 4-ounce pieces; I could exploit the economy of scale by buying a full side of salmon for about $40 and then smoke it on my kettle grill. I could

HOT-SMOKED WHOLE SIDE OF SALMON

either share it, warm from the grill, with a large group, or I could divide it into pieces and squirrel it away in the freezer for future use. A reunion with my treasured old friend seemed imminent.

The basic method for hot-smoking fish goes like this: Apply salt (and often sugar) to the flesh side of a skin-on fillet and let it sit for a while to season the fish and draw out some moisture, which makes the fish a bit denser and firmer. Rinse the fish and let it dry in the refrigerator. Build a moderate fire on one side of your grill, add some wood chips, and place the salmon opposite the fire. Then put the cover on and let the smoke and the gentle heat waft over the fish until it's just cooked. But how long to cure and how long to dry? Experts disagreed.

To determine the ideal curing time, I divided a 4-pound side of salmon into 1-pound portions and applied a curing mixture to one piece every 2 hours. (One of the things I'd loved about the Scottish salmon was the way its slight sweetness complemented its richness, so I used a mixture that included a hefty amount of sugar: 3 parts kosher salt to 4 parts sugar by weight.) When the last one had been curing for 2 hours, I rinsed all the pieces, patted them dry, and refrigerated them for 30 minutes while I fired up the grill.

My setup was simple—a half chimney of charcoal poured over a small amount of unlit coals for gentle but sustained heat, topped with a cup of dry hickory chips wrapped in a foil packet. The fish went on the opposite side, with a foil sling beneath it to aid maneuverability. A little over an hour later, the pieces were just starting to flake when prodded and they registered 125 degrees, so I took them off the grill.

All the samples were juicy inside and lightly smoky on the outside. But the exteriors of the two samples that had been cured the longest—6 hours and 8 hours—were dry and chewy and tasted too salty, while the sample that had been cured for only 2 hours was a little underseasoned. I'd go with a 4-hour cure.

The next step in the process is to rinse off the cure and allow the fish to air-dry in the fridge. The salt and sugar in the cure dissolve some of the proteins in the salmon and draw them to the surface, and as water evaporates during the drying period, these proteins bond together in a sticky film. That's ideal, because when the fish goes out to the grill, you want it moist enough to capture the flavorful vapors in the smoke but not so wet that the smoke simply slides off. I found that a drying time anywhere from 4 to 20 hours dried out the surface of the salmon just enough to ensure admirably robust smoke flavor.

Finally it was time to smoke a full side. I'd spent $40 on the fish and pennies on charcoal, wood chips, sugar, and salt. Now I had flaky, rich, smoky salmon for about one-quarter of the retail price and about 20 minutes of active work. Hello, old friend.

—ANDREA GEARY, *Cook's Illustrated*

Hot-Smoked Whole Side of Salmon
SERVES 16

We used Diamond Crystal kosher salt here. If using Morton's kosher salt, which is denser, use only 6 tablespoons. We developed this recipe with farmed salmon. If you would like to use wild fish, we recommend king salmon. The recipe can be halved, using a 2-pound center-cut fillet and half as much sugar and salt in the cure; the cooking time will be roughly the same as with a full side of salmon. We offer a wide time range for drying the salmon; choose what works best for your schedule. We prefer hickory chips for our salmon, but any kind of hardwood chips will work. Try the salmon on its own, in our Hot-Smoked Salmon Kedgeree (recipe follows), flaked over a salad, mixed into a quiche filling, or stirred into just-set scrambled eggs.

½ cup sugar for curing

½ cup kosher salt for curing

1 (4-pound) skin-on side of salmon, thin end of tail removed and reserved for another use, pin bones removed, and belly fat trimmed

1–1½ cups wood chips

1. Mix sugar and salt together in small bowl. Place salmon on wire rack set in rimmed baking sheet. Spread sugar mixture evenly over surface of fillet, pressing gently to adhere. Refrigerate, uncovered, for 4 hours.

2. Rinse salmon under cold water and return to rack. Pat dry with paper towels. Refrigerate, uncovered, until surface of fillet is tacky and matte, 4 to 20 hours.

3. Using large piece of heavy-duty aluminum foil, wrap chips (1 cup if using charcoal; 1½ cups if using gas) in 8 by 4½-inch foil packet. (Make sure chips do not poke holes in sides or bottom of packet. If using gas, make sure there are no more than 2 layers of foil on bottom of packet.) Cut 3 evenly spaced 2-inch slits in top of packet.

4A. FOR A CHARCOAL GRILL: Open bottom vent halfway. Light large chimney starter half filled with charcoal briquettes (3 quarts). Place 6 unlit briquettes on 1 side of grill. When top coals are partially covered with ash, pour into steeply banked pile over unlit briquettes. Place wood chip packet on coals with slits facing up. Set cooking grate in place, cover, and open lid vent halfway. Heat grill until hot and wood chips are smoking, about 5 minutes.

4B. FOR A GAS GRILL: Remove cooking grate and place wood chip packet directly on primary burner. Set grate in place; turn primary burner to high (leave other burners off); cover; and heat grill until hot and wood chips are smoking, 15 to 25 minutes. Turn primary burner to medium. (Adjust primary burner as needed to maintain grill temperature between 275 and 300 degrees.)

5. Clean and oil cooking grate. Fold large piece of heavy-duty foil into 18 by 6-inch rectangle. Spray lightly with vegetable oil spray. Place foil rectangle on cooler side of grill (on gas grill arrange foil parallel to primary burner, spaced 8 to 10 inches from heat source) and place salmon on foil. Cover grill (positioning lid vent over salmon if using charcoal) and cook until center of thickest part of fillet registers 125 degrees and is still translucent when cut into with paring knife, 50 minutes to 1 hour 10 minutes.

6. Using foil as sling, transfer salmon to platter. Carefully slide foil out from beneath salmon. Serve. (Salmon can be cut into pieces, cooled completely, wrapped tightly in plastic wrap, and frozen for up to 2 months.)

Hot-Smoked Salmon Kedgeree
SERVES 6 TO 8

We like basmati rice here for its delicate fragrance, but any long-grain white rice will work. This recipe works best with day-old rice; alternatively, cook the rice a

---

NOTES FROM THE TEST KITCHEN

BEST PRACTICES FOR SMOKING ON A GAS GRILL

Grill smoking over charcoal is straightforward: Wrap the wood chips in foil to create a packet, cut some slits in the top, and place it atop your lit coals. But getting a packet of wood chips to smoke on a gas grill can be a bit more challenging. The first step is to place the chip packet directly on the heat diffusers so that it is as close as possible to the flame. But because these don't emit as much heat as burning coals, sometimes the chips still don't smoke enough—or even at all. The diffusers also don't offer the most stable place for the packet. Here are some tips for maximizing smoke and ensuring that the process goes smoothly.

1. DON'T OVERWRAP PACKET: Make sure that you have no more than two layers of foil on the bottom of the packet; this will minimize the amount of air that can get trapped between the layers, insulating the chips from heat and keeping them from smoking.

2. WIDEN SLITS IF NECESSARY: If the chips aren't smoking, use the tip of a paring knife to gently widen the slits on top of the packet to let in more oxygen and encourage smoking.

3. MOLD PACKET GENTLY OVER DIFFUSER: Heat diffusers are often shaped like inverted V's. Take advantage of foil's flexibility so that the packet won't fall to the bottom of the grill.

4. IF NEED BE, DON'T REPLACE GRATE: If the packet doesn't fit easily under the cooking grate, don't bother putting it back. In most cases, smoked food doesn't sit directly above the chip packet, so the grate isn't needed.

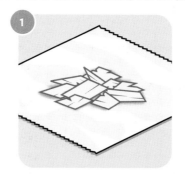

couple hours ahead, spread it on a rimmed baking sheet, and let it cool completely before chilling it for 30 minutes. Use the large holes on a box grater to grate the eggs. Kedgeree is a comforting meal that can be served at any time of day.

5 tablespoons unsalted butter

1 large onion, chopped

1¼ teaspoons table salt, divided

Pinch cayenne pepper (optional)

6 cups cooked basmati rice

8 ounces Hot-Smoked Whole Side of Salmon, broken into 1-inch flakes

6 hard-cooked large eggs, peeled and grated

⅓ cup chopped fresh parsley

⅓ cup chopped fresh chives

5 tablespoons lemon juice (2 lemons), plus lemon wedges for serving

½ teaspoon pepper

1. Melt butter in 12-inch nonstick skillet over medium-low heat. Add onion; ¼ teaspoon salt; and pinch cayenne, if using, and cook, stirring occasionally, until onion is soft but not browned, 10 to 12 minutes. Add rice and remaining 1 teaspoon salt and increase heat to medium-high. Cook, stirring frequently to break up clumps and coat rice with butter, until rice is heated through, about 10 minutes. Add salmon and cook, stirring frequently, until salmon is heated through, about 5 minutes.

2. Transfer mixture to large bowl. Add eggs, parsley, chives, lemon juice, and pepper and toss to combine. Season with salt to taste. Transfer to platter and serve, passing lemon wedges separately.

CHILE-GARLIC SHRIMP

✔ WHY THIS RECIPE WORKS   We were after a Mexican-inspired meal of plump, juicy shrimp simmered in a deeply flavored, garlicky, chile-infused sauce. To start, we toasted dried guajillo chiles to bring out their fruity, lightly spicy flavor. We then blended the chiles with garlic, Worcestershire sauce, and water to make a thick, crimson sauce. To control the cooking of the shrimp, we cooked them partially in two batches to lightly caramelize their exteriors. We then finished cooking them by gently simmering them in the bold chile sauce. A couple pats of butter added richness, and a squirt of lime juice and a sprinkling of fresh cilantro provided welcome freshness.

It's Wednesday night, but that doesn't mean I'm willing to make compromises when planning dinner. Enter this bold, exciting, Mexican-inspired meal of plump, juicy shrimp simmered in a deeply flavorful, garlicky, chile-infused sauce.

The first building block of this dish is dried guajillo chiles. These long, lanky chiles are fruity and lightly spicy. As a big fan of dried chiles, I knew to seed them, cut them into pieces, and toast the pieces in a skillet to bring out their flavor and add a subtle smokiness. Next, I tossed the toasted chiles into my blender, which I used as a makeshift spice grinder. It turned the guajillos into a vibrant, complex homemade chile powder that packed way more depth than a supermarket version would. I blended in water, Worcestershire sauce, and fresh garlic to make a thick, crimson-colored sauce.

To tackle the shrimp, I first tossed them with cumin, salt, and cayenne pepper. I tried searing 2 pounds of shrimp (to feed four people) in one batch, but the shrimp overcrowded the pan and steamed rather than seared. For the next round, I sautéed the shrimp in two batches, browning just one side and then getting them out of the pan before they finished cooking (they'd finish cooking in the sauce momentarily). This method gave the shrimp a lightly caramelized exterior without overcooking them and turning them rubbery.

Now it was time to unite the shrimp and the sauce. To add another layer of flavor, I doubled down on the garlic (which I'd already added to the sauce) by sautéing sliced garlic in a little oil. I then added my chile sauce and the shrimp and let the shrimp finish cooking through. Off the heat, I stirred in a squirt of lime juice, a couple pats of butter, and some fresh cilantro. Perfection.

—MORGAN BOLLING, *Cook's Country*

Chile-Garlic Shrimp

SERVES 4

One ounce of guajillo chiles is about four chiles. New Mexican chiles can be substituted for the guajillos. We prefer untreated shrimp—those not treated with sodium or additives such as sodium tripolyphosphate. Most frozen E-Z peel shrimp have been treated (check

CHILE-GARLIC SHRIMP

the ingredient list). If you're using treated shrimp, omit the ½ teaspoon of salt for seasoning the shrimp in step 3. Serve with warm tortillas or rice.

1 ounce dried guajillo chiles

½ cup water

1 tablespoon Worcestershire sauce

6 garlic cloves (2 chopped, 4 sliced thin)

1 teaspoon table salt, divided

2 pounds extra-large shrimp (21 to 25 per pound), peeled, deveined, and tails removed

½ teaspoon ground cumin

¼ teaspoon cayenne pepper

3 tablespoons extra-virgin olive oil, divided

2 tablespoons lime juice

2 tablespoons unsalted butter, cut into 2 pieces

2 tablespoons chopped fresh cilantro

1. Using kitchen shears, stem guajillos, cut in half lengthwise, and discard seeds. Cut guajillos into 1-inch pieces. Place guajillos in 12-inch nonstick skillet and cook over medium heat, stirring often, until fragrant, 3 to 5 minutes.

2. Transfer guajillos to blender jar and process until finely ground, about 2 minutes. Add water, Worcestershire, chopped garlic, and ½ teaspoon salt and blend until smooth, about 2 minutes; set aside.

3. Pat shrimp dry with paper towels and sprinkle with cumin, cayenne, and remaining ½ teaspoon salt. Heat 1 tablespoon oil in now-empty skillet over high heat until just smoking. Add half of shrimp in even layer and cook, without stirring, until beginning to brown on underside but still raw on top, about 2 minutes. Transfer to bowl. Repeat with 1 tablespoon oil and remaining shrimp, then transfer to bowl with first batch.

4. Reduce heat to low and add remaining 1 tablespoon oil and sliced garlic to now-empty skillet. Cook until garlic is fragrant and golden brown, about 2 minutes. Stir in reserved chile sauce and shrimp and cook until shrimp is just cooked through, about 1 minute. Off heat, stir in lime juice and butter until butter is melted, about 1 minute. Transfer to serving dish. Sprinkle with cilantro and serve.

PAN-SEARED SHRIMP WITH PEANUTS, BLACK PEPPER, AND LIME

✔ **WHY THIS RECIPE WORKS** Shrimp are so small that it's hard to brown them before they overcook. We started by briefly salting them so that they retained moisture even as they were seared over high heat. Sprinkling sugar on the shrimp (patted dry after salting) and waiting to add the sugar until just before searing them boosted browning and underscored the shrimp's sweetness. To cook them, we arranged the shrimp in a single layer in a cold skillet (nonstick or carbon-steel to ensure that the flavorful browning would stick to the shrimp, not the pan) so that they made even contact with the surface. They heated up gradually with the skillet, so they didn't buckle and thus browned uniformly; slower searing also created a wider window for ensuring that they didn't overcook. Once the shrimp were spotty brown and pink at the edges on the first side, we removed them from the heat and quickly turned each one, letting residual heat gently cook them the rest of the way. A flavorful spice mixture for seasoning the shrimp came together in the same skillet we used to cook them.

What could be easier than pan-searing shrimp so that they brown deeply and cook up juicy and tender? In some ways, pan-searing just about anything else.

Don't get me wrong: Pan searing is an inherently quick way to cook shrimp and should be really simple. But when it comes to achieving that ideal combination of deep, flavorful browning on the outside and snappy, succulent meat on the inside, shrimp might be the hardest protein to get right. For one thing, they're tiny and best cooked to a relatively low 120 degrees, so it's almost impossible to get any color on them before they dry out and turn rubbery.

But if you've ever had truly well-browned, juicy shrimp, you know that they're just the thing for bulking up rice or noodle bowls or salads, and they pair well with a host of bold seasonings. My goal was to figure out how to pan-sear them well—and as it turned out, the solution was right in my wheelhouse. The problems with pan-searing shrimp, I realized after flashing them in a hot, oiled skillet as per usual and producing tough results, are just exacerbated versions of the ones I've encountered when coming up with the best way to pan-sear other relatively quick-cooking proteins such as steak and salmon. All I had to do here was modify those methods so that the cooking happened more gently. Here's my method—which is, indeed, really simple.

First, salt the shrimp briefly and then add the sugar just before cooking. Salting the shrimp for 15 minutes (up to 30 minutes is fine) helps them retain moisture even as they're seared, but it doesn't introduce extra moisture like brining does, so the shrimp's exteriors still brown beautifully. Salt also seasons the shrimp. Sprinkling sugar on the shrimp (patted dry after salting) boosts browning and underscores their sweetness. The trick is waiting to sprinkle it until just before searing so that it doesn't get wiped off when you dry the shrimp.

Next, lightly oil the shrimp to ensure that they are evenly coated. Arrange them in a single layer in a cold nonstick or carbon-steel skillet so that they make even contact with the pan. Oiling the shrimp and cooking them in a nonstick skillet ensures that flavorful browning sticks to the food and not to the pan. And a cold start offers more control. Since the shrimp heat up gradually with the skillet, they don't buckle (good for browning) and are less likely to overcook.

Finally, once the shrimp are spotty brown and pink at the edges on the first side, cut the heat and quickly turn each piece, letting residual heat gently cook the shrimp the rest of the way.

—ANDREW JANJIGIAN, *Cook's Illustrated*

Pan-Seared Shrimp with Peanuts, Black Pepper, and Lime

SERVES 4

We prefer untreated shrimp; if yours are treated with additives such as sodium tripolyphosphate, skip the salting in step 1. You can substitute jumbo shrimp (16 to 20 per pound) for the extra-large shrimp; if substituting, increase the cooking time by 1 to 2 minutes. To use the plain seared shrimp as a neutral protein in rice bowls or salads, skip steps 2 and 4.

1½ **pounds extra-large shrimp (21 to 25 per pound), peeled, deveined, and tails removed**

1 **teaspoon kosher salt, divided**

2 **teaspoons coriander seeds**

1 **teaspoon black peppercorns**

1 **teaspoon paprika**

1 **garlic clove, minced**

1⅛ **teaspoons sugar, divided**

⅛ **teaspoon red pepper flakes**

4 **teaspoons vegetable oil, divided**

½ **cup fresh cilantro leaves and tender stems, chopped**

1 **tablespoon lime juice, plus lime wedges for serving**

3 **tablespoons dry-roasted peanuts, chopped coarse**

1. Toss shrimp and ½ teaspoon salt together in bowl; set aside for 15 to 30 minutes.

2. Meanwhile, grind coriander seeds and peppercorns using spice grinder or mortar and pestle until coarsely ground. Transfer to small bowl. Add paprika, garlic, 1 teaspoon sugar, pepper flakes, and remaining ½ teaspoon salt and stir until combined.

3. Pat shrimp dry with paper towels. Add 1 tablespoon oil and remaining ⅛ teaspoon sugar to bowl with shrimp and toss to coat. Add shrimp to cold 12-inch nonstick or well-seasoned carbon-steel skillet in single layer and cook over high heat until undersides of shrimp are spotty brown and edges turn pink, 3 to 4 minutes. Remove skillet from heat. Working quickly, use tongs to flip each shrimp; let stand until second side is opaque, about 2 minutes. Transfer shrimp to platter.

4. Add remaining 1 teaspoon oil to now-empty skillet. Add spice mixture and cook over medium heat until fragrant, about 30 seconds. Off heat, return shrimp to skillet. Add cilantro and lime juice and toss to combine. Transfer to platter; sprinkle with peanuts; and serve, passing lime wedges separately.

VARIATION

Pan-Seared Shrimp with Fermented Black Beans, Ginger, and Garlic

Omit spice mixture of coriander seeds, peppercorns, paprika, garlic, 1 teaspoon sugar, ½ teaspoon salt, and red pepper flakes. Omit cilantro, lime, and peanuts. Combine 2 scallion whites, sliced thin; 1 tablespoon fermented black beans, rinsed, drained, and chopped coarse; 1 tablespoon grated fresh ginger; 2 minced garlic cloves; and 1 teaspoon sugar in small bowl. In step 4, add black bean mixture to skillet instead of spice mixture and cook until ginger is just starting to brown, about 45 seconds. Add 2 scallion greens, sliced thin on bias; 1 tablespoon soy sauce; and 2 teaspoons toasted sesame oil to skillet with shrimp.

PAN-SEARED SHRIMP WITH PEANUTS, BLACK PEPPER, AND LIME

GERMAN APPLE PANCAKE WITH BROWN SUGAR SOUR CREAM

BREAKFAST, BRUNCH, AND BREADS

EGG SANDWICHES

✓ **WHY THIS RECIPE WORKS** For egg sandwiches with tender, creamy eggs that stayed put inside the bread, we skipped frying and scrambling. Inspired by a recipe from restaurateur and cookbook author Joanne Chang, we whisked water into the eggs, seasoned them lightly, and then gently baked them in a water bath. This hands-off method produced a custardy-smooth, silky egg filling. We then placed squares of the baked eggs on lightly toasted bread, layering savory ingredients (such as kimchi and salami), creamy spreads (like mayonnaise and yogurt), and fresh accents (such as tomatoes and herbs) for sandwiches with varied textures and flavors.

Just down the promenade from our office is an outpost of Joanne Chang's Flour Bakery, whose offerings have inspired a number of recipes for *Cook's Illustrated*, including Andrea Geary's Chocolate-Espresso Dacquoise and my Best Lemon Bars. But my favorite item on the menu, my go-to lunch when I can't scavenge something from the test kitchen, has always been the egg sandwich.

What makes it so special? Instead of a runny fried egg that drips and oozes with every bite, a scramble that tumbles out from between the bread, or—the worst scenario—a microwaved slab that's rubbery and dense, it features an "egg soufflé." While the food nerd in me isn't quite on board with this term (there's no air beaten into the egg mixture), I love everything else about it. It's soft, creamy, custardy, and delicately seasoned, and it stays neatly in place while I devour the sandwich.

Chang tucks a portion of the egg into a house-made focaccia roll along with bacon, cheddar, tomato, and arugula for a satisfying package of flavors and textures. After months of working from home because of the COVID-19 pandemic, I really missed that sandwich. So I looked up Chang's method for the eggs (find it, along with many other excellent recipes, in her 2013 cookbook *Flour, Too*) and set out to make my own version.

Chang's recipe turned out to have a couple hidden benefits that I wasn't aware of: It produces four portions at a time and can be made ahead. She starts by whisking ¾ cup of half-and-half into nine eggs along with a touch of salt. The mixture is poured into a round cake pan that's been coated with vegetable oil spray and then baked (covered with foil for the first half of the cooking time) in a water bath in a 300-degree oven. Partway through cooking, after the eggs have begun to set, fresh thyme and ground black pepper are added. Once the eggs are baked, they can be cut into sandwich portions and served right away or cooled completely and later reheated in the microwave.

As good as this recipe was, as a professional cook myself, I couldn't help finding a few things I wanted to change that would make the dish my own. First, the inclusion of half-and-half. Since I don't typically keep it on hand, I tried swapping in whole milk instead. The resulting eggs tasted a little less rich—and more eggy—and that was great. They were destined for egg sandwiches, after all. And milk still made their texture as velvety and smooth as half-and-half had. That's because dilution is the key here, not the type of liquid. As eggs cook, they form a tight mesh. Adding liquid puts space between the proteins, opening up the mesh, which results in tender, silky eggs. This being the case, I wondered if I should just use water. If the eggs were even leaner, I could pair them with rich toppings and still make them a regular part of my lunch (or breakfast or dinner) routine.

After a bit of fiddling, I settled on eight eggs beaten together with ⅔ cup of water and just ¼ teaspoon of salt. This small amount of salt was adequate because the other components in my sandwich would be highly seasoned. I also omitted the pepper and thyme, since a neutral base would allow me to experiment with a variety of toppings.

I chose to bake the mixture in an 8-inch square metal baking pan. Its sharp, clean edges would let me divide the eggs into four neat squares that would fit tidily on bread, without any of the waste that comes from trimming quadrants cut from a round pan. And unlike glass or ceramic, the metal would heat up and cool down quickly, keeping the baking time to about 40 minutes and helping prevent carryover cooking.

I placed the baking pan on a rimmed baking sheet and poured 1½ cups of water around the pan before setting the assembly on the middle rack of the oven. The shallow bath didn't reach even halfway up the sides of the pan, but the egg mixture wasn't deep, so it still prevented the edges from overcooking by lowering the temperature surrounding the pan. Because the bath was so shallow, it was easy to transfer the sheet to the oven without much sloshing.

With the smooth, custardy squares under way for now or later, I considered the bread. There were a few points to keep in mind. First, I needed something large

EGG, SALAMI, AND TOMATO SANDWICHES

enough to support a 4-inch square piece of egg. Second, thick breads needed to be airy and easily compressed; otherwise, I had trouble biting into the sandwich. (Read: no bagels.) Third, light toasting created a thin, crisp crust, whereas an aggressive approach resulted in a hard shell that required a lot of force to bite through, thus squeezing out the filling. Ultimately, I had success with English muffins, kaiser rolls, bulkie rolls, hamburger buns, and sandwich bread.

For the fixings, I mimicked Chang's style, combining contrasting yet complementary flavors and textures.

I started with a classic ham and cheddar cheese combo and then turned it on its head with a spread of sweet apricot jam and a smattering of spicy, crunchy pepperoncini. My next creation paired gutsy kimchi with cool, creamy avocado; another combined lightly peppery salami with fresh tomato and basil; and a third highlighted silky smoked salmon with fresh dill and crisp slices of pungent red onion, all held in place by slices of toasted rye.

Whether you try one of my riffs or create your own, I know you'll fall in love with this approach.

—LAN LAM, *Cook's Illustrated*

NOTES FROM THE TEST KITCHEN

PRINCIPLES FOR EGG SANDWICH PERFECTION

INGREDIENT SELECTION

ANCHOR THE FLAVOR: Build the sandwich around a well-seasoned, savory ingredient such as ham, smoked salmon, kimchi, or salami.

ADD RICHNESS: Mayonnaise, cheese, Greek yogurt, or avocado contributes fat and creaminess.

LAYER IN ACCENTS: Acidic, pungent, and/or fresh choices such as herbs, tomatoes, onion, and jam work well.

ASSEMBLY

MITIGATE MOISTURE: Excess juices don't just drip; they also lubricate the other ingredients, making them prone to slipping out with every bite. Pat wet ingredients dry and avoid superjuicy ones in the first place.

DON'T STACK SLIPPERY INGREDIENTS: Items such as multiple tomato slices will slide around and fall out of the sandwich.

TOAST BREAD LIGHTLY: Crunchy, heavily toasted bread will cause ingredients to slide out when bitten.

USE CREAMY INGREDIENTS AS GLUE: They will hold lighter ingredients such as chopped herbs in place.

Baked Eggs for Sandwiches
SERVES 4

This recipe requires an 8-inch square metal baking pan. Avoid using a ceramic or glass dish, which will increase the cooking time and could cause the eggs to overcook during cooling. Each of our sandwich recipes calls for a salty component; if you omit it, you may want to season the eggs with additional salt after baking. For maximum efficiency, prepare your sandwich fillings while the eggs cook, and toast the bread while the eggs cool. Alternatively, let the eggs cool completely after cutting them, stack them in an airtight container, and refrigerate them for up to three days. To reheat, arrange the egg squares on a large plate and microwave at 50 percent power until they're warm (about 45 seconds for a single square or 2 to 3 minutes for four squares).

8 large eggs
¼ teaspoon table salt

1. Adjust oven rack to middle position and heat oven to 300 degrees. Whisk eggs and salt in large bowl until well combined. Whisk in ⅔ cup water. Spray 8-inch square baking pan with vegetable oil spray. Pour egg mixture into prepared pan and set pan on rimmed baking sheet. Add 1½ cups water to sheet. Transfer sheet to oven and bake until eggs are fully set, 35 to 40 minutes, rotating pan halfway through baking. Remove pan from sheet, transfer to wire rack, and let cool for 10 minutes.

2. Run knife around edges of pan and, using dish towel or oven mitts, invert eggs onto cutting board (if eggs stick to pan, tap bottom of pan firmly to dislodge). Cut into 4 equal squares.

Egg, Kimchi, and Avocado Sandwiches
SERVES 4

We like the flavor and texture of kaiser rolls for these sandwiches, but you can substitute 4-inch bulkie rolls, English muffins, or burger buns, if desired. Blot the kimchi dry while the eggs bake.

¼ cup mayonnaise
4 kaiser rolls, halved and lightly toasted
¼ cup chopped fresh cilantro
1 recipe Baked Eggs for Sandwiches
1 ripe avocado, halved, pitted, and sliced thin
¾ cup cabbage kimchi, drained, chopped coarse, and blotted dry with paper towels

Spread mayonnaise on roll bottoms. Sprinkle cilantro over mayonnaise. Using spatula, transfer 1 egg square to each sandwich. Top each egg square with avocado and then kimchi. Set roll tops over kimchi and serve.

Egg, Smoked Salmon, and Dill Sandwiches
SERVES 4

We like the flavor and texture of rye bread for these sandwiches, but you can substitute 4-inch bulkie rolls, kaiser rolls, English muffins, or burger buns, if desired. Soak the onion while the eggs bake.

½ small red onion, sliced thin
¼ cup plain Greek yogurt
8 slices hearty rye sandwich bread, lightly toasted, divided
2 tablespoons chopped fresh dill
1 recipe Baked Eggs for Sandwiches
4 ounces smoked salmon

1. Place onion in bowl, cover with ice water, and let sit for 15 minutes. Drain onion well and pat dry.

2. Spread yogurt on 4 slices of toast. Sprinkle dill over yogurt. Using spatula, transfer 1 egg square to each sandwich. Top each egg square with smoked salmon and then onion. Set remaining 4 slices of toast over onion and serve.

Egg, Ham, and Pepperoncini Sandwiches
SERVES 4

We like the flavor and texture of English muffins for these sandwiches, but you can substitute 4-inch bulkie rolls, kaiser rolls, or burger buns, if desired.

¼ cup apricot jam
4 English muffins, split and lightly toasted
1 recipe Baked Eggs for Sandwiches
4 slices deli cheddar cheese (4 ounces)
4 slices deli ham (4 ounces)
¼ cup pepperoncini, sliced and blotted dry

Spread jam on muffin bottoms. Using spatula, transfer 1 egg square to each sandwich. Top each egg square with cheddar, then ham, and then pepperoncini. Set muffin tops over pepperoncini and serve.

Egg, Salami, and Tomato Sandwiches
SERVES 4

We like the flavor and texture of bulkie rolls for these sandwiches, but you can substitute 4-inch kaiser rolls, English muffins, or burger buns, if desired.

¼ cup mayonnaise
4 bulkie rolls, halved and lightly toasted
¼ cup chopped fresh basil
1 recipe Baked Eggs for Sandwiches
12–16 thin slices salami (4 ounces)
4 thin tomato slices

Spread mayonnaise on roll bottoms. Sprinkle basil over mayonnaise. Using spatula, transfer 1 egg square to each sandwich. Top each egg square with salami and then 1 tomato slice. Set roll tops over tomato and serve.

BANANA MUFFINS

✅ **WHY THIS RECIPE WORKS** In pursuit of banana muffins with potent flavor, we added plenty of mashed bananas to our batter. To prevent the extra liquid and mass from weighing down the crumb and making our muffins dense and gummy, we used bread flour instead of all-purpose flour; its higher protein content not only makes it more absorbent and better able to accommodate the moisture but also provides extra strength, so our muffins had a uniformly light crumb. Adding extra baking powder ensured that each muffin's volume was maximized. Baking the muffins at a higher-than-normal temperature caused the edges to set before the middle, resulting in dramatic peaks on these quick, homemade muffins.

BANANA MUFFINS WITH COCONUT AND MACADAMIA

It's a familiar scenario: You bought bananas a week ago, planning to enjoy them when they attained perfect ripeness, but life got in the way, so there they sit on your counter, fragrant and guilt-inducing, their once-sparse speckles now merging into uniformity. Banana bread is an option, but you've walked that road so many times. May I suggest muffins?

A dozen muffins come together as swiftly as a loaf of quick bread, but because muffins are smaller, they take less than 20 minutes to bake, making them the speediest possible route from countertop eyesore to satisfying snack. But to make muffins that look and taste great—stately, with potent banana flavor—you need a reliable recipe.

Quick breads and muffins use the same mixing method: Combine the wet ingredients in one bowl and the dry ingredients in another, and then stir them together. Scoop the batter into a loaf pan or the wells of a muffin tin and bake. Easy.

I figured I had a head start because I developed a really good banana bread recipe years ago. It's a little quirky, as I took some unusual measures to pack in as many bananas as possible: I microwaved five peeled bananas until they released lots of liquid and then reduced that liquid, both to concentrate its flavor and to prevent it from weighing down my bread. Then I mixed and baked. The resulting loaf was hefty and fine crumbed—and delicious out of all proportion to the small amount of extra effort required.

I thought I could make the same batter and scoop it into a muffin tin instead of a loaf pan and my muffin recipe would be done. I was mistaken. Most quick bread batters can be transformed into muffin batter with just an equipment switcheroo, but not this particular one, since all the fruit made it particularly heavy. These muffins were dense, rose very little, and had no peaks to speak of.

NOTES FROM THE TEST KITCHEN

SWEET SPOTS
For moist, deeply flavorful muffins, it's essential to use very ripe fruit. In lab tests, we found that heavily speckled bananas had nearly three times the amount of fructose as less-spotty ones. What's more, sugar behaves like a liquid in baked goods, so muffins made with ripe bananas will not only have better banana flavor but also be more moist.

For my next batch, I decreased the number of bananas to three and skipped the microwaving, draining, and reducing steps. With fewer bananas to be lifted, the crumb opened up a bit. But the muffins still didn't have the kind of loft I was hoping for, nor did they have peaks—a sign that maximum rise has been achieved—and the banana flavor was weak.

Maybe using four bananas would boost the flavor without weighing down the crumb? No dice. I liked the deeper flavor, but these muffins were squat, and they each had a slim layer of raw-looking batter near the bottom. They appeared to have too much moisture. Or not enough structure. Or both.

Cake flour and bread flour were both worth trying. Cake flour has absorptive properties, but swapping it in only eliminated the raw layer; these muffins still had poor volume. Bread flour seemed more promising: Its high protein level also makes it more absorbent than all-purpose flour, so it could also handle the moisture, but the extra protein would lead to better structure as well. Sure enough, bread-flour muffins baked up with a loftier, more uniform crumb (no squidgy layer).

Finally, I broke out the baking powder. My banana bread recipe called for only a small amount of baking soda to react with the acidic ingredients in the mix, but here I also stirred in baking powder, which is activated by heat and moisture, to produce an even coarser, more open crumb.

My recipe was close. The muffins had plenty of banana flavor; good volume; and a fluffy, slightly coarse crumb. Adding some walnuts to the batter and sprinkling some sugar on the tops right before baking made them even more special, but the shape wasn't quite right: They had gently rounded domes rather than the tall peaks I wanted. So I did some research on what makes some muffins rounded and others pointy.

It's all about heat: Because a metal muffin tin is an efficient conductor of heat energy, the batter that sits next to the tin (the sides and bottom of each muffin) heats up faster and sets rapidly. The center takes longer to heat and set, so it continues to rise, resulting in a peak. The hotter the oven, the more pronounced the temperature differential and the more dramatic the peak. Indeed, when I increased the oven temperature from 375 to 425 degrees, the edges set long before the centers, resulting in dramatic pointy tops.

Now that I had the banana muffin of my dreams, I wanted to make sure that I had plenty of variations to rotate through. A coconut and macadamia version emphasizes the tropical origins of the fruit, while a peanut butter one harkens back to childhood banana sandwiches. And a sesame variation, bolstered by earthy tahini and flecked with chunks of bittersweet chocolate, makes a more sophisticated snack.

—ANDREA GEARY, *Cook's Illustrated*

Banana-Walnut Muffins

MAKES 12 MUFFINS

Be sure to use bananas that are very heavily speckled or even black; less-ripe bananas will produce dry muffins with less flavor. You can substitute thawed frozen bananas; be sure to add any juice that is given off as the bananas thaw. We like the classic pairing of banana and walnuts here, but you can substitute chopped toasted pecans or omit the nuts altogether if you prefer. (Nut-free muffins will be slightly smaller.)

1⅔	cups (9⅛ ounces) bread flour
1	tablespoon baking powder
½	teaspoon baking soda
½	teaspoon table salt
4-5	very ripe large bananas, peeled and mashed (2 cups)
¾	cup (5¼ ounces) plus 2 tablespoons sugar, divided
2	large eggs
⅓	cup vegetable oil
2	teaspoons vanilla extract
⅓	cup chopped toasted walnuts

1. Adjust oven rack to middle position and heat oven to 425 degrees. Grease 12-cup muffin tin. Whisk flour, baking powder, baking soda, and salt together in medium bowl.

2. Whisk bananas, ¾ cup sugar, eggs, oil, and vanilla in large bowl until fully combined. Add flour mixture and whisk until fully combined. Stir in walnuts. Using portion scoop or large spoon, divide batter evenly among prepared muffin cups (about ½ cup batter per cup; cups will be very full). Sprinkle with remaining 2 tablespoons sugar.

3. Bake until tops are golden brown and toothpick inserted in center comes out clean, 14 to 18 minutes. Let muffins cool in muffin tin on wire rack for 10 minutes. Remove muffins from muffin tin and let cool for at least 5 minutes. Serve warm or at room temperature.

VARIATIONS

Banana Muffins with Coconut and Macadamia
Substitute ⅓ cup finely chopped toasted macadamia nuts and ⅓ cup toasted sweetened flaked coconut for walnuts. Decrease sugar in muffins to ½ cup. Reserve 2 tablespoons macadamia nut mixture for sprinkling atop muffins and decrease sprinkling sugar to 1 tablespoon.

Banana Muffins with Sesame and Chocolate Chunks
Substitute ⅓ cup toasted sesame seeds and 2 ounces bittersweet chocolate, cut into ¼-inch chunks, for walnuts and reserve 2 tablespoons seeds for sprinkling atop muffins. Whisk ⅓ cup tahini with banana mixture in step 2. Decrease sprinkling sugar to 1 tablespoon. Omit vanilla.

Peanut Butter–Banana Muffins
Substitute ½ cup dry-roasted peanuts, chopped fine, for walnuts and reserve 2 tablespoons for sprinkling atop muffins. Whisk ⅓ cup creamy peanut butter with banana mixture in step 2. Decrease sprinkling sugar to 1 tablespoon.

NOTES FROM THE TEST KITCHEN

WHY BREAD FLOUR WORKS BEST

When muffins mixed with all-purpose flour baked up short, with a gummy crumb, we switched to bleached cake flour. Bleaching changes the structure of flour granules, enabling them to accommodate extra moisture; thus, the wetness vanished. But cake flour has fewer of the proteins that combine to form the gluten network that gives baked goods structure, so it couldn't support robust expansion. Bread flour was the answer. It too has absorptive properties, but it also has lots of protein, so it develops a strong gluten network. The upshot: a fluffy crumb with the strength to support the weight of four to five bananas.

GERMAN APPLE PANCAKE

✔ **WHY THIS RECIPE WORKS** This simple (yet impressive) skillet pancake starts with an easy stir-together batter of flour, milk, eggs, brown sugar, salt, and a touch of vanilla. The batter is looser than a typical pancake batter, which allows it to puff dramatically while it bakes. The extra moisture turns to steam in the oven, causing the pancake to balloon, especially around the edges where it touches the hot skillet. For our version, we wanted tender, flavorful apples baked right into the pancake. Caramelizing Granny Smith apples in butter with brown sugar and cinnamon gave us the perfect sweet-tart flavor to stand up to the rich, custardy pancake. A tangy sauce of sour cream and brown sugar made this breakfast extra-special.

Also known as a Dutch baby, a German pancake features a giant puffed rim that makes for a festive presentation—and it comes together in a flash. It's traditionally made by pouring a thin, eggy batter into a hot skillet and baking it; the heat from the skillet and oven convert moisture in the batter to steam, which causes the pancake to balloon dramatically (and then fall). The end result, like Yorkshire pudding or popovers, features a creamy, custardy center surrounded by a crispy browned lip. Classic versions include apples baked right in.

I started with a batter of flour, milk, eggs, brown sugar, salt, and vanilla, which I stirred together by hand. Pancakes from early tests with raw or only lightly cooked apples baked up too wet, and bites of crunchy apples were jarring against the soft-textured pancake, so I began by cooking down apples until they had softened and some of their moisture had evaporated. My tasters liked tart Granny Smith apples, which were an excellent foil for the rich pancake. To coax out extra complexity, I added butter, brown sugar, and cinnamon to the skillet and cooked the apples until they began to brown and their juices reduced to a caramel-like glaze.

I poured the batter around the apples, put the skillet in a 425-degree oven, and held my breath. Every single time I make this pancake, the doubt starts to creep in, and I fear that the steam science will somehow fail me. But it never does! I watched the pancake puff before my eyes and pulled out a gorgeously rumpled, golden-brown pancake with a towering rim just about 20 minutes later.

The finishing touch was a tasty, if unconventional, accompaniment: a dollop of sour cream sweetened with a bit of brown sugar. It was creamy, tangy, and just right.

—JESSICA RUDOLPH, *Cook's Country*

German Apple Pancake with Brown Sugar Sour Cream
SERVES 4 TO 6

You can substitute low-fat or skim milk for the whole milk, if desired, but the pancake will taste slightly eggier. You will need a 12-inch ovensafe skillet for this recipe. We do not recommend using a nonstick or cast-iron skillet here, as the bottom of the pancake will get too dark. The pancake will puff up during baking and deflate shortly after it comes out of the oven—that's supposed to happen. The interior will be no less delicious.

½   cup sour cream
½   cup packed (3½ ounces) brown sugar, divided
¾   cup (3¾ ounces) all-purpose flour
1   teaspoon table salt, divided
5   large eggs
1   cup whole milk
1   teaspoon vanilla extract
4   tablespoons unsalted butter
1¼ pounds Granny Smith apples, peeled, cored, halved, and sliced ¼ inch thick
¼   teaspoon ground cinnamon
    Confectioners' sugar

1. Adjust oven rack to lowest position and heat oven to 425 degrees. Combine sour cream and 2 tablespoons brown sugar in small bowl; set aside.

2. Whisk flour, ¾ teaspoon salt, and 2 tablespoons brown sugar together in large bowl. Whisk eggs, milk, and vanilla together in separate bowl. Whisk half of egg mixture into flour mixture until no lumps remain. Slowly whisk in remaining egg mixture until smooth; set aside batter.

3. Melt butter in 12-inch ovensafe skillet over medium-high heat. Add apples, cinnamon, remaining ¼ cup brown sugar, and remaining ¼ teaspoon salt. Cook, stirring frequently, until apples are softened, browned, and glazy, 8 to 10 minutes.

SPANISH MIGAS WITH FRIED EGGS

4. Scrape any apples off sides of skillet and distribute evenly over bottom of skillet. Working quickly, pour batter around and over apples. Immediately transfer skillet to oven and bake until edges of pancake are browned and have risen above skillet, about 18 minutes.

5. Transfer skillet to wire rack. Cut pancake into wedges in skillet and dust with confectioners' sugar. Serve hot from skillet with sour cream mixture.

SPANISH MIGAS WITH FRIED EGGS

✔ **WHY THIS RECIPE WORKS** Spanish migas is made by frying bread crumbs (and larger pieces of bread) in pork fat to create a rich, satisfying hash. For our version we started by kneading water that we'd seasoned with salt and smoked paprika into the bread, adding extra water as needed for the bread to soften appropriately. We then fried a mixture of soft Spanish-style chorizo sausage, thick-cut bacon, and smashed garlic cloves until the bacon fat had rendered, the bacon had crisped, and the oil had taken on the garlic's flavor. We used most of the oil and rendered bacon fat to fry the bread until the smallest pieces were browned and crisped throughout and larger pieces were crisped on the outside but still moist within. We then fried a mixture of Cubanelle and red bell peppers until they blistered and softened, returned the meat to the skillet, and added sherry vinegar for brightness and parsley for color. Finally, we topped the dish with sunny-side up fried eggs.

Like most bakers, I typically have a hunk (or three) of stale bread lying around my kitchen. As such, I am well acquainted with the satisfaction that comes from breathing new life into a hardened loaf. A prime example is the outstanding Spanish dish known as migas ("migas" means "crumbs"). It involves moistening crumbs (and larger pieces) of bread with water and then frying them in fat along with lots of garlic, Spanish-style chorizo sausage, and smoked paprika. Some of the water evaporates as the bread sizzles, but much of it is pushed into the bread starch, creating crisp and chewy morsels imbued with the flavors of garlic and pork. It's great stuff.

Some cooks include a second pork product such as pork belly, bacon, or Spanish ham for depth (and more fat); others fold in produce like peppers, hearty greens, mushrooms, or even grapes. The mix-ins are cut into bite-size pieces and tossed with the bread to create a filling hash that can be served as tapas or topped with eggs for breakfast, brunch, or dinner.

Making great migas is primarily about getting the bread just right: The proper texture, which I fondly refer to as "crunchewy," is best accomplished by starting with a rustic, crusty loaf; removing the thick bottom crust; and soaking it in water. After some testing, I came up with a method that works with bread of any degree of freshness: Begin with ⅓ cup of water for 5 cups of cubed bread, and then gently knead the bread until the pieces break down. If the bread cubes resist falling apart, add water 1 tablespoon at a time until they yield. Now the texture was right, but the bread needed more flavor, so I first seasoned the water with a little smoked paprika and salt before adding the bread.

With the bread ready to go, I fried slices of soft Spanish-style chorizo in olive oil (harder, more aged sausage dried out too quickly during frying) with smashed whole garlic cloves. I included thick-cut bacon to provide an extra layer of smokiness as well as extra fat for frying the bread, which I did after removing the meat and garlic from the pan with a slotted spoon. Once the pieces were golden and crisp on the outside, I sautéed red bell and Cubanelle peppers—the former offered sweetness, and the latter provided a slight bitter counterpoint—with a little more smoked paprika. Once I returned the meat to the pan, I drizzled on sherry vinegar to help balance the richness and added a colorful shower of minced parsley.

Finally, I topped the migas with fried eggs cooked sunny-side up so that the softly set yolks would spill onto the porky, garlicky bread. Not a bad way to use up a leftover loaf.

—ANDREW JANJIGIAN, *Cook's Illustrated*

Spanish Migas with Fried Eggs
SERVES 4 TO 6

Fresh or stale bread can be used here. Buy fully cooked Spanish-style chorizo that is somewhat soft; if you can't find it, substitute linguica. Anaheim chiles can be used in place of the Cubanelles. Serve as a hearty breakfast or brunch or with a salad for dinner.

⅓ cup water, plus extra as needed

1 teaspoon table salt, divided

1 teaspoon smoked paprika, divided

5 (¾-inch-thick) slices rustic, crusty bread (9 ounces), bottom crust removed, cut into ½- to ¾-inch cubes (5 cups)

6 large eggs, divided

¼ cup extra-virgin olive oil

6 ounces Spanish-style chorizo sausage, halved lengthwise and sliced ¼ inch thick

2 slices thick-cut bacon, cut into ½-inch pieces

4 garlic cloves, smashed and peeled

2 Cubanelle peppers, stemmed, seeded, and cut into ½-inch pieces

1 red bell pepper, stemmed, seeded, and cut into ½-inch pieces

½ teaspoon sherry vinegar

1 tablespoon minced fresh parsley, divided

1. Whisk water, ½ teaspoon salt, and ½ teaspoon paprika in large bowl until salt is dissolved. Add bread and knead gently with your hands until liquid is absorbed and half of bread has broken down into smaller pieces. If bread does not break down, add extra water, 1 tablespoon at a time, and continue to knead until you have mix of bigger and smaller pieces interspersed with a few crumbs. Set aside. Crack 3 eggs into small bowl. Repeat with remaining 3 eggs and second small bowl. Set aside eggs.

2. Heat oil, chorizo, bacon, and garlic in 12-inch nonstick or carbon-steel skillet over medium heat, stirring frequently, until bacon fat is rendered and bacon is just beginning to crisp at edges, 6 to 8 minutes. Using slotted spoon, transfer chorizo and bacon to medium bowl; discard garlic. Reserve 2 tablespoons fat. Pour remaining fat over bread mixture and toss to combine. Add bread to now-empty skillet and cook over medium-high heat, stirring frequently, until smallest pieces are browned and crisp throughout and larger pieces are crisp on exterior and moist within, 12 to 15 minutes. Return bread mixture to bowl.

3. Add 1 tablespoon reserved fat, Cubanelle and bell peppers, remaining ½ teaspoon salt, and remaining ½ teaspoon paprika to now-empty skillet. Cook over high heat until peppers are softened and slightly blistered, 3 to 5 minutes. Return chorizo mixture to skillet with peppers and cook, stirring frequently, until heated through, about 30 seconds. Sprinkle with vinegar and

2 teaspoons parsley and toss to combine. Transfer to bowl with bread and toss to combine. Transfer to wide serving bowl.

4. Heat remaining 1 tablespoon reserved fat in now-empty skillet over medium-high heat until shimmering. Swirl to coat skillet. Working quickly, pour 1 bowl of eggs in 1 side of skillet and second bowl of eggs in other side. Cover and cook for 1 minute. Remove skillet from heat and let sit, covered, for 15 to 45 seconds for runny yolks (white around edge of yolk will be barely opaque), 45 to 60 seconds for soft but set yolks, and about 2 minutes for medium-set yolks. Transfer eggs to top of migas, sprinkle with remaining 1 teaspoon parsley, and serve.

CORNED BEEF AND CABBAGE HASH

✓ **WHY THIS RECIPE WORKS** We wanted a recipe for this diner staple that was easy to make in every home kitchen. In a large bowl we tossed together ½-inch cubes of cooked corned beef from the deli counter; unpeeled russet potatoes; and carrots, which offered pretty pops of color. We also added shredded cabbage and sliced onion and combined the entire mixture with garlic, thyme, a few spices, and vegetable oil. We transferred the contents of the bowl to a nonstick skillet and cooked them, covered, until the potatoes were tender. We then removed the skillet from the heat and mashed the ingredients into a cohesive mass with a potato masher. After adding little nubs of butter all around the sides, we returned the skillet to the heat to brown the hash. Flipping the hash in sections with a spatula gave us control over how much browning was achieved and allowed browning on both sides. The finished hash was bound by creamy potatoes; webbed with cabbage; and studded with salty, tender corned beef and subtly sweet carrots.

Hashes, or meals made from ingredients that are chopped up and cooked in a skillet, have been around forever. One common version found across the United States, corned beef hash, rose to popularity in New England during the 19th century. Home cooks made it with ingredients left over from big boiled dinners of corned beef, potatoes, and cabbage. By the mid-20th century, it was also a canned-goods staple in grocery stores.

CORNED BEEF AND CABBAGE HASH

For my own version, I wanted to skip the can but achieve the flavors of a classic hash without having to make the corned beef (heavily seasoned preserved beef, often brisket) from scratch.

Luckily my local deli sells cooked corned beef, so I bought some and cut it into ½-inch pieces. I did the same with a pound of russet potatoes and two carrots, which offered a bit of sweetness and pretty pops of color. Shredded cabbage and sliced onion joined these ingredients in a large bowl with garlic, thyme, a few spices, and some vegetable oil for a quick toss.

I added the mixture to a nonstick skillet and cooked it, covered, until the potatoes were tender. Then I removed the skillet from the heat and mashed the ingredients together with a potato masher. I pressed everything into one solid mass that looked almost like a pancake, added little nubs of butter all around the sides, and returned it to the heat to brown. Flipping sections with a spatula gave me control over how much browning was achieved and allowed browning on both sides.

My hash was bound by creamy potatoes and woven in a web of cabbage, with salty, tender corned beef and subtly sweet carrots in every bite. I tinkered with the mix of spices (dry mustard, black pepper, and allspice) until I had beautifully amplified flavor throughout the hash. It was just right for a hearty breakfast—or, for that matter, lunch or dinner.

—MARK HUXSOLL, *Cook's Country*

Corned Beef and Cabbage Hash

SERVES 4 TO 6

Corned beef is sold both raw and fully cooked. Purchase fully cooked corned beef from the deli counter—ask the butcher to slice it ½ inch thick. You can also use cooked corned beef left over from a boiled dinner. About one-quarter of a head of green cabbage will yield 3 cups. Serve with hot sauce and a fried egg, if desired.

- 1 **pound russet potatoes, unpeeled, cut into ½-inch dice**
- 12 **ounces cooked corned beef brisket, cut into ½-inch dice**
- 3 **cups shredded green cabbage**
- 1 **cup thinly sliced onion**
- 2 **carrots, peeled and cut into ½-inch dice (½ cup)**
- 2 **tablespoons vegetable oil**
- 2 **garlic cloves, sliced thin**
- 2 **teaspoons coarsely chopped fresh thyme**
- 2 **teaspoons pepper**
- 1½ **teaspoons dry mustard**
- 1 **teaspoon table salt**
- ½ **teaspoon ground allspice**
- 4 **tablespoons unsalted butter, cut into 16 pieces**

1. Toss potatoes, beef, cabbage, onion, carrots, oil, garlic, thyme, pepper, mustard, salt, and allspice together in large bowl. Transfer mixture to 12-inch nonstick skillet and set over medium heat (skillet will be very full, but contents will cook down). Cover and cook until potatoes are tender, 15 to 20 minutes, stirring occasionally.

2. Remove skillet from heat and, using potato masher, mash ingredients into coarse, cohesive mass. Spread corned beef mixture into even layer and place butter pieces along sides of skillet all around hash. Return to medium heat and cook, uncovered and undisturbed, until well browned on bottom, 5 to 7 minutes.

3. Flip spatula-size portions of hash and lightly repack in skillet. Cook until browned on second side, about 2 minutes. Flip again and brown bottom once more, about 2 minutes. Serve.

BOLOS LÊVEDOS (PORTUGUESE MUFFINS)

✓ **WHY THIS RECIPE WORKS** Though they look a lot like English muffins, bolos lêvedos are denser and richer, with a fair amount of sweetness and a rich crumb from whole milk, eggs, and butter. After visiting Central Bakery, a Portuguese bakery in Tiverton, Rhode Island, that's known for its bolos lêvedos, we set out to create our own recipe. We wanted to ensure that the dough would be hydrated enough to produce a tender muffin, so we turned to a method called tangzhong, which involves quickly heating a small portion of the flour and liquid (in this case, water) to form a paste. The paste then gets mixed in with the rest of the ingredients. This helped hydrate the dough quickly and created a more workable dough (it also helped the cooked bolos stay fresh longer). To further ensure full hydration and tender bolos, we included an autolyse step, which entailed mixing everything together (except for the sugar and salt) and letting it rest for 15 minutes to fully hydrate and get a jump start on gluten development. After a traditional two-stage rise, we browned our muffins in a skillet and finished cooking them in the oven, which yielded slightly sweet, moist cakes fit for breakfast, lunch, and dinner.

Bolos lêvedos, at first glance, look a lot like English muffins. But these Portuguese treats ("bolos" means "cakes," and "lêvedos" means "yeast"), originally from the Azores, are denser, sweeter, and richer than English muffins, thanks to whole milk, eggs, and butter. To get their classic look, they are cooked on two sides on a dry griddle or skillet. They're often eaten for breakfast, but they can also be used as burger buns or sandwich bread.

Inspired by a visit to Central Bakery, a Portuguese bakery in Tiverton, Rhode Island, that turns out hundreds of bolos lêvedos a day, I set out to create a small-scale recipe for the home kitchen.

After a few experiments with existing recipes, I zeroed in on some techniques we've used with other rich yeasted doughs that I knew would help here.

First, to ensure that the dough would be well hydrated enough to create a tender finished product, I followed a method called tangzhong, which involves heating a small portion of flour and liquid to form a paste before mixing in the rest of the ingredients. This method helped the flour more readily absorb the liquid from the milk, eggs, and butter, creating a more workable dough and more tender and moist bolos (it also helped the cooked bolos stay fresh longer).

Second, I found that the additions of sugar and salt, essential to bolos, were impeding the absorption of the liquid. To solve the issue, I introduced an autolyse step, mixing everything together (except for the sugar and salt) and allowing it to rest for 15 minutes to fully hydrate and get a head start on gluten development. Only then did I incorporate the sugar and salt and finish kneading the dough.

With these two extra steps, plus a traditional two-part rise (first all together and then in individual portions), I was able to brown my bolos in a nonstick skillet for that signature exterior color and then transfer them to a baking sheet and finish them off in the oven. You wouldn't believe how incredible my kitchen smelled as they baked; waiting for them to cool down was almost intolerable.

—MARK HUXSOLL, *Cook's Country*

Bolos Lêvedos (Portuguese Muffins)

MAKES 8 MUFFINS

If you don't own a microwave, the flour paste can also be made in a small saucepan over medium heat. Just be sure to whisk it constantly so that the ingredients don't scorch. Split the muffins with a knife. Serve them with butter or use them as sandwich bread or burger buns.

FLOUR PASTE

⅔ cup water

¼ cup (1¼ ounces) all-purpose flour

NOTES FROM THE TEST KITCHEN

BUILDING THE BOLOS

1. PORTION: After first rise, divide dough into 8 equal pieces.

2. ROUND: Cup each piece and roll in circles to create taut dough balls.

3. FLATTEN: Use your hand to flatten each ball into disk.

4. WEIGHT: Top with baking sheet so disks don't puff too much before browning.

BOLOS LÊVEDOS (PORTUGUESE MUFFINS)

DOUGH

- 6 tablespoons whole milk
- 4 tablespoons unsalted butter, cut into 4 pieces and softened
- 2 large eggs
- 3 cups (15 ounces) all-purpose flour, plus extra for shaping
- 1 teaspoon instant or rapid-rise yeast
- ½ cup (3½ ounces) sugar
- 1 teaspoon table salt
- 1 teaspoon vegetable oil

1. FOR THE FLOUR PASTE: Whisk water and flour in medium bowl until no lumps remain. Microwave, whisking every 20 seconds, until mixture thickens to stiff, smooth, pudding-like consistency, 40 to 80 seconds. Transfer paste to bowl of stand mixer.

2. FOR THE DOUGH: Whisk milk into flour paste in bowl of stand mixer until combined. Whisk in butter until fully incorporated. Whisk in eggs until fully incorporated.

3. Add flour and yeast to paste mixture. Fit mixer with dough hook and mix on low speed until dough comes together and no dry flour remains, about 2 minutes. Turn off mixer, cover bowl with dish towel or plastic wrap, and let dough stand for 15 minutes.

4. Add sugar and salt to dough and mix on low speed until incorporated, about 1 minute. Increase speed to medium and mix until dough is elastic and pulls away from sides of bowl but still sticks to bottom (dough will be sticky), about 8 minutes. Transfer dough to greased large bowl; cover tightly with plastic wrap; and let rise until doubled in size, about 1½ hours.

5. Line rimmed baking sheet with parchment paper. Turn out dough onto clean counter and divide into 8 equal pieces, about 4 ounces each. Working with 1 piece of dough at a time, cup dough with your palm and roll against counter in circular motion into smooth, tight ball.

6. Sprinkle ¼ cup flour on counter. Working with 1 dough ball at a time, turn dough ball in flour and press with your hand to flatten into 3½- to 4-inch disk. Transfer dough disks to prepared sheet. Lay second sheet of parchment over dough disks, then place second rimmed baking sheet on top to keep disks flat during second rise. Let rise for 30 minutes. Adjust oven rack to middle position and heat oven to 350 degrees.

7. Heat oil in 12-inch nonstick skillet over medium-low heat until shimmering. Using paper towels, carefully wipe out oil from skillet.

8. Transfer 4 dough disks to skillet and cook until deeply browned on both sides, 2 to 4 minutes per side. Return toasted disks to sheet. Repeat with remaining 4 dough disks.

9. Bake until muffins register 190 degrees in center, 11 to 14 minutes. Transfer muffins to wire rack and let cool for 30 minutes. Serve. (Muffins can be stored in airtight container for up to 3 days or frozen for up to 1 month.)

VARIATION

Bolos Lêvedos (Portuguese Muffins) with Lemon and Cinnamon
Add 1½ teaspoons grated lemon zest and ¼ teaspoon ground cinnamon with flour in step 3.

OATMEAL DINNER ROLLS

✔ **WHY THIS RECIPE WORKS** For dinner rolls that boast nutty whole-grain flavor and are also fluffy and moist, we started by soaking old-fashioned rolled oats in hot water. During a short rest the oats absorbed most of the water, effectively locking it away. We stirred in whole-wheat flour to boost the nutty flavor profile, white bread flour for structure, and molasses for its complexity and sweetness. And we added even more water, making a dough that contains a very high proportion of water to flour yet can be rolled into balls without sticking to our hands. Nestling the dough balls close together in a cake pan ensured that they supported each other in upward rather than outward expansion. That mutual support, along with the transformation of water to steam during the bake, yielded dinner rolls that contained the best of both worlds: light, soft, plush texture along with whole-grain complexity. The added liquid also extended the rolls' shelf life, so they could be enjoyed for a few days or even frozen for later.

Years ago, I developed a popular recipe for light, fluffy dinner rolls. The key to the recipe's success? A baking technique commonly called by its Chinese name, tangzhong, thanks to being widely popularized by Taiwanese cook Yvonne Chen in her recipe for fluffy Hokkaido milk bread. The term, which loosely translates as "hot-water roux," refers to a pudding-like mixture made by cooking a small amount of flour in water until the two form a gel. Mixing that gel into my dough enabled me to add a high proportion of water without making the dough unworkably soft and sticky, because some of the water was effectively "locked away" in the gel. When the rolls hit the oven, that abundance of water turned to steam and inflated the rolls, making them light and soft. The gel also extended the shelf life of the rolls, so they remained moist even the next day.

I've made those rolls at home more times than I can count, and the *Cook's Illustrated* team has gone on to apply the tangzhong technique to other classic white breads such as sticky buns and challah. But recently I started wondering: Why stop at white bread? Wouldn't it be great to use tangzhong to add moisture and softness to breads that often lack those qualities, specifically breads with added whole grains? And then I realized I already had.

Back in cooking school, I learned to make a recipe that went like this: Pour boiling water over steel-cut oats and let the mixture sit until the oats have absorbed the water. Then build your dough by adding bread flour, more water, a bit of brown sugar, yeast, and salt. After rising for about an hour, the dough was easy to shape into a loaf—not too sticky or soft. The resulting bread was surprisingly moist and plush, and it stayed soft longer than most other breads—even longer than my Fluffy Dinner Rolls. When I recently analyzed the recipe, I noticed that the proportion of water to flour in

that dough was higher than in most dinner rolls. In fact, it approached 70 percent, a hydration I associate with wet, sticky, unmanageable doughs. But this dough was easy to work with because using the soaked oats acted similarly to tangzhong, with all its associated virtues. (When I did a little investigating, I found out that oats are even more effective than refined white flour at holding on to water in a dough.) That old recipe seemed like a promising starting point for a new dinner roll: one with a plush crumb and an extended shelf life that still offered complexity in terms of flavor and texture.

I made the steel-cut oat dough as I had learned it decades ago, but instead of shaping it into a single loaf that I baked in a loaf pan, after the first rise, I divided it into 12 pieces, which I rolled into balls and arranged in a greased 9-inch round cake pan. (High-moisture doughs can spread if they're baked free-form; placing the rolls close together would allow them to support each other and encourage upward rather than outward expansion.) I let the dough rise again and then baked the rolls. It was a good start: The crumb was fluffy and soft. But I'd had to wait 45 minutes for the coarse steel-cut oats to absorb that first addition of water, and sometimes oats near the surface of the bread dried out in the oven and became a little hard. The solution was to use rolled oats. These hydrated so quickly, in fact, that the mixture was still too hot to add the yeast. To be safe, I incorporated some cold water along with the rest of the ingredients.

When the rolls were baked, the oats in the dough mostly melted into the bread but left a subtle and pleasant nubby texture; the oats I'd sprinkled on top

NOTES FROM THE TEST KITCHEN

HOW OATS MAKE MOISTER BREAD THAT LASTS LONGER
Given the high hydration of this dough, one might expect that it would be extremely soft and too sticky to handle. Here's why it isn't: The recipe contains oats, and before adding them to the other ingredients, we soak them in some of the water (boiled first), which causes them to gel and essentially lock away this moisture. This technique is called tangzhong, and we've employed it in other bread recipes, but only with refined white flour.

It turns out that oats are even better at "hiding" extra liquid in a dough. That's because, as a whole-grain product, oats contain more pentosans—a type of carbohydrate—than refined white flour, which has had its pentosan-rich bran layer milled away.

Pentosans are more absorbent than starch and can hold up to 10 times their weight in water. The upshot for our oatmeal rolls: With so much water in the dough, the rolls bake up exceptionally moist and stay that way longer.

UNSOAKED OATS
Loose, sticky dough

SOAKED OATS
Stiffer, drier dough

delivered a crisp texture and toasty flavor. Still, these rolls looked and tasted a lot like my fluffy dinner rolls. That wasn't a bad thing, but I was after something a little heartier and nuttier here.

I was using bread flour because I needed its higher protein for lift (the oats have no gluten-forming proteins to contribute structure, so they're freeloaders in this formula), but was there room for something with a bit more personality? I replaced one-third of the bread flour with whole-wheat flour, which turned out to be a good move. It provided more nutty flavor and a heartier texture, but it didn't noticeably compromise the rolls' lift. I was getting there.

For the next batch, I added just a bit of richness in the form of butter. Rather than leave it to soften at room temperature or melt it in the microwave, I added it with the oats so that the hot water would melt it while the oats were hydrating. Finally, I considered the brown sugar. Presumably it had been added to that old cooking school recipe because, with its molasses notes, it provided a bit more character to the bread than white sugar would have. But why not go whole hog? I swapped the brown sugar for molasses itself, which added even more moisture; a complex, bittersweet flavor; and a rich color.

I still love my original fluffy white dinner rolls, but it's nice to have options.

—ANDREA GEARY, *Cook's Illustrated*

Oatmeal Dinner Rolls

MAKES 12 ROLLS

For an accurate measurement of boiling water, bring a kettle of water to a boil and then measure out the desired amount. We strongly recommend measuring the flour by weight. Avoid blackstrap molasses here, as it's too bitter. If you prefer, you can portion the rolls by weight in step 2 (2¼ ounces of dough per roll). To make 24 rolls, double this recipe and bake the rolls in two 9-inch round cake pans. These rolls freeze well; thaw them at room temperature and refresh in a 350-degree oven for 8 minutes.

¾ cup (2¼ ounces) old-fashioned rolled oats, plus 4 teaspoons for sprinkling

⅔ cup boiling water, plus ½ cup cold water

2 tablespoons unsalted butter, cut into 4 pieces

1½ cups (8¼ ounces) bread flour

¾ cup (4⅛ ounces) whole-wheat flour

¼ cup molasses

1½ teaspoons instant or rapid-rise yeast

1 teaspoon table salt

1 large egg, beaten with 1 teaspoon water and pinch table salt

1. Stir ¾ cup oats, boiling water, and butter together in bowl of stand mixer and let sit until butter is melted and most of water has been absorbed, about 10 minutes. Add cold water, bread flour, whole-wheat flour, molasses, yeast, and salt. Fit mixer with dough hook and mix on low speed until flour is moistened, about 1 minute (dough may look dry). Increase speed to medium-low and mix until dough clears sides of bowl (it will still stick to bottom), about 8 minutes, scraping down dough hook halfway through mixing (dough will be sticky). Transfer dough to counter, shape into ball, and transfer to lightly greased bowl. Cover with plastic wrap and let rise until doubled in volume, 1 to 1¼ hours.

2. Grease 9-inch round cake pan and set aside. Transfer dough to lightly floured counter, reserving plastic. Pat dough gently into 8-inch square of even thickness. Using bench scraper or chef's knife, cut dough into 12 pieces (3 rows by 4 rows). Working with 1 piece of dough at a time, form dough pieces into smooth, taut balls. (To round, set piece of dough on unfloured counter. Loosely cup your lightly floured hand around dough and, without applying pressure to dough, move your hand in small circular motions. Tackiness of dough against counter and circular motion should work dough into smooth ball.) Arrange seam side down in prepared pan, placing 9 dough balls around edge of pan and remaining 3 dough balls in center. Cover with reserved plastic and let rise until rolls are doubled in size and no gaps are visible between them, 45 minutes to 1 hour.

3. When rolls are nearly doubled in size, adjust oven rack to lower-middle position and heat oven to 375 degrees. Brush rolls with egg wash and sprinkle with remaining 4 teaspoons oats. Bake until rolls are deep brown and register at least 195 degrees at center, 25 to 30 minutes. Let rolls cool in pan on wire rack for 3 minutes; invert rolls onto rack, then reinvert. Let rolls cool for at least 20 minutes before serving.

BLUEBERRY BISCUITS

BLUEBERRY BISCUITS

✔ **WHY THIS RECIPE WORKS** Inspired by the Bo-Berry Biscuits at Bojangles, the Southern fast-food chain, we set out to create our own recipe for blueberry biscuits. We wanted to be careful to keep these in the realm of flaky biscuits, with a light, tender texture that almost melts in the mouth. We were after the delicious sweet and slightly salty flavor of the fast-food biscuits, but of course we wanted to use real blueberries. We started by mixing together all-purpose flour, a little sugar, baking powder, baking soda, and salt. Then we smashed in some chilled butter with our fingertips, a step that gives biscuits their signature flaky interior crumb; the large pieces of butter melt in the oven and produce steam that helps create a light texture. Finally, we folded in tangy buttermilk and plenty of fresh blueberries. To avoid dirtying the kitchen counter and rolling and stamping out biscuits, we used our "pat-in-the-pan" biscuit method to shape the dough. This method calls for pressing the biscuit dough into an 8-inch square baking pan and cutting it into squares instead of traditional circles. After baking the biscuits, we brushed them with a lightly salted honey butter while they were still hot.

Bojangles, the Southern fast-food chain, has a menu item I used to love called Bo-Berry Biscuits. These breakfast treats have the fluffy texture of a biscuit and the sweetness of a muffin and are studded with something called Bo-Berries (faux blueberries). I haven't had these biscuits in many years, but I distinctly remember that the "berries" didn't taste much like blueberries (to me, they tasted more like candy, or part of a sweet breakfast cereal). I loved them nonetheless. I've always had a sweet tooth, and the motivation of Bo-Berry Biscuits got me out the door many mornings throughout middle school.

Inspired by my memories, I set off to make a recipe for blueberry biscuits. I wanted to be careful to keep these in the realm of fluffy biscuits, with a light, tender texture that almost melts in your mouth. I was after the delicious sweet and slightly salty flavor of the fast-food biscuits, but of course I wanted to use real blueberries (I'm pretty sure that even our crack shopping team would have a hard time finding Bo-Berries).

Here at *Cook's Country*, we know our way around a biscuit. I started pulling elements from a few of our

existing recipes, using a mix of all-purpose flour, baking powder, baking soda, and salt. I then used my fingers to smash in some chilled butter, a step that gives biscuits their signature fluffy interior crumb; the large pieces of butter melt in the oven and produce steam that helps create a light texture. Finally, I folded in tangy buttermilk and plenty of fresh blueberries. It was time to roll out the dough and stamp out biscuits. Or was it?

Our recipe for Pat-in-the-Pan Buttermilk Biscuits calls for baking the biscuits in an 8-inch square baking pan and cutting the biscuits into squares instead of circles. Yes, it's a different look from the traditional round shape. But this technique avoids dirtying the kitchen counter and rolling and stamping out biscuits. And there is no need to reroll the scraps, a step that can overwork the dough and lead to tough biscuits. So I decided to use this technique and baked my first batch in a 450-degree oven. The texture was great—moist and fluffy—but the biscuits weren't sweet enough, and the blueberries felt out of place.

I added some sugar to the dough and in turn lowered the oven temperature to prevent the biscuits from burning (sugar encourages browning). And because the biscuits I grew up eating had a sweet glaze drizzled on them, I played around with a lemon glaze and a buttermilk glaze, but ultimately I landed on brushing the hot biscuits with a lightly salted honey butter. Easy and delicious.

Turns out, a buttery blueberry biscuit is still a strong motivation for me to get out of bed in the morning. And without the need to clean up a floured counter or use a food processor, the recipe actually feels easy enough to pull off as the coffee is brewing.

—MORGAN BOLLING, *Cook's Country*

Blueberry Biscuits

SERVES 9 (MAKES 9 BISCUITS)

We prefer the flavor of fresh blueberries here, but you can also use 7½ ounces (1½ cups) of frozen blueberries that have been thawed, drained, and then patted dry with paper towels. If you have leftover buttermilk, it can be frozen in ice cube trays, transferred to zipper-lock freezer bags, and frozen for up to a month. Upon thawing, the whey and the milk solids will separate; simply whisk the buttermilk back together before using it.

BISCUITS

- 1 tablespoon unsalted butter, melted, plus
- 10 tablespoons unsalted butter, cut into ½-inch pieces and chilled
- 3 cups (15 ounces) all-purpose flour
- ½ cup (3½ ounces) sugar
- 2 teaspoons baking powder
- ½ teaspoon baking soda
- 1¼ teaspoons table salt
- 7½ ounces (1½ cups) blueberries
- 1⅔ cups buttermilk, chilled

HONEY BUTTER

- 2 tablespoons unsalted butter
- 1 tablespoon honey
- Pinch table salt

1. FOR THE BISCUITS: Adjust oven rack to middle position and heat oven to 425 degrees. Brush bottom and sides of 8-inch square baking pan with melted butter.

2. Whisk flour, sugar, baking powder, baking soda, and salt together in large bowl. Add chilled butter to flour mixture and smash butter between your fingertips into flat, irregular pieces. Add blueberries and toss with flour mixture. Gently stir in buttermilk until no dry pockets of flour remain.

NOTES FROM THE TEST KITCHEN

KEY TECHNIQUES FOR OUR EASY, FLUFFY BLUEBERRY BISCUITS

1. Add chilled butter to flour mixture and smash butter between your fingertips into flat, irregular pieces.

2. Press dough into pan, then cut into 9 equal squares with bench scraper before baking.

---

3. Using rubber spatula, transfer dough to prepared pan and spread into even layer and into corners of pan. Using bench scraper sprayed with vegetable oil spray, cut dough into 9 equal squares (2 cuts by 2 cuts), but do not separate. Bake until browned on top and paring knife inserted into center biscuit comes out clean, 40 to 45 minutes.

4. FOR THE HONEY BUTTER: Meanwhile, combine butter, honey, and salt in small bowl and microwave until butter is melted, about 30 seconds. Stir to combine; set aside.

5. Remove pan from oven and let biscuits cool in pan for 5 minutes. Turn biscuits out onto baking sheet, then reinvert biscuits onto wire rack. Brush tops of biscuits with honey butter (use all of it). Let cool for 10 minutes. Using serrated knife, cut biscuits along scored marks and serve warm.

BANANA BREAD

✔ **WHY THIS RECIPE WORKS** We wanted a dead-simple recipe for banana bread that was big on banana flavor and that wasn't all that "bready." We were seeking a slice that was tender, moist, buttery, just the right amount of sweet, and heavy with the aroma and flavor of bananas. To get there, we started by adding more bananas than we thought was possible, and then we added even more. After extensive testing, we arrived at a recipe that called for more than a pound of sweet, very ripe bananas and that was as easy as mixing the wet and dry ingredients together in a bowl. This version packs in a bit more butter and loads more bananas than the average recipe. What's more, we think it tastes a lot better, and we think you'll agree.

What makes a really good banana bread? That's what my colleagues and I asked ourselves as we dug into the five banana breads I'd baked to kick off testing for this recipe. After studying dozens of recipes, I had prepared five so that we could zero in on what we wanted.

The consensus after much tasting and discussing was that we overwhelmingly prefer banana breads that are big on banana flavor and that aren't really "bready" at all. We were after a slice that was tender, moist, buttery, just the right amount of sweet, and (most important) heavy with the aroma and flavor of bananas. So I took a look at our favorite sample (not surprisingly

BANANA BREAD AND DOUBLE-CHOCOLATE BANANA BREAD

the one with the most bananas in it) and asked myself a question: "Can it take even more bananas?"

Some 30 or so loaves later, the answer was a resounding yes; this version includes more than a pound of them. It also includes just a bit more butter, four fewer ingredients, and a simplified method (no more stand mixer). What's more, we think it tastes a lot better, too.

With our master recipe down, we decided to introduce some chocolate. Our Double-Chocolate Banana Bread has cocoa powder in the batter and chunks of bittersweet chocolate mixed in for the perfect balance of chocolate and banana.

—MATTHEW FAIRMAN, *Cook's Country*

Banana Bread
MAKES 1 LOAF

Be sure to use very ripe, heavily speckled (or even black) bananas here. Use a potato masher to thoroughly mash the bananas. The test kitchen's preferred loaf pan measures 8½ by 4½ inches; if you use a 9 by 5-inch loaf pan, start checking for doneness 5 minutes earlier than advised in the recipe.

- 1½ cups (7½ ounces) all-purpose flour
- 1¼ teaspoons baking soda
- ¾ teaspoon table salt
- 2½ cups mashed very ripe bananas (about 5 bananas)
- 1 cup packed (7 ounces) dark brown sugar
- 10 tablespoons unsalted butter, melted and cooled slightly
- 2 large eggs
- 2 tablespoons granulated sugar

1. Adjust oven rack to middle position and heat oven to 350 degrees. Spray 8½ by 4½-inch loaf pan with vegetable oil spray.

2. Whisk flour, baking soda, and salt together in bowl. Whisk bananas, brown sugar, melted butter, and eggs in large bowl until thoroughly combined, making sure to break up any clumps of brown sugar with whisk. Add flour mixture to banana mixture and whisk gently until just combined (batter will be lumpy).

3. Place prepared pan on rimmed baking sheet. Transfer batter to prepared pan and sprinkle granulated sugar over top. Bake until toothpick inserted in center comes out clean, about 1 hour 10 minutes.

4. Let bread cool in pan on wire rack for 30 minutes. Tilt pan and gently remove bread. Let bread continue to cool on wire rack at least 30 minutes longer. Serve warm or at room temperature. (Cooled bread can be wrapped tightly in plastic wrap and stored at room temperature for up to 5 days.)

Double-Chocolate Banana Bread
MAKES 1 LOAF

Be sure to use very ripe, heavily speckled (or even black) bananas here. Use a potato masher to thoroughly mash the bananas. The test kitchen's preferred loaf pan measures 8½ by 4½ inches; if you use a 9 by 5-inch loaf pan, start checking for doneness 5 minutes earlier than advised in the recipe.

- 1¼ cups (6¼ ounces) all-purpose flour
- ¼ cup (¾ ounce) Dutch-processed cocoa powder
- 1¼ teaspoons baking soda
- ¾ teaspoon table salt
- 2 cups mashed very ripe bananas (about 4 bananas)
- 1 cup packed (7 ounces) dark brown sugar
- 10 tablespoons unsalted butter, melted and cooled slightly
- 2 large eggs
- 4 ounces bittersweet chocolate, chopped
- 2 tablespoons granulated sugar

1. Adjust oven rack to middle position and heat oven to 350 degrees. Spray 8½ by 4½-inch loaf pan with vegetable oil spray.

2. Whisk flour, cocoa, baking soda, and salt together in bowl. Whisk bananas, brown sugar, melted butter, and eggs in large bowl until thoroughly combined, making sure to break up any clumps of brown sugar with whisk. Add flour mixture to banana mixture and whisk gently until just combined (batter will be lumpy). Fold in chocolate.

3. Place prepared pan on rimmed baking sheet. Transfer batter to prepared pan and sprinkle granulated sugar over top. Bake until toothpick inserted in center comes out clean, about 1 hour 10 minutes.

4. Let bread cool in pan on wire rack for 30 minutes. Tilt pan and gently remove bread. Let bread continue to cool on wire rack at least 30 minutes longer. Serve warm or at room temperature. (Cooled bread can be wrapped tightly in plastic wrap and stored at room temperature for up to 5 days.)

POPOVERS

✔ **WHY THIS RECIPE WORKS** The ideal popover has a crisp, well-browned exterior and a hollow interior, with lush, custardy walls. Bread flour's extra gluten-forming proteins made the batter stretchy enough to accommodate the expanding steam within the popover. Though many recipes call for preheating the pan to jump-start the "pop," we found it equally effective to warm the batter instead by adding heated milk. Greasing the pan very lightly allowed the batter to "climb" the sides of the cups for bases that were full and round instead of shrunken. Most recipes call for lowering the oven temperature after the popovers reach their maximum height to prevent the outsides from burning, but we zeroed in on the ideal baking temperature to ensure a perfect bake inside and out, with less fuss.

I made a lot of popovers when I was in high school, which might give you the impression that I was a very sophisticated teen. I wasn't. I made them because the recipe was easy and required only inexpensive pantry ingredients, which made popovers a perfect after-school snack. I mixed milk, eggs, flour, and salt; poured the mixture into the wells of a preheated, greased muffin tin (we didn't have a popover pan); and baked them, turning down the temperature halfway through baking to prevent the outsides from burning while the insides finished cooking. When all went well, the batter ballooned dramatically into crisp, hollow shells with creamy, custardy interiors. I felt like I had invented fire.

But it didn't always go well, even with the same recipe. About 25 percent of the time my popovers were squat and spongy, like damp, bland muffins. Other times I'd lift seemingly perfect popovers out of the tin only to reveal bases that were comically shrunken. Over the years, I grew exasperated with my frequent inexplicable failures, so I stopped making popovers. But now that developing foolproof recipes is my job, I felt ready to confront the challenge anew. I'd figure out what makes popovers pop (or not pop), and I'd test all aspects of their production to find a formula and baking method that guaranteed success every time.

Our science research editor, Paul Adams, confirmed my suspicion that the science behind what makes popovers pop is similar to that of pitas and cream puffs: The oven's heat rapidly gels the surface of the batter so that when the moisture inside turns to steam and

expands, that surface is able to stretch to retain it, leaving a growing hollow inside. Eventually the exterior dries out so much that the protein in the eggs and flour forms a rigid shell, halting expansion. The inner walls, protected from the heat, remain moist. Equipped with this insight, I made five recipes that varied in their choice of flour and milk, number of eggs, mixing methods, and baking temperatures.

Two batches—those made with the thickest batter and with the runniest batter—resembled my teenage failures: stunted, squishy, and sad. Was batter viscosity the variable that made the difference? A series of tests in which I varied only the amount of flour convinced me that it played a large part. Thin mixtures made weak popovers that couldn't contain their steam, while thick mixtures never generated enough steam for lift.

As a kid, I had measured my flour by volume, so I was probably adding subtly different amounts each time, which led to the occasional failure. Going forward I'd make sure to weigh it so that I'd have the proper ratio of flour to liquid. My working formula—I landed on 6¾ ounces of all-purpose flour, a bit of salt, 1½ cups of whole milk, and three large eggs—produced popovers that popped reliably, though they weren't as tall as I'd hoped. Tweaking the ingredients might help.

Newly understanding popover mechanics, I suspected the extra gluten-forming protein in bread flour would make the batter stretchier and produce loftier popovers. It did. Not only were popovers made with bread flour about 30 percent taller than those made with all-purpose, but their higher walls were also thinner, making them more crisp, and that crispness held up as they cooled. Bread flour was in. Next up: milk.

Whole milk is our default, but, wondering if low-fat or skim milk might be better, I made three batches of popovers, each with milk of a different fat level. There wasn't a huge difference in stature, but there was a slight difference in texture: The lower the proportion of milk fat, the more crisp the popover. Skim milk made slightly more crisp popovers, and whole milk softer ones. But the differences were so slight that I went with low-fat because that's what many cooks are likely to have on hand. And besides, the next ingredient under consideration—butter—had a bigger impact. Though many recipes call for adding melted butter to the batter, I found it to have a greater softening effect than higher-fat milk. I'd save the butter for spreading on my baked popover, where I could really appreciate it.

POPOVERS

But about those popover-pan cups: Should they be hot? Greased? My standard high school MO was to combine these: Heat the pan with fat in each cup and then pour in the batter. This method yielded light, expanded, crisp popovers but also the greatest number of shrunken bases. The pan's heat seemed to jump-start the rise, but the hot fat prevented the batter from gaining purchase on the sides of the cups. Adding cold batter to cold, very lightly greased cups ensured just enough grip for the popovers to have full, round bases, but overall they weren't as tall.

Early heat clearly helped the rise, but maybe that heat could come from the batter. That could be the principle behind recipes that called for room-temperature milk and eggs, whose popovers tended to rise higher than those made with cold ingredients. But I was reluctant to have to think that far ahead when I made popovers. My solution: use fridge-cold eggs, but warm the milk to 120 degrees in the microwave. This made towering popovers. Now to refine the baking method.

Most popover recipes call for starting hot to make the most of that initial pop and then lowering the heat to prevent burning. But because some ovens lose heat more quickly than others, lowering the temperature halfway through can throw off the timing. I prefer to bake at a single, constant temperature: My sweet spot was 400 degrees.

Buttered popovers are a great accompaniment to dinner. Or drizzled with honey or smeared with jam, they make a delightful breakfast, brunch, or snack. With a recipe this straightforward and reliable, I can easily see myself returning to my teenage levels of popover production.

—ANDREA GEARY, *Cook's Illustrated*

Popovers

MAKES 6 POPOVERS

This batter comes together quickly, so start heating your oven before gathering your ingredients and equipment. Our recipe works best in a six-cup popover pan, but you can substitute a 12-cup muffin tin, distributing the batter evenly among the 12 cups; start checking these smaller popovers after 25 minutes. Whole or skim milk can be used in place of the low-fat milk. We strongly recommend weighing the flour for this recipe. Do not open the oven during the first 30 minutes of baking; if possible, use the oven window and light to monitor the popovers.

1¼ cups (6¾ ounces) bread flour

¾ teaspoon table salt

1½ cups 2 percent low-fat milk, heated to 110 to 120 degrees

3 large eggs

   Salted butter

1. Adjust oven rack to middle position and heat oven to 400 degrees. Lightly spray cups of popover pan with vegetable oil spray. Using paper towel, wipe out cups, leaving thin film of oil on bottom and sides.

2. Whisk together flour and salt in 8-cup liquid measuring cup or medium bowl. Add milk and eggs and whisk until mostly smooth (some small lumps are OK). Distribute batter evenly among prepared cups in popover pan. Bake until popovers are lofty and deep golden brown all over, 40 to 45 minutes. Serve hot, passing butter separately. (Leftover popovers can be stored in zipper-lock bag at room temperature for up to 2 days; reheat directly on middle rack of 300-degree oven for 5 minutes.)

MANA'EESH ZA'ATAR (ZA'ATAR FLATBREADS)

✔ **WHY THIS RECIPE WORKS** We used the food processor's high-speed blades to bring the dough together quickly, creating a chewy, tender crust. Baking the flatbread on a preheated baking stone in a 500-degree oven gave it a crispy bottom, and tapping the dough all over with our fingertips before baking helped prevent uneven puffing. We spread a mixture of za'atar, olive oil, and salt over the dough for tangy, herbal flavors.

Flatbreads play a vital role in many Middle Eastern cuisines, often served alongside meals or as vehicles for dips or pools of olive oil. In Lebanon, mana'eesh are found both as a street food and as a specialty of dedicated bakeries. According to Maroun (Mario) Ellakis, owner of Mario's Lebanese Bakery in Fall River, Massachusetts, they are eaten at nearly every Lebanese meal.

A man'oushe is typically topped with olive oil and za'atar, a combination of sumac; thyme; sesame seeds; and sometimes oregano, coriander, cumin, and salt. In Lebanese, the word "man'oushe" means "engraved" and refs to the indentations in the bread made by tapping the dough with your fingertips just before baking it. This keeps the dough from puffing too much in the oven as it bakes and also creates pockets for the za'atar and oil.

After watching Mario spend his morning baking off several dozen mana'eesh, I bought a bag of his Lebanese za'atar to try my hand at making mana'eesh at home.

A food processor does the work of a stand mixer in a fraction of the time and is perfect for smaller amounts of dough. I wanted three flatbreads, enough to serve my family of five. The basic dough ingredients are flour, water, salt, and yeast, and I eventually opted for the inclusion of olive oil, which is found in some recipes and makes the baked mana'eesh tender.

To mimic Mario's 1,200-degree brick oven, I heated a baking stone at 500 degrees for a good hour before baking the dough. The high heat encouraged slight bubbles to form on top with delicate bits of char while the bottom turned an even golden brown.

These mana'eesh come together in a snap and emerge from the oven bubbly, hot, and chewy. Very rewarding for the amount of effort involved.

—BRYAN ROOF, *Cook's Country*

Mana'eesh Za'atar (Za'atar Flatbreads)

SERVES 4 TO 6 (MAKES THREE 9-INCH FLATBREADS)

You can purchase za'atar in many grocery stores or online, or you can make our recipe below.

DOUGH

2½ cups (12½ ounces) all-purpose flour
1½ teaspoons instant or rapid-rise yeast
1 teaspoon table salt
¾ cup plus 2 tablespoons cold water
2 tablespoons extra-virgin olive oil

TOPPING

3 tablespoons za'atar
3 tablespoons extra-virgin olive oil
½ teaspoon table salt

1. FOR THE DOUGH: Process flour, yeast, and salt in food processor until combined, about 3 seconds. Combine cold water and oil in liquid measuring cup.

With processor running, slowly add water mixture and process until dough forms sticky ball that clears sides of bowl, 30 to 60 seconds.

2. Transfer dough to clean counter and knead into cohesive ball, about 1 minute. Place dough in greased bowl. Cover bowl with plastic wrap and let dough rise at room temperature until almost doubled in size, 2 to 2½ hours. One hour before baking, adjust oven rack to middle position, set baking stone on rack, and heat oven to 500 degrees.

3. FOR THE TOPPING: Meanwhile, combine za'atar, oil, and salt in bowl.

4. On clean counter, divide dough into 3 equal pieces, about 7 ounces each. Shape each piece of dough into ball; cover loosely with plastic and let rest for 15 minutes.

5. Working with 1 dough ball at a time on lightly floured counter, coat lightly with flour and flatten into 6- to 7-inch disk using your fingertips.

6. Using rolling pin, roll dough into 9- to 10-inch circle. Slide dough round onto floured baking peel. Spread one-third of za'atar mixture (about 1½ table-spoons) over surface of dough with back of dinner spoon, stopping ½ inch from edge.

7. Firmly tap dough all over with your fingertips, about 6 times. Slide dough onto baking stone and bake until lightly bubbled and brown on top, about 5 minutes. Using baking peel, transfer man'oushe to wire rack. Repeat with remaining dough and za'atar mixture. Slice or tear and serve.

Za'atar

MAKES ABOUT ⅓ CUP

Za'atar can be stored in an airtight container at room temperature for up to one year.

2 tablespoons dried thyme
1 tablespoon dried oregano
1½ tablespoons sumac
1 tablespoon sesame seeds, toasted
¼ teaspoon table salt

Grind thyme and oregano using spice grinder or mortar and pestle until finely ground and powdery. Transfer to bowl and stir in sumac, sesame seeds, and salt.

MANA'EESH ZA'ATAR (ZA'ATAR FLATBREADS)

REALLY GOOD KEY LIME PIE

CHAPTER 7

DESSERTS

Yellow Sheet Cake with Chocolate Frosting   230

Raspberry Pound Cake   231

Rhubarb Upside-Down Cake   235

Maple Cheesecake   236
  Maple-Pecan Skillet Granola

Vegan Chocolate-Espresso Tart   240
  Coconut Whipped Cream

Cranberry Curd Tart with Almond Crust   243

Peach Zabaglione Gratin   244

Strawberry Galette   246
  Tangy Whipped Cream

Really Good Key Lime Pie   249
  Failproof Whipped Cream

Endless Summer Peach Pie   251
  Salted Butterscotch Sauce

Choux au Craquelin   256
  Colorful Choux au Craquelin
  Mocha Choux au Craquelin

Nutella Rugelach   259
  Cinnamon-Walnut Rugelach
  Jam Rugelach

Anzac Biscuits   262

Two Chocolate Chip Cookies   265

M&M Cookies   266

YELLOW SHEET CAKE WITH CHOCOLATE FROSTING

✓ **WHY THIS RECIPE WORKS** For a tender cake with a fine, plush texture, we started by using bleached cake flour. Its altered starch is more absorbent than the starch in unbleached flour, so it can accommodate more liquid, sugar, and fat (we used butter for flavor and vegetable oil for moistness) without collapsing under the extra weight. We combined the ingredients using the reverse-creaming method: First we mixed the dry ingredients—flour, sugar, leavener, and salt—with the fat, and then we beat in the eggs and liquid ingredients. Only a small amount of air was incorporated during mixing, resulting in a superfine texture. For a frosting that would hold its shape even in warm weather, we whipped up a modified American buttercream. Adding hot water reduced the grittiness of the confectioners' sugar, and a combination of cocoa powder and bittersweet chocolate yielded a frosting with a rich, multidimensional chocolate flavor.

Yellow sheet cake is a darling of American desserts: It's classic, universally liked, and just right for serving by the square. And yet it never seems to realize its full potential. The crumb is usually OK—moist and relatively coarse—but there's no reason that a sheet cake can't have a truly special texture. I'm talking about an extraordinarily fine, uniform crumb, the kind so tender that it practically dissolves on the palate. I wanted to combine this plush texture with fresh, buttery flavor. And for a cake this good, only a rich, creamy chocolate frosting would do.

The unique crumb I'm referring to shows up in what is known as a "high-ratio" cake. Most cake formulas are low ratio, meaning they have slightly less sugar by weight than flour, but some are high ratio, meaning—you guessed it—they have more sugar by weight than flour. And that's key because sugar doesn't just sweeten a cake; it also adds moisture and makes the crumb finer and more tender.

Quick experiment: I increased the sugar in a low-ratio yellow cake recipe by 20 percent so that it outweighed the flour. Quick result: The cake collapsed right after I took it out of the oven. This is where bleached cake flour, the signature ingredient in high-ratio cake, comes in. Bleached cake flour differs from all-purpose in three ways: It's more finely milled, it has less protein, and (surprise) it's bleached. The first

characteristic helps the flour disperse and absorb moisture more evenly, and the second helps make cakes tender. But it's the bleaching that's really important here. Although it whitens the flour, that's not the primary objective: It also alters the starch in such a way that the cake doesn't fall under the weight of extra sugar, liquid, or fat.

I searched for a few high-ratio cake recipes, and the one I liked best went like this: Cream 12¼ ounces of sugar together with butter, whip in the eggs and the liquid (which in this case was buttermilk with a generous amount of vanilla), and then mix in the dry ingredients (9 ounces of bleached cake flour, plus baking powder, baking soda, and salt). Pour the batter into a greased and floured pan and bake it for about 30 minutes.

The vanilla flavor, so important to the subtle profile of a yellow cake, was suitably strong. But the crumb was a bit dry and crumbly, and I noticed something odd with how it looked as I served it.

When I cut into the cooled cake, I found damp, subtly shaded areas in the crumb, mostly toward the bottom half of the cake. What was happening? Turns out, some of the liquid in the batter was settling as it baked.

An emulsifier would help the liquid in the cake stay evenly distributed throughout baking. Luckily, I always keep a superstrong emulsifier in my fridge. You probably do, too—it's called egg yolk. Yolks contain lecithin, a powerful emulsifier. When I added two extra egg yolks to my batter, the "shadow" that had marred my earlier cake disappeared.

I now had quintessential yellow cake flavor: all butter and vanilla and egg yolks. But the crumb was still a little dry and a little more open and crumbly than I wanted.

To address the dryness, I replaced some of the butter with vegetable oil. Not only would this produce a moister cake, but the cake would stay that way for longer. But this meant that I needed to reconsider my mixing method. The conventional creaming method requires beating the butter and sugar together until the mixture is light and fluffy before adding the remaining ingredients. Half the fat in my new cake was liquid (oil), which can't hold air the way that solid fat (butter) can, so creaming was no longer viable. But reverse creaming? That's different.

Reverse creaming is simple. Just combine the sugar, flour, leavening, and salt in the bowl of your stand mixer, and then add the fat. Mix it until it's combined.

YELLOW SHEET CAKE WITH CHOCOLATE FROSTING

Next, add the liquid and eggs and beat the heck out of it, turning up the speed once the mixture is combined. Only a small amount of air gets incorporated during mixing, resulting in a superfine texture. It worked beautifully. The cake had a tender, moist, and fine-grained crumb. On to the frosting.

This cake is especially perfect for casual summer meals, so it was important that the frosting could stand up to warm, humid weather. American chocolate buttercream, the simple mixture of butter, confectioners' sugar, milk or cream, and cocoa powder and/or melted bittersweet chocolate, holds up well, but I had reservations. Its fine sugar crystals can sometimes feel a little coarse on the tongue.

I came up with a solution: In addition to softened butter, I beat ¼ cup of hot water (instead of milk) into the confectioners' sugar and cocoa powder, which dissolved some of the sugar crystals for a smoother frosting. When the butter was well incorporated, I added a couple ounces of melted bittersweet chocolate for deep, dark flavor. At first, the frosting looked far too loose to be spreadable, but after sitting for a few minutes, it was thick and creamy, ready to be smoothed over the top of my cake.

This classic dessert had been upgraded in exactly the way that I had envisioned: Here was a tender, fine-textured cake full of butter and vanilla, topped with rich chocolate frosting.

—ANDREA GEARY, *Cook's Illustrated*

NOTES FROM THE TEST KITCHEN

WHY USE BLEACHED CAKE FLOUR?

It's vital to use bleached cake flour for this cake. That's because exposure to chlorine gas (or other bleaching methods) not only whitens flour but also alters its starch in such a way that the cake doesn't shrink or fall once it is baked. It works in two ways: First, bleaching makes the starch in flour better able to absorb the extra sugar (which dissolves during baking), liquid, and fat present in high-ratio cakes such as this one, thus creating a thicker batter that can hold tiny air bubbles to support a fine, plush texture. Second, bleaching promotes the gelatinization of the starch in the flour, which also develops structure in the crumb.

BLEACHED CAKE FLOUR
Cake stands tall

UNBLEACHED CAKE FLOUR
Cake sags

Yellow Sheet Cake with Chocolate Frosting

SERVES 12 TO 15

Use a metal baking pan for this recipe; a glass baking dish will cause the edges of the cake to overbake as it cools. It's important to use bleached cake flour here; substituting unbleached cake flour or a combination of all-purpose flour and cornstarch will cause the cake to fall. To ensure the proper texture, weigh the flour. Our favorite bittersweet chocolate is Ghirardelli 60% Cacao Bittersweet Chocolate Premium Baking Bar.

CAKE

- 4 large eggs plus 2 large yolks
- ½ cup buttermilk
- 1 tablespoon vanilla extract
- 2¼ cups (9 ounces) bleached cake flour
- 1¾ cups (12¼ ounces) granulated sugar
- 1¼ teaspoons baking powder
- ¼ teaspoon baking soda
- ½ teaspoon table salt
- 8 tablespoons unsalted butter, softened
- ½ cup vegetable oil

FROSTING

- 2¼ cups (9 ounces) confectioners' sugar
- ½ cup (1½ ounces) unsweetened cocoa powder
- 8 tablespoons unsalted butter, softened
- ¼ cup hot water
- ¼ teaspoon table salt
- 2 ounces bittersweet chocolate, melted

1. FOR THE CAKE: Adjust oven rack to middle position and heat oven to 350 degrees. Grease and flour 13 by 9-inch baking pan. Combine eggs and yolks, buttermilk, and vanilla in 2-cup liquid measuring cup and whisk with fork until smooth.

2. Combine flour, sugar, baking powder, baking soda, and salt in bowl of stand mixer fitted with paddle.

Mix on low speed until combined, about 20 seconds. Add butter and oil and mix on low speed until combined, about 30 seconds. Increase speed to medium and beat until lightened, about 1 minute. Reduce speed to low and, with mixer running, slowly add egg mixture. When mixture is fully incorporated, stop mixer and scrape down bowl and paddle thoroughly. Beat on medium-high speed until batter is pale, smooth, and thick, about 3 minutes. Transfer batter to prepared pan and smooth top. Tap pan firmly on counter 5 times to release any large air bubbles.

3. Bake until toothpick inserted in center comes out with few crumbs attached, 28 to 32 minutes. Let cake cool completely in pan on wire rack, about 2 hours.

4. FOR THE FROSTING: Combine sugar, cocoa, butter, hot water, and salt in bowl of stand mixer fitted with whisk attachment. Mix on low speed until combined, about 20 seconds. Increase speed to medium and continue to mix until smooth, about 1 minute longer, scraping down bowl as necessary. Add melted chocolate and whip on low speed until incorporated. Let sit at room temperature until thickened to spreadable consistency, 30 to 40 minutes.

5. Frost cake. Refrigerate until frosting is set, about 20 minutes, before serving.

RASPBERRY POUND CAKE

✔ **WHY THIS RECIPE WORKS** We wanted a truly excellent pound cake—tender, rich, and sweet—with a tart, fruity raspberry filling swirled throughout. For the cake batter, we started with a tried-and-true test kitchen vanilla pound cake recipe that we've adored for years. The secret to this version is baking the cake in a relatively low oven (300 degrees), which ensures a crust that's just browned but still tender and slices that are moist and evenly baked throughout. A generous spoonful of vibrant lemon zest helped balance the rich batter. We swirled in a simple raspberry filling for a fresh fruit element that would spread juicy textural contrast and a lovely ruby color throughout the cake. Cooking the berries briefly with sugar and just enough cornstarch to thicken the sauce ensured that the surrounding cake wouldn't become soggy. The result was a buttery loaf with a tender crumb thoroughly marbled with sweet-tart raspberry ribbons.

A slice of truly excellent pound cake—tender, rich, and sweet—can transform an ordinary moment into one that borders on sublime. For generations, cooks have dressed up pound cake batter with sour cream, cream cheese, chocolate, and brown sugar or served warm slices slathered with salted butter or topped with fresh berries. But my favorite pound cake addition is a tart, fruity raspberry filling swirled throughout.

When I was a kid, my grandmother used to pick pounds of the perfectly ripe blackberries and raspberries growing behind her house, toss them with a touch of sugar, and freeze them for my brother and me to enjoy whenever we visited. I can still remember eagerly scraping at the thawing berries with a spoon.

I wanted to create a treat that would capture that joy. For the cake batter, I started with a test kitchen vanilla pound cake recipe that I've adored for years. The genius of this version is baking the cake in a relatively low, 300-degree oven, ensuring a just-browned, still-tender crust and a slice that's moist and evenly baked throughout. Adding a generous spoonful of vibrant lemon zest helped balance and round out the rich batter. (Remember: Pound cake originally got its name because the recipe involved baking 1 pound each of its essential ingredients: flour, butter, sugar, and eggs.)

For a fresh fruit element that would spread juicy textural contrast and a lovely ruby color throughout the pleasantly dense cake, I swirled in a raspberry filling that was so uncomplicated I knew my grandma would approve. Cooking the berries briefly with sugar and just enough cornstarch to thicken the sauce ensured that the surrounding cake wouldn't become soggy.

The result is this decadent loaf, with a buttery, tender crumb thoroughly marbled with gorgeous sweet-tart raspberry ribbons.

—MATTHEW FAIRMAN, *Cook's Country*

Raspberry Pound Cake
SERVES 8

We prefer using frozen raspberries for this recipe because they are more consistently sweet than fresh. If you have access to very good fresh berries, use them instead. The ideal temperature for the eggs and butter is 60 degrees. The test kitchen's preferred loaf pan measures 8½ by 4½ inches; if you use a 9 by 5-inch loaf pan, start checking for doneness 5 minutes earlier than advised in the recipe.

RASPBERRY POUND CAKE

RASPBERRY FILLING

- **1 teaspoon cornstarch**
- **1 teaspoon water**
- **8 ounces (about 1⅔ cups) frozen raspberries**
- **¼ cup (1¾ ounces) sugar**
- **¼ teaspoon table salt**

POUND CAKE

- **5 large eggs, room temperature**
- **2 teaspoons vanilla extract**
- **1¾ cups (8¾ ounces) all-purpose flour**
- **¾ teaspoon table salt**
- **½ teaspoon baking powder**
- **⅓ cup sour cream**
- **2 tablespoons milk**
- **14 tablespoons unsalted butter, softened but still cool**
- **1¼ cups (8¾ ounces) sugar**
- **1 tablespoon grated lemon zest**

1. FOR THE RASPBERRY FILLING: Stir cornstarch and water together in bowl; set aside. Cook raspberries, sugar, and salt in small saucepan over medium heat, stirring occasionally, until mixture is slightly thickened and measures scant 1 cup, 8 to 10 minutes.

2. Stir cornstarch mixture to recombine, then stir into raspberry sauce. Cook until thickened, about 1 minute. Transfer filling to bowl and refrigerate, uncovered, until no longer warm, about 1 hour. (Filling can be covered and refrigerated for up to 2 days.)

3. FOR THE POUND CAKE: Adjust oven rack to lower-middle position and heat oven to 300 degrees. Grease and flour 8½ by 4½-inch loaf pan. Whisk eggs and vanilla together in 2-cup liquid measuring cup. Whisk flour, salt, and baking powder together in bowl. Whisk sour cream and milk together in second bowl.

4. Using stand mixer fitted with paddle, beat butter, sugar, and lemon zest on medium-high speed until pale and fluffy, 5 to 7 minutes, scraping down bowl as needed.

5. Reduce speed to medium and gradually add egg mixture in slow, steady stream. Scrape down bowl and continue to mix on medium speed until uniform, about 1 minute longer (batter may look slightly curdled).

6. Reduce speed to low and add flour mixture in 3 additions, alternating with sour cream mixture in 2 additions, scraping down bowl as needed. Give batter final stir by hand.

7. Transfer half of batter (about 2 cups) to prepared pan. Stir raspberry filling to loosen. Spoon half of raspberry filling over length of batter in pan, leaving ½ inch border. Using butter knife, thoroughly swirl filling throughout batter, taking care to not leave any big deposits of filling in center or along sides of pan.

8. Transfer remaining batter to pan and repeat spooning and swirling with remaining raspberry filling. Tap pan on counter twice to release air bubbles.

9. Bake until toothpick inserted 1 inch to side of split in center of cake comes out clean (very top center of cake may seem underdone; this is OK), 1½ hours to 1 hour 40 minutes, rotating pan halfway through baking.

10. Run thin knife around edges of pan. Let cake cool in pan on wire rack for 15 minutes. Remove cake from pan and let cool completely on rack, about 2 hours. Slice and serve. (Cooled cake can be wrapped tightly in plastic wrap and stored at room temperature for up to 3 days or frozen for up to 1 month.)

RHUBARB UPSIDE-DOWN CAKE

WHY THIS RECIPE WORKS This recipe combines the best attributes of two of our favorite rhubarb cakes: a Scandinavian-style cake and an upside-down cake. An almond streusel reminiscent of the sugary almond topping of the former provided a substantial, crunchy foundation, and lemon and cardamom in the batter delivered warm, floral notes to highlight the tart, vegetal rhubarb. Enriching the cake with butter, eggs, and sour cream yielded a rich, tender texture with enough structure to support the generous rhubarb topping. Making this cake in an upside-down style encouraged the rhubarb to break down and achieve a sweet, compote-like consistency.

In Scandinavia, the arrival of rhubarb signals the close of a long winter. The prolific perennial is used in pies, crumbles, soups, and jams. It is fermented into wine, and its juice is sipped fresh. Purists even eat stalks raw, dipping them in sugar to quiet their bracing tartness. But perhaps the finest celebration of rhubarb is the making of rich butter cakes that are dotted with chunks of the crimson-green stems, perfumed with cardamom and lemon, and speckled with sugar and crisp almonds.

The treat is a far cry from the rustic rhubarb upside-down cake I enjoyed as a kid in rural Vermont, where the plants grew wild at the edge of our neighbor's property. No, the flavor of the Nordic cake is more sophisticated—and the texture more intriguing.

That said, I enjoy the heavy use of rhubarb in the upside-down style, which creates an incredibly appealing compote-like layer atop the cake. So why choose? Instead, I got to work on a culinary mash-up using our Apple Upside-Down Cake as a template. That cake is rich with butter, sour cream, and brown sugar, and it would take well to the spice and citrus flavorings.

Having worked with rhubarb a lot over the years, I knew that it would soften quickly in the oven, so I skipped the stovetop parcooking step that the apple cake recipe calls for. I cut a full pound of stalks into planks; tossed them with melted butter, brown sugar, and some lemon zest to help balance their slight savoriness (rhubarb is a vegetable, after all); and organized the planks into neat perpendicular stacks to create a geometric arrangement in an 8-inch square pan. Along with vanilla, I spiked the cake batter with ground cardamom and lemon zest and juice. I poured the batter on top of the scarlet slices, slid the pan into a 350-degree oven, and baked the cake for about 45 minutes.

After the cake cooled, I turned it out onto a platter. I expected the artfully arranged rectangles to resemble garnet stained glass, but instead I got a different type of stain: The brown sugar that had worked so well with the apples had turned the blushing rhubarb a murky brown. Plus, the rhubarb had wept as it baked, making the crumb soggy. Finally, the long planks were stringy,

so they were tricky to cut, never mind eat gracefully.

A handful of fixes really paid off: To start, I abandoned the finicky slices of rhubarb and simply diced the stalks and packed them into the bottom of the pan. This produced an attractive mosaic design with zero fuss. To help preserve the color of the chunks, I swapped the brown sugar for granulated (to keep things simple, I switched to granulated in the cake, too). I also sprinkled in 1½ teaspoons of cornstarch to help the juices gel during baking.

The cake now baked up with a fruity, lightly thickened topping. The rhubarb pieces were no longer brown, but their rosy color had still faded a bit, so after the cake cooled, I dabbed on some melted red currant jelly to restore a crimson shine.

Now, what to do with the almonds? Their nutty crunch contrasted nicely with the plush cake and soft compote, but the angular slices looked awkward perched atop the rhubarb layer. My solution was a topsy-turvy one: I arranged the rhubarb in the bottom of the pan, added the batter, and then sprinkled a mix of sugar and sliced almonds on top. Once the cake was baked and inverted, the nuts formed a crispy base.

I was on the right track, but the delicate sliced almonds were hard to notice underneath the rest of the dessert. For my next try, I turned the almonds and sugar into a substantial streusel by adding melted butter and flour. The cake baked up with a generous nutty base, and my gastronomic merger was complete.

—STEVE DUNN, *Cook's Illustrated*

NOTES FROM THE TEST KITCHEN

A TASTY, TEXTURE-RICH TRIO
We not only add a third component to the usual cake and fruit but also turn up the flavors a notch.

FRUITY TOPPING
A full pound of raw rhubarb (along with sugar, butter, cornstarch, and lemon zest) is transformed into a sweet-tart jammy layer as the cake bakes.

BUTTERY CAKE
The moist, tender crumb is rich with sour cream and butter and scented with vanilla, cardamom, and lemon.

CRUNCHY STREUSEL
A blend of sliced almonds, flour, butter, and sugar sprinkled atop the batter before it's baked becomes a crisp streusel base for the cake once it is inverted.

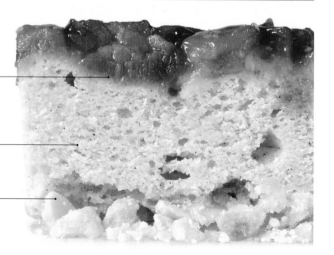

Rhubarb Upside-Down Cake

SERVES 8

You can substitute thawed, drained frozen rhubarb for the fresh. Serve the cake with unsweetened whipped cream, if desired. Red currant jelly is worth seeking out; strawberry and raspberry jam won't produce the same effect.

STREUSEL

½ cup (2½ ounces) all-purpose flour

½ cup sliced almonds

¼ cup (1¾ ounces) sugar

4 tablespoons unsalted butter, melted

¼ teaspoon table salt

RHUBARB

¾ cup (5¼ ounces) sugar

1½ teaspoons cornstarch

1 teaspoon grated lemon zest

1 pound rhubarb, trimmed and cut into ½-inch pieces

2 tablespoons unsalted butter, melted

CAKE

1 cup (5 ounces) all-purpose flour

1½ teaspoons ground cardamom

1 teaspoon baking powder

½ teaspoon table salt

1 cup (7 ounces) sugar

2 large eggs

6 tablespoons unsalted butter, melted and cooled

½ cup sour cream

1 teaspoon grated lemon zest plus 1 tablespoon juice

1 teaspoon vanilla extract

2 tablespoons red currant jelly

1. Adjust oven rack to lower-middle position and heat oven to 350 degrees. Grease 8-inch square baking pan, line bottom with parchment paper, and grease parchment.

2. FOR THE STREUSEL: Stir all ingredients in medium bowl until well combined. Set aside.

3. FOR THE RHUBARB: Whisk sugar, cornstarch, and lemon zest together in large bowl. Add rhubarb and stir well to coat. Drizzle with melted butter and stir to incorporate. Transfer rhubarb mixture to prepared pan and press rhubarb pieces into bottom of pan, making sure there are no large gaps (pieces may not fit in single layer).

4. FOR THE CAKE: Whisk flour, cardamom, baking powder, and salt together in medium bowl; set aside. Whisk sugar and eggs in large bowl until thick and homogeneous, about 45 seconds. Whisk in melted butter until combined. Add sour cream, lemon zest and juice, and vanilla; whisk until combined. Add flour mixture and whisk until just combined. Pour batter into pan and spread evenly over rhubarb mixture. Break up streusel with your hands and sprinkle in even layer over batter. Bake until cake is golden brown and toothpick inserted in center comes out clean, 45 to 50 minutes.

5. Transfer pan to wire rack and let cool for 20 minutes. Run knife around edges of pan to loosen cake, then invert onto serving platter. Let cool for about 10 minutes. Microwave jelly in small bowl until fluid, about 20 seconds. Using pastry brush, gently dab jelly over rhubarb topping. Serve warm or at room temperature.

MAPLE CHEESECAKE

✓ **WHY THIS RECIPE WORKS** We were after a velvety and smooth cheesecake using maple syrup instead of sugar for an autumnal twist. We loved the way a handful of pecans added to our favorite graham cracker crust provided a nutty accent to the maple-y filling. Some flour ensured the crisp texture of this crust, combining with melted butter to waterproof the graham cracker crumbs and prevent the crust from getting soggy. For maximum maple impact, we needed to use a lot of maple syrup (not pancake syrup, which is corn syrup–based and cloying). Through several rounds of testing, we landed on 1¼ cups of syrup for 2 pounds (four bricks) of cream cheese. A 225-degree oven cooked the cheesecake superslowly, setting the filling to a just barely firm, custardy texture that was completely free of cracks, without the need for a fussy water bath. A border of crunchy granola plus an extra drizzle of maple syrup made for a stunning finish to this festive cheesecake.

A simple cheesecake is, in my mind, the ultimate dessert: velvety and smooth, with a crisp, buttery crust and a richness that's restrained by an underlying tang. But for Thanksgiving this year, I wanted to give the classic an autumnal twist, and sweetening the cheesecake with maple syrup instead of sugar was just the way to get there.

But first, the crust. I tried a basic graham cracker crust as well as a few unorthodox variations; we loved the way a handful of pecans added to our tried-and-true graham cracker crust provided a nutty accent to the maple-y filling. To make it, grind up graham crackers and pecans in a food processor until they're fine crumbs. To this, add sugar, salt, and flour (the flour is the key to the crisp texture of this crust, as it combines with the butter to waterproof the cracker crumbs and prevent the crust from sogging out). After moistening this mixture with melted butter, tumble it into a greased 9-inch springform pan (the pop-off collar will make unmolding a breeze when it's time to serve) and press it into an even, compact layer on the bottom of the pan—the flat bottom of a dry measuring cup is a great tool for this, but a straight-edged drinking glass works, too. Bake it until it's toasty and crisp, let it cool while making the filling, and drop the oven temperature down to ensure a gentle bake on the cheesecake.

For maximum maple impact, you need to use a lot of maple syrup. Through several rounds of testing, I landed on 1¼ cups of syrup for 2 pounds (that's four bricks) of cream cheese.

The cheesecake batter couldn't be easier to make. Start by blitzing the syrup and cream cheese together in the food processor. Once the mixture is totally smooth, add four eggs, one at a time, until they're incorporated (adding them individually helps ensure even blending), and then pour this batter into your cooled crust. Rap the pan on the counter, let the mixture settle for 10 minutes to release air bubbles, and then drag a fork across the surface to pop them (it's not essential to eliminate every single bubble; the cheesecake will still be delicious with a less-than-smooth top!).

Once your oven has cooled to 225 degrees (use an oven thermometer to be sure), pop the cheesecake in and bake it for about 3 hours. The low oven temperature cooks the cheesecake superslowly, setting the filling to a just barely firm, custardy texture that's completely free of cracks, without the need for a sloshy water bath.

After chilling completely, this beauty is ready to wow at your next dinner party as is. But to make it extra-spectacular, a border of crunchy granola (after all, we already borrowed the syrup from the breakfast table) plus an extra drizzle of maple syrup will make the cheesecake look as stunning as it tastes.

—JESSICA RUDOLPH, *Cook's Country*

Maple Cheesecake

SERVES 12 TO 16

Do not substitute pancake syrup for the maple syrup. Reduce the oven temperature as soon as the crust is finished baking, and use an oven thermometer to check that it has dropped to 225 degrees before you bake the cheesecake. Thoroughly scrape the processor bowl as you make the filling to eliminate lumps. For the topping, you can use store-bought granola or make our Maple-Pecan Skillet Granola (recipe follows).

CRUST

- 4 whole graham crackers, broken into pieces
- ¼ cup pecans
- ½ cup (2½ ounces) all-purpose flour
- ⅓ cup (2⅓ ounces) sugar
- ¼ teaspoon table salt
- 4 tablespoons unsalted butter, melted

CHEESECAKE

- 2 pounds cream cheese, softened
- 1¼ cups maple syrup
- 4 large eggs

TOPPING

- ⅓ cup granola
- ½ cup maple syrup

1. FOR THE CRUST: Adjust oven rack to middle position and heat oven to 325 degrees. Grease bottom and side of 9-inch springform pan. Process cracker pieces and pecans in food processor until finely ground, about 30 seconds. Add flour, sugar, and salt and pulse to combine, about 2 pulses. Add melted butter and pulse until crumbs are evenly moistened, about 5 pulses.

2. Using your hands, press crumbs into even layer on bottom of prepared pan. Using bottom of dry measuring cup, firmly pack crumbs into pan. Bake until crust smells toasty and is browned around edges, about 18 minutes. Reduce oven temperature to 225 degrees. Let crust cool completely.

3. FOR THE CHEESECAKE: In clean, dry processor bowl, process cream cheese and maple syrup until smooth, about 2 minutes, scraping down sides of bowl as needed. With processor running, add eggs, one at a time, until just incorporated, about 30 seconds total. Pour batter onto cooled crust.

MAPLE CHEESECAKE

4. Firmly tap pan on counter and set aside for 10 minutes to allow air bubbles to rise to top. Gently draw tines of fork across surface of batter to pop air bubbles that have risen to surface.

5. Once oven has reached 225 degrees, bake cheesecake on aluminum foil–lined rimmed baking sheet until edges are set and center jiggles slightly when shaken and registers 165 degrees ½ inch below surface, about 3 hours.

6. Transfer pan to wire rack and let cool completely, about 2 hours. Refrigerate cheesecake, uncovered, until cold, about 6 hours. (Once fully chilled, cheesecake can be covered with plastic wrap and refrigerated for up to 4 days.)

7. To unmold cheesecake, run tip of paring knife between cake and side of pan; remove side of pan. Slide thin metal spatula between crust and pan bottom to loosen, then slide cheesecake onto serving platter. Let cheesecake stand at room temperature for 30 minutes.

8. FOR THE TOPPING: Sprinkle granola around top edge of cheesecake. Drizzle maple syrup inside ring of granola. Spread with back of spoon, as needed, to fill area inside granola ring.

9. Warm knife under hot water, then wipe dry. Cut cheesecake into wedges and serve.

Maple-Pecan Skillet Granola
SERVES 4 (MAKES ABOUT 3 CUPS)

Do not substitute quick or instant oats in this recipe; old-fashioned oats provide the perfect amount of chew. It's important to stir the granola frequently in step 3 to ensure that the mixture cooks evenly.

- ¼ **cup maple syrup**
- 1 **teaspoon vanilla extract**
- ½ **teaspoon ground cinnamon**
- ¼ **teaspoon table salt**
- 2 **tablespoons vegetable oil**
- ½ **cup pecans, chopped coarse**
- 1½ **cups (4½ ounces) old-fashioned rolled oats**

1. Combine maple syrup, vanilla, cinnamon, and salt in bowl; set aside. Line baking sheet with parchment paper.

2. Heat oil in 12-inch nonstick skillet over medium heat until shimmering. Add pecans and cook, stirring frequently, until fragrant and just starting to darken in color, about 4 minutes. Add oats and cook, stirring frequently, until oats are golden and pecans are toasted, about 6 minutes.

3. Add maple syrup mixture to skillet and cook, stirring frequently, until absorbed and mixture turns shade darker, about 3 minutes. Transfer granola to prepared sheet, spread into even layer, and let cool for 20 minutes. Break granola into bite-size pieces and serve.

VEGAN CHOCOLATE-ESPRESSO TART

✓ **WHY THIS RECIPE WORKS** "Showstopping" and "dead easy" are terms rarely used to describe the same dessert. But this pull-out-all-the-stops chocolate tart with a dreamy espresso "meringue" is so elegant and sophisticated yet so simple that even we science-based test cooks thought it must be magic. We started with our vegan tart dough, which we rolled out to fit the tart pan; docking it and baking it with pie weights kept it in good shape. Next, we made the simplest "water ganache," an emulsion of chocolate and hot water (instead of the usual heavy cream) that became smooth and silky with a little whisking, set up beautifully glossy at room temperature, and sliced like a dream. Finally, the crowning touch: a three-ingredient espresso "meringue" inspired by coffee whipped cream. Instant espresso crystals, when dissolved in water with sugar and then whipped, created a billowy, glossy foam that could be piped or dolloped as an elegant decoration.

So much of baking relies on dairy. What are cookies without butter or custard without milk? A chocolate tart is no exception: Butter provides the crust with its pleasantly crumbly texture and nutty flavor, and heavy cream helps the filling set into a rich, sliceable ganache. When I was assigned the desserts chapter for *The Complete Plant-Based Cookbook*, I wanted to develop a recipe for an elegant dessert that would challenge what people thought about plant-based baking. A vegan chocolate tart was the obvious choice.

I started at the bottom—with the crust. My colleague had been working on a savory tart dough for the cookbook, so I thought I'd pick up where she left off. The recipe called for some of the usual suspects—sugar, all-purpose flour, and salt—but it replaced the butter with melted coconut oil. Coconut oil contains less water than butter does, so a few tablespoons of water are added to prevent the dough from being too crumbly. I increased the amount of sugar to 3 tablespoons to bring the dough into dessert territory.

My colleague's working recipe was a pat-in-the-pan dough, but it baked up with a lot of cracks. Rolling out the dough between two sheets of parchment paper brought it together into a more cohesive round. To get the dough into the pan, I simply lifted off the top sheet of parchment, flipped the dough into the pan, and tucked it into the corners and up the fluted sides. This dough had a tendency to become misshapen and shrink in the oven, so I docked it all over with a fork before chilling it for 30 minutes. I also filled the tart shell with pie weights for the first half of baking.

Most tart shells can be made ahead, so I baked off my dough and popped it into the refrigerator so that I could work on the filling the next day. But when I removed the tart shell from the fridge, it was rock-hard—and it stayed that way, even after hours at room temperature. I knew that a dairy-free filling was going to be a challenge, but now I'd have to develop a dairy-free filling that didn't require refrigeration to set.

My research uncovered a technique invented by French chemist Hervé This. Known as a chocolate Chantilly, the technique involves melting chocolate

NOTES FROM THE TEST KITCHEN

FITTING TART DOUGH INTO THE PAN

1. Ease dough into tart pan by lifting dough and gently pressing it into corners and fluted sides of pan.

2. Run rolling pin over top of pan to remove any excess dough.

with an abundant amount of water and then whipping the mixture into a mousse. The result is a rich dessert in which the chocolate flavor comes through loud and clear, unobscured by dairy or eggs. I wasn't after a mousse-like texture for my filling, so I needed to tweak This's method. I also wanted to streamline the technique, which involved melting the chocolate and water over a double boiler before whipping it over an ice bath.

After extensive testing I landed on a mixture of 10½ ounces of bittersweet chocolate and ¾ cup of water. These proportions ensured a filling that set to a sliceable consistency at room temperature. I made sure to use bittersweet chocolate with 60 to 70 percent cacao, which set faster, and I added ¼ cup of sugar and ¼ teaspoon of table salt to balance the chocolate's bitterness. The high ratio of chocolate to water eliminated the fussy double boiler and ice bath; I simply brought the water to a boil, poured it over the chopped chocolate, and whisked the mixture until it was smooth. I then transferred the filling to the baked tart shell and let it set up at room temperature, which took only 2 hours.

I was searching for a topping to finish off the tart when my colleague came across an intriguing video from the YouTube channel emmymade. Emmy makes a "magic" coffee whipped cream by whipping instant coffee powder, sugar, and water in a stand mixer for 3 minutes. The resulting mixture resembles a thick, glossy meringue, which Emmy uses to pipe over brownies. Variations on this whipped coffee can be found throughout the world; it's often used to top iced coffee or milk. I knew that it would make an excellent vegan topping for my tart, as its bittersweet flavor would nicely complement the dark chocolate filling.

I played with the amounts of coffee powder and sugar and found that increasing the sugar resulted in a glossier, thicker foam. Switching from coffee powder to espresso powder tempered the sweetness of the extra sugar. After whipping the mixture to soft peaks in my stand mixer, I piped it over the chocolate filling. A light dusting of cocoa powder was a delicate finishing touch. My vegan chocolate tart had it all: a crisp crust; a rich, silky dark chocolate filling; and an airy espresso topping that brought the chocolate flavor into focus. Baking doesn't have to rely on dairy.

—CAMILA CHAPARRO, *America's Test Kitchen Books*

Vegan Chocolate-Espresso Tart

SERVES 10 TO 12

Not all brands of bittersweet chocolate are vegan, so check ingredient lists carefully. We used bittersweet chocolate with 60 to 70 percent cacao for the filling (higher-percentage cacao will set faster). We had the best results using a stand mixer to whip the topping; you can skip the topping if you like and just dust the tart with cocoa powder or confectioners' sugar, or add a dollop of Coconut Whipped Cream (recipe follows) or dairy whipped cream. For an accurate measurement of boiling water, bring a kettle of water to a boil and then measure out the desired amount.

CRUST

1¾ cups (8¾ ounces) all-purpose flour

3 tablespoons sugar

¼ teaspoon table salt

½ cup refined coconut oil, melted and cooled slightly

3 tablespoons water

FILLING

10½ ounces bittersweet chocolate, chopped fine

¼ cup (1¾ ounces) sugar

¼ teaspoon table salt

¾ cup boiling water

TOPPING

6 tablespoons (2⅔ ounces) sugar

¼ cup ice water

4 teaspoons instant espresso powder

Unsweetened cocoa powder (optional)

1. FOR THE CRUST: Whisk flour, sugar, and salt together in bowl. Add melted oil and water and stir with rubber spatula until dough forms. Roll dough into 12-inch circle between 2 large sheets of parchment paper. Remove top sheet of parchment and, working quickly, gently invert dough (still on bottom sheet of parchment) onto 9-inch tart pan with removable bottom. Center dough over pan, letting excess dough hang over edge, and remove remaining parchment. Ease dough into pan by gently lifting edge of dough with your hand while pressing into corners and fluted sides of pan with your other hand. Run rolling pin over top of pan to remove any excess dough. Prick dough all over with fork, then wrap pan loosely in plastic wrap and refrigerate for 30 minutes. (Dough-lined tart pan can be refrigerated for up to 24 hours or frozen for up to 1 month.)

2. Adjust oven rack to middle position and heat oven to 350 degrees. Line chilled tart shell with double layer of aluminum foil and fill with pie weights. Bake on rimmed baking sheet until tart shell is evenly pale and dry, 30 to 35 minutes, rotating sheet halfway through baking.

3. Remove foil and weights and continue to bake tart shell until light golden brown and firm to touch, about 20 minutes, rotating pan halfway through baking. Set aside to cool completely. (Cooled crust can be wrapped in plastic wrap and stored at room temperature for up to 24 hours. Do not refrigerate or crust will become hard.)

4. FOR THE FILLING: Place chocolate, sugar, and salt in bowl. Pour boiling water over chocolate mixture and let sit for 30 seconds, then whisk until mixture is completely smooth. Transfer filling to cooled tart shell, popping any large bubbles that form with toothpick, and let tart sit at room temperature until chocolate is set, at least 2 hours or up to 24 hours. (Do not refrigerate or crust will become hard.)

5. FOR THE TOPPING: Using stand mixer fitted with whisk attachment, whip sugar, ice water, and espresso powder on high speed until soft peaks form, 2 to 3 minutes. Transfer mixture to pastry bag fitted with star tip (or use zipper-lock bag with corner snipped off) and pipe decoratively over filling. Dust with cocoa, if using, and serve.

Coconut Whipped Cream

MAKES ABOUT 2 CUPS

The cream from canned coconut milk easily whips into delicately flavored soft-peaked billows.

4 (14-ounce) cans coconut milk

2 tablespoons sugar

2 teaspoons vanilla extract

Refrigerate unopened cans of coconut milk for at least 24 hours to ensure that 2 distinct layers form. Skim top layer of cream from each can and measure out 2 cups cream (save any extra cream and milky liquid for another use). Using stand mixer fitted with whisk attachment, whip coconut cream, sugar, and vanilla on low speed until well combined, about 30 seconds. Increase speed to high and whip until mixture thickens and soft peaks form, about 2 minutes. (Coconut whipped cream can be refrigerated for up to 4 days.)

CRANBERRY CURD TART WITH ALMOND CRUST

✔ **WHY THIS RECIPE WORKS** Our cranberry curd tart showcases cranberries' bold flavor and brilliant color while making use of their ample pectin content. We started by quickly simmering the cranberry filling, which softened the berries and released their acids and pectin. We immediately pureed the berries with egg yolks and cornstarch, using the berries' heat to cook the eggs and thicken the cornstarch. Then, while the filling rested, we stirred together the dough for our crust. The combination of almond flour and cornstarch kept the crust thin but sturdy and gluten-free. After pressing the dough into a tart pan, we baked it until it was golden. Then we pureed butter into the cooled filling, strained it, and poured the mixture over the baked crust. This method prevented the filling from developing a thick, rubbery skin. Finally, we whisked up a whipped cream topping stabilized by a small amount of the pectin-rich puree. This topping could be piped onto the tart hours in advance without breaking or weeping.

When I first encountered a tart made with cranberry curd (a recipe by David Tanis in the *New York Times*), I was bowled over by its gorgeousness. I loved seeing cranberries in the limelight, since they're so often relegated either to a relish or to an accent role in apple pie or crisp. I got to work showcasing their vivid color and unapologetic tartness in my own version of this dazzling alternative to a lemon curd tart. At the same time, I discovered how to make a sturdy yet delicate almond crust that just happens to be gluten-free, along with a whipped cream topping that doesn't weep or deflate.

I thought a nut crust would complement the astringent cranberry filling more than plain pastry, and almond seemed like a good choice since I could enhance its flavor with the nut's sweet, perfumed extract. So I stirred almond flour together with melted butter, sugar, salt, and almond extract; pressed the dough into a tart pan; and baked it in a 350-degree oven. It was rich and beautifully golden—but so fragile that it crumbled apart when I sliced the finished tart. Plus, some of the curd (a placeholder recipe for now) had seeped through to the pan, indicating that I needed something to bind up the crumb. Both flour and cornstarch worked nicely, so I chose the latter to keep the shell gluten-free.

Tangy, luscious curd is usually made by heating citrus juice (lemon is classic) with sugar, eggs, and butter until the mixture turns thick and glossy. When the curd will be used as a filling rather than as a spread, flour or cornstarch is added to thicken it to a sliceable consistency. It's then strained to ensure a satiny-smooth texture, transferred to a tart or pie shell, and baked until it's fully set.

Cranberry curd, however, is typically made using the whole fruit, including its pectin-rich flesh and skin. Pectin is a potent gelling agent, so the filling doesn't need the usual number of eggs (six or more per ½ cup of juice) or as much of the flavor-dulling, starchy thickeners to make it sliceably firm. (Any curd made with citrus juice alone, which contains relatively little pectin, requires more thickeners.) So I ran a bunch of tests, simmering a pound of berries with sugar and water, buzzing the syrupy mixture in the food processor, and heating it again with varying amounts of yolks and cornstarch (plus butter for silky richness). I found that just three yolks and 2 teaspoons of cornstarch provided all the thickening help my curd needed.

But there were a couple other advantages to making curd with cranberries that I hadn't anticipated. For one thing, I didn't need to pour the fruit puree back into the saucepan and heat it with the yolks and cornstarch to ensure that it solidified and gelled; the cranberry puree was a piping hot 180 degrees, so I could add the thickeners directly to the food processor and let them cook in the puree's residual heat. The other perk was that the berries' abundance of pectin tightened the curd so effectively that there was no need to bake the filling in the tart shell; it was perfectly set by the time it cooled to room temperature.

The only problem I ran into was cosmetic: As it cooled, the curd developed an unattractive skin—a dry barrier that forms when water evaporates and proteins and sugar concentrate near the surface. Short of pressing a sheet of parchment over the curd, which would wreck its appearance when I pulled it off, I couldn't prevent a skin from forming. But I had an idea for how

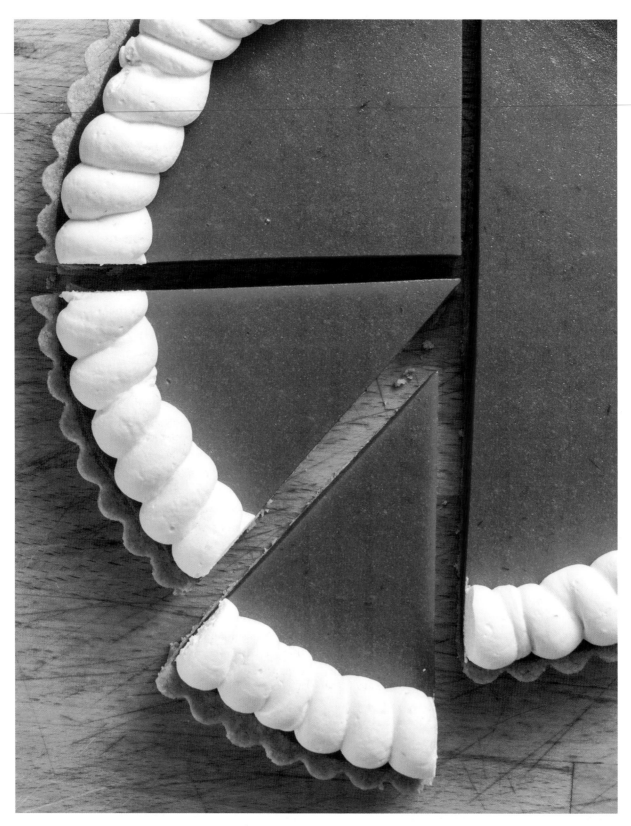

CRANBERRY CURD TART WITH ALMOND CRUST

to get rid of it before I even transferred the filling to the tart shell: After processing in the eggs and cornstarch, I left the mixture to cool in the processor bowl. When a skin spread over its surface and the temperature dropped to 125 degrees—cool enough that little further evaporation would occur—I processed the puree again (adding the butter first for efficiency's sake), obliterating all signs of the skin. I strained the filling, poured it into the baked shell, and left it to fully cool. When I tried a bite, it was uniformly silky from top to bottom.

Rich, billowy whipped cream piped into a pretty design would be perfect for topping my tart, but since it doesn't hold its shape for very long, I'd have to pipe it just before serving. Then I had an idea: Why not make use of the pectin in the filling to help stabilize the whipped cream? It wouldn't take much, since the calcium in dairy also helps strengthen pectin. And that way, I could pipe it well in advance of the meal. I reserved 2 tablespoons of the curd before pouring the rest into the tart shell. Once the tart had cooled, I whipped the reserved curd with a cup of heavy cream and piped the faintly rosy mixture into a simple yet elegant pattern around the filling's perimeter.

With that, the tart was perfect. I savored its three contrasting elements: the crisp, golden, nutty crust with sweet, floral overtones; the satiny magenta filling full of sharp, fruity flavors; and the velvety whipped cream that tempered the whole thing. When the holidays roll around, join me in giving cranberries a stunning breakout moment. You'll be glad you did.

—LAN LAM, *Cook's Illustrated*

Cranberry Curd Tart with Almond Crust

SERVES 8

You'll need a 9-inch tart pan with a removable bottom for this recipe. We strongly recommend weighing the almond flour and cornstarch for the crust. If preferred, you can use a stand mixer or handheld mixer to whip the cream in step 4. The tart crust will be firm if you serve the tart on the day that it's made; if you prefer a more tender crust, make the tart through step 3 up to two days ahead. The test kitchen's favorite almond extract is Nielsen-Massey Pure Almond Extract.

FILLING

1 pound (4 cups) fresh or frozen cranberries

1¼ cups (8¾ ounces) plus 1 tablespoon sugar, divided

½ cup water

   Pinch table salt

3 large egg yolks

2 teaspoons cornstarch

4 tablespoons unsalted butter, cut into 4 pieces and softened

CRUST

1 cup (4 ounces) almond flour

½ cup (2 ounces) cornstarch

⅓ cup (2⅓ ounces) sugar

½ teaspoon table salt

6 tablespoons unsalted butter, melted and cooled

¾ teaspoon almond extract

1 cup heavy cream

1. FOR THE FILLING: Bring cranberries, 1¼ cups sugar, water, and salt to boil in medium saucepan over medium-high heat, stirring occasionally. Adjust heat to maintain very gentle simmer. Cover and cook until all cranberries have burst and started to shrivel, about 10 minutes. While cranberries cook, whisk egg yolks and cornstarch in bowl until smooth. Transfer hot cranberry mixture to food processor. Immediately add yolk mixture and process until smooth (small flecks of cranberry skin will be visible), about 1 minute, scraping down sides of bowl as necessary. Let mixture cool in processor bowl until skin forms and mixture registers 120 to 125 degrees, 45 minutes to 1 hour. While mixture cools, make crust.

2. FOR THE CRUST: Adjust oven rack to middle position and heat oven to 350 degrees. Whisk flour, cornstarch, sugar, and salt in bowl until well combined. Add melted butter and almond extract and stir with wooden spoon until uniform dough forms. Crumble two-thirds of mixture over bottom of 9-inch tart pan with removable bottom. Press dough to even thickness in bottom of pan. Crumble remaining dough and scatter evenly around edge of pan. Press crumbled dough into sides of pan. Press edges to even thickness. Place pan on rimmed baking sheet and bake until crust is golden brown, about 20 minutes, rotating pan halfway through baking.

3. Add softened butter to cranberry puree and process until fully combined, about 30 seconds. Strain mixture through fine-mesh strainer set over bowl, pressing on solids with rubber spatula to extract puree. Transfer 2 tablespoons puree to medium bowl, then stir in cream and remaining 1 tablespoon sugar. Cover and refrigerate. Transfer remaining puree to crust (it's OK if crust is still warm) and smooth into even layer. Let tart sit at room temperature for at least 4 hours. (Cover tart with large bowl and refrigerate after 4 hours if making ahead.)

4. Whisk cream mixture until stiff peaks form, 1 to 3 minutes. Transfer to pastry bag fitted with pastry tip. Pipe decorative border around edge of tart. Transfer any remaining whipped cream to small serving bowl.

5. To serve, remove outer metal ring of tart pan. Slide thin metal spatula between tart and pan bottom to loosen tart. Carefully slide tart onto serving platter. Slice into wedges, wiping knife clean between cuts if necessary, and serve, passing extra whipped cream separately. (Leftovers can be covered and refrigerated for up to 3 days.)

PEACH ZABAGLIONE GRATIN

✓ **WHY THIS RECIPE WORKS** For a dessert that would evoke a "peaches and cream" vibe, we took inspiration from an Italian classic, fruit with zabaglione (which is also called "sabayon" in French cuisine). Zabaglione is a dairy-free custard made by cooking egg yolks, sugar, and sweet wine in a double boiler to get a silky texture. Constant whisking traps air as the temperature rises and the egg yolks slowly cook, lightening the zabaglione. Cooking the custard until it registers 165 to 170 degrees removes much of the guesswork. We used freestone peaches at their peak ripeness and treated them simply, macerating them in sugar, a drinking-quality Marsala wine, and a little vanilla. For a refined finishing touch, after spooning the luscious zabaglione over the peaches, we used a broiler (or blowtorch) to toast the top, which gave the custard a roasted-marshmallow character.

Peach pie, peach cobbler, peach jam—all are delicious treats that celebrate perfectly ripe peaches at their seasonal peak. But this adaptation of "peaches and cream" takes inspiration from an Italian classic, fruit with zabaglione (which is also called "sabayon" in French cuisine). The elegant dessert is perfect served after a light meal on warm summer nights.

Zabaglione is a dairy-free custard made with egg yolks, sugar, and sweet wine; I cooked my version in a double boiler to achieve a silky consistency. The classic cooking method involves setting a bowl over a pot of simmering water—without the bowl touching the water—and constantly whisking the mixture until it thickens. Constant, gentle whisking traps air, keeping the sauce light as the mixture comes up to the desired temperature—anywhere from 165 to 170 degrees. Reaching the target temperature and watching for visual cues takes the guesswork out of knowing when the zabaglione is done and minimizes the danger of curdling the eggs.

To make a complete dessert, I tossed the best peaches I could find with sugar, sweet Marsala wine, vanilla, and a touch of salt. The sugar drew out the natural sweetness of the fruit, while the Marsala added a nutty quality and the vanilla imparted richness. Macerating the peaches instead of cooking them maintained their shape; plus, the process yielded an incredible sweet peach nectar that I used to flavor the egg yolk base.

For a refined finishing touch, I arranged the peaches in a baking dish and then spooned the zabaglione on top before broiling, which created a toasted sugar crown that reminded me of a perfectly browned marshmallow. Fresh peaches never had it so good.

—MARK HUXSOLL, *Cook's Country*

Peach Zabaglione Gratin
SERVES 4 TO 6

For the best results, use in-season, ripe peaches here. A ripe peach will be fragrant and yield slightly when pressed with your thumb. We like to use freestone peaches if they're available, because they're easier to prepare. Don't use cooking Marsala in this recipe—use a drinking-quality Marsala instead. Other sweet wines such as moscato and port can be substituted for the Marsala, if desired. Note that depending on the type of bowl you use, the timing of the zabaglione in step 3 will vary by several minutes. The finished zabaglione should have the texture of soft whipped cream.

1½	**pounds ripe peaches, halved, pitted, and cut into ¾-inch wedges**
½	**cup (3½ ounces) sugar**
¼	**cup sweet Marsala**

1 teaspoon vanilla extract

¼ teaspoon table salt

4 large egg yolks

1. Gently toss peaches, sugar, Marsala, vanilla, and salt together in bowl. Let sit for 30 minutes, stirring occasionally. Set colander in medium bowl. Transfer peach mixture to colander and let drain for 2 minutes; reserve accumulated peach liquid.

2. Remove colander from bowl and whisk egg yolks into accumulated peach liquid. Set bowl with egg yolk mixture over large saucepan with 1 inch of barely simmering water (water should not touch bottom of bowl).

3. Cook, whisking constantly, until zabaglione is thickened to point where ribbons sit on top of mixture when drizzled from whisk and mixture registers 165 to 170 degrees, 10 to 15 minutes for metal bowl or about 20 minutes for glass bowl.

4. Arrange peaches in single layer in shallow 1½-quart gratin dish. Spoon zabaglione over peaches to cover completely.

NOTES FROM THE TEST KITCHEN

KEY STEPS TO MAKING PEACH ZABAGLIONE GRATIN

1. Macerate peach wedges in sugar, Marsala, vanilla, and salt, then drain.

2. Gently cook custard using double boiler.

3. Brown top under broiler element in oven or using blowtorch.

5A. FOR A BROILER: Adjust oven rack 6 inches from broiler element and heat broiler. Broil until top is well browned, 30 to 60 seconds.

5B. FOR A BLOWTORCH: Ignite torch and continuously sweep flame above zabaglione until well browned, about 2 minutes.

6. Serve immediately.

STRAWBERRY GALETTE

✓ **WHY THIS RECIPE WORKS** We wanted a foolproof recipe for a simple free-form galette with a crisp, buttery, flaky crust and a juicy (not soupy) filling full of concentrated strawberry flavor. We made a few key decisions to guard against a soggy, leaky galette. First, to ensure a uniformly sturdy, flaky crust (rather than a short, crumbly one that might leak), we turned to a method called fraisage, which entails smearing flour, chilled butter, and ice water against the counter with the heel of your hand to form a dough. This method converts the butter pieces into thin sheets that are layered between the flour and water. Second, we tossed the strawberries with ¼ cup of sugar—just enough to highlight their natural sweetness and tame some of their tartness—and drained off the juice. Less juice in the galette meant less chance of leaking. Finally, we stirred the strawberries together with a bit of strawberry jam, 1½ tablespoons of cornstarch, and ¼ teaspoon of salt. The jam not only boosted the strawberry flavor but, along with the cornstarch, also helped thicken the juice, creating a leakproof tart with a jammy strawberry filling.

Although strawberries are delightful eaten out of hand—especially at the peak of ripeness in late spring—they become something truly sublime when baked into a dessert. Their flavor concentrates and intensifies as the liquid inside them cooks off.

My go-to fresh fruit dessert is always a free-form galette. It's everything that's lovable about a fruit pie but with much less fuss. However, as with any baked fresh fruit filling, the juiciness of the fruit can cause some structural problems if left unchecked. This is especially so with strawberries, which seem to have hidden reservoirs of ruby juice within them. It's all too easy to toss some strawberries with a bit of sugar, place them in the pastry, slide it all into the oven, and then come back to a strawberry juice lake overflowing your crust's soggy shores.

For this recipe, I made a few key decisions to guard against that truly disappointing outcome. First, to ensure a uniformly sturdy, flaky crust (rather than a short, crumbly one that might leak), I turned to a method called fraisage: a technique I first encountered when making quiche and free-form caramelized onion tarts for a French bakery. This is the process of working the crumbles of flour, butter, and water together into a dough by smearing them against the counter with the heel of your hand, thereby spreading the butter pieces into thin sheets between layers of flour and water. It makes for a sturdy, flaky crust.

Second, after hulling and slicing my strawberries, I tossed them with ¼ cup of sugar—just enough to accent their natural sweetness and mellow some of their tartness—and let them sit while my pastry dough chilled. Then I drained off the juice, reserving some to brush back onto the formed galette to help my final sprinkling of sugar stick. Less juice in the galette would lead to less chance of leaking.

Finally, just before placing my fruit on the rolled-out pastry crust, I stirred the berries together with a bit of strawberry jam and 1½ tablespoons of cornstarch. The jam not only added extra strawberry flavor but, along with the cornstarch, also helped thicken the juice, creating a leakproof free-form tart with a juicy, jammy strawberry filling.

—MATTHEW FAIRMAN, *Cook's Country*

Strawberry Galette

SERVES 6

Quarter any strawberries larger than a Ping-Pong ball. Do not combine the macerated strawberries with the jam mixture until you're ready to form and bake the galette; they may release more juice and make it hard to shape the dough around the fruit. Serve with Tangy Whipped Cream (recipe follows), if desired.

DOUGH

- 1½ cups (7½ ounces) all-purpose flour
- ½ teaspoon table salt
- 10 tablespoons unsalted butter, cut into ½-inch cubes and chilled
- 6 tablespoons ice water

FILLING

- 1½ pounds strawberries, hulled, halved if small or quartered if large (5 cups)
- ¼ cup (1¾ ounces) plus 1 tablespoon sugar, divided
- ⅓ cup strawberry jam
- 1½ tablespoons cornstarch
- ¼ teaspoon table salt

1. FOR THE DOUGH: Process flour and salt in food processor until combined, about 3 seconds. Scatter butter over top and pulse until mixture resembles coarse sand and butter pieces are size of small peas, about 10 pulses. Add ice water to flour mixture and pulse until dough begins to form small curds and holds together when pinched with your fingers, about 5 pulses.

2. Transfer mixture to lightly floured counter. Using bench scraper, gather dough into rough rectangular mound about 12 inches long and 4 inches wide. Starting at farthest end, use heel of your hand to smear small amount of dough against counter, pushing firmly down and away from you, to create separate pile of dough (flattened pieces of dough should look shaggy). Continue processing until all dough has been worked. Gather dough into rough 12 by 4-inch mound and repeat smearing process.

3. Form dough into 6-inch disk, wrap tightly in plastic wrap, and refrigerate for at least 1 hour or up to 2 days. (Wrapped dough can be frozen for up to 1 month. If frozen, let dough thaw completely on counter before rolling.)

4. FOR THE FILLING: One hour before rolling out dough, toss strawberries with ¼ cup sugar in bowl. Set aside for 1 hour. Reserve 1 tablespoon strawberry juice. Drain strawberries in colander in sink. Leave strawberries in colander while rolling out dough.

5. Adjust oven rack to lower-middle position and heat oven to 375 degrees. Line rimmed baking sheet with parchment paper. Roll dough into 12-inch circle on lightly floured counter, then transfer to prepared sheet. Cover dough loosely with plastic and refrigerate until firm, about 10 minutes.

6. Whisk jam, cornstarch, and salt in large bowl until combined. Add strawberries and toss gently to coat. Mound fruit in center of dough, leaving 2-inch border. Carefully grasp 1 edge of dough and fold up 2 inches over fruit. Repeat around circumference of galette, overlapping dough every 2 inches; firmly pinch pleated dough to secure, but do not press dough into fruit.

STRAWBERRY GALETTE

7. Brush top of dough with reserved strawberry juice and sprinkle dough and filling with remaining 1 tablespoon sugar.

8. Bake until crust is deep golden brown and fruit is bubbling, 1 hour to 1 hour 10 minutes. Let galette cool on baking sheet for 10 minutes. Using parchment, carefully slide galette onto wire rack. Remove parchment and let cool on rack until just warm, about 30 minutes. Serve.

Tangy Whipped Cream
SERVES 6 (MAKES 2 CUPS)

 1   cup heavy cream, chilled
¼   cup sour cream, chilled
¼   cup packed (1¾ ounces) light brown sugar
⅛   teaspoon vanilla extract

1. Using stand mixer fitted with whisk attachment, whip all ingredients on medium-low speed until foamy, about 1 minute.

2. Increase speed to high and whip until soft peaks form, 1 to 3 minutes. Serve.

REALLY GOOD KEY LIME PIE

WHY THIS RECIPE WORKS We set out to create a great key lime pie with a soft yet set filling that perfectly balanced sweetness and tartness. We started with what's commonly held as the go-to recipe for key lime pie filling: the one on the back of the bottle of Nellie & Joe's Famous Key West Lime Juice. We increased the ingredient amounts and added heavy cream to make an impressively tall, extra-luscious pie. For further embellishment, we bolstered a sturdy graham cracker crust with crushed pretzel twists. The pretzels added a saltiness that balanced the rich filling. A pillowy meringue topping added a contrasting lightness and a stunning look.

However and wherever key lime pie was born, the pie has become a point of pride in Florida, where it's the official state pie. But even within the Sunshine State, the dessert inspires heated opinions. In the 1960s, state representative Bernie Papy Jr. called to impose a $100

fine on anyone calling their dessert "key lime pie" without using real key limes. And while no one has pushed this legislation, many believe that green food coloring ruins the pie. A graham cracker crust and a whipped cream topping are common elements, but plenty of Floridians adamantly defend a traditional pastry crust and/or a meringue top.

So going into this recipe, we knew that we wouldn't be able to satisfy everyone. But we set off to create a pie with a soft yet set filling that straddled the fine line between sweet and tart.

We started with what many think of as the go-to recipe for key lime pie filling: the one on the back of the bottle of Nellie & Joe's Famous Key West Lime Juice. This recipe calls for mixing sweetened condensed milk, egg yolks, and lime juice and then baking the mixture. After some trial and error, we decided to nearly double the ingredient amounts and add some heavy cream to make an impressively tall slice of pie that's extra-luscious.

Next, we wondered whether the tiny, yellow-hued key limes were truly better than regular supermarket limes (aka Persian limes), which are generally easier to find. We baked three pies to find out: one using bottled key lime juice, another using freshly squeezed key lime juice, and a final with fresh Persian lime juice.

The bottled-juice version had a bitter aftertaste and lacked brightness. But both pies made with fresh juice were deliciously tangy. Sure, there were some differences; the key lime version was floral and nuanced. But the key lime custard was also a little astringent, and juicing those 18 tiny limes—as opposed to six Persian limes—was not an easy task.

For some embellishment to our already nontraditional pie, we bolstered a sturdy graham cracker crust with pulverized pretzels. The pretzels added a buttery saltiness that balanced the sweet-tart filling. Topping the pie with a light, fluffy meringue was a good way to use up some of the egg whites left over from making the filling. Plus, the pillowy meringue added a contrasting texture and a stunning look.

One thing not worth debating: This delicious, creamy, not-necessarily-key lime pie is just the thing to bring a little sunshine to your table.

—LINDSAY AUTRY WITH MORGAN BOLLING,
Cook's Country

Really Good Key Lime Pie

SERVES 8

Note that two egg whites are used to make the meringue topping—don't discard them when separating the eggs for the filling. Be sure to zest the limes to get the 2 teaspoons of zest needed for the garnish before juicing them. We do not recommend using a disposable aluminum pie plate here; those plates are shallow and the volume of the filling is too much for them. We like the meringue on this pie, but you can top it with Failproof Whipped Cream (recipe follows) instead. You'll need to buy two 14-ounce cans of sweetened condensed milk to yield the 1½ cups for this recipe. We call for regular fresh lime juice here, but if you'd prefer to use key lime juice you'll need to squeeze about 18 key limes to get ¾ cup of juice.

CRUST

   6   ounces graham crackers, broken into
        1-inch pieces (about 11 crackers)
   2   ounces mini pretzel twists (about 35 twists)
   ¼   cup packed (1¾ ounces) light brown sugar
   ¼   teaspoon table salt
   8   tablespoons unsalted butter, melted

FILLING

   1½ cups sweetened condensed milk
   ¾   cup lime juice (6 limes)
   6   tablespoons heavy cream
   4   large egg yolks
   ⅛   teaspoon table salt

MERINGUE

   2   large egg whites
   ¼   teaspoon table salt
   ¼   teaspoon cream of tartar
   ½   cup (3½ ounces) granulated sugar
   ¼   cup water
   1   tablespoon vanilla extract
   2   teaspoons grated lime zest

1. FOR THE CRUST: Adjust oven rack to middle position and heat oven to 350 degrees. Process cracker pieces, pretzels, sugar, and salt in food processor until finely ground, about 30 seconds. Add melted butter and pulse until combined, about 8 pulses.

2. Transfer cracker mixture to 9-inch pie plate. Using bottom of dry measuring cup, press crumbs firmly into bottom and up sides of plate. Place plate on baking sheet and bake until crust is fragrant and set, about 17 minutes. Transfer sheet to wire rack.

3. FOR THE FILLING: Whisk all ingredients in bowl until fully combined. With pie plate still on sheet, carefully pour filling into crust (crust needn't be cool). Transfer sheet to oven and bake pie until edge of filling is set but center still jiggles slightly when shaken, about 30 minutes.

4. Place pie on wire rack and let cool completely, about 1 hour. Refrigerate until fully chilled, at least 4 hours, or cover with greased plastic wrap and refrigerate for up to 24 hours.

5. FOR THE MERINGUE: Combine egg whites, salt, and cream of tartar in bowl of stand mixer fitted with whisk attachment. Whip on medium-high speed until soft peaks form, 2 to 4 minutes.

6. Combine sugar and water in small saucepan. Bring to rolling boil over medium-high heat and cook until syrup registers 240 degrees, 1 to 3 minutes.

7. Working quickly, turn mixer to medium speed. With mixer running, slowly and carefully pour hot syrup into egg white mixture (avoid pouring syrup onto whisk, if possible). Add vanilla. Increase speed to medium-high and whip until shiny, stiff peaks form, about 2 minutes.

8. Spread meringue over pie filling, leaving 1-inch border. Working gently, use spatula or spoon to create swirls and cowlicks over surface of meringue. Sprinkle meringue with lime zest. Slice pie into wedges with wet knife, wiping knife clean between slices. Serve.

Failproof Whipped Cream

SERVES 6 TO 8 (MAKES ABOUT 2 CUPS)

If your kitchen is particularly warm, it's helpful to chill the mixer bowl and whisk attachment in the freezer for 20 minutes before whipping the cream. This recipe can be doubled or tripled, if desired.

   1   cup heavy cream, chilled
   ¼   cup (1¾ ounces) sugar
   ½   teaspoon vanilla extract

Using stand mixer fitted with whisk attachment, whip cream, sugar, and vanilla on medium-low speed until foamy, about 1 minute. Increase speed to medium-high and whip until stiff peaks form, 1 to 3 minutes.

ENDLESS SUMMER PEACH PIE

ENDLESS SUMMER PEACH PIE

✓ **WHY THIS RECIPE WORKS** We sidestepped the typical obstacles to a great peach pie (such as mushy filling and soupy slices) by using frozen peaches: They're convenient, consistent, and easily accessible year-round. To give the frozen slices a much-needed flavor boost, we precooked them with sugar, simmering them to drive off excess moisture and concentrate their fruity flavors. Once cooled, the peaches needed little more than a lively spritz of lemon juice to taste summer-fresh. We used a flaky, buttery pie dough, adding in some sour cream for richness and to make it even more workable, and we kept the classic lattice top but made it extra-achievable by using fewer, thicker strips. With a generous topping of crunchy turbinado sugar, this pie is delicious all on its own, but it is even better when drizzled with a salted butterscotch sauce and dolloped with whipped cream.

Is there a more highly anticipated time of year than peach season? I don't think so. And once it's here, the best way to celebrate is to capture the essence of a perfectly ripe peach in a freshly baked pie . . . right?

The sad truth is that all of a fresh peach's best qualities can become roadblocks to a great pie. The juices you love when they're running down to your elbows can make a pie a soupy mess. Those subtle floral and creamy flavors you crave in the fresh fruit tend to flatten out when baked. And not every peach is sweet and juicy, even in peak season. How can you best account for the variability in sweetness, tartness, and juiciness in less-than-perfect peaches?

Good news! We have the ideal fix at our disposal: frozen peaches. While they're not as lively or rewarding as fresh peaches when eaten straight, frozen peaches are a far more consistent product and are available anytime, anywhere. And with a little care, they make a dynamite pie.

To bolster the muted flavor of the frozen peaches, I had to first drive off excess moisture, which concentrated their fruity taste. I did this by cooking down frozen peaches in a Dutch oven with some sugar and a pinch of salt. As the peaches cooked, they thawed and released liquid, which then reduced with the sugar and turned syrupy and glazy, lightly candying the peaches. Unlike fresh peaches, frozen peach slices start out quite firm and will hold their shape without breaking down while simmering.

Once cooked and cooled, the peaches needed little more than a squeeze of lemon to perk them up, plus some cornstarch to thicken the remaining liquid and ensure a sliceable finished pie.

Tucked into a simple, buttery pie crust and topped with a decorative lattice and a sprinkle of satisfyingly crunchy turbinado sugar, the peaches baked into a beautiful, fragrant pie that could sway even the most die-hard of fresh seasonal peach fans. Endless summer, indeed.

—JESSICA RUDOLPH, *Cook's Country*

Endless Summer Peach Pie
SERVES 8 TO 10

When purchasing frozen peaches, look for a no-sugar-added product; we like Earthbound Farm, Cascadian Farm, or Welch's frozen peaches. There is no need to thaw the frozen peaches. If you can't find turbinado sugar, simply omit the sugar topping (do not substitute granulated sugar). Plan ahead: The pie filling needs to cool for at least 2 hours and the dough needs to chill for at least an hour before rolling. This pie is best when baked a day ahead of time and allowed to rest overnight. Serve with Salted Butterscotch Sauce (recipe follows) and whipped cream.

FILLING
- 3 pounds frozen sliced peaches
- 1 cup (7 ounces) granulated sugar
- ¾ teaspoon table salt
- 2 tablespoons cornstarch
- 1½ tablespoons lemon juice
- 2 tablespoons unsalted butter, cut into ½-inch pieces

PIE DOUGH
- 7 tablespoons ice water
- ¼ cup sour cream
- 2½ cups (12½ ounces) all-purpose flour
- 1 tablespoon granulated sugar
- 1 teaspoon table salt
- 16 tablespoons unsalted butter, cut into ½-inch pieces and chilled
- 1 large egg, lightly beaten
- 2 tablespoons turbinado sugar

1. FOR THE FILLING: Combine peaches, sugar, and salt in Dutch oven. Cook peach mixture over medium-high heat, stirring occasionally, until juice is reduced

HOW TO MAKE AN EASY LATTICE TOP

You don't need a degree in physics or an origami manual to get this simple lattice right.

1. Cut six 2-inch-wide strips of dough, chill, then lay first strip across pie.

2. Make cross with second strip.

3. Lay third strip parallel to first.

4. Lay fourth strip below first.

5. Fold back left side of first strip and lay fifth strip in place.

6. Unfold first strip to cover.

7. Fold back right side of first strip and lay final strip in place.

8. Unfold and seal lattice pieces to bottom dough.

to thick syrup and spatula dragged through mixture leaves trail that doesn't fill in immediately, 25 to 30 minutes. Transfer to large bowl and refrigerate until completely cooled, at least 2 hours. (Filling can be refrigerated for up to 3 days.)

2. FOR THE PIE DOUGH: Meanwhile, mix ice water and sour cream in bowl. Process flour, granulated sugar, and salt in food processor until combined, about 5 seconds. Scatter butter over top and pulse until butter pieces are no larger than peas, about 10 pulses.

3. Add half of sour cream mixture to flour mixture and pulse until incorporated, about 4 pulses. Scrape down sides of bowl; add remaining sour cream mixture; and pulse until dough forms large clumps and no dry flour remains, about 6 pulses.

4. Transfer dough to counter and knead briefly until it comes together. Divide dough in half. Form 1 half into 5-inch disk and second half into 5-inch square, pressing any cracked edges back together. Wrap separately in plastic wrap and refrigerate for 1 hour. (Wrapped dough can be refrigerated for up to 2 days or frozen for up to 1 month. If frozen, let dough thaw completely on counter before rolling.)

5. Adjust oven rack to lowest position and heat oven to 375 degrees. Let chilled dough sit on counter to soften slightly before rolling, about 10 minutes. Roll dough disk into 13-inch circle on lightly floured counter. Loosely roll dough around rolling pin and gently unroll it onto 9-inch pie plate, letting excess dough hang over edge. Ease dough into plate by gently lifting edge of dough with your hand while pressing into plate bottom with your other hand.

6. Wrap dough-lined plate loosely in plastic and refrigerate until dough is firm, about 30 minutes. Roll dough square into 13 by 11-inch rectangle on lightly floured counter, with long side parallel to counter's edge. Using pizza wheel or chef's knife, trim ½ inch of dough from short sides of rectangle (sides perpendicular to counter's edge) to create clean edges. Cut six 2-inch-wide strips of dough perpendicular to counter's edge. Transfer strips to parchment paper–lined baking sheet, cover with plastic, and refrigerate for 30 minutes.

7. Stir cornstarch and lemon juice together in small bowl, add to cooled peach mixture, and stir to combine. Transfer peach mixture to dough-lined pie plate, spread into even layer, and dot with butter.

8. To make lattice, lay 1 dough strip across center of pie, parallel to counter's edge. Lay second strip across center of pie to form cross. Lay 2 strips across pie, parallel to counter's edge, on either side of middle parallel strip, about ¾ inch away from middle strip.

9. Fold back left side of middle parallel strip. Lay 1 strip across left side of pie, perpendicular to counter's edge, about ¾ inch away from middle perpendicular strip. Unfold middle parallel strip to cover. Repeat with right side of middle parallel strip and remaining dough strip.

10. Shift strips as needed so they are evenly spaced over top of pie. Pinch edges of lattice strips and bottom crust together firmly. Trim overhang to ½ inch beyond lip of plate. Tuck overhang under itself; folded edge should be flush with edge of plate. Crimp dough evenly around edge of plate using your fingers.

11. Brush lattice top and crimped edge with egg and sprinkle with turbinado sugar. Set pie on parchment-lined baking sheet. Bake until well browned and juices bubble around outer edge between lattice strips, about 1 hour, rotating sheet halfway through baking. Let cool on wire rack for at least 6 hours. Slice and serve.

Salted Butterscotch Sauce

SERVES 8 TO 10 (MAKES 1½ CUPS)

We like to serve this sauce warm with our Endless Summer Peach Pie, but it can also be drizzled over ice cream, bread pudding, or cake.

    1   cup packed (7 ounces) light brown sugar
    ½   cup heavy cream
    8   tablespoons unsalted butter, cut into 8 pieces and
        chilled, divided
    ½   teaspoon table salt
    ½   teaspoon vanilla extract

1. Combine sugar, cream, 4 tablespoons butter, and salt in medium saucepan. Cook over medium-high heat, stirring often with heat-resistant rubber spatula, until large bubbles burst on surface of sauce, about 4 minutes. Remove from heat.

2. Carefully stir in vanilla and remaining 4 table-spoons butter until fully combined, about 1 minute. Carefully transfer sauce to bowl and let cool for 30 minutes (sauce will thicken as it cools). Serve. (Sauce can be refrigerated for up to 1 week. Reheat in microwave before serving.)

CHOUX AU CRAQUELIN

WHY THIS RECIPE WORKS For our choux au craquelin recipe—airy, crispy shells encasing smooth, lush pastry cream—we began by making our pastry cream, which we reinforced with a little extra flour so that it could be lightened with whipped cream later on. While it chilled and set, we mixed the craquelin dough—a simple combination of flour, butter, and sugar—and rolled it into a thin sheet from which we cut 24 disks before freezing the dough. For the shells, incorporating both milk and water ensured that our puffs baked up crisp and browned nicely, and using the food processor made it easy to incorporate eggs into the choux paste. Before sliding the piped mounds of batter into the oven, we topped them with the slim disks of craquelin dough, which transformed into crackly shells as the puffs baked. Slitting the baked puffs released steam before we returned them to the turned-off oven for 45 minutes to ensure crispness.

I've always loved cream puffs (called choux à la crème in France). The contrast between the minimally sweetened, delicately crisp pastry with its simple eggy flavor and the voluptuous, vanilla-scented filling makes the combination magical. I'd never considered that there could be anything to improve upon the formula.

But then I discovered choux au craquelin. These puffs are capped with a thin, cookie-like layer (craquelin translates as "cracker") that not only helps smooth out the shape of the puffs so that they're more uniformly round and pretty but also adds buttery taste and some extra crunch that makes this dessert even more delectable. And if that weren't enough, the craquelin also helps the crisp, sweet pastry balloon hold its texture for hours after it's loaded with cream.

There's also something magical about how the craquelin creates that nubbly, delicately brittle layer. You roll out a dough stirred together from flour, butter, sugar, and a little salt and cut it into rounds that you freeze. You pipe the choux paste and then top the mounds with the hardened disks. As the puffs inflate in the oven, the craquelin melts, molding itself against their tops and sides, and then sets into a deeply golden, finely fissured shell.

All I had to do was figure out the most streamlined way to make all three components—choux, craquelin, and cream—and then put them together.

Since the filling would have to cool for a while, I decided to make it first. Pastry cream is standard in cream puffs, but I wanted to go for something more ethereal—a crème diplomate, in which that pudding-like filling is lightened by whipped cream.

I heated milk in a saucepan, and while it came to a simmer, I whisked flour (more than usual to ensure that the filling wouldn't be too loose once I folded in whipped cream), sugar, and salt together in a bowl. I added egg yolks and cold milk. Then I whisked in some of the simmering milk to warm the eggs. This maneuver is called tempering, and it's safer than adding the mixture straight into the saucepan, which could cause the eggs to curdle. I combined everything over the heat, and I stirred. And stirred.

When making pastry cream, it's worth taking your time. The flour needs to fully gelatinize, which means that the granules swell with water until they burst and dissolve; it's what makes the pastry cream thick. And the eggs need to get hot enough to deactivate an enzyme called amylase, which could otherwise break down the starch and leave the pastry cream runny. So I slowly brought the mixture to a boil, knowing that, since everything was now well combined, the starch would prevent the eggs from curdling.

Thanks to the extra flour, the mixture was very thick when I removed it from the heat. I whisked in some butter and vanilla, transferred the pastry cream to a bowl, and let it cool while I moved on to the craquelin and choux (I'd add the whipped cream just before serving so that it wouldn't deflate).

Making the craquelin was a breeze. I mixed nearly equal weights of flour and sugar (I chose light brown for its warm color), some softened butter, and a pinch of salt and stirred the mixture together in a bowl. To make it easy to roll out the dough and transfer it to the freezer, I scraped it onto a sheet of parchment, placed another sheet on top, and rolled the mass into a thin rectangle. I removed the top layer of parchment; cut out 24 disks with a small round cutter; replaced the parchment; and slid the whole thing onto a rimless baking sheet, which I placed in the freezer. While the craquelin chilled, I made the puffs.

I heated water, butter, milk, sugar, and salt in a saucepan; when it came to a full boil, I stirred in flour to make a thick paste. I cooked the paste, stirring all the while, until it came together in a shiny, cohesive mass. Then I took it off the heat so that I could incorporate the eggs: two whole eggs and an extra white. We've found that an added white improves crispness and provides more water, which turns to steam and helps the choux puff even more.

Traditionally, the eggs are mixed in by hand, and in fact that's how I learned to do it in cooking school, so I can tell you: Slippery raw eggs and a warm thick paste do not want to combine. It's much easier to move the paste to a food processor and blend in the eggs there. After about a minute, the eggy dough was thoroughly mixed. I transferred it to a pastry bag and piped 24 mounds onto a rimmed baking sheet, which I'd prepped in advance with a clever trick: I oiled and floured the sheet to prevent sticking and then used my round cutter to mark circles I could use as a guide for piping. Then I retrieved the craquelin disks from the freezer and balanced one atop each mound.

Choux are baked in three stages. First, a really hot oven causes the water in the dough to turn to steam, which expands and inflates the puffs. Then the oven temperature is lowered so that the shells can finish cooking without burning. Finally, the puffs are pierced to allow any steam to escape, and they're returned to the oven—now turned off—to finish drying out and firming up. (During the first stage of baking, I recommend peering through the glass oven door to see the craquelin do its satisfying thing: thaw and mold itself over each choux as it puffs.) When I removed the shells from the oven, they were all I hoped for: crisp, golden, and nicely rounded. It was time to fill them.

But first, I needed to turn the cooled pastry cream into crème diplomate, which was as simple as gently whisking the thick mixture just until it was smooth and then folding in a cup of cream I'd whipped to stiff peaks. I piped this airy, satiny filling into the puffs through the vent hole I'd poked in each one.

When I ate a couple of the choux right after filling them, I found that the lightened pastry cream was a perfect foil for the crisp puffs and their sweet crackly coating. I ate a couple more a few hours later—and yep, the choux buns were still good and crisp. And the next morning, after breakfast? Still delicious, inside and out.

—ANDREA GEARY, *Cook's Illustrated*

CHOUX AU CRAQUELIN

Choux au Craquelin

MAKES 24 CHOUX

You'll need a 2-inch round cutter, a pastry bag, and two pastry tips—one with a ¼-inch round opening and one with a ½-inch round opening—for this recipe. If desired, this recipe can be made over two days: Make the pastry cream and craquelin on day 1 and the puffs on day 2. We strongly recommend measuring the flour by weight. We prefer whole milk in the pastry cream, but you can use low-fat milk; do not use skim milk. Use a mixer to whip the cream if you prefer.

PASTRY CREAM

2½ cups whole milk, divided

⅔ cup (3⅓ ounces) all-purpose flour

½ cup (3½ ounces) granulated sugar

¼ teaspoon table salt

6 large egg yolks

4 tablespoons unsalted butter, cut into 4 pieces and chilled

1 tablespoon vanilla extract

CRAQUELIN

½ cup packed (3½ ounces) light brown sugar

6 tablespoons unsalted butter, softened

¾ cup (3¾ ounces) all-purpose flour

Pinch table salt

CHOUX

2 large eggs plus 1 large white

6 tablespoons water

5 tablespoons unsalted butter, cut into ½-inch pieces

2 tablespoons milk

1½ teaspoons granulated sugar

¼ teaspoon table salt

½ cup (2½ ounces) all-purpose flour

1 cup heavy cream

1. FOR THE PASTRY CREAM: Heat 2 cups milk in medium saucepan over medium heat until just simmering. Meanwhile, whisk flour, sugar, and salt in medium bowl until combined. Add egg yolks and remaining ½ cup milk to flour mixture and whisk until smooth. Remove saucepan from heat and, whisking constantly, slowly add ½ cup heated milk to yolk mixture to temper. Whisking constantly, add tempered yolk mixture to milk in saucepan.

2. Return saucepan to medium heat and cook, whisking constantly, until mixture thickens slightly, about 1 minute. Reduce heat to medium-low and continue to simmer, whisking constantly, for 8 minutes. Increase heat to medium and cook, whisking vigorously, until very thick (mixture dripped from whisk should mound on surface), 1 to 2 minutes. Off heat, whisk in butter and vanilla until butter is melted and incorporated. Transfer to wide bowl. Press lightly greased parchment paper directly on surface and refrigerate until set, at least 2 hours or up to 24 hours.

3. FOR THE CRAQUELIN: Mix sugar and butter in medium bowl until combined. Mix in flour and salt. Transfer mixture to large sheet of parchment and press into 6-inch square. Cover with second piece of parchment and roll dough into 13 by 9-inch rectangle (it's fine to trim and patch dough to achieve correct dimensions). Remove top piece of parchment and use 2-inch round cutter to cut 24 circles. Leaving circles and trim in place, replace top parchment and transfer to rimless baking sheet. Freeze until firm, at least 30 minutes or up to 2 days.

4. FOR THE CHOUX: Adjust oven rack to middle position and heat oven to 400 degrees. Spray rimmed baking sheet with vegetable oil spray and dust lightly and evenly with flour, discarding any excess. Using 2-inch round cutter, mark 24 circles on sheet. Fit pastry bag with ½-inch round tip. Beat eggs and white together in 2-cup liquid measuring cup.

NOTES FROM THE TEST KITCHEN

WHAT CRAQUELIN DOES FOR CREAM PUFFS
A simple craquelin layer not only adds sweetness and lasting crunch to your cream puffs but also controls the expansion of the choux in the oven so that they're more uniformly rounded instead of whimsically shaped. Here's how it works: The craquelin consists of a buttery dough that's cut into disks and frozen before being placed atop the mounds of choux. In the oven, as the craquelin thaws, it blankets the choux, helping smooth out their contours. At the same time, the butter (of which there is a large amount in the dough) melts, creating fissures in the craquelin that widen as the choux expand.

5. Bring water, butter, milk, sugar, and salt to boil in small saucepan over medium heat, stirring occasionally. Off heat, stir in flour until incorporated. Return saucepan to low heat and cook, stirring constantly and using smearing motion, until mixture looks like shiny, wet sand, about 3 minutes (mixture should register between 175 and 180 degrees).

6. Immediately transfer hot mixture to food processor and process for 10 seconds to cool slightly. With processor running, add beaten eggs in steady stream and process until incorporated, about 30 seconds. Scrape down sides of bowl and continue to process until smooth, thick, sticky paste forms, about 30 seconds longer.

7. Fill pastry bag with warm mixture and pipe into 1½-inch-wide mounds on prepared sheet, using circles as guide. Using small, thin spatula, transfer 1 frozen craquelin disk to top of each mound. Bake for 15 minutes; then, without opening oven door, reduce oven temperature to 350 degrees and continue to bake until golden brown and firm, 7 to 10 minutes longer.

8. Remove sheet from oven and cut ¾-inch slit into side of each pastry with paring knife to release steam. Return sheet to oven, turn off oven, and prop open oven door with handle of wooden spoon. Let pastries dry until center is mostly dry and surface is crisp, about 45 minutes. Transfer pastries to wire rack and let cool completely.

9. Fit pastry bag with ¼-inch round tip. In large bowl, whisk cream to stiff peaks. Gently whisk pastry cream until smooth. Fold pastry cream into whipped cream until combined. Transfer one-third of mixture to pastry bag. To fill choux buns, insert pastry tip ¾ inch into opening and squeeze gently until cream just starts to appear around opening, about 2 tablespoons cream per bun. Refill bag as needed. Serve. (Choux are best eaten up to 2 hours after filling. Leftovers can be refrigerated for up to 3 days but will soften over time.)

VARIATIONS

Colorful Choux au Craquelin
Substitute granulated sugar for brown sugar in craquelin. Add gel or paste food coloring to craquelin dough until desired color is achieved.

Mocha Choux au Craquelin
Add 5 teaspoons instant espresso powder to hot milk for pastry cream. Decrease flour in craquelin to ⅔ cup and add 1 tablespoon unsweetened cocoa powder.

NUTELLA RUGELACH

✔ **WHY THIS RECIPE WORKS** There are at least two distinct varieties of rugelach, the sweet rolled cookies popular in Jewish bakeries around the world. The first is made with a yeasted dough and most often found in Israel and among Mizrahi and Sephardic Jewish communities in many countries. The second version, the one we chose to emulate for this recipe, is made from a dough that's enriched with cream cheese and is much more common in the United States. We wanted a rugelach dough that was rich, supple, and easy to roll out and had a mellow, buttery sweetness along with the mild tang of cream cheese. We used the food processor to make easy work of cutting the butter and cream cheese into the flour, and then we brought the dough together with a final addition of sour cream, further enhancing the dough's tanginess. To shape our rugelach, we rolled the dough flat into circles, spread on some Nutella, and then used a pizza wheel to cut the circle into wedges. Rolling the wedges beginning with the wide ends created adorable little croissant-shaped cookies. A finishing touch of egg wash and demerara sugar applied just before baking imparted a gorgeous sheen and a sweet, crunchy textural contrast to these golden treats.

Rugelach, sweet rolled cookies popular in Jewish bakeries around the world, come in at least two distinct variations. The first is built on a yeasted dough and is most often found in Israel and among Mizrahi and Sephardic Jewish communities in many countries. The second is made from a dough that's highly enriched with cream cheese and is much more common in the United States. Both share the same name, rugelach, which is derived from the Yiddish and connotes the idea of a "twist."

I first fell in love with rugelach as a kid, when the bakery attendant at my local grocery store would slip me (and other well-behaved youngsters) a cookie. On lucky days, it would be a chocolate-filled rugelach, the kind made with cream cheese in the dough. I brought these memories with me into the test kitchen as I began work on my own recipe.

I started, of course, with the dough. After researching several recipes and carefully adjusting the amounts of flour, fat, and sugar, I had a dough that was slightly sweet with a pleasant tanginess from the cream cheese (and some sour cream, too). The dough came together quickly in the food processor. I set it in the refrigerator to chill for an hour.

RUGELACH

I rolled the chilled dough into a 12-inch circle, spread it with Nutella, and then used a pizza wheel to cut the circle into 16 equal wedges. I then rolled up each wedge from the edge to the center of the circle, creating the little "twists." Brushed with egg wash for shine and sprinkled with demerara sugar for sparkle, my rugelach baked up to a deep golden brown, and my Nutella filling didn't ooze. Picture perfect.

—MARK HUXSOLL, *Cook's Country*

Nutella Rugelach

SERVES 8 (MAKES 32 COOKIES)

The demerara sugar adds a nice crunch to these rugelach, but they are still great without it. If you have packets of Sugar in the Raw at home, you can use those in place of the demerara. When brushing the rugelach with the egg wash, brush only a few cookies at a time and then sprinkle them with the demerara sugar immediately. If you brush the egg wash onto all the rugelach at once, it will begin to dry by the time you get to the last rugelach, and the sugar won't stick.

1½	cups (7½ ounces) all-purpose flour
¼	cup (1¾ ounces) granulated sugar
¼	teaspoon table salt
6	ounces cream cheese, cut into 3 pieces and chilled
10	tablespoons unsalted butter, cut into ½-inch pieces and chilled
¼	cup sour cream
⅔	cup Nutella, divided
1	large egg, beaten with 1 tablespoon water
1	tablespoon demerara sugar

1. Process flour, granulated sugar, and salt in food processor until combined, about 3 seconds. Add cream cheese and pulse until large, irregularly sized chunks of cream cheese form with some small pieces interspersed throughout, about 5 pulses. Scatter butter over top and pulse until butter is size of large peas, 5 to 7 pulses.

2. Add sour cream and process until dough forms little clumps that hold together when pinched with your fingers (dough will look crumbly), about 10 seconds.

3. Transfer dough to clean counter and knead briefly until dough just comes together, about 3 turns. Divide dough in half (each piece should weigh about 11 ounces) and form each piece into 4-inch disk. Wrap disks individually in plastic wrap and refrigerate for at least 1 hour or up to 2 days.

4. Adjust oven rack to middle position and heat oven to 375 degrees. Line baking sheet with parchment paper. Roll 1 dough disk into 12-inch circle on lightly floured counter. Using offset spatula, spread ⅓ cup Nutella evenly over entire surface of circle. Using pizza wheel or sharp knife, cut through center of circle to form 16 equal wedges. Starting at wide edge of each wedge, roll dough toward point and transfer to prepared sheet, seam side down.

5. Wipe counter clean, dust counter with additional flour, and repeat with remaining dough disk and remaining ⅓ cup Nutella. Arrange rugelach in 8 rows of four on sheet.

6. Working with few rugelach at a time, brush tops with egg wash, then sprinkle with demerara sugar. Bake until golden brown, 30 to 35 minutes. Let cookies cool completely on sheet, about 20 minutes. Serve.

VARIATIONS

Cinnamon-Walnut Rugelach

Omit Nutella. Pulse ½ cup walnuts, ½ cup packed brown sugar, 1½ teaspoons ground cinnamon, and ¼ teaspoon table salt in food processor until finely ground, about 20 pulses. Sprinkle half of filling over each dough circle.

Jam Rugelach

Substitute raspberry or apricot jam for Nutella. (If jam contains large chunks of fruit, process jam in food processor to smooth, spreadable consistency before using.) Be sure to check for doneness at 30 minutes; jam tends to accelerate browning on bottom of rugelach.

NOTES FROM THE TEST KITCHEN

RUGELACH CONSTRUCTION

We use a pizza wheel to cut equal-size wedges for rolling up.

ANZAC BISCUITS

✓ **WHY THIS RECIPE WORKS** Both a distinct symbol of patriotism in New Zealand and Australia and an everyday sweet, Anzac biscuits are simple oatmeal cookie–like confections with distinctly rich caramel flavor and color, cobbled together from pantry staples that were available during the First World War: rolled oats; flour; sugar; butter; baking soda dissolved in a little hot water; and a viscous, amber-toned liquid sweetener called golden syrup. To produce our ideal version—crisp at the edges and evenly chewy in the middle, with the nuttiness of coconut and the lightly caramelized, distinctly Anzac sweetness of golden syrup—we started by loading up on golden syrup, adding roughly triple the amount called for in traditional Anzac recipes. The golden syrup added sweetness and moisture, loosened up the dough so that it spread more, and promoted chewiness. Increasing the amount of flour prevented the dough from spreading too much and turning candy-like. Lots of oats provided welcome substance and toasty flavor, and sweetened flaked coconut added the fruit's distinct richness and sweetness.

If you want to get a sense of just how deeply Antipodeans cherish their Anzac biscuits, you can start by consulting the regulations outlined by the Protection of the Word "Anzac" Act 1920. Issued by the Australian government's Department of Veterans' Affairs, the law states that any biscuits bearing that name must "generally conform to the traditional recipe and shape" and must never be referred to as "Anzac cookies." Doing so, it says, would suggest "non-Australian overtones."

Ironically, there isn't much consensus on what defines a traditional Anzac biscuit. The basic idea has always been a simple oatmeal cookie–like confection with distinctly rich caramel flavor and color, cobbled together from pantry staples that were available during the First World War: rolled oats; flour; sugar; butter; baking soda; and a viscous, amber-toned liquid sweetener called golden syrup. (Eggs, which were scarce during the war, were usually omitted.) Treacly and much more palatable than the hardtack that sustained soldiers on the move (ANZAC is the acronym used during the First World War for the Australian and New Zealand Army Corps), the biscuits were care-package fodder for overseas forces. Their accessible ingredients and stir-together method made it possible for soldiers' wives and women's groups in both nations to regularly bake and ship their own versions to soldiers.

No doubt, that widespread popularity led to the eclectic mix of biscuits called Anzac today. Many modern versions contain flaked coconut, and some are embellished with nuts or raisins or dipped in chocolate. But in most cases the distinction comes down to the proportions of the ingredients: Depending on the precise amounts of dry mix, water, fat, and sugar, they bake up thick, thin, dense, lacy, crisp, or chewy.

Hoping that the Anzac world had room for one more interpretation, I got to work on a version that boasted the texture of my favorite oatmeal cookie—crisp at the edges and evenly chewy within—with the nutty richness of coconut and the lightly caramelized, distinctly Anzac sweetness of golden syrup.

I started by trying the most common approach, a ratio formula: 1 cup each of rolled oats, flour, sugar, and unsweetened coconut. After stirring together the dry mix, I melted a stick of butter with a tablespoon or two of golden syrup and dissolved a teaspoon of baking soda in a couple tablespoons of hot water—an unusual step that almost all recipes include. Then I stirred the baking soda mixture into the butter mixture (the two components reacted and foamed up) and added the dry mix directly to the saucepan I'd melted the butter in (as convenient a vessel to mix the dough as a bowl). Then I dropped spoonfuls of the dough onto a baking sheet, flattened them, and baked them until they were golden.

I could feel how little moisture there was in the dough as I was mixing it, so I wasn't surprised when the biscuits baked up dry and dense, with virtually no chewiness. Adjusting the flour and/or golden syrup would address that, but I decided to zero in on the coconut first. I'd been using the unsweetened kind that most Anzac recipes call for, but it seemed pretty absorbent—almost like dry flour. That made me wonder if sweetened coconut might behave differently, since the sugar it contains is hygroscopic (retains water). I tried a one-for-one swap, and the biscuits baked up thinner, moister, and (of course) sweeter, which was great since sweetened coconut is more widely available in the States than unsweetened. I stuck with it and liked the results even more when I cut back on the sweetened coconut by 25 percent.

From there I circled back to the golden syrup: Its caramel-like flavor and color hadn't been prominent enough, and I'd done enough baking with corn syrup (a close relative) to know that it's also invaluable for ramping up moisture and chewiness.

ANZAC BISCUITS

I turned out several more batches with increasingly higher amounts of syrup. Each one was moister, chewier, and more flavorful than the last, but when I got to ⅓ cup, I stopped: The crumb of that batch was rich and gold-toned, but that much syrup caused the dough to spread so much that the biscuits were wafer-thin and lacy like Florentine cookies and so chewy that they bordered on candy—and, in combination with the sugar and coconut, it made the biscuits much too sweet.

If I wanted to keep that much syrup in the biscuits for its flavor and color, I needed to adjust the other ingredients. I spent the next several tests pushing and pulling at the amounts of granulated sugar, coconut, oats, and flour. Ultimately, I cut back on the sugar to tone down the biscuits' sweetness and chewiness, added a bit more flour to reduce the dough's spread, and added lots more oats so that the biscuits baked up with more substance and toasty flavor.

Whether my biscuits would pass muster with the Australian government, I can't say. But they're crisp at the edges and chewy within; boast robust caramel-like richness, loads of oats, and lots of nutty-sweet coconut; and come together on a whim. What more could I ask from a ~~drop cookie~~ biscuit?

—DAVID PAZMIÑO, *Cook's Illustrated*

Anzac Biscuits

MAKES 24 BISCUITS

Golden syrup is important to achieving the proper appearance and texture in these biscuits. Look for Lyle's brand in the baking aisle of your supermarket or with the honey. Regular old-fashioned rolled oats work best here. Do not use extra-thick rolled oats; they will make a dry, tough biscuit. To ensure that the biscuits spread properly, weigh the flour and oats.

1¼	**cups (6¼ ounces) all-purpose flour**
½	**cup (3½ ounces) sugar**
¼	**teaspoon table salt**
1½	**cups (4½ ounces) old-fashioned rolled oats**
¾	**cup (2½ ounces) sweetened flaked coconut**
8	**tablespoons unsalted butter**
⅓	**cup golden syrup**
2	**tablespoons hot water**
1	**teaspoon baking soda**

1. Adjust oven rack to middle position and heat oven to 350 degrees. Line 2 rimmed baking sheets with parchment paper. Whisk flour, sugar, and salt together in medium bowl. Add oats and coconut and whisk to combine evenly, breaking up any coconut clumps.

2. Heat butter and golden syrup in medium saucepan over medium heat, stirring occasionally, until butter is melted and mixture begins to bubble, 2 to 3 minutes. Meanwhile, stir hot water and baking soda in small bowl until combined. Off heat, stir baking soda mixture into butter mixture (mixture will foam and bubble). Add flour mixture to saucepan and stir until evenly combined.

3. Divide dough into 24 equal portions, about 1 mounded tablespoon each (or use #40 portion scoop, or weigh out 1 ounce per portion), stirring remaining dough after first 12 portions to ensure even distribution of oats. Space rounded portions evenly on prepared sheets, 12 portions per sheet. Let dough portions rest until surface is slightly dry to touch, about 5 minutes. Using fork, gently press each portion into 2-inch disk. (Rinse and dry fork if it becomes sticky.)

NOTES FROM THE TEST KITCHEN

THE SODA-SYRUP REACTION

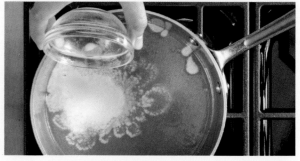

Most modern baking recipes call for adding chemical leaveners such as baking soda to the dry mix. But almost all Anzac biscuit recipes suggest mixing the soda into a little hot water and then stirring that solution into a mixture of melted butter and golden syrup, causing a bubbly reaction. Historically, bakers did this to break up clumps of baking soda (early formulations didn't contain anticaking agents). But this method also makes for a biscuit that's pleasantly dense and chewy, since activating the soda before adding it to the dough blows off some of its leavening power, so it's less able to aerate the dough. What's more, it deepens the crumb's color and flavor: When the alkaline soda reacts with the acidic syrup's plant pigments (which respond dramatically to pH change), the syrup darkens, and the darker dough develops more flavorful Maillard browning as it bakes.

4. Bake biscuits, 1 sheet at a time, until orange brown and edges are set, 10 to 12 minutes, rotating sheet after 5 minutes. Let biscuits cool completely on sheet, 45 minutes to 1 hour. Use wide metal spatula to remove biscuits from sheets. Serve. (Biscuits can be stored in airtight container for up to 1 week.)

TWO CHOCOLATE CHIP COOKIES

✔ **WHY THIS RECIPE WORKS** Sometimes you just want to treat yourself to some freshly baked chocolate chip cookies. You might not have the time or patience to make an entire batch, but two cookies? Two is perfect. But drastically scaling down a recipe often results in head-scratching measurements, such as half an egg, so we did the heavy lifting for you, figuring out how to scale back without the fuss. We relied solely on brown sugar instead of both brown sugar and granulated sugar for caramelized flavor and just-right texture. There was no need for a mixer or even measuring cups and, best of all, the cookies could be baked right in the toaster oven—no waiting to heat up a conventional oven. These cookies have crispy edges and soft, chewy interiors, giving them truly the best of both ends of the cookie-texture spectrum.

Most cookie recipes make a dozen or more cookies, but what if you're baking for one and want only a couple cookies? Enter this recipe for two chocolate chip cookies that involves an easy prep process, calls for ingredients you probably already have on hand, and can even be prepared in your toaster oven. For our *Cooking for One* book, we recognized that leftovers can be a double-edged sword if you're flying solo: A big batch of cookies can get old when you're still eating them a week later. Sometimes it really is possible to have too much of a good thing. With personal-size desserts such as this one, you can prep and eat enough to satisfy your cookie craving but not make a huge batch that you'll get sick of by the time they're gone. There are a lot of recipes for desserts that are simple to scale down to feed one— mug cakes, small fruit crumbles, or ice cream sundaes—but cookies seemed to be an unfulfilled need among dessert recipes for one.

I was determined to tackle the fun challenge of a small-batch chocolate chip cookie recipe. Scaling down

a regular-size chocolate chip cookie recipe can be a nightmare, as you end up with awkward measurements such as half an egg, so I wanted to make a foolproof cookie recipe that was scaled down already. My goals: a crisp-on-the-outside, chewy-on-the-inside chocolate chip cookie; an uncomplicated prep process; and a one-serving recipe that uses ingredients that you probably already have on hand.

For the testing process, I started out with two strategies that proved unsuccessful: simply cutting down one of our other chocolate chip cookie recipes to make a small-batch recipe and trying to bake one giant cookie. I quickly realized that the measurements were too messy and complicated when I tried just scaling down a regular-size cookie recipe, so I switched to just building my own from the ground up with typical chocolate chip cookie ingredients. Likewise, baking one big cookie gave me a disappointing, unevenly baked cookie, so I switched to dividing the dough into two normal-size cookies. My final recipe doesn't use an electric mixer, doesn't use any measuring cups (just measuring spoons), and doesn't include any chilling for the easiest, quickest prep. While testing, I had the idea of trying the recipe in the toaster oven so that I could skip preheating the oven, and I was thrilled when it worked perfectly. Another way to make the recipe even simpler and quicker!

I had a solid start by sticking to typical chocolate chip cookie ingredients, so from there it was a question of tweaking each component until I had my ideal cookie. The main variables I needed to figure out were the fat, sugar, and chocolate. The choice of fat was the biggest stumbling block at first. I started out with a few possibilities: butter, both melted and softened, and vegetable oil. Vegetable oil was a bust—it tasted too oily, and we missed the buttery flavor that we associate with chocolate chip cookies. A cookie made with vegetable oil and granulated sugar was a huge failure. It was basically a meringue cookie, with a shiny and crisp outside and a soft inside. Melted butter made an extremely wet dough that was impossible to form into balls, and cookies with melted butter and brown sugar came out supercakey—not what I was looking for. The sweet spot was softened butter instead of melted and brown sugar instead of granulated. I found that brown sugar brought great caramelized flavor and cookies with exactly the texture I was aiming for. I went with a typical creaming method for the sugar and softened butter but did the

TWO CHOCOLATE CHIP COOKIES

creaming with a spatula instead of an electric mixer to make the recipe easier and minimize dirty dishes.

The final decision was which kind of chocolate to use. We really liked a batch made with mini chocolate chips but decided to call for regular-size chocolate chips since cooks are more likely to have those on hand. That said, this recipe is flexible—you can make it with whatever chocolate you have around; use mini chocolate chips, a chopped-up chocolate bar, white chocolate chips, or even M&M'S. For additional ingredients, I added a touch of vanilla for nostalgic cookie flavor and another caramelized note to complement the brown sugar. The dough had lift from the baking soda already, so I skipped the whole egg and went with just an egg yolk for additional fat and moisture. I had perfected my ingredient list to use ingredients I already had on hand and to add up to the best cookie possible. In the end, I had the foolproof small-batch cookie recipe I'd been dreaming of: two flawlessly baked chocolate chip cookies ready in a flash, with effortless prep, a straightforward ingredient list, and no leftovers.

—SAMANTHA BLOCK, *America's Test Kitchen Books*

Two Chocolate Chip Cookies

SERVES 1

A pinch is equal to 1/16 teaspoon. You can use a regular rimmed baking sheet if you don't have a quarter-sheet pan, though you'll have to use your oven instead of a toaster oven. You can use any type of chocolate (a chopped bar or chips) that you have on hand. Or try other sweet stir-ins (M&M'S, Reese's Pieces, white chocolate chips, or butterscotch chips) in place of the chocolate.

  3 **tablespoons all-purpose flour**
     Pinch baking soda
     Pinch table salt
  1 **tablespoon unsalted butter, softened**
  2 **tablespoons packed brown sugar**
  1 **large egg yolk**
 ⅛ **teaspoon vanilla extract**
  2 **tablespoons chocolate chips**

1. Adjust toaster oven or oven rack to middle position and heat oven to 325 degrees. Line small rimmed baking sheet with parchment paper. Whisk flour, baking soda, and salt together in bowl. Using rubber spatula, mash butter and sugar together in separate bowl until well combined and lightened in color. Add egg yolk and

vanilla and mix until combined. Stir in flour mixture until just combined, then stir in chocolate chips.

2. Divide dough into 2 portions, then roll into balls. Place on prepared sheet, spaced about 2 inches apart. Bake until edges of cookies are set and beginning to brown but centers are still soft and puffy, 8 to 12 minutes. Let cookies cool on sheet for 10 minutes. Serve.

M&M COOKIES

✔ **WHY THIS RECIPE WORKS** For our version of this nostalgic cookie recipe, we wanted M&M cookies that were big and colorful, soft and chewy, sweet and buttery, and just salty enough to make us want to eat another one. To start, we skipped the traditional creaming of the butter and sugar because that adds extra air that produces taller, more tender cookies. Instead we whisked together brown sugar, granulated sugar, and melted butter; the extra moisture in the brown sugar made for moist, chewy cookies. Following the advice of an M&M cookie expert we visited in Portland, Oregon, we increased the baking soda, upped the oven temperature to 425 degrees, and pulled the cookies out of the oven sooner (after only 8 minutes). Each of these strategies resulted in cookies that stayed soft and chewy longer.

For a few years as a teenager I had a flawless routine for Friday lunch at school. I'd hit up the cafeteria for two slices of cheese pizza and then, instead of sitting down with the other kids to eat, my best friend and I would carry our lunches straight to the library. Because as soon as the bell rang for lunch, the cheerleaders would start setting up the bake sale in the library, and if you wanted to get one of Katie Johnson's M&M cookies, you needed to get there early. I can still remember feeling for the coins in my pocket as I walked over there, searching for the ridged edges of the quarters, nervous to talk to the cheerleaders but glad to have an excuse all the same. I always made sure I had exactly seventy-five cents so that I could keep the exchange brief, because for me, talking to Katie Johnson was something like running into the ocean in January. Get in, gasp for air, get out. Totally worth it.

I'd all but forgotten about those Friday lunches until, just recently, I walked into a little bakery in Portland, Oregon, where they were selling M&M cookies. In my memory, there wasn't a cookie baked that could be better than Katie Johnson's. But, to my surprise, these cookies were.

They were big and colorful, soft and chewy, sweet and buttery, and just salty enough to bring me back to the counter to buy some more. The crackly contrast of the M&M shells immediately rocketed me back to high school. When the cashier handed me my change, I asked her why the cookies were so delicious. She smiled and said that she was the pastry chef. She said the real answer is probably that they have more salt, butter, and sugar than other versions, but that if you wanted to get technical, then you needed to increase the oven temperature and add more baking soda so that the cookies puff up quickly and then deflate for just the right texture. And then, with keen enthusiasm she exclaimed: "And you need to take them out of the oven way before you think they're done. Way before!" All these choices, she explained, made for soft, chewy cookies that would stay chewy for days.

And so that's the inspiration for the recipe here. Back in the test kitchen, I followed her advice, but without her recipe, I needed to employ some test kitchen know-how and techniques. To start, I skipped the creaming of butter and sugar because that produces taller, tender cookies. Instead I simply whisked together light brown sugar, granulated sugar, and melted butter; the extra moisture in the brown sugar makes for moist, chewy baked goods. And by not creaming the butter and sugar, I was avoiding adding the extra air that results in taller, less chewy cookies.

And, as the pastry chef in Portland had instructed me to do, I added ¼ teaspoon more baking soda and ½ teaspoon more salt to the dough; I raised the oven temperature to 425 degrees; and I pulled the cookies out of the oven after only 8 minutes. The pastry chef gave good advice, and now I pass it on to you. Follow this advice, and I'd be willing to bet you could get a lot more than just seventy-five cents per cookie at your next bake sale.

—MATTHEW FAIRMAN, *Cook's Country*

M&M Cookies
MAKES 16 COOKIES

Use standard, not mini, M&M'S in this recipe. The cookies will seem underdone when you pull them from the oven. This is OK; they will continue to bake as they cool on the baking sheet for 5 minutes. This method ensures that the cookies remain chewy once they are cooled.

2¼	cups (11¼ ounces) all-purpose flour
1	teaspoon table salt
¾	teaspoon baking soda
12	tablespoons unsalted butter, melted
1	cup packed (7 ounces) light brown sugar
½	cup (3½ ounces) granulated sugar
1	large egg plus 1 large yolk
2	teaspoons vanilla extract
1¼	cups (9 ounces) M&M'S

1. Adjust oven rack to middle position and heat oven to 425 degrees. Line 2 baking sheets with parchment paper. Combine flour, salt, and baking soda in bowl.

2. Whisk melted butter, brown sugar, and granulated sugar in large bowl until thoroughly combined, about 30 seconds. Whisk in egg and yolk and vanilla until fully combined and mixture looks emulsified, about 30 seconds. Stir in half of flour mixture with rubber spatula or wooden spoon. Stir in candies and remaining flour mixture.

3. Divide dough into sixteen 2¼-ounce portions, about 2 heaping tablespoons each; divide any remaining dough evenly among dough portions. Roll dough portions between your hands to make smooth balls.

4. Evenly space dough balls on prepared sheets, 8 balls per sheet. Using your hand, flatten balls to ¾-inch thickness.

5. Bake cookies, 1 sheet at a time, until centers of cookies are puffed and still very blond, about 8 minutes; cookies will seem underdone. Let cookies cool on sheet for 5 minutes. Using spatula, transfer cookies to wire rack and let cool for 10 minutes before serving.

TO MAKE AHEAD: At end of step 4, transfer flattened dough balls to parchment paper–lined plate and freeze until very firm, at least 1 hour. Transfer balls to 1-gallon zipper-lock bag and freeze for up to 1 month. Bake from frozen, increasing baking time to 12 minutes.

M&M COOKIES

TEST KITCHEN RESOURCES

* Not all products we tested are listed in these pages. Web subscribers can find complete listings and information on all products tested and reviewed at AmericasTestKitchen.com.

BEST KITCHEN QUICK TIPS

CLEAN UP MESSY SPILLS WITH SALT

If Rose Smythe of San Francisco, Calif., spills oil or accidentally drops an egg, she cleans up the mess with salt. She covers the spill with a generous amount of table or kosher salt (for eggs, she removes any large shell pieces first) and lets the mixture sit until the moisture has been soaked up, about 5 minutes. Once a paste has formed, she scoops it up with a paper towel or dustpan before cleaning the area with soap and water.

EASIER HERB PLUCKING WITH A COLANDER

Plucking the leaves from a bunch of tender herbs such as cilantro and dill can be tedious and time-consuming. Carly Helmetag of Somerville, Mass., has found that threading the herb stems through the holes of her colander (starting from the inside and pulling them through) makes quick work of the task—plus, the bowl collects the leaves.

AVOIDING A "FOOT" ON CHOCOLATE-DIPPED TREATS

Nancy Annis of Henniker, N.H., enjoys making chocolate-dipped treats such as buckeyes and chocolate-covered strawberries but dislikes when a "foot" (a puddle of excess chocolate) forms where the chocolate touches the surface under the treats. To prevent this, she inserts a toothpick into each treat to serve as a handle, dips the treat into the chocolate, gently shakes off the excess, and then spears the free end of the toothpick into a piece of Styrofoam covered with aluminum foil. This way, the treat dries upside down without touching a flat surface that would cause it to form a foot and the foil catches drips, making cleanup easy.

SPREADING COLD BUTTER

Cecelia Rooney of Point Pleasant, N.J., often runs into this common problem: She wants butter for her toast, but it's too cold and firm to spread easily. Crisis averted. She has discovered that a vegetable peeler will cut a thin ribbon of butter that's easy to spread.

MAKE SEEDLESS JALAPEÑO RINGS WITH A VEGETABLE PEELER

To create neat rings of jalapeños without the seeds or spicy ribs when garnishing nachos and the like, Nate Cobb of Jamaica Plain, Mass., employs a vegetable peeler.

1. Cut off stem end of jalapeño with knife, then insert peeler into chile. Using circular motion, core jalapeño and pull out ribs and seeds.

A SMART PLACE TO HOLD A SHOPPING LIST

When shopping for groceries, Pam Wells of Milwaukie, Ore., would get frustrated with losing her list while shopping. To keep her list front and center, she punches a hole in the paper and then uses a twist tie to secure it to the handle of the shopping cart.

milk
eggs
bread
broccoli
pears

POT HOLDERS GET A GRIP ON CORN SILK

Bart McSpadden of Edmond, Okla., has found a handy tool for removing the fine hairs from fresh corn: a silicone pot holder. Rubbing the grippy mat around the shucked ear from one end to the other loosens and grabs the silky strands.

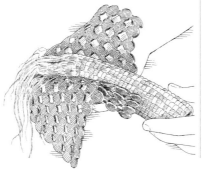

2. Shake any remaining seeds out of jalapeño, then slice into rings.

A GRATE IDEA FOR HARD BROWN SUGAR

When Gloria Lynch of Colorado Springs, Colo., finds that her brown sugar has turned from granules into a solid brick, she pulls out her grater. Running the block along the tool's sharp holes quickly breaks down the hard sugar into a measurable state.

MAKESHIFT MUFFIN TIN

Bonnie Ruger of Scotts Valley, Calif., came up with this tip for baking muffins or cupcakes without a muffin tin: Set canning-jar rings atop their lids on a rimmed baking sheet, and then place a paper muffin-tin liner inside each ring. The rings will prevent heavy batters from spreading out so that the baked goods emerge nicely domed. The lids add a bit of protection to the bottoms of the baked goods so that they don't overbrown.

PATCHING CRACKED SHELLS

Rather than throw away pie dough trimmings, Melissa Borrell of Annville, Pa., saves the scraps for patchwork. If there are any cracks or holes in a pie shell after she prebakes it, she spackles them with the leftover dough, pressing it into place, and then finishes baking according to the recipe.

MAKING THE MOST OUT OF SPONGES

When Jordan Jungwirth of Roseburg, Ore. buys new sponges, he immediately cuts some of them in half. Not only does this make his sponge supply last longer, but the half-sponges are ideal for cleaning smaller items such as drinking glasses.

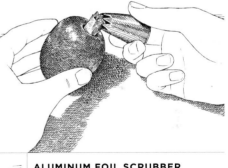

BUNDT PAN AS VERTICAL ROASTER STAND-IN

While we like vertical roasters because they produce evenly cooked poultry with crispy skin, many cooks don't own one. A tall beer can is a good substitute, but Julianne Douglas of Providence, R.I., has found another stand-in: a Bundt pan. She slides the chicken onto the center post of the pan, legs facing down, so that the chicken stands upright. She then places the pan on a rimmed baking sheet and transfers it to the oven.

FASTER TOMATO CORING WITH A PASTRY TIP

Dawn Jacobson of Vallejo, Calif., found another use for the large star pastry tip she gets out just once a year to make spritz cookies: coring tomatoes. She pierces the tomato at the stem scar with the pointed end of the tip, twists the tip to cut, and then lifts it to remove the core.

ALUMINUM FOIL SCRUBBER

When she runs out of steel wool but needs to get tough, baked-on food off a glass baking dish or her oven rack, Allison Brown of San Francisco, Calif., uses dishwashing liquid and a crumpled-up ball of aluminum foil. Using the craggy foil, which is more abrasive than a sponge, is also a great way to repurpose used—but still clean—sheets of foil.

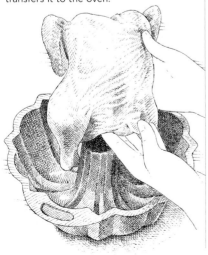

QUICKLY DICE BUTTER WITH AN EGG SLICER

Carolyn Winslow of Bellingham, Wash., uses an egg slicer to cut butter into small pieces for pie dough and biscuits. She places up to 4 tablespoons of butter in an egg slicer and pushes down on the slicer to create planks. She then rotates the butter a quarter turn and pushes down again to create small pieces.

BEST KITCHEN QUICK TIPS

CLEANING CAST IRON WITH SUPERSTALE BREAD

When day(s)-old bread becomes too dry for croutons, Lance Johnson of Salt Lake City, Utah, cuts it into sections to clean cast-iron and carbon-steel pans. The dry, exposed edges are abrasive enough to remove adhered food without damaging the seasoning.

SAVE YOUR SMOOTHIE LEFTOVERS

If Tzipora Einbinder of Pikesville, Md., can't finish the smoothie she made, she doesn't throw out the extra left in the blender—rather, she freezes the leftovers in an ice cube tray, so the cubes can be used in place of ice for a future smoothie.

PASTA WATER SUBSTITUTE

Carla Landry of Baton Rouge, La., used to kick herself when she forgot to save pasta water for thinning sauce and instead poured it all down the drain. Now when this happens, she has an easy fix: She thoroughly mixes ¼ teaspoon of cornstarch with 1 cup of water and microwaves it for 1 to 2 minutes until it's hot. Just a splash or two of the slightly thickened liquid creates a sauce with just the right consistency.

QUICKLY MEASURING SALAD DRESSING

Instead of dirtying her measuring cups, spoons, and whisk every time she wants to make her favorite vinaigrette, Elizabeth Zeller Montgomery of Brooklyn, N.Y., came up with this practical solution. Separately measure out the oil and vinegar (we like a 3:1 ratio), and then pour them into a clear plastic bottle, using a permanent marker to mark the level of the mixture after you've added each ingredient. As long as you keep the bottle, you'll never again have to dirty a measuring cup or spoon for these components. Add any solid ingredients (such as garlic, herbs, or mustard), close the bottle, and shake it until the dressing is thoroughly mixed.

BETTER FLOUR DUSTER

When rolling out biscuits, pie pastry, or pizza dough, Latrice Gainey of Timmonsville, S.C., was covering her counter with drifts of wasted flour until she figured out a better method. She now keeps a clean, dry cheese shaker filled with flour and sprinkles just what she needs.

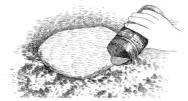

EASY-ROLL PIE DOUGH

Instead of wrapping pie dough in plastic wrap, Hannah Grinberg of Mendocino, Calif., refrigerates it in an empty 2-gallon zipper-lock bag. When the dough is chilled, she sprinkles in a bit of flour and rolls out the dough right in the bag. This way, there's a built-in guide, so the dough round is just the right size and her counter and rolling pin stay clean. She can easily transfer the dough to a pie plate by cutting the bag open along the sides.

WAITING TO REMOVE DOUGH RESIDUE

When cleaning up after kneading dough on the counter, Brianna Walter of Dobbs Ferry, N.Y., has found that a little patience goes a long way. Rather than vigorously scrub the surface to remove dried bits of dough, she pours a little cold water onto the stuck-on bits and lets them soak for a few minutes. Then she can easily wipe the counter clean with a towel.

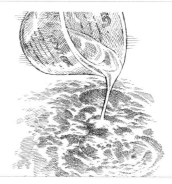

PITTING OLIVES THE FUN(NEL) WAY

A common way to remove pits from olives without an olive pitter is to smash them on a cutting board. For a more elegant—and equally effective—alternative, Marci Abbrecht of Wellesley, Mass., places a funnel upside down on the counter; stands one end of the olive on the spout; and presses down, allowing the pit to fall through the funnel.

WHIPPING PUDDING INTO SHAPE

If a pudding or pastry cream has become lumpy during cooking, Patricia Williams of Houston, Texas, turns to a restaurant trick to smooth things out: She uses an immersion blender to quickly blend the pudding until it's smooth and then passes the pudding through a fine-mesh strainer to remove any remaining solid bits.

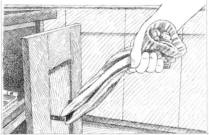

TRASH BIN TOWEL HANDLE

Ed Michaelson of Orange, Conn., loops a clean dish towel through the handle of his pull-out trash drawer when he is working with raw meat, fish, or poultry. Instead of using his dirty hand to pull on the handle to access the trash, he pulls on the towel, which can be easily removed and washed.

AN ARTISTIC WAY TO ORGANIZE KITCHEN TOOLS

When he travels or rents a home for vacation, Geoff Poulet of Cambridge, Mass., likes to make sure that he has a well-equipped kitchen. So he bought a paintbrush roll and neatly packed it with small tools such as a spatula, a thermometer, a rasp-style grater, and a pair of tongs for easy, organized transport.

A DRYING RACK FOR PRODUCE

Lisa Carter of Birmingham, Ala., has a nifty way to dry fruits and vegetables after she's washed them. She puts them on a wire rack that she's placed over one side of her sink. Smaller items such as berries go into a strainer set atop the rack.

A BANANA'S BUILT-IN CUTTING BOARD

To avoid dirtying a cutting board when slicing bananas for a morning bowl of cereal, Michael Bibeault of Austin, Texas, uses this trick: Partially peel the banana, leaving a strip of peel running down its length. Then place the banana peel side down on the counter and slice the banana.

WHEN THE CORK CRUMBLES

Use one of these remedies to eliminate the frustration of fishing out bits of cork that have fallen into a wine bottle.

A. ADD A STRAINER

1. Sorcha Byrne of San Francisco, Calif., recommends cutting cheesecloth into a 2-inch square, fitting it over the bottle, and securing it with a rubber band.

2. Next, pour the wine through the cheesecloth, which will catch any bits of cork.

B. USE A STRAW

Ellen Malmon of New Canaan, Conn., removes the pieces individually by inserting a straw into the neck of the bottle, over the cork crumb, and then placing a finger over the end of the straw and lifting it out. This creates a vacuum that traps the cork crumb for removal.

THE FRENCH (PRESS) WAY TO HYDRATE MUSHROOMS

ANOTHER USE FOR A FAT SEPARATOR

A bottom-draining fat separator isn't just useful for skimming stocks and pan juices. Alexandra Samis of Chicago, Ill., uses hers to portion batter for pancakes and crepes. She just pulls the handle to dispense as much—or as little—batter as is needed.

Dried mushrooms are so light that they often bob to the surface of the water being used to hydrate them, causing the pieces to soften unevenly. To keep the pieces submerged, Georgia Spaulding Edwards of Santa Barbara, Calif., uses a French press coffee maker. She places the mushrooms in the clean carafe, fills it with hot water, and uses the press to submerge the mushrooms.

HOW TO MAKE PRO-CALIBER ICE CREAM

Ice cream distills some of the most complex culinary science into cold, creamy magic, but it's actually simple to make yourself. Here's everything you need to know to get churning.

When we think about ice cream, we usually think about flavors such as chocolate, vanilla, coffee, and strawberry. But what makes or breaks great ice cream is texture—how smooth, cold, and refreshing it feels in your mouth. Getting it right hinges on two main factors: controlling the water in the base and freezing that base as quickly as possible.

MIX UP JUST THE RIGHT BASE

Ice cream is mostly water, which freezes during the churning process and thickens the base so that it becomes solid and refreshing. The key is controlling the size of the ice crystals that form as the water freezes and that can continue to grow over time in the freezer. When ice cream is grainy, it's because the crystals are noticeably large, while smooth, high-quality ice cream contains ice crystals so small that our tongues can't detect them.

Each ingredient in the base influences the properties of the water and the size—and our perception—of the ice crystals. Classic formulations include just heavy cream, milk, and sugar. (Adding egg yolks produces a rich, custard-style ice cream; omitting them, as we do here, yields a cleaner-tasting base that allows other flavors to shine.) Our base also includes corn syrup, nonfat milk powder, and cornstarch—unusual additions that are essential to our ice cream's smooth consistency. Here's a breakdown of each ingredient's role in our formula.

SWEETENERS

Sugar sweetens the base, but it also ensures that the ice cream is soft enough to scoop straight out of the freezer by keeping a portion of the water in the mix from turning to ice. Adding just the right amount of sugar is crucial to achieving that properly dense but still scoopable consistency.

NOT ENOUGH SUGAR
Rock-hard

TOO MUCH SUGAR
Soupy

Corn syrup is a less sweet form of sugar, so it provides the textural benefits of sugar without making the ice cream sweeter than we want.

FAT

More fat (heavy cream and whole milk) in the base means there's less water to freeze, but too much fat can form flecks of butter during churning; it can also dull the ice cream's cold, refreshing mouthfeel. Fourteen percent fat is considered the sweet spot. Fat also lubricates the tongue so that ice crystals aren't as noticeable, and it solidifies when chilled, trapping air during churning.

STABILIZERS

These ingredients increase the viscosity of the base, so there's less chance for ice crystals to cluster into larger, more perceptible crystals.

Nonfat dry milk powder not only replaces liquid milk in the mix, effectively decreasing the amount of freezable water, but also traps some of the water so that it can't freeze, minimizing ice crystals.

Cornstarch also traps water so that it can't freeze.

FAST FREEZING = SMOOTH RESULTS

There are three basic steps to freezing the base as quickly as possible, which ensures small (less than 50 microns), imperceptible ice crystals.

CHILL: To shorten the time it takes for the base to freeze, it's important to chill it down to 40 degrees—when it's cold but still fluid—before it goes into the ice cream maker. (Chill the ice cream maker's canister for at least 24 hours before adding the base and churning so that it's as cold as possible.)

CHURN: Churning partially freezes the base and incorporates air into it through the whipping action of the paddle (also called a dasher blade). The process takes about 30 minutes; you'll know it's time to stop when the base is the texture of thick soft serve and registers 21 degrees.

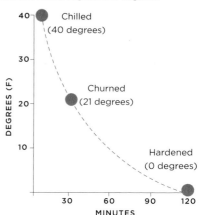

HARDEN: After churning, about 50 percent of the water is frozen; the rest of the freezing and hardening happens when the base is packed into a container and left in the freezer for at least a couple of hours.

HERE'S THE SCOOP

Zeroll Original Ice Cream Scoop

PRICE: $18.44
COMMENTS: Its gently curved bowl forms perfect round orbs, and as your hand warms the heat-conductive handle, the metal slightly melts the ice cream or sorbet so that it's particularly easy to scoop.

BEFORE YOU BEGIN

This recipe can be used to make sweet cream ice cream or used as a base for making other flavors (see recipes below). If using a canister-style ice cream maker, be sure to freeze the empty canister for at least 24 hours (or preferably 48 hours) before churning. For self-refrigerating ice cream makers, prechill the canister by running the maker for 5 to 10 minutes before pouring in the base. We prefer Carnation Instant Nonfat Dry Milk. Some base may stick to the bottom of the saucepan when pouring it into the strainer in step 3; simply scrape it into the strainer with the rest of the base and press it through with a spatula. This ice cream can be frozen for up to five days.

Sweet Cream Ice Cream

SERVES 8 (MAKES ABOUT 1 QUART)
TOTAL TIME: 20 MINUTES, PLUS 9 HOURS
CHILLING

- ½ cup plus ⅓ cup nonfat dry milk powder
- ⅓ cup (2⅓ ounces) sugar
- ¼ teaspoon kosher salt
- 1½ cups whole milk, divided
- 1½ cups heavy cream
- ¼ cup corn syrup
- 5 teaspoons cornstarch

1. Whisk milk powder, sugar, and salt together in small bowl. Whisk 1¼ cups milk, cream, corn syrup, and sugar mixture together in large saucepan. Cook over medium-high heat, whisking frequently to dissolve sugar and break up any clumps, until tiny bubbles form around edge of saucepan and mixture registers 190 degrees, 5 to 7 minutes.

2. Meanwhile, whisk cornstarch and remaining ¼ cup milk together in small bowl.

3. Reduce heat to medium. Whisk cornstarch mixture to recombine, then whisk into milk mixture in saucepan. Cook, constantly scraping bottom of saucepan with heat-resistant rubber spatula, until mixture thickens, about 30 seconds. Immediately pour ice cream base through fine-mesh strainer into large bowl; let cool until no longer steaming, about 20 minutes. Cover bowl; transfer to refrigerator; and chill until base registers 40 degrees, at least 6 hours. (Base can be chilled overnight. Alternatively, base can be chilled to 40 degrees in about 1½ hours by placing bowl in ice bath of 6 cups ice, ½ cup water, and ⅓ cup table salt.)

4. Churn base in ice cream maker until mixture resembles thick soft serve and registers 21 degrees, about 30 minutes. Transfer ice cream to airtight container, pressing firmly to remove air pockets; freeze until firm, at least 2 hours. Serve.

FOUR FAVORITE FLAVORS

VANILLA BEAN

In step 1, process milk with 1 vanilla bean, cut in half lengthwise and then cut crosswise into 3 pieces, in blender on high speed until vanilla bean is reduced to specks, about 1 minute. Do not strain. Proceed with recipe, whisking vanilla milk with cream, corn syrup, and sugar mixture.

WHITE COFFEE CHIP

At end of step 1, stir 2 cups whole dark-roast coffee beans into milk mixture, cover, and let steep for 1 hour. Using slotted spoon, discard coffee beans. Return mixture to 190 degrees over medium-high heat and proceed with step 2, whisking extra ½ cup milk (for total of ¾ cup milk) into cornstarch. Before churning base, microwave 4 ounces finely chopped bittersweet chocolate in bowl, stirring frequently, until melted, about 2 minutes; set aside and let cool. Churn base as directed; when base registers 21 degrees, with maker running, slowly drizzle chocolate into ice cream and continue to churn until incorporated, 1 to 2 minutes longer. Proceed with recipe.

STRAWBERRY RIPPLE

While base chills, combine 6 ounces hulled fresh strawberries, ½ cup plus 1 tablespoon sugar, and 1 cup (½ ounce) freeze-dried strawberries in blender; process on high speed until smooth, about 1 minute.

Transfer to airtight container and refrigerate until ready to use. In step 4, when base registers 21 degrees, spread one-quarter of base on bottom of airtight container and top with ¼ cup strawberry mixture. Repeat 3 more times, then proceed with recipe.

PEANUT BUTTER CUP CRUNCH

In step 1, place ⅓ cup chunky natural peanut butter in large bowl while milk mixture cooks. In step 3, strain base into bowl with peanut butter and whisk thoroughly to combine. In step 4, when base registers 21 degrees and with maker running, add 2 cups halved and frozen mini peanut butter cups and continue to churn until incorporated, 1 to 2 minutes longer. Proceed with recipe.

OUR FAVORITE ICE CREAM MAKER

Cuisinart Frozen Yogurt, Ice Cream & Sorbet Maker

PRICE: $53.99

COMMENTS: Inexpensive, lightweight, and simple to use, this canister-style model churns out velvety ice cream with the push of a button.

THE SALTY, SWEET, SMOKY SCIENCE OF BACON

We dig into the mystique behind America's favorite cured meat; plus, we offer tips for decoding package labels, splatter-free cooking, and even making your own.

When cooks first cured pork bellies thousands of years ago, their purpose was preservation: The salt deprived harmful microbes of water, effectively killing them so that the uncooked meat could be kept for months without spoiling. Later, sugar, smoke, and the curing salt called sodium nitrite were added to the preservation process. But once refrigeration arrived, bacon became purely indulgent.

There's serious science behind its primal appeal. As it cures and cooks, the pork undergoes a storm of chemical reactions, which results in its unmistakable aroma and flavor. We'll explain all that and leave you with a recipe for home-cured bacon—a project that's easier than you think and that all bacon aficionados should try at least once.

THE CURE

Manufacturers use one or both of the following methods to cure the pork before it's smoked.

DRY CURE (also called "dry rub"; slower, pricier, and used mostly by artisanal producers): The pork is rubbed with a mixture of salt, sodium nitrite, and a handful of seasonings and left to sit for at least a week, during which time a variety of savory flavor compounds start to develop.

WET CURE (faster and cheaper; the most common commercial method): The pork is submerged in or injected with a brine; injection mimics the dry-cured effect in a matter of hours. Note that wet cures leave more water in the bacon, which you pay for in the price per pound and which causes the bacon to splatter more during cooking.

SALT deprives bacteria and mold of water while also restructuring the muscle fibers so that the bacon is pleasantly dense, tender, and concentrated in flavor.

CURING SALT which contains sodium nitrite and sometimes sodium nitrate, slows rancidity and bacteria growth and gives bacon its pink blush and "cured" flavor.

SUGAR (often a flavorful kind such as brown or maple) balances the flavor of the salt and helps draw out water.

THE FINE PRINT ABOUT "UNCURED" BACON

Bacon that is labeled "uncured," "nitrite-free," or "nitrate-free" might sound like it avoids the risks associated with curing salts, but those terms are misleading. When we tested cured and "uncured" bacon for nitrite content, we found that the "uncured" bacon contained at least as much nitrite as the cured. The confusion rests in the labeling laws of the U.S. Department of Agriculture (USDA): Producers of "uncured" bacon are not using any additives that the USDA recognizes as curing agents; they're using natural ingredients such as celery juice or celery juice powder that are packed with nitrites and that also have the potential to turn into carcinogenic compounds when the bacon is fried. Legally, manufacturers must label the product as uncured, but the chemical process is the same, as are the potential risks.

THE MEAT

PORK BELLY which is cut from the pig's underside, features alternating layers of meat and fat. Most bacon today features a roughly 60:40 ratio of fat to meat.

WHY BACON SMELLS SO GOOD

Much of what we find enticing about bacon is tied to its scent, and roughly 150 aromatic compounds have been detected in the aroma of fried bacon. Chief among them are meaty-smelling pyridines and pyrazines, created when the pork is cured and then volatilized as it sizzles. Together with the other compounds, they give off the characteristic smell of bacon.

THE SMOKE

Smoke flavor can be applied using wood (logs, chips, or sawdust), liquid smoke, or a combination of both methods.

DRY SMOKE: The pork is cooked whole in a low-temperature convection oven with smoldering wood logs, chips, or sawdust. Because the smoke deposits on the exterior of the pork, thick-cut bacon, with its greater surface area per slice, has more smoke flavor than thin-cut bacon. Dry-smoked bacon can also be labeled "naturally smoked" or "hardwood smoked."

LIQUID SMOKE: If the phrase "smoke flavor" appears on the packaging, that's a sign that liquid smoke has been injected along with the cure—and that's not necessarily a bad thing. Liquid smoke is simply condensed wood smoke that's been filtered to remove tar and resins, and when used in proper proportions, it can actually produce decent smoke flavor.

BRING HOME THE BEST BACON

REGULAR

Oscar Mayer Naturally Hardwood Smoked Bacon

PRICE: $6.99 per lb
COMMENTS: "Classic" bacon that "hits all the right notes" and boasts "a good balance of chew and crispness"

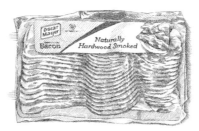

THICK-CUT

SUGARDALE Thick Sliced Bacon

PRICE: $4.39 per lb
COMMENTS: "Very meaty" and mildly smoky with a "distinct maple" taste

ARTISANAL

VANDE ROSE Applewood Smoked Artisan Dry Cured Bacon

PRICE: $29.07 per lb, including shipping
COMMENTS: "Perfectly balanced salt, sugar, and smoke"

TURKEY

WELLSHIRE All Natural Uncured Turkey Bacon

PRICE: $6.99 per 12 oz
COMMENTS: More like Canadian bacon than the conventional pork kind, with some of the big smoky, salty, sweet flavors we associate with good bacon

OUR FAVORITE WAYS TO COOK BACON

OVEN

This method allows you to cook up to 12 slices of bacon at a time and avoids stovetop splatter. Place bacon on rimmed baking sheet and bake at 400 degrees for about 15 minutes, rotating sheet halfway through baking.

STOVETOP

The key is to cook the bacon with a little water in the pan (3 tablespoons for a 12-inch skillet), which keeps the temperature low enough that the fat renders thoroughly and the whole strip cooks evenly. Once water comes to boil, reduce heat to medium. When all water has evaporated, reduce heat to medium-low and continue to cook until bacon is crispy and well browned.

Home-Cured Bacon

MAKES ABOUT 3½ POUNDS
TOTAL TIME: 4 HOURS, PLUS 7 DAYS CURING

It takes at least one week for the bacon to cure. You will need a smoker for this recipe. Do not use iodized salt—we developed this recipe using Diamond Crystal Kosher Salt. If you use Morton Kosher Salt, which has denser crystals, use ⅓ cup for this recipe. Pink curing salt #1, which can be purchased online or in stores specializing in meat curing, is a mixture of table salt and sodium nitrite; it is also called Prague Powder #1, Insta Cure #1, or DQ Curing Salt #1. (Do not substitute Morton's Tender Quick or Insta Cure #2.) Maple sugar, which is made from maple syrup, is available in many grocery stores and online from King Arthur Baking Company and various New England maple farms. You can substitute brown sugar for the maple sugar.

1 cup maple sugar

½ cup kosher salt

1 tablespoon black peppercorns, cracked

2 teaspoons minced fresh thyme

¾ teaspoon pink curing salt #1

1 bay leaf, crumbled

1 (4-pound) pork belly, skin removed

4 medium hickory wood chunks

1. Combine sugar, kosher salt, peppercorns, thyme, pink salt, and bay leaf in small bowl. Place pork in 13 by 9-inch baking dish and rub pork all over with sugar mixture. Cover dish tightly with plastic wrap and refrigerate until pork feels firm yet still pliable, 7 to 10 days, flipping pork every other day.

2. Soak wood chunks in water for 1 hour, then drain. Thoroughly rinse pork with cold water and pat dry with paper towels.

3. Open bottom vent of smoker completely. Arrange 1½ quarts unlit charcoal briquettes in center of smoker in even layer. Light large chimney starter three-quarters filled with charcoal briquettes (4½ quarts). When top coals are partially covered with ash, pour evenly over unlit coals. Place wood chunks on coals. Assemble smoker and fill water pan with water according to manufacturer's instructions. Cover smoker and open lid vent completely. Heat smoker until hot and wood chunks are smoking, about 5 minutes.

4. Clean and oil smoking grate. Place pork meat side down in center of smoker. Cover (positioning lid vent over pork) and smoke until pork registers 150 degrees, 1½ to 2 hours.

5. Remove bacon from smoker and let cool completely before slicing. Unsliced bacon can be wrapped tightly with plastic and refrigerated for up to 1 month or frozen for up to 2 months.

OUR FAVORITE HOLIDAY COOKIES

Behold, five of our best, most festive treats—each with a practical tip—to fill your cookie tin.

Chocolate Crinkle Cookies

MAKES 22 COOKIES
TOTAL TIME: 1¼ HOURS, PLUS 20 MINUTES
COOLING

Unsweetened chocolate and cocoa powder (plus a boost from espresso powder) give these cookies brownie-like richness and depth. Rolling the dough in granulated and then confectioners' sugar yields the perfect crackly exterior.

- 1 cup (5 ounces) all-purpose flour
- ½ cup (1½ ounces) unsweetened cocoa powder
- 1 teaspoon baking powder
- ¼ teaspoon baking soda
- ½ teaspoon table salt
- 1½ cups packed (10½ ounces) brown sugar
- 3 large eggs
- 4 teaspoons instant espresso powder (optional)
- 1 teaspoon vanilla extract
- 4 ounces unsweetened chocolate, chopped
- 4 tablespoons unsalted butter
- ½ cup (3½ ounces) granulated sugar
- ½ cup (2 ounces) confectioners' sugar

UNDERBAKE FOR PROPER CHEW

Underbaking is key for producing cookies with chewy centers, but gauging exactly when to take them out is tricky. Your best bet is a visual cue: For crackly cookies like these, look for cracks that appear shiny.

1. Adjust oven rack to middle position and heat oven to 325 degrees. Line 2 baking sheets with parchment paper. Whisk flour, cocoa, baking powder, baking soda, and salt together in bowl.

2. Whisk brown sugar; eggs; espresso powder, if using; and vanilla together in large bowl. Combine chocolate and butter in bowl and microwave at 50 percent power, stirring occasionally, until melted, 2 to 3 minutes.

3. Whisk chocolate mixture into egg mixture until combined. Fold in flour mixture until no dry streaks remain. Let dough sit at room temperature for 10 minutes.

4. Place granulated sugar and confectioners' sugar in separate shallow dishes. Working with 2 tablespoons dough (or use #30 scoop) at a time, roll into balls. Drop each ball into granulated sugar directly after shaping and roll to coat. Transfer dough balls to confectioners' sugar and roll to coat evenly. Evenly space dough balls on prepared sheets, 11 dough balls per sheet.

5. Bake cookies, 1 sheet at a time, until puffed and cracked and edges have begun to set but centers are still soft (cookies will look raw between cracks and seem underdone), about 12 minutes, rotating sheet halfway through baking. Let cool completely on sheet before serving.

Thick and Chewy Gingerbread Cookies

MAKES ABOUT 20 COOKIES
TOTAL TIME: 1 HOUR, PLUS 1½ HOURS
CHILLING AND COOLING

Lots of butter and brown sugar give these cookies a satisfying chewiness. Rolling the dough thin—but not too thin—and baking the cookies until their edges are just set ensures that they're soft but flat and even. Cinnamon, ginger, and cloves add robust but balanced flavor and warmth. If you want to decorate the cookies, our stiff, glossy Decorative Icing (recipe follows) pipes neatly into clearly defined lines.

- 3 cups (15 ounces) all-purpose flour
- ¾ cup packed (5¼ ounces) dark brown sugar
- 1 tablespoon ground cinnamon
- 1 tablespoon ground ginger
- ¾ teaspoon baking soda
- ½ teaspoon ground cloves
- ½ teaspoon table salt
- 12 tablespoons unsalted butter, melted
- ¾ cup molasses
- 2 tablespoons milk

1. Process flour, sugar, cinnamon, ginger, baking soda, cloves, and salt in food processor until combined, about 10 seconds. Add melted butter, molasses, and milk and process until soft dough forms and no streaks of flour remain, about 20 seconds, scraping down sides of bowl as needed.

2. Spray counter lightly with baking spray with flour; transfer dough to counter; and knead until dough forms cohesive ball, about 20 seconds. Divide dough in half. Form each half into 5-inch disk, wrap disks tightly in plastic wrap, and refrigerate for at least 1 hour or up to 24 hours.

3. Adjust oven racks to upper-middle and lower-middle positions and heat oven to 350 degrees. Line 2 rimmed baking sheets with parchment paper. Working with 1 disk of dough at a time, roll disk ¼ inch thick

CHILL THE DOUGH

To keep cookies from spreading and to make shaping easier, refrigerate the dough for at least 1 hour before using it. If you're rerolling cut-out scraps of dough, cover the scraps with plastic wrap and rechill them before using them again.

between 2 large sheets of parchment. (Keep second disk refrigerated.) Remove top piece of parchment. Using 3½-inch cookie cutter, cut dough into shapes. Peel away scraps from around shapes and space shapes ¾ inch apart on prepared sheets. Wrap scraps in plastic and refrigerate for at least 30 minutes. Repeat rolling and cutting with scraps.

4. Bake cookies until puffy and just set around edges, 9 to 11 minutes, switching and rotating sheets halfway through baking. Let cookies cool on sheets for 10 minutes, then transfer to wire rack. Let cookies cool completely before serving. (Cookies can be stored in wide, shallow airtight container, with sheet of parchment or waxed paper between layers, at room temperature for up to 3 days.)

Decorative Icing

MAKES 1⅓ CUPS TOTAL TIME: 10 MINUTES

- 2⅔ **cups (10⅔ ounces) confectioners' sugar**
- 2 **large egg whites**

Using stand mixer fitted with whisk attachment, whip sugar and egg whites on medium-low speed until combined, about 1 minute. Increase speed to medium-high and whip until glossy, soft peaks form, 2 to 3 minutes, scraping down bowl as needed. Transfer icing to pastry bag fitted with small round pastry tip. Decorate cookies and let icing harden before serving or storing.

Florentine Lace Cookies

MAKES 24 COOKIES
TOTAL TIME: 2¼ HOURS, PLUS 30 MINUTES
CHILLING

Part confection, part cookie, these lacy, orange-flavored almond disks are made by cooking a loose dough in a saucepan and then baking the rounds until they're deeply caramelized. Our easy method for tempering chocolate makes the elegant zigzag of shiny, snappy chocolate—a Florentine's decorative hallmark—surprisingly simple to pull off.

- 2 **cups slivered almonds**
- ¾ **cup heavy cream**
- ½ **cup (3½ ounces) sugar**
- 4 **tablespoons unsalted butter, cut into 4 pieces**
- ¼ **cup orange marmalade**
- 3 **tablespoons all-purpose flour**
- 1 **teaspoon vanilla extract**
- ¼ **teaspoon grated orange zest**
- ¼ **teaspoon table salt**
- 4 **ounces bittersweet chocolate, chopped fine, divided**

1. Adjust oven racks to upper-middle and lower-middle positions and heat oven to 350 degrees. Line 2 baking sheets with parchment paper. Process almonds in food processor until they resemble coarse sand, about 30 seconds.

2. Bring cream, sugar, and butter to boil in medium saucepan over medium-high heat. Cook, stirring frequently, until mixture begins to thicken, 5 to 6 minutes. Continue to cook, stirring constantly, until mixture begins to brown at edges and is thick enough to leave trail that doesn't immediately fill in when spatula is scraped along saucepan bottom, 1 to 2 minutes longer (it's OK if some darker speckles appear in mixture). Off heat, stir in almonds, marmalade, flour, vanilla, orange zest, and salt until combined.

3. Drop 6 level tablespoons dough at least 3½ inches apart on each prepared sheet. When cool enough to handle, use your damp fingers to press each portion into 2½-inch circle. (Don't worry if some butter separates from dough while you're portioning cookies.)

4. Bake until deep brown from edge to edge, 15 to 17 minutes, switching and rotating sheets halfway through baking. Transfer cookies, still on parchment, to wire racks and let cool. Let sheets cool for 10 minutes, line with fresh parchment, and repeat portioning and baking with remaining dough.

5. Microwave 3 ounces chocolate in bowl at 50 percent power, stirring frequently, until about two-thirds melted, 1 to 2 minutes. Remove bowl from microwave, add remaining 1 ounce chocolate, and stir until melted, returning to microwave for no more than 5 seconds at a time to complete melting if necessary. Transfer chocolate to small zipper-lock bag and snip off corner, making hole no larger than 1/16 inch.

6. Transfer cooled cookies directly to wire racks. Pipe zigzag of chocolate over each cookie, distributing chocolate evenly

among all cookies. Refrigerate until chocolate is set, about 30 minutes, before serving. (Cookies can be stored at cool room temperature for up to 4 days.)

TEMPER CHOCOLATE THE EASY WAY

Microwave three-quarters of the chocolate at 50 percent power, stirring frequently so that it doesn't get much warmer than body temperature, until it is about two-thirds melted, 1 to 2 minutes. Stir in the remaining chocolate.

Ultranutty Pecan Bars

MAKES 24 BARS
TOTAL TIME: 1 HOUR, PLUS 1½ HOURS COOLING

Unlike most pecan bars that are dominated by sugary goo, these are packed with nuts—a full pound of them—that are lightly bound together by a dump-and-stir topping that's not too sweet. The crust is easy, too: a pat-in-the-pan dough that doesn't even require parbaking.

CRUST

- 1¾ **cups (8¾ ounces) all-purpose flour**
- 6 **tablespoons (2⅔ ounces) sugar**
- ½ **teaspoon table salt**
- 8 **tablespoons unsalted butter, melted**

TOPPING

- ¾ cup packed (5¼ ounces) light brown sugar
- ½ cup light corn syrup
- 7 tablespoons unsalted butter, melted and hot
- 1 teaspoon vanilla extract
- ½ teaspoon table salt
- 4 cups (1 pound) pecans, toasted
- ½ teaspoon flake sea salt (optional)

1. FOR THE CRUST: Adjust oven rack to lowest position and heat oven to 350 degrees. Make foil sling for 13 by 9-inch baking pan by folding 2 long sheets of aluminum foil; first sheet should be 13 inches wide and second sheet should be 9 inches wide. Lay sheets of foil in pan perpendicular to each other, with extra foil hanging over edges of pan. Push foil into corners and up sides of pan, smoothing foil flush to pan. Lightly spray foil with vegetable oil spray.

2. Whisk flour, sugar, and salt together in medium bowl. Add melted butter and stir with wooden spoon until dough begins to form. Using your hands, continue to combine until no dry flour remains and small portion of dough holds together when squeezed in palm of your hand. Evenly scatter tablespoon-size pieces of dough over surface of pan. Using your fingertips and palm of your hand, press and smooth dough into even thickness in bottom of pan.

3. FOR THE TOPPING: Whisk sugar, corn syrup, melted butter, vanilla, and table salt in medium bowl until smooth (mixture will look separated at first but will become homogeneous), about 20 seconds. Fold pecans into sugar mixture until evenly coated.

4. Pour topping over crust. Using spatula, spread topping over crust, pushing to edges and into corners (there will be bare patches). Bake until topping is evenly distributed and rapidly bubbling across entire surface, 23 to 25 minutes.

5. Transfer pan to wire rack and lightly sprinkle with flake sea salt, if using. Let bars cool completely in pan on rack, about 1½ hours. Using foil overhang, lift bars out of pan and transfer to cutting board. Cut into 24 bars. (Bars can be stored at room temperature for up to 5 days.)

BAKE BAR COOKIES IN METAL PANS

Glass dishes retain heat longer, which can lead to overbaking. Plus, the straight sides and crisp corners of metal vessels produce bars with well-defined, professional-looking edges. Our favorite 8-inch square baking pan is Fat Daddio's ProSeries Square Cake Pan; our favorite 13 by 9-inch pan is the Williams Sonoma Goldtouch Nonstick Rectangular Cake Pan, 9" x 13".

Almond Biscotti

MAKES 30 COOKIES
TOTAL TIME: 1¾ HOURS, PLUS 50 MINUTES COOLING

These biscotti are appropriately hard and crunchy but not jawbreakers, thanks to ample butter creating tenderness, whipped eggs that aerate the dough, and not too much gluten. These cookies keep well for up to a month—a real boon for holiday bakers.

- 1¼ cups whole almonds, lightly toasted, divided
- 1¾ cups (8¾ ounces) all-purpose flour
- 2 teaspoons baking powder
- ¼ teaspoon table salt
- 2 large eggs, plus 1 large white beaten with pinch table salt
- 1 cup (7 ounces) sugar
- 4 tablespoons unsalted butter, melted and cooled
- 1½ teaspoons almond extract
- ½ teaspoon vanilla extract
  Vegetable oil spray

1. Adjust oven rack to middle position and heat oven to 325 degrees. Using ruler and pencil, draw two 8 by 3-inch rectangles, spaced 4 inches apart, on piece of parchment paper. Grease rimmed baking sheet; place parchment on sheet, pencil side down.

2. Pulse 1 cup almonds in food processor until coarsely chopped, 8 to 10 pulses; transfer to bowl and set aside. Process remaining ¼ cup almonds until finely ground, about 45 seconds. Add flour, baking powder, and salt; process to combine, about 15 seconds. Transfer flour mixture to second bowl. Process 2 eggs in now-empty processor until lightened in color and almost doubled in volume, about 3 minutes. With processor running, slowly add sugar until thoroughly combined, about 15 seconds. Add melted butter, almond extract, and vanilla and process until combined, about 10 seconds. Transfer egg mixture to medium bowl. Sprinkle half of flour mixture over egg mixture and, using spatula, fold gently until just combined. Add remaining flour mixture and chopped almonds and fold gently until just combined.

3. Divide batter in half. Using your floured hands, form each half into 8 by 3-inch rectangle, using lines on parchment as guide. Spray each loaf lightly with oil spray. Using rubber spatula lightly coated with oil spray, smooth tops and sides of rectangles. Gently brush tops of loaves with egg-white wash. Bake until loaves are golden and just beginning to crack on top, 25 to 30 minutes, rotating sheet halfway through baking.

4. Let loaves cool on sheet for 30 minutes. Transfer loaves to cutting board. Using serrated knife, slice each loaf on slight bias ½ inch thick. Lay slices, cut side down, about ¼ inch apart on wire rack set in rimmed baking sheet. Bake until crisp and golden brown on both sides, about 35 minutes, flipping slices halfway through baking. Let cool completely before serving. Biscotti can be stored in airtight container for up to 1 month.

TOAST NUTS BEFORE BAKING TO DEEPEN THEIR FLAVOR

Spread nuts in single layer on rimmed baking sheet and toast in preheated 350-degree oven until fragrant and slightly darkened, 8 to 12 minutes, shaking sheet halfway through toasting to prevent burning.

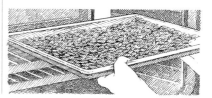

COOKING WITH BUTTER

This stick of (mostly) fat is one of the most versatile ingredients in any kitchen.

Butter production is so common and industrialized today that it's remarkable to think that it might have been born out of serendipity some 9,000 years ago. Allegedly, milk in an animal-skin sack sloshed around so vigorously during transport that its fat separated from its water and aggregated into divinely rich globs.

However butter came about was undeniably good fortune—culinary happenstance that writer Elaine Khosrova describes as "Rumpelstiltskin-like magic" in her book, *Butter: A Rich History* (2016). But more plainly than that, butter is evidence of science at work, from the organic way it forms to the innumerable ways it functions. We cooks are indebted to both its utility and its luxury, marveling at—and relying on—its ability to shape-shift from a stiff block that laminates pastry dough to a creamy mass that captures air in cakes and cookies; an opaque liquid that blooms spices and glosses flatbreads; or a complex, nut-brown sauce that is spooned over countless dishes.

THE BUTTER BREAKDOWN

Butter is an emulsion of fat, water, and milk solids—specifically, a water-in-oil emulsion in which tiny droplets of water and trace amounts of milk solids are suspended throughout the butterfat. Together, these components give butter the potential to be a remarkable multitasker: a high heat–tolerant cooking fat, a source of moisture, and a flavor powerhouse.

FAT
By law, butter manufactured in the United States must have at least 80 percent fat. (Premium butters contain between 82 and 86 percent fat.) Because butterfat is highly saturated, butter is solid and its emulsion is stable well above room temperature.

WATER
Butter can contain no more than 16 percent water, which is suspended in the fat, creating a solid mass. The water droplets are coated in a small amount of protein, which keeps them from coalescing until the butter is completely melted; when that happens, the emulsion "breaks," meaning that the water and milk solids separate from the fat.

MILK SOLIDS
About 4 percent of butter is made up of milk solids that include proteins, lactose, and salts.

BUY THE BEST

UNSALTED
CHALLENGE Unsalted Butter
PRICE: $4.49 for 1 lb ($0.28 per oz)

SALTED
LURPAK Slightly Salted Butter
PRICE: $3.59 for 8 oz ($0.45 per oz)

HOW TEMPERATURE CHANGES BUTTER

One of the great benefits (and challenges) of cooking with butter is that its texture and flavor change rapidly and dramatically with temperature. Over a span of about 200 degrees, it transforms from a firm, milky mass to a deeply aromatic mahogany liquid—and hits a handful of other milestones along the way. Here's a "map" of that temperature progression.

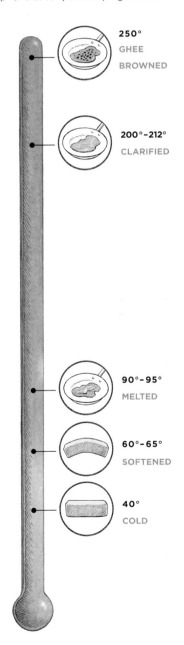

250°
GHEE
BROWNED

200°–212°
CLARIFIED

90°–95°
MELTED

60°–65°
SOFTENED

40°
COLD

COLD

HOW IT WORKS: Fridge-cold butter is a must for making flaky pastry. When you layer cold butter and dough and bake the pastry, the butterfat melts, releasing water that turns to steam; that steam helps puff and separate the layers of dough, creating literally hundreds of flaky layers. It's also key for making glossy—not greasy—pan sauces: Since cold butter melts slowly, swirling it into a sauce allows you to thoroughly break the butterfat into tiny droplets that can be dispersed throughout the water in the sauce, creating a stable emulsion.

Ultimate Flaky Buttermilk Biscuits

MAKES 9 BISCUITS
TOTAL TIME: 1¾ HOURS, PLUS 30 MINUTES RESTING

- **3 cups (15 ounces) King Arthur all-purpose flour**
- **2 tablespoons sugar**
- **4 teaspoons baking powder**
- **½ teaspoon baking soda**
- **1½ teaspoons table salt**
- **16 tablespoons (2 sticks) unsalted butter, frozen for 30 minutes**
- **1¼ cups buttermilk, chilled**

1. Line rimmed baking sheet with parchment paper and set aside. Whisk flour, sugar, baking powder, baking soda, and salt together in large bowl. Coat sticks of butter in flour mixture, then grate 7 tablespoons from each stick on large holes of box grater directly into flour mixture. Toss gently to combine. Set aside remaining 2 tablespoons butter.

2. Add buttermilk to flour mixture and fold with spatula until just combined (dough will look dry). Transfer dough to liberally floured counter. Dust surface of dough with flour; using your floured hands, press dough into rough 7-inch square.

3. Roll dough into 12 by 9-inch rectangle with short side parallel to edge of counter. Starting at bottom of dough, fold into thirds like business letter, using bench scraper or metal spatula to release dough from counter. Press top of dough firmly to seal folds. Turn dough 90 degrees clockwise. Repeat rolling into 12 by 9-inch rectangle, folding into thirds, and turning clockwise 4 more times, for total of 5 sets of folds. After last set of folds, roll dough into 8½-inch square

about 1 inch thick. Transfer dough to prepared sheet, cover with plastic wrap, and refrigerate for 30 minutes. Adjust oven rack to upper-middle position and heat oven to 400 degrees.

4. Transfer dough to lightly floured cutting board. Using sharp, floured chef's knife, trim ¼ inch of dough from each side of square; discard. Cut remaining dough into 9 squares, flouring knife after each cut. Arrange biscuits at least 1 inch apart on sheet. Melt reserved butter; brush tops of biscuits with melted butter.

5. Bake until tops are golden brown, 22 to 25 minutes, rotating sheet halfway through baking. Transfer biscuits to wire rack and let cool for 15 minutes before serving.

SOFTENED

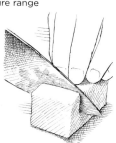

HOW IT WORKS: In this temperature range (60–65 degrees), butter is the perfect consistency for creaming with sugar: soft enough to capture air bubbles that expand in the oven, giving baked goods lightness and lift, yet firm enough to support those air bubbles so that they don't collapse. It's also ideal for whipping into frostings such as buttercream.

SPEEDY SOFTENING

FOR CREAMING: Cut the stick into 1-tablespoon pieces (more exposed surface area helps the butter warm quickly and evenly) and arrange them on a plate. The pieces will soften in about 20 minutes.

FOR SPREADING OR MIXING WITH FLAVORINGS: Microwave the pieces at 50 percent power in 10-second increments until the butter is still solid but yields completely to pressure. It's OK if the butter melts a little; stir it together until it's uniform. Don't use the microwave method for baking applications; oversoftened butter can compromise baked goods.

Creamy Butterscotch Frosting

MAKES ABOUT 2¼ CUPS
TOTAL TIME: 30 MINUTES

The frosting can be made up to 24 hours in advance and refrigerated in an airtight container. When ready to frost, place

frosting in a microwave-safe container and microwave until just slightly softened, 5 to 10 seconds. Once warmed, stir until creamy.

- **½ cup packed (3½ ounces) dark brown sugar**
- **2 large egg whites**
- **½ teaspoon table salt**
- **12 tablespoons unsalted butter, cut into 1-tablespoon pieces and softened**
- **½ teaspoon vanilla extract**

1. Combine sugar, egg whites, and salt in bowl of stand mixer; place bowl over saucepan of simmering water. Whisking gently but constantly, heat until mixture is slightly thickened and foamy and registers 150 degrees, 2 to 3 minutes.

2. Fit mixer with whisk attachment and whip mixture on medium speed until consistency of shaving cream and slightly cooled, 1 to 2 minutes. Add butter, 1 piece at a time, and whip until smooth and creamy. (Frosting may look curdled after half of butter has been added; it will smooth out with additional butter.) Once all butter is added, add vanilla; mix until combined. Increase speed to medium-high and whip until light, fluffy, and thoroughly combined, about 30 seconds, scraping whisk attachment and bowl with rubber spatula as necessary.

3. If frosting seems too thick, warm bowl briefly over saucepan of simmering water. Return bowl to mixer and whip on medium-high speed until creamy.

MELTED

HOW IT WORKS: When butterfat reaches its melting point (94 degrees), it liquefies and the emulsion "breaks," causing the water and milk solids to separate out. That free water is available to hydrate the flour in doughs and batters, creating a stronger gluten network—and thus a more pliable, resilient texture—than cold or softened butter would.

Chewy Peanut Butter Cookies

MAKES 24 COOKIES
TOTAL TIME: 50 MINUTES, PLUS 30 MINUTES COOLING

To ensure that the cookies have the proper texture, use a traditional creamy peanut butter here; do not substitute chunky or natural peanut butter. We developed this recipe with Skippy Creamy Peanut Butter. For the best results, be sure to weigh the flour, sugar, and peanut butter. You can substitute light brown sugar for the dark, but your cookies will be lighter in color.

1½ cups (7½ ounces) all-purpose flour
1 teaspoon baking soda
½ teaspoon table salt
1½ cups packed (10½ ounces) dark brown sugar
1 cup (9 ounces) creamy peanut butter
2 large eggs
4 tablespoons unsalted butter, melted and cooled
2 tablespoons honey
1 teaspoon vanilla extract
½ cup dry-roasted peanuts, chopped fine

1. Adjust oven rack to middle position and heat oven to 350 degrees. Line two 18 by 13-inch rimmed baking sheets with parchment paper. Whisk flour, baking soda, and salt together in medium bowl.

2. In large bowl, whisk sugar, peanut butter, eggs, melted butter, honey, and vanilla until smooth. Add flour mixture and stir with rubber spatula until soft, homogeneous dough forms. Stir in peanuts until evenly distributed.

3. Working with 2 tablespoons dough at a time (or using #30 portion scoop), roll dough into balls and evenly space on prepared sheets (12 dough balls per sheet). Using your fingers, gently flatten dough balls until 2 inches in diameter.

4. Bake cookies, 1 sheet at a time, until edges are just set and just beginning to brown, 10 to 12 minutes, rotating sheet after 6 minutes. Let cookies cool on sheet for 5 minutes. Using wide metal spatula, transfer cookies to wire rack and let cool completely before serving.

CLARIFIED BUTTER

WHAT IT IS: Butter that has been heated until its water evaporates and then skimmed of its milk solids, leaving clear, relatively shelf-stable, mild-tasting fat.

HOW IT'S USED: As a high heat–tolerant (up to 400 degrees) fat for sautéing and frying; as a gloss for phyllo in dishes such as baklava and spanakopita; and for dipping shellfish and artichokes.

HOW WE MAKE IT: Cut butter into 1-inch chunks and then melt it either in a small saucepan over medium-low heat or in the microwave at 50 percent power. Let the melted butter sit for 10 minutes, then skim off the milk solids floating at the top with a soupspoon. Transfer the butter to a bowl if melted in a saucepan. Cover and refrigerate until the fat solidifies, at least 4 hours. The solidified butter can then be popped out of the bowl, where the water (and trace amounts of other dissolved ingredients) will remain. Blot the bottom of the fat dry with paper towels and store in the refrigerator. (You can clarify butter faster by skipping the initial refrigeration step and skimming the fat off the layer of water using a spoon, but this approach is less effective at removing water, so the result won't be as shelf-stable.)

BROWNED BUTTER

WHAT IT IS: Butter that has been heated until its water evaporates and its milk solids undergo the Maillard reaction, creating hundreds of new, complex-tasting flavor compounds.

HOW IT'S USED: As the foundation of countless sauces; in baked goods, where it offers unrivaled depth.

HOW WE MAKE IT: Melt butter in a pan with a light-colored interior, such as a stainless-steel or enameled cast-iron skillet (better for monitoring browning than a pan with a dark-colored interior), until sputtering subsides. Using a heatproof spatula, stir and scrape constantly as the solids brown so that none stick to the pan. Immediately pour the butter into a heatproof bowl, scraping out the browned bits, to stop the cooking.

Bacon and Browned Butter Vinaigrette

SERVES 4 (MAKES ABOUT 1 CUP)
TOTAL TIME: 25 MINUTES

Use this to dress a hearty salad or grilled seafood.

8 tablespoons unsalted butter, divided
1 slice bacon, chopped fine
3 tablespoons sherry vinegar
3 tablespoons vegetable oil
1 shallot, minced
1 tablespoon maple syrup
2 teaspoons Dijon mustard

1. Melt 6 tablespoons butter in 10-inch skillet over medium-high heat. Cook, swirling skillet constantly, until butter is dark golden brown and has nutty aroma, 1 to 3 minutes. Remove skillet from heat and transfer browned butter to large heatproof bowl. Stir remaining 2 tablespoons butter into hot butter to melt. Wipe skillet clean with paper towel.

2. Cook bacon in now-empty skillet over medium heat until crispy, 5 to 7 minutes. Using slotted spoon, transfer bacon to paper towel–lined plate. Pour off any bacon fat into browned butter. Add vinegar, oil, shallot, maple syrup, and mustard to browned butter mixture; whisk until emulsified, about 30 seconds. Stir in bacon.

GHEE

WHAT IT IS: Butter (usually cultured) that has been heated until its water evaporates and its milk solids undergo the Maillard reaction and then strained of the brown solids, leaving nutty-tasting, shelf-stable fat (cooking the milk solids forms antioxidants that help prevent rancidity) with an ultrahigh smoke point.

HOW IT'S USED: As a high heat–tolerant fat in South Asian cooking for sautéing, stir-frying, and deep frying; as a more flavorful alternative in any application that calls for clarified butter.

HOW WE MAKE IT: Place 1 to 2 pounds of unsalted butter in a Dutch oven and cook, uncovered, on the lower-middle rack of a 250-degree oven until all the water evaporates and the milk solids are golden brown, 2 to 3 hours. Let cool slightly and strain ghee through fine-mesh strainer lined with cheesecloth. Pour into a clean glass jar, let cool completely, and seal. Store, sealed, in a cool, dark place for up to 3 months or refrigerate for up to 1 year. (Commercial ghee is also available in many supermarkets, usually stocked near the oils.)

HOW TO HARNESS THE FLAVOR OF GARLIC

As cooks, we hold all the power over garlic flavor. Here, we'll teach you how to use it well.

Sniff an intact clove of garlic, and you won't smell anything. But smash that same clove, and it comes to life, unleashing a ripe, complex pungency that defies its small size and plays an integral role in just about every cuisine around the world.

That transformative nature, and its tremendous range of flavor and aroma, is what makes garlic so compelling to cooks. Depending on how you prepare it, garlic can be the hot sting in aioli and mojo; the aromatic depth in countless stir-fries, curries, and braises; or a mellow, creamy, caramelized spread for slathering on bread or mixing into doughs or sauces. It has been a culinary staple since as far back as ancient Mesopotamia—scholars have uncovered references to garlic and other alliums in recipes chiseled in cuneiform script on tablets—as well as a respected form of medicine and the subject of great lore and legend.

HOW GARLIC FLAVOR WORKS

At the root of garlic flavor is an enzyme called alliinase, which is released the moment the cloves' cells are damaged and jump-starts a pivotal chemical reaction. The alliinase acts on a sulfur-containing molecule called alliin, converting it to a harsh-tasting molecule called allicin. Allicin in turn immediately starts to change into a variety of other, often more mellow-tasting compounds, all of which in tandem are responsible for the flavor of garlic.

Manipulating garlic flavor is all about controlling the creation and subsequent evolution of allicin, and the following four variables are some of the tools cooks have to make that happen.

SUBTLE

KNIFE WORK **STRENGTHENS FLAVOR** The more you break down garlic cells by chopping, the more allicin is produced. One minced clove of garlic has more flavor than one sliced clove of garlic, which has more flavor than one crushed clove of garlic.

CRUSHED

SLICED

MINCED

MINCED TO A PASTE

STRONG

HEAT **MELLOWS FLAVOR; INTRODUCES COMPLEXITY AND SWEETNESS** Heating an intact clove of garlic to above 140 degrees deactivates the enzyme alliinase—the thing that starts the whole reaction in the first place—so cutting that garlic won't produce any additional garlic flavor. Heat also tames garlic's intensity after chopping, converting its raw-tasting compounds to mellower ones called polysulphides. Its sugars and amino acids undergo the Maillard reaction, turning the garlic flavor complex and sweet (see "Cooked and Raw Garlic at Work"); just beware of overbrowning garlic, which will produce bitter-tasting compounds.

ACID **MELLOWS FLAVOR:** Steeping just-minced garlic in an acidic liquid (such as lemon juice) inhibits the alliinase so that less harsh-tasting allicin is developed. This technique is especially handy when applied to preparations such as Caesar dressing and hummus, where there's no cooking to tame it and you want just a hint of raw-garlic bite.

TIME **INTRODUCES COMPLEXITY; STRENGTHENS FLAVOR** If you let cut garlic sit, more and more allicin will be produced and evolve into other compounds, making it taste more complex as well as stronger. Even a 10-minute rest before cooking will increase garlic's complexity. Just know that in raw garlic applications like aioli, while the allium's flavor will grow more complex with time, it will also intensify and may eventually become unpalatable.

COOKED AND RAW GARLIC AT WORK

In this recipe, which is loosely based on classic aglio e olio, we use both slow-cooked and raw minced garlic to deliver assertive but balanced garlic flavor.

COOKED
Complex and sweet

RAW
Sharp and pungent

Garlicky Spaghetti with Lemon and Pine Nuts

SERVES 4 TOTAL TIME: 1 HOUR

- ¼   cup extra-virgin olive oil
- 2   tablespoons plus ½ teaspoon minced garlic, divided
- ¼   teaspoon red pepper flakes
- 1   pound spaghetti
    Table salt for cooking pasta
- 2   teaspoons grated lemon zest plus 2 tablespoons juice
- 1   cup chopped fresh basil
- 1   ounce Parmesan cheese, grated (½ cup), plus extra for serving
- ½   cup pine nuts, toasted

1. Combine oil and 2 tablespoons garlic in 8-inch nonstick skillet. Cook over low heat, stirring occasionally, until garlic is pale golden brown, 9 to 12 minutes. Off heat, stir in pepper flakes; set aside.

2. Bring 2 quarts water to boil in large pot. Add pasta and 2 teaspoons salt and cook, stirring frequently, until al dente. Reserve 1 cup cooking water, then drain pasta and return it to pot. Add lemon zest and juice, reserved garlic-oil mixture, reserved cooking water, and remaining ½ teaspoon garlic to pasta in pot. Stir until pasta is well coated with oil and no water remains in bottom of pot. Add basil, Parmesan, and pine nuts and toss to combine. Season with salt and pepper to taste. Serve, passing extra Parmesan separately.

GARLIC GUIDELINE

DON'T BUY GARLIC THAT SMELLS LIKE GARLIC

A head of fresh garlic should not have any aroma, since its characteristic pungency is produced only when the cloves' cells are damaged. Strong-smelling garlic has likely been mishandled during transport or storage. To demonstrate this, we put a few heads of garlic in a plastic bag and whacked at them with a rolling pin (forcefully but not so much that it left visible damage). After a day in storage, they were pungent, while heads that we hadn't mistreated had no aroma at all.

KEEP GARLIC COOL, DRY, AND IN THE DARK

Garlic is highly sensitive to temperature and the amount of sunlight it is exposed to. Following harvest, garlic should be stored away from direct sunlight in low humidity to prevent sprouting and spoilage. Garlic should not be refrigerated, as the combination of low temperature and moisture will initiate spoilage.

YES, YOU CAN COOK WITH SPROUTED GARLIC

Raw garlic sprouts don't taste harsh, but the cloves that surround them are especially fiery and sharp. That's because as garlic ages, it loses moisture, and much of its sugar is used to grow the sprouts, so the cloves themselves taste more intense and less sweet. That said, we've found that sprouted garlic's more pronounced flavor is perceptible only in dishes that call for loads of garlic (such as aglio e olio) or where garlic is the primary flavoring (such as aioli).

MAKE MINCING EASY AND EVEN WITH A PRESS

Squeezing a clove of garlic in a press isn't just the fastest way to mince garlic; it also produces a particularly fine, uniform result that cooks evenly and distributes nicely throughout a dish—factors that add up to balanced garlic flavor. Our favorite press, from Kuhn Rikon, offers sturdy stainless-steel construction and comfortable handles that make the job especially easy.

PEEL GARLIC THE FAST, EASY WAY

To remove the outer papery skin of a garlic head, place the head in a 2-cup wide-mouth Mason jar, screw on the lid, and vigorously shake the jar for 30 seconds. Pour out the cloves and inspect them. If any still have skins, put them back in the jar and repeat.

TAKE ADVANTAGE OF PREPEELED CLOVES

If you go through a lot of garlic, using prepeeled cloves is a convenient alternative to skinning fresh ones yourself, and their flavor can be perfectly acceptable. Just be wary of their shelf life, which tends to be shorter than that of a head of garlic properly stored in a cool, dry place (about two weeks versus several weeks, in our testing). Also make sure to carefully inspect what you buy: The cloves should look firm and white with a matte finish; avoid any that look yellow or shriveled or give off an overly pungent aroma.

DON'T DIS GARLIC POWDER

Garlic powder gets a bad rap—but it shouldn't. The sandy powder (which is simply dehydrated ground garlic) isn't meant to be a replacement for the fresh stuff but rather a toasty, subtly sweet-savory seasoning that works well in concert with fresh garlic as well as alongside other spices in everything from dry rubs to chili, mashed potatoes, and garlic bread.

The trick to using garlic powder effectively is hydrating it before cooking, which can be done by mixing it with a little water before adding it to a dish or will happen naturally when it's applied to wet foods such as raw meat. Hydrating the powder before heating "awakens" the flavor-producing enzyme, alliinase, which goes dormant when producers dry the garlic (drying happens below 140 degrees to avoid deactivating the alliinase), whereas heating the powder before hydrating it would kill the enzyme—and any potential for garlic flavor.

BUILD YOUR BEST BURGER

Of course, top-quality proteins handled with care make for the tastiest, juiciest patties. But it's when you refine every other component—the bun, the cheese, the fixings—that you really up your burger game.

THE CHEESE

Unless you're topping a burger with crumbled feta or blue cheese or slathering on a soft spread such as pimento cheese, the biggest consideration for cheeseburger cheese is meltability. These simple tips will ensure perfectly gooey results.

PICK A GOOD MELTER

Relatively young cheeses such as Monterey Jack, Colby, Swiss, Havarti, and mild cheddar melt smoothly because they contain plenty of moisture that helps them "flow" and because their casein protein matrix is relatively loose and flexible, allowing the cheese to melt with only minimal heat so that its fat doesn't separate and turn greasy.

SHRED BLOCK CHEESE

At home, it's hard to slice cheese as thin as a commercially sliced product. Shredding on the large holes of a box grater is the best option if you're working with block cheese. (To prevent a semifirm cheese such as Monterey Jack from smearing on or clogging the grater, firm up the block by freezing it for 30 minutes before shredding.)

TIME THE MELT

Don't add cheese until the burgers are nearly done—the patties should have 2 minutes to go on the grill or 90 seconds on the stovetop.

TRAP THE HEAT

To help cheese melt quickly and evenly, cover grilled burgers with an overturned disposable aluminum roasting pan and stovetop burgers with a lid.

THE BUN

A good bun should be soft and fresh-tasting and support a thick, juicy burger without falling apart. There's a perfect style for every patty, and supermarkets offer a good range of options. But for the ultimate experience, we like to make our own. It's fun and satisfying, and a fresh-baked bun will immeasurably improve the whole package.

POTATO BUNS

Potato starch soaks up loads of water and makes the crumb exceptionally soft and moist. Martin's is our favorite brand.

BEST FOR: Thinner, fast food–style patties

BRIOCHE BUNS

Rich with butter and eggs, the crumb is tender and easy to bite through but sturdy enough to soak up flavorful meat juices without falling apart.

BEST FOR: Thick, juicy patties

KAISER ROLLS

These attractive twisted rolls boast a thin, crisp, golden exterior and a sturdy, faintly sweet crumb.

BEST FOR: Hefty, heavily topped patties that need a sturdy bun to stay intact

WHY AND HOW WE TOAST BURGER BUNS

Toasting provides some additional flavor and exterior crispness, but the primary (albeit lesser-known) benefit is that it softens the interior of the bun, turning it plush and moist. Why? Heating bread to at least 140 degrees temporarily reverses retrogradation, the process that stales bread and other starch-based foods, by releasing water that gradually gets trapped within the crumb's starch crystals as the bread sits. Once it's released, that water is then available to hydrate the crumb, making it taste more moist and fresh. Here's how we toast indoors and out.

OVEN Broil split buns 6 inches from broiler element until lightly toasted.

GRILL While burgers rest, grill split buns until lightly toasted, 30 to 60 seconds.

LETTUCE, ONION, TOMATO

Treating these basics just right allows their freshness, acidity, and bite to come through.

LETTUCE

CHOOSE WISELY: Shredded iceberg offers fresh crunch; Bibb, ultratenderness; and red and green leaf, a combination of structure and tenderness.

DRY THOROUGHLY: After washing the lettuce, spin or pat it dry to remove any excess moisture that could sog out the bun.

ONION

SOAK BRIEFLY: Soaking thinly sliced onion in ice water for 15 minutes will mellow its bite without dulling its crunch. Blot dry before use.

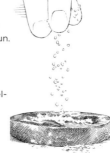

TOMATO

DON'T FORGET THE SALT: Seasoning tomato slices makes their bright flavor pop. Salt just before serving to avoid drawing out moisture.

Toppings have the power to determine the profile of the whole burger package, and ketchup and mustard are just the beginning. Make yours smoky, crispy, tangy—or all of the above. The key is choosing a balance of flavors and textures.

Microwave-Fried Shallots

(CRISPY)

SERVES 4 TO 6
TOTAL TIME: 25 MINUTES

Combine **3 thinly sliced shallots** and **½ cup vegetable oil** in medium bowl. Microwave for 5 minutes. Stir and continue to microwave 2 minutes longer. Repeat stirring and microwaving in 2-minute increments until beginning to brown (4 to 6 minutes). Repeat stirring and microwaving in 30-second increments until deep golden brown (30 seconds to 2 minutes). Using slotted spoon, transfer shallots to paper towel–lined plate; season with salt to taste. Let drain and crisp, about 5 minutes.

Spicy Red Pepper Relish

(TANGY)

SERVES 16 (MAKES ABOUT 1 CUP)
TOTAL TIME: 40 MINUTES, PLUS 20 MINUTES COOLING

1. Stem, seed, and cut **2 red bell peppers** and **2 jalapeño chiles** into 1-inch pieces. Pulse bell peppers and jalapeños in food processor until chopped into ¼-inch pieces, 8 to 10 pulses; transfer to large bowl. Pulse **1 small chopped onion and 3 peeled garlic cloves** in now-empty processor until chopped into ¼-inch pieces, about 10 pulses; transfer to bowl with bell pepper mixture.

2. Bring **½ cup distilled white vinegar, ½ cup sugar, 1 teaspoon yellow mustard seeds, and ½ teaspoon table salt** to boil in Dutch oven over medium-high heat. Add vegetable mixture; reduce heat to medium; and simmer, stirring occasionally, until mixture is thickened, 15 to 18 minutes.

3. Let relish cool slightly, then transfer to airtight container and let cool completely. (Relish can be refrigerated for up to 3 months; flavor will deepen over time.)

Grilled Shiitake Mushroom Topping

(SAVORY)

SERVES 4 (MAKES ABOUT ¾ CUP) TOTAL TIME: 1 HOUR

1. Combine **2 tablespoons sour cream, 2 tablespoons mayonnaise, 2 tablespoons buttermilk, 1 tablespoon cider vinegar, 1 tablespoon minced fresh chives, 2 teaspoons Dijon mustard, ½ teaspoon table salt, ¼ teaspoon sugar, and ⅛ teaspoon pepper** in medium bowl. Set aside.

2. Toss **8 ounces shiitake mushrooms,** stemmed, with **2 tablespoons vegetable oil** in large bowl. Grill mushrooms over hot fire until lightly charred and softened, 2 to 4 minutes per side. Return to bowl and let cool for 5 minutes. Slice mushrooms thin, then transfer to bowl with sour cream mixture. Toss to combine and season with salt and pepper to taste.

Classic Burger Sauce

(CREAMY)

SERVES 6 (MAKES ABOUT ¼ CUP) TOTAL TIME: 10 MINUTES

Whisk together **2 tablespoons mayonnaise, 1 tablespoon ketchup, ½ teaspoon sweet pickle relish, ½ teaspoon sugar, ½ teaspoon distilled white vinegar, and ¼ teaspoon pepper** in small bowl.

Peppered Bacon

(SMOKY)

SERVES 4 TOTAL TIME: 35 MINUTES

Adjust oven rack to middle position and heat oven to 375 degrees. Arrange **6 slices bacon** on rimmed baking sheet and sprinkle with **2 teaspoons coarsely ground pepper.** Place second rimmed baking sheet on top of bacon and bake until bacon is crispy, 15 to 20 minutes. Transfer bacon to paper towel–lined plate and let cool. Cut bacon in half crosswise.

Caramelized Onion Jam

(SWEET)

SERVES 16 (MAKES ABOUT 1 CUP) TOTAL TIME: 50 MINUTES, PLUS 20 MINUTES COOLING

1. Heat **3 tablespoons extra-virgin olive oil** in Dutch oven over medium-high heat until shimmering. Add **1¼ pounds halved and thinly sliced onions, 1 bay leaf, ½ teaspoon minced fresh rosemary, ½ teaspoon table salt, and ¼ teaspoon pepper.** Cover and cook, stirring occasionally, until onions have softened, about 10 minutes.

2. Stir in **2 smashed and peeled garlic cloves.** Reduce heat to medium-low and cook, uncovered, scraping up any browned bits, until onions are golden brown, about 15 minutes.

3. Stir in **¼ cup balsamic vinegar, ¼ cup water, and 2 tablespoons sugar,** scraping up any browned bits. Increase heat to medium-high and simmer until mixture is thickened and heat-resistant rubber spatula or wooden spoon leaves distinct trail when dragged across bottom of pot, about 2 minutes.

4. Discard bay leaf. Transfer onion mixture to food processor and pulse to jam-like consistency, about 5 pulses. Transfer onion jam to airtight container and let cool completely. (Onion jam can be refrigerated for up to 4 days.)

MEAT-FREE BURGERS

A meatier burger. A perfect burger. A meat lover's burger. This doesn't sound like marketing for vegetarian burgers, but it is. There's a seismic shift happening in the world of vegetarian, or plant-based, "meat." Companies are shaking their health-store reputations and targeting consumers who like meat but want to eat less of it. More products than ever before are intended to mimic the taste, texture, and experience of eating meat. We wanted to know: Does the next generation of meat-free burgers taste good? And can they really appeal to both vegetarians and meat eaters? To find out, we purchased eight products that were clearly positioned as meat-like. Six were sold as preformed burger patties, and two were "ground" products that we shaped into burgers ourselves. (For consistency, we'll refer to all the products in our lineup as "burgers" because that's how we ate them.) We cooked the burgers on the stovetop and held two blind tastings: plain, and on buns with ketchup and lettuce. Prices shown were paid in Boston-area supermarkets. Scores were averaged, and the top four products are listed below in order of preference.

HIGHLY RECOMMENDED

IMPOSSIBLE FOODS Impossible Burger
PRICE: $10.39 for 12 oz ($0.87 per oz)
FORMAT: Ground
FAT: 14 g SUGAR: < 1 g
SODIUM: 370 mg PROTEIN: 19 g
INGREDIENTS: Water, soy protein concentrate, coconut oil, sunflower oil, natural flavors, 2% or less of: potato protein, methylcellulose, yeast extract, cultured dextrose, food starch modified, soy leghemoglobin, salt, soy protein isolate, mixed tocopherols (vitamin E), zinc gluconate, thiamine hydrochloride (vitamin B1), sodium ascorbate (vitamin C), niacin, pyridoxine hydrochloride (vitamin B6), riboflavin (vitamin B2), vitamin B2
COMMENTS: This product's flavor, texture, and appearance are remarkably similar to ground beef. Its mineral-y flavor and blood-red color are due largely to the company's pioneering use of heme protein from soy leghemoglobin, an iron-containing molecule naturally found in soy roots and made on a large scale by inserting the DNA from the roots into yeast and fermenting it. The coarse texture and bits of solid coconut oil resemble beef flecked with fat. One taster noted: "If I didn't know that this was made from plants, I would think it was meat."

RECOMMENDED

BEYOND MEAT Beyond Burger
PRICE: $5.99 for 8 oz ($0.75 per oz)
FORMAT: Patties
FAT: 18 g SUGAR: 0 g
SODIUM: 350 mg PROTEIN: 20 g
INGREDIENTS: Water, pea protein isolate, expeller-pressed canola oil, refined coconut oil, rice protein, natural flavors, cocoa butter, mung bean protein, methylcellulose, potato starch, apple extract, salt, potassium chloride, vinegar, lemon juice concentrate, sunflower lecithin, pomegranate fruit powder, beet juice extract (for color)
COMMENTS: These patties had a slightly more coarse, irregular texture than the bulk ground product sold by the same brand. Tasters liked that their interiors "really resembled ground beef" and that their exteriors developed good crunch. Their flavor was rich and savory, but not quite as impressively so as the Impossible Burger. The cooked burgers were slightly purple, likely due to the beet juice extract added for coloring. That said, they are still an excellent meat-free option likely to satisfy vegetarians and meat eaters alike.

RECOMMENDED *(continued)*

BEYOND MEAT Beyond Beef
PRICE: $9.99 for 16 oz ($0.62 per oz)
FORMAT: Ground
FAT: 18 g SUGAR: 0 g
SODIUM: 390 mg PROTEIN: 20 g
INGREDIENTS: Water, pea protein isolate, expeller-pressed canola oil, refined coconut oil, rice protein, natural flavors, cocoa butter, mung bean protein, methylcellulose, potato starch, apple extract, salt, potassium chloride, vinegar, lemon juice concentrate, sunflower lecithin, pomegranate fruit powder, beet juice extract (for color)
COMMENTS: Although we preferred the slightly more coarse, irregular texture of this company's preformed burger patties, we very much enjoyed this bulk product as well. When formed into burgers and cooked, it had a texture that was still "meat-like," and it developed a "nice crunchy crust on the exterior." Like the preformed burgers made by the same company, the burgers made with this product retained a slightly purple hue when cooked. It lacked the distinctly iron-y, beefy flavor of the Impossible Burger, but it was satisfyingly "meaty" in flavor.

RECOMMENDED WITH RESERVATIONS

QUORN MEATLESS Gourmet Burgers
PRICE: 4.99 for 11.3 oz ($0.44 per oz)
FORMAT: Patties
FAT: 10 g SUGAR: 1 g
SODIUM: 649 mg PROTEIN: 14 g
INGREDIENTS: Mycoprotein (37%), egg white, wheat flour, onion, palm oil, canola oil, milk protein concentrate, contains 2% or less of natural flavor, roasted barley malt extract, salt, maltodextrin, dextrose, calcium chloride, calcium acetate, potassium chloride, citric acid, sugar, potato dextrin, yeast, coconut oil, black pepper
COMMENTS: These burgers were packed with sweet, savory, salty flavor. Some tasters thought they were very satisfying, but others found their intensity overwhelming, comparing the flavor to such packaged foods as barbecue potato chips and beef jerky. It's likely the company used a generous amount of malt extract and yeast, which amp up the umami, or savory, quality of foods. The texture of the burgers was softer and smoother than our favorites. This product, which contains egg white, is vegetarian but not vegan.

TOASTED SESAME OIL

We love toasted sesame oil in the test kitchen. Just a teaspoon or two adds distinctive toasty, nutty, roasted flavor to various recipes, from meats to vegetables to salads and stir-fries. Because toasted sesame oil is such an important element in so many of our recipes, we bought eight top-selling products, priced from about $0.40 to about $1.60 per ounce, to discover which tasted best. Twenty-one America's Test Kitchen staffers sampled them in two blind tastings, first plain and then in Rice Salad with Peas and Mushrooms. We were surprised by how much the oils differed in taste. Tasters described flavors that ranged from "nutty, toasty, tasty," and "a touch smoky," with an "almost oaky or bourbon quality," to "a bit too delicate" or, worse, "fishy" and "too intense." The lowest-ranked oils had stronger off-flavors that persisted in the rice salad, leaving acrid, bitter impressions with our tasters. Because we add toasted sesame oil specifically for its flavor, whether it's in a simple dressing or dipping sauce or in another application where it is not cooked, we preferred oils that tasted great both plain and in a recipe. Prices shown were paid in Boston-area supermarkets. Scores were averaged, and the top six products are listed below in order of preference.

RECOMMENDED

OTTOGI Premium Roasted Sesame Oil
PRICE: $11.99 for 10.82 oz ($1.11 per oz)
COUNTRY OF ORIGIN: China
COMMENTS: With a "much more nutty, almost roasted-peanut flavor" than other samples, this oil had "strong sesame flavor, with a tahini-like aroma" and was "not bitter or burnt"-tasting, whether we tried it plain or in rice salad. With "lovely complexity," it struck tasters as "buttery," with "gorgeous," "round" flavor and "golden color." "OMG, so sweet and nutty and flavorful I could drink a whole cup of this," one taster raved. "I found myself going back for a few bites," another agreed. We appreciate that it is sold in a light-blocking, nonreactive amber glass bottle that protects the oil's fresh flavor.

DYNASTY Premium Sesame Oil (100% Pure)
PRICE: $5.62 for 5 oz ($1.12 per oz)
COUNTRY OF ORIGIN: Japan
COMMENTS: "Very roasted and toasted in flavor," this oil "definitely tastes like sesame" and is "slightly bitter" with a "nice aroma." It was "one of the more palatable stronger-flavored ones." In rice salad it had "a nice toasty flavor" and was "very bold-tasting." One taster summed it up: "Very nice level of toasting and flavor. I wanted to love this the most, but it had just a hint of a bitter taste in the back that made me dock points."

KADOYA Pure Sesame Oil
PRICE: $8.97 for 11 oz ($0.82 per oz)
COUNTRY OF ORIGIN: Japan
COMMENTS: "Nutty, toasty, tasty. The sesame flavor really shines," wrote one taster, and many others agreed, finding it "a touch smoky," with an "almost oaky or bourbon quality" and a "slightly bitter finish." A few found it slightly too "delicate" or "muted." The "flavor was nice, just not strong enough," one taster concluded.

RECOMMENDED (continued)

LA TOURANGELLE Toasted Sesame Oil
PRICE: $6.99 for 8.45 oz ($0.83 per oz)
COUNTRY OF ORIGIN: Japan, Mexico
COMMENTS: Tasters reported that this oil had "delicate, elegant, toasted sesame flavor." It was "light, almost sweet, buttery," and "a bit too delicate." "I'm missing some toasted flavor," one taster noted. ("What sesame oil?" one quipped when tasting the rice salad.) But overall most tasters approved this sample as "mild, creamy, and rich." We liked that this oil is sold in a nonreactive, light-blocking steel tin that helps preserve fresh flavor.

IMPERIAL DRAGON 100% Pure Sesame Oil
PRICE: $7.86 for 5 oz ($1.57 per oz)
COUNTRY OF ORIGIN: Japan
COMMENTS: Featuring a "caramelly coffee aroma with nutty bitter tastes that are immediately apparent," this "smoky," "very toasty, and thick" oil was "a little too severe," "way too bitter," and "acrid" when tasted plain, but when served in the rice salad with mushrooms and peas, it was another story: "Fantastic! Tasted the sesame in every bite but not in a bitter way. Truly delicious flavor." This sample was "a standout," with "a bold, nutty smell. It was incredibly flavorful and really tasty."

LEE KUM KEE Pure Sesame Oil
PRICE: $5.99 for 15 oz ($0.40 per oz)
COUNTRY OF ORIGIN: Confidential
COMMENTS: Tasters generally approved of this oil, but some had mixed reactions, commenting: "a bit too delicate but I still like it." "Pretty subtle," with a "pleasant nuttiness," this oil was "toasty, nutty but not too much so." It lost points for some "plasticky" off-flavors. In rice salad, it was "pleasant" but a bit too subtle: "I could hardly taste the sesame flavor at all; it was overpowered by the rice," said one taster, and another remarked that they "wish this was toasted a bit more."

BONE BROTH

Once a niche offering, bone broth has become more mainstream. Boxed versions now sit alongside traditional broths in the supermarket soup aisle. Proponents of bone broth claim that it is a nutritional superfood. These claims mostly center on how the longer simmering time of bone broth extracts more protein and nutrients from the bones than the shorter simmering time of traditional stock. However, little scientific research has been done into the actual health benefits of bone broth. Many manufacturers use the long cooking time and purported health benefits of bone broth to justify making it more expensive than regular chicken stock. We've seen a wide range in the pricing of supermarket bone broth—from prices that are on par with our favorite chicken stock (about $0.10 per ounce) to up to four times that amount. What are you getting for the extra money, and, from a cooking perspective, is bone broth really all that different from regular stock? To find out, we tasted five top-selling supermarket chicken bone broths, priced from about $0.10 to about $0.50 per ounce. Since manufacturers suggest heating it before sipping it, we tried all the broths warmed and served plain in a blind tasting with 21 tasters. We then used the top-rated bone broth in recipes that call for chicken stock to better understand how (and if) bone broth can be used for cooking. Our takeaway: Bone broth is great for sipping on its own or using to cook and season simple foods such as rice, but for most recipes we prefer regular chicken stock, which provides a more neutral base for building more complex, nuanced flavors. Prices shown were paid in Boston-area supermarkets. Scores were averaged, and products appear below in order of preference.

HIGHLY RECOMMENDED

COLLEGE INN Chicken Bone Broth
PRICE: $3.99 for 32 oz ($0.12 per oz)
SODIUM: 560 mg
PROTEIN: 10 g
INGREDIENTS: Chicken bone broth, contains less than 2% of the following: salt, natural flavors, vegetable stock (concentrates of onion, celery root and carrot), sugar, black pepper, turmeric, bay leaf
COMMENTS: This broth was "rich" and "well seasoned," with a "meaty," "umami" flavor and a "hint of black pepper." Though it had the highest sodium level per serving of all the broths we tasted, it tasted "balanced" and "gently salted." Tasters also remarked that this product had a "nice brightness" and "freshness" that was "very homemade-tasting."

SWANSON Chicken Bone Broth
PRICE: $4.29 for 32 oz ($0.13 per oz)
SODIUM: 350 mg
PROTEIN: 8 g
INGREDIENTS: Chicken stock, carrots, cabbage, celery, onions, salt, tomato paste, parsley, thyme
COMMENTS: This product, from the brand that makes our favorite regular chicken stock, was "deeply savory," with "good chicken flavor." It had a "clean," slightly "herbal" flavor with "hints of carrots and stewed vegetables." While most tasters thought it was "well seasoned," a few "wished it had a bit more salt."

RECOMMENDED

KITCHEN BASICS Chicken Bone Broth
PRICE: $5.49 for 32 oz ($0.17 per oz)
SODIUM: 380 mg
PROTEIN: 10 g
INGREDIENTS: Chicken broth (made from bones), mirepoix (onion, carrots, celery), sea salt & spice and herbs (black pepper, bay leaf, thyme)
COMMENTS: This broth was "savory" and "vegetal," with a "mild" chicken flavor. Tasters liked its "earthy" notes of celery and onion, though a few noted that it was short on chicken flavor. We also thought that, like other products, it "could use more salt."

NOT RECOMMENDED

IMAGINE Chicken Bone Broth
PRICE: $4.32 for 32 oz ($0.14 per oz)
SODIUM: 300 mg
PROTEIN: 9 g
INGREDIENTS: Chicken stock, organic chicken flavor (contains organic chicken), sea salt
COMMENTS: Although this broth had the shortest ingredient list of all the ones we tried, with no added vegetables or spices, most tasters thought it was "hard to discern any chicken flavor" from this product. Many thought it tasted "overly roasted" and "bland," like "dry chicken." Others picked up on a "bitter," almost "burnt" aftertaste, likely from the process of roasting the bones before boiling.

KETTLE & FIRE Chicken Bone Broth
PRICE: $6.99 for 16.9 oz ($0.41 per oz)
SODIUM: 240 mg
PROTEIN: 10 g
INGREDIENTS: Chicken bones and feet, celery, roasted poblano pepper, green pepper, onions, carrots, garlic, scallions, tomato puree, herbs, spices, sea salt, apple cider vinegar
COMMENTS: A "lack of salt" (it had the least sodium of all the products we tried) was just the start of this broth's issues. Tasters thought it was "lacking in chicken flavor" and "overpowered by seasoning ingredients" such as apple cider vinegar and poblano and green peppers, which made the liquid taste "tart" and "tannic," like "bad vegetables." A number of tasters remarked that it tasted overwhelmingly of "old oregano" or "pizza," thanks to the unusual addition of tomato puree.

SHREDDED SHARP CHEDDAR CHEESE

In the test kitchen, we've long sung the praises of shredding cheese by hand (or in a food processor). Preshredded cheese is coated with additives such as cellulose or cornstarch to keep it from clumping, which can affect its mouthfeel and meltability. Still, preshredded cheese is an incredible shortcut: It saves time, it saves your hands from wrestling with a sharp grater, and it saves you from extra cleanup. Could we find a good shredded cheddar? We chose six shredded cheddar cheeses, priced from about $3.00 to about $4.00 per 8-ounce bag. We focused on sharp cheddar, which is the kind of cheddar we call for most often in our recipes. Three of the products were orange, and three were white; all were "traditional," "thick," or "farmstyle" cut—we didn't include any "fancy cut" or "finely" shredded cheeses, since thicker shreds most closely resemble what we get from shredding by hand or in the food processor. We sampled the six products plain and melted atop nachos. So when should you opt for preshredded cheese? If you have the time, we still recommend shredding block cheese by hand or in a food processor for the best results. However, we were able to recommend all the products we tried, so for dishes where the cheese will be melted or combined with other ingredients, we think the shredded stuff makes a perfectly acceptable shortcut. Prices shown were paid in Boston-area supermarkets. Scores were averaged, and the top five products are listed below in order of preference.

RECOMMENDED

KRAFT Sharp Cheddar Shredded Natural Cheese
PRICE: $3.29 for 8 oz ($0.41 per oz)
COLOR: Orange
SODIUM: 170 mg
INGREDIENTS: Cheddar cheese (pasteurized milk, cheese culture, salt, enzymes, annatto [color]), modified cornstarch added to prevent caking, natamycin (a natural mold inhibitor)
COMMENTS: Our favorite cheese was "bright" and "sweet," with a subtle sharpness and a hint of "tang." The cheese melted easily and was "mellow" and "mild" atop nachos. When tasted plain, the strands had a slightly dry texture.

CRYSTAL FARMS Shredded Wisconsin Sharp Cheddar Cheese
PRICE: $3.49 for 8 oz ($0.44 per oz)
COLOR: White
SODIUM: 170 mg
INGREDIENTS: Cheddar cheese (cultured pasteurized milk, salt, enzymes), potato starch, starch and powdered cellulose to prevent caking, natamycin (mold inhibitor)
COMMENTS: These long, thin white shreds were subtly sharp and slightly sweet. Despite containing three types of anticaking agents, this cheese felt a little "tacky" and "sticky" in our fingers and clumped a bit in the bag. When melted, the cheese was "mellow" and "sweet," with just a hint of sharpness.

KRAFT Sharp White Cheddar Shredded Natural Cheese
PRICE: $3.29 for 8 oz ($0.41 per oz)
COLOR: White
SODIUM: 170 mg
INGREDIENTS: Cheddar cheese (pasteurized milk, cheese culture, salt, enzymes), modified cornstarch added to prevent caking, natamycin (a natural mold inhibitor)
COMMENTS: The white version of our favorite product by Kraft, this cheese was similar in flavor, with the same "long, thin" strands. Like the orange version, this product uses cornstarch to prevent caking. As a result, it was a bit dry when tasted plain.

RECOMMENDED *(continued)*

SARGENTO Shredded Sharp Cheddar Cheese Traditional Cut
PRICE: $3.29 for 8 oz ($0.41 per oz)
COLOR: Orange
SODIUM: 180 mg
INGREDIENTS: Cheddar cheese (pasteurized milk, cheese culture, salt, enzymes, annatto [vegetable color]), potato starch (to prevent caking), powdered cellulose (to prevent caking), natamycin (a natural mold inhibitor)
COMMENTS: These "chunky" orange shreds were "thick" and "hearty," with an appearance that reminded tasters of "hand-shredded" cheese. Though the chunkier shreds were a bit harder to sprinkle on nachos, they tasted pleasantly "milky" and "slightly sweet" and melted easily. As with most of the products, the addition of cellulose and potato starch left a "chalky" texture when the cheese was eaten plain.

TILLAMOOK Farmstyle Cut Sharp Cheddar Shredded Cheese
PRICE: $3.19 for 8 oz ($0.40 per oz)
COLOR: Orange
SODIUM: 200 mg
INGREDIENTS: Sharp cheddar cheese (cultured milk, salt, enzymes, annatto [color]), potato starch (added to prevent caking), natamycin (natural mold inhibitor)
COMMENTS: Named "farmstyle cut" after the short, "thick" shreds reminiscent of cheese shredded off the block, these "chunky" strips were "mellow" and a bit "tangy" both when eaten plain and when melted. While they were a tad "dry" when tasted plain, they were perfectly "melty" atop nachos. We also found the thicker shreds a bit more difficult to sprinkle when making nachos.

JARRED MEDIUM SALSA

We always have a jar (or two) of salsa in our pantries for when we need a quick snack or condiment. We especially like medium-heat salsas because they provide bold flavor without scorching our palates. There are tons of options at the store, and new brands have entered the market since we last tasted them. We wondered which medium-heat salsa should become our new go-to. We first identified 10 top-selling, nationally available salsa brands. Many of these brands make multiple versions of medium-heat salsa, so we rounded up all the options from each company, tasted them against each other, and included our favorite from each brand in our final lineup of 10 salsas. A group of 21 staffers sampled the salsas plain and with our favorite tortilla chips and compared their flavors, textures, and heat levels. Even though all the salsas we tasted were labeled as medium heat, some were considerably spicier than others. The flavors of the salsas also varied a lot. The most important variables were the type of pepper used in the salsa, the amount of sodium per serving, and the presence of additional spices or seasonings. The textures of the salsas in our lineup also varied, from thick and chunky to pureed. Some were almost saucy, like marinara. Fortunately, we found something we liked in each of the salsas we tasted. Instead of picking a favorite, we've listed tasting notes for each one so that you can find the salsa that's right for you. Products are ordered from hottest to mildest. Prices shown were paid in Boston-area supermarkets.

RECOMMENDED

MATEO'S Gourmet Medium Salsa
PRICE: $5.99 for 16 oz
PEPPER TYPE: Jalapeño
AMOUNT OF LIQUID SHED: ¾ cup
BUY THIS IF YOU LIKE: A pureed salsa with intense heat and strong garlic and cumin flavors

GREEN MOUNTAIN Gringo Medium Salsa
PRICE: $4.99 for 16 oz
PEPPER TYPE: Jalapeño, pasilla
AMOUNT OF LIQUID SHED: ⅔ cup
BUY THIS IF YOU LIKE: A thinner salsa that starts sweet and has a strong heat that builds

PACE Medium Chunky Salsa
PRICE: $2.99 for 16 oz
PEPPER TYPE: Jalapeño
AMOUNT OF LIQUID SHED: ½ cup
BUY THIS IF YOU LIKE: Salsa with crunchy pieces ofvegetables and a good amount of heat

CHI-CHI'S Thick & Chunky Salsa Medium
PRICE: $2.99 for 16 oz
PEPPER TYPE: Jalapeño
AMOUNT OF LIQUID SHED: ½ cup
BUY THIS IF YOU LIKE: Chunky salsa with a bit of sweetness and bright tomato flavor

TOSTITOS Chunky Salsa (Medium)
PRICE: $3.79 for 15.5 oz
PEPPER TYPE: Jalapeño
AMOUNT OF LIQUID SHED: ½ cup
BUY THIS IF YOU LIKE: A thick salsa with medium-diced vegetables and moderate heat

RECOMMENDED *(continued)*

LA VICTORIA Thick 'n Chunky Salsa Medium
PRICE: $3.49 for 16 oz
PEPPER TYPES: Jalapeño, green chiles
AMOUNT OF LIQUID SHED: ½ cup
BUY THIS IF YOU LIKE: A thicker, marinara-like salsa with a touch of smoke and mild heat

ON THE BORDER Original Salsa, Medium
PRICE: $2.99 for 16 oz
TYPE OF PEPPER: Jalapeño
AMOUNT OF LIQUID SHED: ⅔ cup
BUY THIS IF YOU LIKE: A thinner salsa and a sweet-and-smoky flavor combination

FRONTERA Double Roasted Gourmet Tomato Salsa
PRICE: $4.29 for 16 oz
PEPPER TYPE: Fire-roasted jalapeño
AMOUNT OF LIQUID SHED: Slightly less than 1 cup
BUY THIS IF YOU LIKE: A thin salsa with roasted, smoky, charred flavors

NEWMAN'S OWN Medium Salsa
PRICE: $2.99 for 16 oz
PEPPER TYPE: Green chili, green bell, red jalapeño, red bell
AMOUNT OF LIQUID SHED: ½ cup
BUY THIS IF YOU LIKE: A thick salsa with tender pieces of tomato and mild heat

HERDEZ Salsa Casera Medium
PRICE: $3.49 for 16 oz
PEPPER TYPE: Chile
AMOUNT OF LIQUID SHED: Slightly more than 1 cup
BUY THIS IF YOU LIKE: A thinner salsa that tastes mild and fresh like pico de gallo

REMOTE-PROBE THERMOMETERS

Babysitting food can be a real slog; remote-probe thermometers untether you from the oven or grill and let you monitor your food's temperature from afar. There are two types: pager-style thermometers, which send their temperature data via radio frequency from the base to a handheld monitor, and smartphone-connected thermometers, which rely on Wi-Fi or Bluetooth to transmit temperature data from the base to an app on your phone. To find the best remote-probe thermometer, we tested a mix of models, including two pager-style and five smartphone-connected models. We used each to monitor pork butt on a gas grill for 4 hours, hamburgers quickly cooked on the stovetop, and whole chickens roasted on a charcoal grill for 1 hour. During each test we walked up to 1,000 feet from the probes, up and down stairs, and behind walls, frequently checking the connection. We also used them in the dark, in the rain, and in an area with limited cell service. The prices listed in this chart are based on shopping at online retailers and will vary. The top three thermometers are listed below in order of preference.

HIGHLY RECOMMENDED	PERFORMANCE	TESTERS' COMMENTS

THERMOWORKS Smoke 2-Channel Alarm
PRICE: $99
MODEL NUMBER: TX-1300-XX (last two digits depend on color of unit)
RANGE: 300 ft
STYLE: Pager
CONNECTION: Radio
POWER TYPE: AA batteries
NUMBER OF PROBES: 2
TEMPERATURE RANGE: –58°F to 572°F
TIME TO TRANSMIT TEMPERATURE TO BASE: 8 sec
TIME TO TRANSMIT TEMPERATURE TO RECEIVER: 13 sec

SETUP ★★★
ACCURACY ★★★
EASE OF USE ★★★
CONNECTIVITY ★★½

Right out of the box the base paired automatically with the receiver, making it ready to use in seconds. Both the base and the receiver had bright, clear displays that could be read easily in both bright and dim light; both also have backlights for operating in the dark. The unit maintains a connection for up to 300 feet and alerts you when you go out of range. When you go back into range, it automatically reconnects, and its alarms were loud and easy to set. While we used it primarily for grilling, this thermometer can read up to 572 degrees and transmits temperature data from the probe to the base in 8 seconds, which also makes it useful for candy making and deep frying. It can be made to work with a smartphone by purchasing the Smoke Gateway ($89); however, setup was difficult and the app was glitchy.

RECOMMENDED

NUTRICHEF Bluetooth Wireless BBQ Grill Thermometer
PRICE: $43.99 **BEST BUY**
MODEL NUMBER: PWIRBBQ80
RANGE: 200 ft
STYLE: Smartphone-connected
CONNECTION: Bluetooth
POWER TYPE: AA batteries
NUMBER OF PROBES: Equipped with 2, can accommodate up to 6
TEMPERATURE RANGE: Up to 482°F
TIME TO TRANSMIT TEMPERATURE TO BASE: 5 sec
TIME TO TRANSMIT TEMPERATURE TO RECEIVER: 0 sec

SETUP ★★½
ACCURACY ★★★
EASE OF USE ★★★
CONNECTIVITY ★★

This smartphone-connected thermometer relies on Bluetooth, and its range maxes out at about 200 feet in open air—plenty of distance to cover most homes. The app and base both display the temperature output in large, clear numbers, and we found this model to be the easiest to pair with an app of all the smart models we tested. Its temperature readings were accurate to within 1 degree (it does not display decimals), it transmitted temperature readings from the probe to the app in 5 seconds, and its app was easy to use. It was also the least expensive of all the models we tried.

RECOMMENDED WITH RESERVATIONS

MEATER+
PRICE: $99
MODEL NUMBER: OSC-MT-MP01
RANGE: 165 ft
STYLE: Wireless smartphone-connected probe
CONNECTION: Bluetooth
POWER TYPE: Charging cable (AAA battery included)
NUMBER OF PROBES: 1
TEMPERATURE RANGE: Up to 527°F
TIME TO TRANSMIT TEMPERATURE TO BASE: n/a (no base)
TIME TO TRANSMIT TEMPERATURE TO RECEIVER: 24 sec

SETUP ★
ACCURACY ★★★
EASE OF USE ★★
CONNECTIVITY ★★

This probe doesn't have wires. Instead, the probe transmits temperature information directly to your phone via Bluetooth. However, you have to keep the charging base near both the probe and your phone, as it contains the Bluetooth transmitter. Pairing was relatively easy, though instructions were minimal and the device has to be charged for at least 4 hours before you can use it. Because it relies on Bluetooth (not Wi-Fi), we found the connection range was fairly limited—only about 165 feet. It did occasionally unpair with our phone when we went out of range, but it was easy enough to reconnect when we were back in range (though it was not always automatic). Overall, we found the wireless design incredibly easy to use, and it's a good option if you don't want to deal with replacing wires that get pinched in an oven or come in contact with a heat source and get fried.

12-INCH CERAMIC NONSTICK SKILLETS

Ceramic nonstick skillets promise to be as slick and reliable as the best regular nonstick skillet. Because manufacturers of Teflon and similar coatings have faced allegations that their coatings are dangerous for cooks and bad for the environment, ceramic pans are often marketed as safer, more environmentally friendly options. To find our favorite product, we purchased seven 12-inch ceramic nonstick skillets and subjected them to our standard battery of evaluations for nonstick cookware. We ran a test that's common in the cookware industry: cooking eggs in a dry skillet back-to-back, stopping either when they began to stick or when we had made 50 consecutive eggs. We did this at the beginning and at the end of testing so that we could see if the coatings deteriorated with use. In between those egg tests, we made stir-fries, frittatas, and fish to help us assess each pan's capacity, browning ability, and maneuverability. We also recruited three additional testers who were unfamiliar with these pans to use them to make sautéed peas. To test the durability of the skillets, we cut in them with a knife; heated them and then plunged them into ice water; and, finally, whacked them three times on a cement block. The prices listed in this chart are based on shopping at online retailers and will vary. The top five skillets are listed below in order of preference.

RECOMMENDED	PERFORMANCE	TESTERS' COMMENTS
GREENPAN Valencia Pro Hard Anodized Nonstick Frypan PRICE: $79.99 MODEL NUMBER: CC002679-001 WEIGHT: 2.60 lb OVENSAFE TO: 600°F INDUCTION COMPATIBLE: Yes COOKING SURFACE DIAMETER: 9½ in	CAPACITY ★★★ EASE OF USE ★★½ DURABILITY ★★ NONSTICK ABILITY ★★★	One of only two pans to pass our test of nonstick coating durability, this pan arrived slick and remained so throughout cooking and abuse tests. It also has a broad cooking surface, gently sloped walls, and a comfortable handle. Because it runs a little hotter than our favorite regular nonstick skillet, you may need to adjust the heat level or cooking time when following recipes. It became scratched when we cut in it.
KYOCERA Ceramic-Coated 12″ Nonstick Frypan PRICE: $40.98 `BEST BUY` MODEL NUMBER: CFP30BK WEIGHT: 2.65 lb OVENSAFE TO: 400°F INDUCTION COMPATIBLE: Yes COOKING SURFACE DIAMETER: 10 in	CAPACITY ★★★ EASE OF USE ★★½ DURABILITY ★★ NONSTICK ABILITY ★★★	This pan remained slick throughout testing and was one of only two pans to do so. However, it resembles a sauté pan more than it does a skillet. Because the sides are fairly tall and steep, it requires more care to slide out a frittata or angle a spatula under an egg or piece of fish. Like our winner, it has a comfortable handle, but the skillet feels a little heavy.

NOT RECOMMENDED		
CUISINART GreenGourmet Hard-Anodized Nonstick 12-Inch Open Skillet PRICE: $49.99 MODEL NUMBER: GG22-30 WEIGHT: 2.45 lb OVENSAFE TO: 400°F INDUCTION COMPATIBLE: No COOKING SURFACE DIAMETER: 9 in	CAPACITY ★★ EASE OF USE ★★½ DURABILITY ★★ NONSTICK ABILITY ★	Until this skillet failed the second dry-egg test after releasing just nine eggs, it was one of our favorites. It's shaped nicely, with a sufficiently broad cooking surface and gently sloped walls. The handle is especially comfortable. In our abuse tests, the cooking surface dented slightly.
BIALETTI Ceramic Pro 11.75 in Sauté Pan PRICE: $43.54 MODEL NUMBER: 07402 WEIGHT: 2.00 lb OVENSAFE TO: 400°F INDUCTION COMPATIBLE: No COOKING SURFACE DIAMETER: 8⅞ in	CAPACITY ★★ EASE OF USE ★★ DURABILITY ★★ NONSTICK ABILITY ★	This pan's cooking surface is a little smaller than our favorite model's, and we had to be careful not to spill when stirring food around. Out of the box, it was one of the slickest models in our lineup. Unfortunately, that slick surface deteriorated as we continued to cook in the pan, and the pan was able to cleanly release only 15 eggs at the end of our testing. It's fairly lightweight and became visibly dented when we whacked it on a hard surface.
TRAMONTINA Ceramic Deluxe 12 In. Fry Pan PRICE: $44.95 MODEL NUMBER: 90110/020DS WEIGHT: 2.95 lb OVENSAFE TO: 350°F INDUCTION COMPATIBLE: No COOKING SURFACE DIAMETER: 9½ in	CAPACITY ★★★ EASE OF USE ★½ DURABILITY ★★ NONSTICK ABILITY ★	The white cooking surface on this model made it easy for us to track browning and see when food started to stick. We also liked its overall size and shape as well as its broad and grippy handle. However, the surface became less slick with use. It was able to successfully turn out only 24 eggs in its second dry-egg test. The pan is not recommended for use in ovens hotter than 350 degrees, and it dented slightly in our abuse tests.

FOOD PROCESSORS

In the test kitchen, our longtime favorite food processor has been the Cuisinart Custom 14 Cup Food Processor, which has performed well for years, but with new competitors on the market, it was time to see if it was still the best choice. We bought a fresh copy of our previous favorite and six competing food processors with capacities from 9 to 14 cups and put them through more than a dozen tests, assessing how well they performed and how easy they were to handle, use, clean, and store. We also evaluated their capacities, noise levels, and the usefulness of their accessories. The prices listed in this chart are based on shopping at online retailers and will vary. The top three food processors are listed below in order of preference.

HIGHLY RECOMMENDED	PERFORMANCE	TESTERS' COMMENTS

CUISINART Custom 14 Cup Food Processor
PRICE: $145.99
MODEL NUMBER: DFP-14BKSY
ACCESSORIES: Chopping S-blade, slicing disk, shredding disk, spatula
BOWL CAPACITY: 14 cups
LIQUID MAXIMUM: 3 cups
WEIGHT OF BASE: 12.45 lb
DISHWASHER-SAFE: Yes

CLEANUP ★★★
EASE OF USE ★★★
PERFORMANCE ★★½

Our previous favorite still excelled with power; precision; and a compact, streamlined design, all at a moderate price. Its smooth, simple bowl and blade design make it easy to handle, monitor during use, and clean. Its unusual feed tube placement allows for increased bowl visibility. It comes with blades for chopping, shredding, and slicing that can all be stored inside the bowl. However, since we last tested it, the chopping blade was redesigned and leaves slightly bigger gaps between it and the bottom and side of the bowl, so it couldn't effectively incorporate egg yolks into single-batch mayonnaise. We didn't discover any other adverse effects from these slightly bigger gaps, which were still narrower than those of lower-ranked models. It did chop mirepoix uniformly and was one of only two models to give us perfectly green-colored yogurt in our dye test. Although it lacks a mini bowl for very small jobs, a double batch of mayonnaise worked well.

RECOMMENDED

BREVILLE Sous Chef 12 Plus Food Processor
PRICE: $329.95
MODEL NUMBER: BFP680BALUSC
ACCESSORIES: Chopping S-blade, slicer with 24 settings, reversible shredder, dough blade, storage case, spatula, mini bowl with small S-blade
LIQUID MAXIMUM: 4 cups
WEIGHT OF BASE: 13.85 lb
BOWL CAPACITIES: 12 cups, 2.5 cups
DISHWASHER-SAFE: Hand-wash only, don't soak bowl; can wash in dishwasher occasionally (top rack only), but will shorten life of plastic

CLEANUP ★★½
EASE OF USE ★★½
PERFORMANCE ★★½

This powerful processor handled nearly every challenge, doing especially well with mincing parsley and grinding beef. Its pulse function is strong, responsive, and short. We loved the ability to set precise thicknesses when slicing, the reversible shredding disk that offers two sizes, and the helpful indicators on the bowl for aligning the lid. It also comes with a 2.5-cup mini bowl for small jobs. While the main bowl has a leakproof gasket, the lid still slides on and off fairly easily, unlike other models with this feature. However, its mixing and chopping fell a bit short of ideal; with gaps between the blade tips and bowl walls, it left small streaks in our yogurt dye test, a bit of yolk in the mayo, and a few chunks of carrot in mirepoix. Its tall profile and accessories box took up storage space, and its bowl's gray tint made it a bit harder to monitor progress. We found its two-part S-blades trickier to handle and clean than other models' single-piece S-blades. Its bowl and parts are hand-wash only.

MAGIMIX Compact 4200 XL White 950 Watt Food Processor
PRICE: $349.93
MODEL NUMBER: 4200XL
ACCESSORIES: Large and small chopping S-blade, adjustable slicer with 24 settings, reversible shredder with 2-mm and 4-mm holes, dough blade, BlenderMix tool for processing creamy liquids, whisk, spatula, storage case, "midi" bowl, mini bowl
BOWL CAPACITIES: 14 cups, 12 cups, 6 cups
LIQUID MAXIMUM: 7 cups (must use Blendermix attachment to prevent leaks)
WEIGHT OF BASE: 14.35 lb
DISHWASHER-SAFE: Yes, but no drying cycle and avoid high temperatures. If washing by hand, do not soak in soapy water

CLEANUP ★★½
EASE OF USE ★★
PERFORMANCE ★★½

We loved the simple lines of this powerful machine by Magimix, whose parent company, Robot-Coupe, is known for its commercial processors. Its pulse duration is short, though slightly longer than that of the two highest-ranking models. It came with tons of accessories, including three sizes of bowls, a ringlike Blendermix tool to help puree without leaks, and a whisk to whip egg whites or cream, with options to buy more, including dicing, juicing, and spiralizing kits. While it sliced, kneaded dough, and processed pie dough perfectly, it did not perform other tasks quite as well—something we'd expect at this price. It left big streaks of color in the yogurt, several irregular pieces of ground meat in the hamburger, a handful of oversize carrot chunks in the mirepoix, and several larger pieces of cheese and carrots after shredding that we discovered in the bowl. We found it frustrating that the lid twists off in the same direction as the bowl so that they both swing loose with the lid still attached.

MULTICOOKERS

When we tested multicookers a few years ago, we named two products our winners. Recently, though, multicookers have undergone some big changes. For starters, manufacturers have added more features to boost the "multi" aspect of this small appliance's name, with some products purporting to sous vide, ferment, and even adjust their capabilities to accommodate cooking at high altitudes. With so many new and updated models, we wondered if our former favorites were still the best on the market. To find out, we selected 13 multicookers, including our previous winners. We included both 8-quart and 6-quart models because our multicooker recipes work equally well in both sizes. In each model, we pressure- and slow-cooked beef stew and Boston baked beans and made white rice. We also evaluated the multicookers' searing and sautéing capabilities, ease of use, and cleanup. The prices listed in this chart are based on shopping at online retailers and will vary. The top three multicookers are listed below in order of preference.

HIGHLY RECOMMENDED	PERFORMANCE	TESTERS' COMMENTS
INSTANT POT Duo Evo Plus 9-in-1 Electric Pressure Cooker, 8-QT **PRICE:** $139.95 **MODEL NUMBER:** Instant Pot 8 Quart Duo Evo Plus **CAPACITY:** 8 qt **SETTINGS:** Pressure Cook, Rice/Grain, Steam, Sauté, Slow Cook, Sous Vide, Yogurt, Bake **COOKING POT INTERIOR:** Stainless steel 	CLEANUP ★★½ EASE OF USE ★★★ RICE COOKING ★★★ SLOW COOKING ★★★ PRESSURE COOKING ★★★ SEARING/SAUTÉING ★★★	This multicooker had advanced features that made it great to cook in and easy to use. It made excellent pressure-cooked beef stew, baked beans, white rice, and pulled pork. Unlike previous Instant Pot models we've tested, it slow-cooked well. Its stainless-steel cooking pot seared food evenly, and its light-colored interior made it easy to monitor browning. We loved its clear, intuitive digital interface and unique pressure-release switch. The silicone handles on the inner pot stayed cool and were easy to grab. While it took extra scrubbing to fully clean the cooking pot, this wasn't a huge issue. This model also had some extra features, including sous vide, yogurt, and bake functions. We tested the sous vide and yogurt functions. The sous vide function took too long to heat and didn't maintain the consistent temperature needed for successful sous vide cooking. We were able to make creamy, fully set yogurt using the yogurt setting and Instant Pot's recipe. Overall, we think this multicooker's performance and ease of use deserved top marks.
INSTANT POT Duo Evo Plus 9-in-1 Electric Pressure Cooker, 6-QT **PRICE:** $119.99 **MODEL NUMBER:** Instant Pot 6 Quart Duo Evo Plus **CAPACITY:** 6 qt **SETTINGS:** Pressure Cook, Rice/Grain, Steam, Sauté, Slow Cook, Sous Vide, Yogurt, Bake **COOKING POT INTERIOR:** Stainless steel 	CLEANUP ★★½ EASE OF USE ★★★ RICE COOKING ★★★ SLOW COOKING ★★★ PRESSURE COOKING ★★★ SEARING/SAUTÉING ★★½	Like the 8-quart version, this multicooker was easy to use and produced excellent pressure- and slow-cooked food. Its controls were identical to the 8-quart model, with all the same features: an intuitive digital display, a lid that sealed automatically, a pressure-release switch, and silicone handles on its cooking pot. It made great beef stew, baked beans, and rice. Its stainless-steel cooking pot seared well, and the light interior made it easy to monitor browning, but it was slightly harder to clean than the nonstick pots. Like all the 6-quart pots, it had a smaller cooking surface, so we had to brown in more batches. However, if you want a smaller, equally capable multicooker, this is an excellent option.

RECOMMENDED

	PERFORMANCE	TESTERS' COMMENTS
ZAVOR LUX LCD 8 QT Multi-Cooker **PRICE:** $179.95 **MODEL NUMBER:** ZSELL03 **CAPACITY:** 8 qt **SETTINGS:** Pressure Cook, Slow Cook, Steam, Brown, Flex (for sous vide), Simmer, Yogurt, Grains, Eggs, Dessert **COOKING POT INTERIOR:** Stainless steel 	CLEANUP ★★½ EASE OF USE ★★½ RICE COOKING ★★★ SLOW COOKING ★★★ PRESSURE COOKING ★★½ SEARING/SAUTÉING ★★★	Our former favorite multicooker again produced excellent food. It made great pressure- and slow-cooked beans and rice. But it didn't get as hot as our top model, and when we compared the pressure-cooked beef stew and pulled pork made in the Instant Pot to the same recipes made in this model, the former featured more tender meat. But the Zavor still did a great job. It seared and sautéed deeply and evenly, and its stainless-steel cooking pot made it easy to monitor browning (but required a bit of scrubbing to clean). We liked its digital interface but found it more complicated than our top-rated model's. Plus, its control knob jumped between settings with even the slightest movement. It also gave its "brown" temperature in degrees, which we found trickier to use than the more familiar stovetop readings "low, medium, high." A helpful feature: Its control panel can be locked so that no one can accidentally cancel cooking or adjust settings.

OVEN MITTS

When you invest in a sturdy chef's knife, cooking immediately becomes easier, safer, and more satisfying. The same thing is true of a good pair of oven mitts. You don't need to worry about burning your hand on a hot skillet handle or dropping a stockpot full of boiling water halfway between the stovetop and kitchen sink. To find our favorite pair of oven mitts, we purchased nine ambidextrous models in a range of styles. Some of the mitts were sold singly and some were sold in sets; we purchased second copies of all the mitts sold singly. We used them to maneuver sheets of cookies, full cake pans, and pie plates lined with pie dough into, around, and out of hot ovens; carry and empty Dutch ovens filled with boiling water; and lift and maneuver ripping-hot cast-iron skillets that each contained a 4-pound roast chicken. We also evaluated how well the mitts protected our hands and forearms from heat and how easy they were to clean. The prices listed in this chart are based on shopping at online retailers and will vary. The top four oven mitts are listed below in order of preference.

HIGHLY RECOMMENDED	PERFORMANCE	TESTERS' COMMENTS
OXO Silicone Oven Mitt **PRICE:** $14.99 each ($29.98 for 2) **MODEL NUMBER:** 11219700 (teal) **STYLE:** Mitt **MATERIALS:** Silicone, cotton, and Cellucotton **DIMENSIONS:** 13 x 6¼ in **CARE INSTRUCTIONS:** Machine-wash, then air-dry **THICKNESS WHEN COMPRESSED:** 3 mm **TIME USER COULD HOLD PREHEATED SKILLET:** 22 sec	CLEANUP ★★½ DEXTERITY ★★★ HEAT PROTECTION ★★★ 	These oven mitts kept our hands comfortably cool and in control when holding hot equipment or reaching into a hot oven. When compressed, they were the thickest of the models with a silicone exterior. The silicone is heavily textured for better grip, and because it flexed with our hands, we could easily pinch thin cookie sheets and small handles or knobs. The fabric lining moved around inside the mitts at times during use, but it stayed put better than the linings of other models. The mitts can be machine-washed, but they have to be laid flat to dry. The silicone became permanently stained.

RECOMMENDED		
BIG RED HOUSE Oven Mitts **PRICE:** $13.99 for set of 2 **MODEL NUMBER:** n/a **STYLE:** Mitt **MATERIALS:** Cotton, silicone, and polyester **DIMENSIONS:** 12¾ x 6 in **CARE INSTRUCTIONS:** Machine-wash, then air-dry **THICKNESS WHEN COMPRESSED:** 5 mm **TIME USER COULD HOLD PREHEATED SKILLET:** 13.5 sec	CLEANUP ★★½ DEXTERITY ★★½ HEAT PROTECTION ★★½ 	With exteriors of thick, red fabric striped with silicone, this set performed reliably. Although another fabric model appeared to be as padded as this set, this pair was slightly thicker when compressed. When we flexed our hands while wearing these mitts, the lining stayed put, but testers noted that their thicker design made them a bit bulkier and blunter at the fingertips than our favorite model. And even though these mitts were thicker than our winner when compressed, we couldn't grip a hot cast-iron skillet for quite as long.

RECOMMENDED WITH RESERVATIONS		
HOMWE Silicone Oven Mitts **PRICE:** $16.97 for set of 2 **MODEL NUMBER:** n/a **STYLE:** Mitt **MATERIALS:** Silicone, cotton, and polyester **DIMENSIONS:** 14½ x 6½ in **CARE INSTRUCTIONS:** Machine-wash, then air-dry **THICKNESS WHEN COMPRESSED:** 2 mm **TIME USER COULD HOLD PREHEATED SKILLET:** 18 sec	CLEANUP ★★½ DEXTERITY ★★ HEAT PROTECTION ★★½ 	These thin and flexible silicone mitts kept our hands comfortable and felt relatively nimble, particularly when we were carrying thin or lightweight bakeware. However, when working with heavier hot items, our hands sometimes felt a bit warmer than they did in the top silicone mitt (but not hot enough to cause alarm). We also noticed that the fabric lining often moved around and bunched up inside the mitts as we were using them. Because their exteriors are made mostly of silicone, we could wash off debris or grease by hand, but we recommend a thorough machine washing as needed.
MASTRAD Silicone Mitt Plus **PRICE:** $13.29 each ($26.58 for 2) **MODEL NUMBER:** 82301 (charcoal) **STYLE:** Mitt **MATERIALS:** Silicone and cotton **DIMENSIONS:** 11½ x 5 in **CARE INSTRUCTIONS:** Dishwasher (silicone shell), machine-wash and machine-dry (removable lining) **THICKNESS WHEN COMPRESSED:** 2.5 mm **TIME USER COULD HOLD PREHEATED SKILLET:** 31.5 sec	CLEANUP ★★ DEXTERITY ★★ HEAT PROTECTION ★★★ 	These cotton-lined silicone mitts provided great heat protection, but we had to sacrifice some dexterity. At times, the cotton liner moved around inside the mitt while we were using it, and the rigid silicone shell didn't flex with our hands as we grasped items and got in our way. Some testers felt that the placement of the thumb (below the fingers instead of next to them) made using these mitts a bit less intuitive than using lobster claw–shaped models. We liked that the mitts can be easily taken apart and cleaned—the silicone shell is dishwasher-safe, and the cotton liner can be machine-washed and machine-dried, but the seam on the liner came loose after just three laundry cycles.

PETTY AND UTILITY KNIVES

Petty and utility knives provide more power and coverage than a paring knife but more precision and control than a chef's knife. Over the years, distinctions between petty and utility knives have blurred somewhat. In practice, both terms refer to any midsize prep knife. Curious to know which of these knives was best for home cooks, we bought 10 petty or utility knives and put them through their paces, using them to slice tomatoes; mince shallots and parsley; quarter mushrooms; break down chickens and debone chicken breasts; and slice salami, firm cheese, and cooked skin-on chicken breasts. We evaluated their sharpness, performance, and ease of use. The prices listed in this chart are based on shopping at online retailers and will vary. The top five knives are listed below in order of preference.

HIGHLY RECOMMENDED	PERFORMANCE	TESTERS' COMMENTS
TOJIRO 150mm Petty R-2 Powder Steel PRICE: $117.00 MATERIALS: R-2 stainless steel, wood composite WEIGHT: 2⅞ oz BLADE LENGTH: 5.9 in SPINE THICKNESS: 1.4 mm KNUCKLE CLEARANCE: 0.6 in HANDLE LENGTH: 4.25 in	SHARPNESS ★★★ PERFORMANCE ★★★ EASE OF USE ★★½ 	Lightweight, and with a medium-size handle, this petty knife felt great in our hands, maneuvering nimbly around chicken joints and bones and making quick work of mushrooms and shallots. It sported the sharpest blade straight out of the box; thin, keen, and just the right length, it was capable of producing near-surgical incisions. One tiny quibble? The plastic handle was just a touch slick when wet.
TOGIHARU PRO Petty 5.9" PRICE: $126.00 MODEL NUMBER: HTO-PROPE-150 MATERIALS: 440 16Cr. molybdenum stain-resistant steel, POM (polyacetal resin) WEIGHT: 2⅞ oz BLADE LENGTH: 6.1 in SPINE THICKNESS: 1.4 mm KNUCKLE CLEARANCE: 0.6 in HANDLE LENGTH: 4.25 in	SHARPNESS ★★★ PERFORMANCE ★★★ EASE OF USE ★★½  	This petty knife felt and performed almost exactly like our winner—perhaps not surprisingly, since they share most of the same specs. Just as agile and nearly as sharp, it made quick work of every task, and felt great in our hands as well. Like our winner, its handle can be a little slick when wet.
MAC PKF-60 Pro Utility 6" PRICE: $71.99 BEST BUY MODEL NUMBER: PKF-60 MATERIALS: Carbon/chromium/molybdenum steel blend, Pakkawood WEIGHT: 2⅞ oz BLADE LENGTH: 6.0 in SPINE THICKNESS: 1.4 mm KNUCKLE CLEARANCE: 0.5 in HANDLE LENGTH: 4.4 in	SHARPNESS ★★★ PERFORMANCE ★★★ EASE OF USE ★★½ 	Very sharp and thin-spined, this knife sailed through food cleanly and precisely. We liked it almost as much as our winner; its blade is just a hair longer, giving us a bit less control, and there's a tiny bit less clearance for your knuckles under the handle. But these are really minor quibbles; this is a great knife, and larger-handed testers will appreciate that its handle has a little extra room for them to grip.
OUL 150mm Wa Petty Ginsanko - Walnut Octagon PRICE: $212.00 BEST SPLURGE MATERIALS: Ginsanko steel, walnut wood WEIGHT: 3⅜ oz BLADE LENGTH: 6.1 in SPINE THICKNESS: 2.3 mm KNUCKLE CLEARANCE: 0.6 in HANDLE LENGTH: 4.9 in	SHARPNESS ★★★ PERFORMANCE ★★½ EASE OF USE ★★★ 	Hand-forged in Sakai, the capital of Japanese knife making, this gorgeous premium petty knife was ultrasharp and capable, slicing and mincing foods beautifully. Its walnut handle was longer than most and felt warm and responsive in our hands; because it had a little grippiness to it, it was also easy to hold when wet. It's just a touch heavier than our top picks, and its spine is a little thicker, so it occasionally wedged into food a tiny bit.
ZWILLING Pro 5.5-Inch Ultimate Prep Knife BEST FOR LARGE-HANDED COOKS PRICE: $69.95 MODEL NUMBER: 38400-143 MATERIALS: Stainless steel, polypropylene WEIGHT: 3⅛ oz BLADE LENGTH: 5.5 in SPINE THICKNESS: 1.4 mm KNUCKLE CLEARANCE: 0.75 in HANDLE LENGTH: 4.5 in	SHARPNESS ★★★ PERFORMANCE ★★★ EASE OF USE ★★½ 	This "prep" knife had a slightly curved blade that allowed us to rock through each slice, rather than cut in a more up-and-down motion, as with our other top choices. And it did a great job with all the foods; its relatively short blade made it very easy to control. While a touch slippery, its handle is on the longer side for these types of knives and provides lots of clearance underneath, making it an excellent choice for large-handed cooks.

FLAT-TOP GRILLS

Like traditional gas grills, flat-top grills are propane powered, have multiple heat zones, and are designed exclusively for outdoor use. But unlike gas or charcoal grills, flat-top grills can't be used for barbecuing or smoking foods. Instead, they're meant for cooking foods that are typically cooked on a griddle—pancakes and fried eggs—as well as foods that are typically grilled but are flattop-friendly—steak, burgers, and sliced vegetables. To find out which flat-top grill was best, we selected four models. Three of the grills had four burners under their rectangular cooking surfaces. One of the grills had just two burners and a round cooking surface. On each grill, we made pancakes, bacon, and eggs over easy; seared smashed burgers and toasted burger buns; and made chopped cheese sandwiches. We also used an infrared thermometer to monitor the temperature of each grill's cooking surface when set at both a high and a low heat setting. The prices listed in this chart are based on shopping at online retailers and will vary. The top three grills are listed below in order of preference.

HIGHLY RECOMMENDED	PERFORMANCE	TESTERS' COMMENTS

NEXGRILL 4-Burner Propane Gas Grill with Griddle Top
PRICE: $299.00
MODEL NUMBER: 720-0786
NUMBER OF SIDE TABLES: 2
ASSEMBLY TIME: 20 min
NUMBER OF WHEELS: 4
DRIP CUP LOCATION: Back center of cooktop
NUMBER OF BURNERS: 4
DIMENSIONS OF COOKTOP: 35.75 x 20.50 in (732.88 sq in)
TEMPERATURE DIFFERENCE BETWEEN HOTTER AND COOLER ZONES: 90°F

CLEANUP ★★★
COOKING ★★★
ASSEMBLY ★★½
CAPACITY ★★★
EASE OF USE ★★★

Our favorite flat-top grill was great to cook on, easy to use, and simple to clean. It made evenly cooked and thoroughly browned food and had the second largest cooktop of the grills we tested, which easily accommodated enough food to feed a crowd. The grill had distinct hotter and cooler zones, making it possible to successfully sear burgers and gently toast burger buns at the same time. It also had four wheels for easy transport, two well-positioned side tables that made it convenient to transfer food to and from the cooktop, and a large opening and drip cup at the back of the grill that made for easy cleanup. Two of the wheels can be locked to ensure that the grill stays in place while it's being used. While it did emerge from its packaging covered in a sticky factory coating, this came off easily as we seasoned the cooktop.

RECOMMENDED

BLACKSTONE 36" Griddle Cooking Station in Classic Black
PRICE: $279.99
MODEL NUMBER: 1554
NUMBER OF SIDE TABLES: 2
ASSEMBLY TIME: 65 min
NUMBER OF WHEELS: 4
DRIP CUP LOCATION: Back center of cooktop
NUMBER OF BURNERS: 4
DIMENSIONS OF COOKTOP: 35.75 x 21.50 in (768.63 sq in)
TEMPERATURE DIFFERENCE BETWEEN HOTTER AND COOLER ZONES: 88°F

CLEANUP ★★★
COOKING ★★
ASSEMBLY ★★
CAPACITY ★★★
EASE OF USE ★★★

This grill produced well-cooked food and was easy to use and clean, but the hotter and cooler cooking zones were not as distinct as our winner's—a large hot spot ran through the middle of the grill, even on low heat, so we had to be very attentive while cooking to avoid burning delicate items such as burger buns or sandwich rolls. It also took more than an hour to assemble. This grill did have a large cooktop, four wheels that made moving the grill easy, and two side tables—all features we appreciated.

RECOMMENDED WITH RESERVATIONS

CAMP CHEF FLAT TOP GRILL
PRICE: $349.00
MODEL NUMBER: FTG600
NUMBER OF SIDE TABLES: 2
ASSEMBLY TIME: 45 min
NUMBER OF WHEELS: 2
DRIP CUP LOCATION: Front left of cooktop
NUMBER OF BURNERS: 4
DIMENSIONS OF COOKTOP: 31.00 x 18.75 in (581.25 sq in)
TEMPERATURE DIFFERENCE BETWEEN HOTTER AND COOLER ZONES: 95°F

CLEANUP ★½
COOKING ★★
ASSEMBLY ★★★
CAPACITY ★★
EASE OF USE ★

While this grill was one of the fastest to assemble, and it browned burgers and ground beef thoroughly and cooked eggs, bacon, and pancakes evenly, it was a bit difficult to use and clean. We disliked having to place our faces close to the grill to peer through the small holes next to the burner knobs to see if each burner was lit. Its regulator was also finicky and needed to be tightened as much as possible and turned very slowly when opened, or we risked triggering the safety mechanism. (Once triggered, the burners will shut off.) The cooktop's drip cup sat below a small circular opening that often clogged and made cleanup difficult. We did, however, appreciate the grill's walls, which facilitated the flipping of pancakes and burgers. And while its cooking surface was relatively small, it still accommodated plenty of food.

BRAISERS

Traditionally defined, braising is a wet-heat cooking method that's used to turn tough cuts of meat tender. Most braising recipes call for a Dutch oven that's large enough to accommodate the food, but a braiser—a round pan that is shallower than a Dutch oven, with sloped sides to contain liquid and a wide cooking surface for browning—can also be used. To find out which braiser is best, we selected five models, priced from about $59 to about $330. While one of the models was ceramic, the rest were made of enameled cast iron (we didn't find any models that were traditional cast iron). We focused on braisers that were about 3.5 quarts, as this size accommodates enough food to serve four. We used each to make braised chicken, meatballs in tomato sauce, braised green beans, roast chicken, and pappardelle with pork. We evaluated the finished food, noting if the braisers were able to brown food thoroughly, cook food evenly, and evaporate moisture adequately. We also judged the pans on how easy it was to monitor our foods' browning while using them, ease of cleanup, and durability. The prices listed in this chart are based on shopping at online retailers and will vary. The top three braisers are listed below in order of preference.

HIGHLY RECOMMENDED	PERFORMANCE	TESTERS' COMMENTS
LE CREUSET Signature Enameled Cast-Iron 3.5-Quart Braiser PRICE: $299.95 MODEL NUMBER: LS2532-305HSS WEIGHT: 12 lb, ½ oz THICKNESS: .47 in MATERIALS: Enameled cast iron, stainless steel WALL HEIGHT: 2.25 in INTERIOR COLOR: Light HANDLE DIMENSIONS: 1.8 x 4.25 in COOKING SURFACE DIAMETER: 10 in	CLEANUP ★★★ COOKING ★★★ DURABILITY ★★★ EASE OF USE ★★★ 	Our top-ranked braiser had several features that contributed to a solid performance in test after test: a light interior that made it easy to monitor browning; a moderately thick bottom that helped ensure good heat retention and even browning; a generous cooking surface that fit every recipe from whole chicken to meatballs to pork ragu without crowding; and large, comfortable looped handles and a stainless-steel lid knob that gave us a secure grip, especially important when the pan was heavy and full of hot food. While pricey, this versatile braiser made great food, was easy to use, and looked good enough to double as a serving dish.

RECOMMENDED		
STAUB Cast Iron 3.5-Quart Braiser PRICE: $329.95 MODEL NUMBER: ME7118 WEIGHT: 12 lb, 4⅞ oz THICKNESS: .50 in MATERIALS: Enameled cast iron, stainless steel WALL HEIGHT: 2.15 in INTERIOR COLOR: Dark HANDLE DIMENSIONS: 1.65 x 3.25 in COOKING SURFACE DIAMETER: 10 in	CLEANUP ★★★ COOKING ★★★ DURABILITY ★★★ EASE OF USE ★★ 	We really liked this enameled cast-iron braiser, which cooked food evenly and browned it thoroughly. It had large handles that were angled upward, which helped distribute weight and made the pan feel lighter to carry—even when loaded with a roast chicken or pork ragu. This braiser was also easy to clean and didn't retain many stains. However, it did have two downsides: a dark interior that made it hard to monitor browning and a lid with a rather small stainless-steel knob, which wasn't as easy to grasp as the knob of our winner.
TRAMONTINA Enameled Cast Iron Covered Braiser PRICE: $61.97 `BEST BUY` MODEL NUMBER: 8013⅛50DS WEIGHT: 13 lb, ⅛ oz THICKNESS: .56 in MATERIALS: Enameled cast iron, stainless steel WALL HEIGHT: 2.3 in INTERIOR COLOR: Light HANDLE DIMENSIONS: 1.55 x 3.5 in COOKING SURFACE DIAMETER: 10.4 in	CLEANUP ★★★ COOKING ★★★ DURABILITY ★★★ EASE OF USE ★½ 	This pan performed just as well as our favorite braiser but had smaller handles that were tough to grasp. Because of its thicker cooking surface, it took a bit longer to heat up and to brown chicken thighs. This braiser had the largest cooking surface area, which ensured proper liquid reduction and a rich, flavorful ragu. It was easy to clean and withstood being whacked with a spoon and having its lid slammed down repeatedly. This pan delivered excellent results at a relatively low price.

ELECTRIC KNIFE SHARPENERS

Our favorite tool for keeping our kitchen knives sharp has long been an electric knife sharpener because a good one can bring the dullest, most damaged blade back to life and then keep it in prime shape with quick touch-ups. You don't need special skills or a lot of time if you have the right electric sharpener, which means that you can take care of your knife in minutes and get back to the real goal: making something good to eat. Our previous favorite, the Chef'sChoice Trizor 15XV Knife Sharpener, has some new competition, so we bought a fresh copy of our winner and six rivals, all priced from about $37 to about $160. Most of the machines in our lineup sharpened blades to 15-degree angles; however, the manufacturer of two of the sharpeners did not reveal the angle to which it sharpens blades, and a sharpener from another manufacturer sharpens blades to 17 degrees. We used each machine to sharpen the blades of brand-new copies of our favorite chef's knife that we'd dulled by dragging them over a whetstone, repeating the dulling-and-resharpening test a total of four times. We assigned one copy of the knife to each machine throughout testing. To evaluate the results after each sharpening, we sliced through sheets of copy paper, our standard sharpness test; used an industrial sharpness-testing machine that assigned a numerical score to the sharpness; and finally circled back to the real world by slicing ripe, juicy tomatoes. The prices listed in this chart are based on shopping at online retailers and will vary. The top three knife sharpeners are listed below in order of preference.

HIGHLY RECOMMENDED	PERFORMANCE	TESTERS' COMMENTS
CHEF'SCHOICE Trizor 15XV Knife Sharpener PRICE: $139.99 MODEL NUMBER: 15 SHARPENING METHOD: Three stages: two diamond-coated steel disks (one coarse, one medium) and flexible stropping disk 	DAMAGE ★★½ EASE OF USE ★★★ CLEANUP ★★★ PERFORMANCE ★★★	Our top-rated sharpener produced truly exceptional and consistent results quickly, neatly, and efficiently. The manual clearly outlined a few specific steps that must be followed each time, and it took about 2 minutes from start to finish to get a polished, razor-sharp edge. Narrow, spring-loaded slots made it easy and unambiguous to maintain a consistent angle as we moved the knife through the three slots. It rapidly removed a notch we cut in the blade and easily sharpened both our everyday chef's knife and pricey carbon-steel chef's knife. We subtracted half a point because the slots left very light cosmetic scratches along the sides of our knives.
CHEF'SCHOICE 315XV Knife Sharpener PRICE: $109.99 **BEST BUY** MODEL NUMBER: 315 SHARPENING METHOD: Two stages: medium-abrasive diamond-coated steel disk and flexible stropping disk  	DAMAGE ★★½ EASE OF USE ★★★ CLEANUP ★★★ PERFORMANCE ★★★	This slightly simplified, more compact version of our top-rated sharpener has one fewer sharpening slot, with the same medium-abrasive diamond abrasive of our winner for shaping, and a flexible stropping disk to polish the edge. As a result, this sharpener created an edge with two reinforcing bevels, as opposed to the three created by the top-rated Trizor model. We noticed only a minor difference in cutting performances between the knife we sharpened in this model and the knife we sharpened in the Trizor, but knives sharpened in this model may require slightly more frequent sharpening to maintain their edges. Like the Trizor, the spring-loaded guides left light cosmetic scratches along the side of our blades.

RECOMMENDED		
WORK SHARP Culinary E5 Kitchen Knife Sharpener with Ceramic Honing Rod PRICE: $159.97 MODEL NUMBER: E5 SHARPENING METHOD: One stage: ceramic oxide abrasive belt, plus separate ceramic honing rod  	DAMAGE ★★ EASE OF USE ★★½ CLEANUP ★★★ PERFORMANCE ★★½	This compact sharpener should be easy to use: You push a button to start a 90-second sharpening cycle. The speed of the rotating abrasive belt changes over the course of the cycle to shape, refine, and polish the blade's edge as you pass the knife through a single set of left and right slots. While the results could be superlative, we didn't find that they were consistently so. It's up to the user to hold the knife in the correct position in the slots, which don't grip the knife or guide the blade's angle against the abrasive belt. We'd often reach the end of sharpening to find that a spot along the knife wasn't quite as sharp as the rest of the blade. Removing the notch took twice as long as it did with our winner, but it eventually worked well. The included honing rod was a great addition for polishing up the edge after a sharpening cycle or for light maintenance between sharpening sessions. One disadvantage: The abrasive belt cut into the Fibrox handle of our chef's knife, leaving it rough and slightly damaged where it joins the blade.

NUTRITIONAL INFORMATION FOR OUR RECIPES

We calculate the nutritional values of our recipes per serving; if there is a range in the serving size, we used the highest number of servings to calculate the nutritional values. We entered all the ingredients, using weights for important ingredients such as meat, cheese, and most vegetables. We also used our preferred brands in these analyses. We did not include additional salt or pepper for food that's "seasoned to taste."

SWEET POTATO SALAD WITH CUMIN, SMOKED PAPRIKA, AND ALMONDS

RECIPE	CALORIES	TOTAL FAT (G)	SAT FAT (G)	CHOL (MG)	SODIUM (MG)	CARBS (G)	FIBER (G)	SUGARS (G)	PROTEIN (G)
CHAPTER 1: SOUPS, SALADS, AND STARTERS									
Phở Gà Miền Bắc (Northern Vietnamese–Style Chicken Pho)	707	32	9	154	1194	59	2	9	44
Phở Gà Miền Nam (Southern Vietnamese–Style Chicken Pho)	509	24	7	116	894	36	2	2	32
Korean-Inspired Spicy Fish Stew	200	6	0.5	40	830	7	1	3	28
Spiced Wild Rice and Coconut Soup	350	25	19	0	330	29	3	3	7
Horiatiki Salata (Hearty Greek Salad)	397	33	11	50	1000	18	5	10	11
Sweet Potato Salad with Cumin, Smoked Paprika, and Almonds	309	17	2	0	473	38	7	8	5
Sweet Potato Salad with Soy Sauce, Sriracha, and Peanuts	*309*	*16*	*2*	*0*	*478*	*37*	*6*	*8*	*5*
Cantaloupe Salad with Olives and Red Onion	54	1	0	0	266	12	2	10	1
Honeydew Salad with Peanuts and Lime	102	4	1	0	449	16	2	12	3
Watermelon Salad with Cotija and Serrano Chiles	153	8	3	15	458	18	1	13	6
Charred Chicken Caesar Salad	930	47	8	180	1220	56	0	6	67
Warm Wheat Berry Salad with Radicchio, Dried Cherries, and Pecans	250	15	3	4	269	26	5	6	6
Warm Spelt Salad with Pickled Fennel, Pea Greens, and Mint	227	9	2	6	281	32	5	6	7
Warm Kamut with Carrots and Pomegranate	190	8	1	0	118	27	5	5	6
Skordalia (Greek Garlic-Potato Puree)	160	14	2	0	176	8	2	1	2
Smoked Salmon Dip	174	16	8	46	299	2	0	1	6
Bagel Chips	*167*	*9*	*1*	*0*	*139*	*17*	*1*	*3*	*3*
Pajeon (Korean Scallion Pancake)	366	23	2	0	619	37	2	3	5
Crispy Fried Shrimp	295	17	3	70	407	30	1	6	6
Pigs in Blankets	58	3	1	21	182	5	1	3	3
CHAPTER 2: SIDE DISHES									
Skillet-Roasted Green Beans with Garlic and Pecorino Romano	207	14	4	15	513	15	5	6	8
Skillet-Roasted Green Beans with Bacon, Black Bean Garlic Sauce, and Tahini	*218*	*16*	*3*	*5*	*209*	*17*	*6*	*6*	*5*
Roasted Fennel	86	7	1	0	209	6	2	3	1
Orange-Honey Dressing	*29*	*2*	*0*	*0*	*16*	*2*	*1*	*2*	*0*
Crunchy Oil-Cured Olives	*4*	*0*	*0*	*0*	*7*	*0*	*1*	*0*	*0*
Parmesan Bread Crumbs	*47*	*3*	*1*	*4*	*24*	*2*	*1*	*0*	*2*
Spiced Cashews	*54*	*5*	*0*	*0*	*24*	*2*	*1*	*1*	*1*
Braised Red Cabbage with Apple, Bacon, and Shallots	167	8	3	13	632	20	5	12	5
Celery Root Puree	156	9	6	28	396	17	3	3	3
Bacon, Garlic, and Parsley Topping	*42*	*4*	*1*	*7*	*65*	*1*	*0*	*0*	*1*
Shallot, Sage, and Black Pepper Topping	*43*	*4*	*2*	*10*	*26*	*2*	*1*	*0*	*0*
Gobi Manchurian	530	36	3	0	706	48	4	6	6
Marinated Zucchini	189	16	4	11	350	5	1	3	7
Kansas City–Style Cheesy Corn	320	24	12	74	714	13	1	6	15
Skillet Squash Casserole	340	27	8	32	520	18	2	6	9
Sweet Potato Fritters with Feta, Dill, and Cilantro	378	25	5	79	455	32	4	6	8

RECIPE	CALORIES	TOTAL FAT (G)	SAT FAT (G)	CHOL (MG)	SODIUM (MG)	CARBS (G)	FIBER (G)	SUGARS (G)	PROTEIN (G)
CHAPTER 2: SIDE DISHES (continued)									
Tourte aux Pommes de Terre (French Potato Pie)	645	44	27	147	607	56	4	2	9
Cheesy Mashed Potato Casserole	470	30	18	88	580	37	4	3	14
Cheesy Mashed Potato Casserole with Blue Cheese, Bacon, and Rosemary	*443*	*31*	*18*	*83*	*562*	*31*	*4*	*3*	*11*
Cheesy Mashed Potato Casserole with Parmesan, Browned Butter, and Sage	*467*	*31*	*19*	*85*	*576*	*33*	*4*	*3*	*17*
Torn and Fried Potatoes	601	43	3	0	485	51	4	2	6
Hung Kao Mun Gati (Thai Coconut Rice)	251	8	7	0	200	40	1	2	4
Arroz con Titoté (Colombian Coconut Rice)	522	22	19	0	604	77	1	14	7
CHAPTER 3: PASTA, PIZZA, SANDWICHES, AND MORE									
Spaghetti Carbonara	814	34	13	201	839	87	4	4	36
Cheeseburger Mac	698	43	21	139	892	35	2	5	40
Pasta e Piselli (Pasta and Peas)	462	18	5	22	734	57	5	8	19
Cashew e Pepe e Funghi	450	16	2.5	0	360	63	1	4	14
Spaghetti with Tuna and Capers	496	19	4	14	362	58	3	2	23
Dan Dan Mian (Sichuan Noodles with Chili Sauce and Pork)	789	36	7	136	677	88	6	4	28
Spinach and Ricotta Gnudi with Tomato-Butter Sauce	427	28	18	87	727	23	3	3	23
Stuffed Pizza	714	37	16	101	1870	61	4	3	33
Lahmajun (Armenian Flatbread)	417	13	3	21	437	62	3	2	13
Cucumber-Tomato Salad	*73*	*6*	*1*	*0*	*267*	*5*	*1*	*2*	*1*
Smashed Burgers	613	43	15	104	703	26	1	4	29
Crispy Fish Sandwiches with Tartar Sauce	1106	85	9	93	980	53	2	5	29
Mumbai Frankie Wraps	630	29	9	0	1340	83	9	7	16
Chapatis (Whole-Wheat Wraps)	*300*	*14*	*2*	*0*	*580*	*40*	*3*	*0*	*7*
Cilantro-Mint Chutney	*10*	*0*	*0*	*0*	*35*	*1*	*0*	*1*	*0*
Quick Sweet-and-Spicy Pickled Red Onions	*20*	*0*	*0*	*0*	*55*	*5*	*0*	*5*	*0*
Tacos al Pastor	369	13	4	53	696	45	7	13	20
Tuna Tostadas	500	30	4.5	50	880	22	2	4	33
Corn Risotto	272	8	4	18	684	44	3	5	8
Kimchi Bokkeumbap (Kimchi Fried Rice)	475	10	1	5	534	84	2	2	10
Chana Masala	291	11	1	0	578	39	11	8	11
Bhature	*513*	*28*	*2*	*4*	*337*	*57*	*2*	*3*	*8*
CHAPTER 4: MEAT									
Easier Prime Rib	555	49	20	111	441	1	0	0	25
Prepared Horseradish	*28*	*0*	*0*	*0*	*203*	*6*	*2*	*4*	*1*
Spice-Crusted Sirloin Steak with Asparagus and Lemon-Shallot Butter	400	26	11	115	510	8	3	3	34
Steakhouse Spice Blend	*15*	*0*	*0*	*0*	*0*	*2*	*1*	*0*	*1*
Tex-Mex Spice Blend	*15*	*0.5*	*0*	*0*	*0*	*2*	*1*	*0*	*1*
Grilled Boneless Beef Short Ribs	364	29	12	110	353	0	0	0	26
Kimchi-Scallion Sauce	*91*	*9*	*1*	*0*	*218*	*1*	*0*	*0*	*1*
Preserved Lemon–Almond Sauce	*128*	*13*	*2*	*0*	*3*	*2*	*1*	*1*	*1*
Glazed Meatloaf for One	670	44	15	310	1570	30	1	10	37

RECIPE	CALORIES	TOTAL FAT (G)	SAT FAT (G)	CHOL (MG)	SODIUM (MG)	CARBS (G)	FIBER (G)	SUGARS (G)	PROTEIN (G)
CHAPTER 4: MEAT *(continued)*									
Palomilla Steak	485	35	13	126	646	10	2	4	35
Beef Wellington	675	41	24	163	744	49	3	6	29
Creamy Green Peppercorn Sauce	*127*	*11*	*7*	*39*	*257*	*2*	*0*	*1*	*2*
Madeira Sauce	*95*	*7*	*4*	*18*	*102*	*5*	*0*	*1*	*2*
Braciole	491	28	9	111	896	17	3	7	38
Keema (Garam Masala–Spiced Ground Beef)	210	13	4	50	376	7	2	3	17
Keema Aloo (Garam Masala–Spiced Ground Beef with Potatoes)	*232*	*13*	*4*	*50*	*378*	*12*	*3*	*3*	*17*
Keema Matar (Garam Masala–Spiced Ground Beef with Peas)	*286*	*21*	*6*	*55*	*400*	*10*	*3*	*4*	*16*
Fresh Bulk Sausage	211	14	5	70	69	0	0	0	20
Breakfast Seasoning	*78*	*1*	*0*	*0*	*5*	*19*	*3*	*13*	*1*
Fresh Garlic Seasoning	*29*	*1*	*0*	*0*	*4*	*6*	*2*	*0*	*1*
Italian Seasoning	*83*	*2*	*0*	*0*	*12*	*18*	*6*	*9*	*2*
Cast Iron Pork Fajitas	542	19	3	82	808	57	4	8	35
Ranch Fried Pork Chops	598	23	5	100	906	56	2	6	40
Choucroute Garnie	732	62	22	133	1864	10	4	3	29
Kansas City–Style Barbecue Ribs	924	73	24	249	790	16	1	13	49
Herbed Leg of Lamb with Fingerling Potatoes and Asparagus	390	14	4.5	110	510	25	5	3	39
Braised Lamb Shanks	887	61	24	221	1484	16	4	5	66
CHAPTER 5: POULTRY AND SEAFOOD									
Broiled Chicken with Gravy	864	57	18	254	1286	17	1	5	65
Poulet au Vinaigre (Chicken with Vinegar)	469	33	10	167	697	6	1	2	28
Khao Man Gai (Thai-Style Chicken and Rice)	749	33	9	145	2183	67	3	7	44
Kombdi, Jira Ghalun (Cumin-Scented Chicken)	494	31	6	205	1068	10	2	3	42
Onion Raita	*30*	*1*	*1*	*5*	*117*	*3*	*0*	*3*	*2*
Grilled Chicken Satay	385	22	3	142	589	14	2	7	33
Lard-Fried Chicken	1444	111	38	312	1598	37	2	0	68
Orange Chicken	1149	69	6	161	1232	89	3	25	40
Cast Iron Chicken and Vegetables	928	61	15	217	1725	36	8	8	59
One-Pan Turkey Breast and Stuffing with Pomegranate-Parsley Sauce	1061	58	14	196	1392	60	5	7	72
Turkey Thigh Confit with Citrus-Mustard Sauce	447	27	9	124	636	20	2	13	31
Moroccan Fish Tagine	387	24	3	73	710	12	4	6	33
24-Hour Preserved Lemons	*271*	*27*	*4*	*0*	*145*	*9*	*1*	*7*	*0*
Broiled Spice-Rubbed Snapper	243	9	1	63	451	3	1	0	35
Hot-Smoked Whole Side of Salmon	261	15	3	62	278	6	0	6	23
Hot-Smoked Salmon Kedgeree	343	15	7	174	438	37	1	1	14
Chile-Garlic Shrimp	338	19	6	301	1336	10	2	4	32
Pan-Seared Shrimp with Peanuts, Black Pepper, and Lime	215	10	1	214	966	6	1	2	25
Pan-Seared Shrimp with Fermented Black Beans, Ginger, and Garlic	*201*	*9*	*1*	*214*	*1342*	*5*	*0*	*2*	*24*

RECIPE	CALORIES	TOTAL FAT (G)	SAT FAT (G)	CHOL (MG)	SODIUM (MG)	CARBS (G)	FIBER (G)	SUGARS (G)	PROTEIN (G)
CHAPTER 6: BREAKFAST, BRUNCH, AND BREADS									
Baked Eggs for Sandwiches	143	10	3	372	233	1	0	0	13
Egg, Kimchi, and Avocado Sandwiches	459	27	6	378	616	35	4	2	19
Egg, Smoked Salmon, and Dill Sandwiches	349	14	4	381	636	30	2	5	25
Egg, Ham, and Pepperoncini Sandwiches	481	23	10	417	978	41	3	10	29
Egg, Salami, and Tomato Sandwiches	520	32	8	408	1034	32	2	2	24
Banana-Walnut Muffins	252	10	1	31	239	38	2	18	4
Banana Muffins with Coconut and Macadamia	*260*	*11*	*2*	*31*	*233*	*37*	*2*	*16*	*4*
Banana Muffins with Sesame and Chocolate Chunks	*325*	*15*	*2*	*31*	*262*	*46*	*3*	*22*	*6*
Peanut Butter–Banana Muffins	*318*	*14*	*2*	*31*	*255*	*43*	*3*	*20*	*7*
German Apple Pancake with Brown Sugar Sour Cream	368	17	9	189	479	44	3	26	9
Spanish Migas with Fried Eggs	452	30	9	217	705	26	3	5	20
Corned Beef and Cabbage Hash	356	25	10	74	447	21	3	3	13
Bolos Lêvedos (Portuguese Muffins)	340	8	4	63	283	57	2	13	8
Bolos Lêvedos (Portuguese Muffins) with Lemon and Cinnamon	*340*	*9*	*4*	*63*	*284*	*57*	*2*	*13*	*8*
Oatmeal Dinner Rolls	170	3	2	21	145	31	2	5	5
Blueberry Biscuits	288	5	3	12	315	55	2	18	7
Banana Bread	257	11	6	56	231	38	2	20	4
Double-Chocolate Banana Bread	287	14	8	56	229	41	2	24	4
Popovers	288	10	5	112	372	38	1	5	11
Mana'eesh Za'atar	323	12	2	0	264	46	2	0	7
CHAPTER 7: DESSERTS									
Yellow Sheet Cake with Chocolate Frosting	473	24	10	88	220	62	2	45	4
Raspberry Pound Cake	521	26	15	368	66	3	3	39	8
Rhubarb Upside-Down Cake	552	25	13	100	295	79	3	53	7
Maple Cheesecake	454	29	15	133	323	43	1	32	7
Maple-Pecan Skillet Granola	*321*	*18*	*2*	*0*	*149*	*37*	*4*	*13*	*6*
Vegan Chocolate-Espresso Tart	340	19	14	0	100	42	2	14	4
Coconut Whipped Cream	*230*	*10*	*9*	*0*	*20*	*35*	*0*	*34*	*1*
Cranberry Curd Tart with Almond Crust	548	34	17	148	183	59	4	44	5
Peach Zabaglione Gratin	153	3	1	123	103	28	2	26	3
Strawberry Galette	432	20	12	51	302	60	3	25	5
Tangy Whipped Cream	*89*	*8*	*5*	*30*	*11*	*4*	*0*	*4*	*1*
Really Good Key Lime Pie	622	26	14	158	519	88	2	55	11
Failproof Whipped Cream	*127*	*11*	*7*	*41*	*11*	*7*	*0*	*7*	*1*
Endless Summer Peach Pie	482	23	14	77	421	65	3	35	6
Salted Butterscotch Sauce	*178*	*14*	*9*	*41*	*88*	*15*	*0*	*14*	*0*
Choux au Craquelin	205	13	8	97	80	18	0	9	3
Colorful Choux au Craquelin	*210*	*13*	*8*	*97*	*79*	*19*	*0*	*10*	*3*
Mocha Choux au Craquelin	*204*	*13*	*8*	*97*	*80*	*18*	*0*	*9*	*3*

RECIPE	CALORIES	TOTAL FAT (G)	SAT FAT (G)	CHOL (MG)	SODIUM (MG)	CARBS (G)	FIBER (G)	SUGARS (G)	PROTEIN (G)
CHAPTER 7: DESSERTS *(continued)*									
Nutella Rugelach	481	31	21	89	176	44	2	22	6
Cinnamon-Walnut Rugelach	*385*	*24*	*14*	*89*	*224*	*38*	*1*	*17*	*5*
Jam Rugelach	*412*	*24*	*14*	*89*	*176*	*46*	*1*	*20*	*5*
Anzac Biscuits	124	5	3	10	71	19	1	5	2
Two Chocolate Chip Cookies	440	22	12	215	120	57	1	38	6
M&M Cookies	292	13	8	37	153	42	1	25	3

PEACH ZABAGLIONE GRATIN

CONVERSIONS & EQUIVALENTS

Some say cooking is a science and an art. We would say that geography has a hand in it, too. Flour milled in the United Kingdom and elsewhere will feel and taste different from flour milled in the United States. So while we cannot promise that the loaf of bread you bake in Canada or England will taste the same as a loaf baked in the States, we can offer guidelines for converting weights and measures. We also recommend that you rely on your instincts when making our recipes. Refer to the visual cues provided. If the bread dough hasn't "come together in a ball" as described, you may need to add more flour—even if the recipe doesn't tell you so. You be the judge.

The recipes in this book were developed using standard U.S. measures following U.S. government guidelines. The charts below offer equivalents for U.S., metric, and imperial (U.K.) measures. All conversions are approximate and have been rounded up or down to the nearest whole number. For example:

1 teaspoon = 4.929 milliliters, rounded up to 5 milliliters

1 ounce = 28.349 grams, rounded down to 28 grams

VOLUME CONVERSIONS

U.S.	METRIC
1 teaspoon	5 milliliters
2 teaspoons	10 milliliters
1 tablespoon	15 milliliters
2 tablespoons	30 milliliters
¼ cup	59 milliliters
⅓ cup	79 milliliters
½ cup	118 milliliters
¾ cup	177 milliliters
1 cup	237 milliliters
1¼ cups	296 milliliters
1½ cups	355 milliliters
2 cups	473 milliliters
2½ cups	591 milliliters
3 cups	710 milliliters
4 cups (1 quart)	1 liter
4 quarts (1 gallon)	4 liters

WEIGHT CONVERSIONS

OUNCES	GRAMS
½	14
¾	21
1	28
1½	43
2	57
2½	71
3	85
3½	99
4	113
4½	128
5	142
6	170
7	198
8	227
9	255
10	283
12	340
16 (1 pound)	454

CONVERSIONS FOR INGREDIENTS COMMONLY USED IN BAKING

Baking is an exacting science. Because measuring by weight is far more accurate than measuring by volume, and thus more likely to achieve reliable results, in our recipes we provide ounce measures in addition to cup measures for many ingredients. Refer to the chart below to convert these measures into grams.

INGREDIENT	OUNCES	GRAMS
Flour		
1 cup all-purpose flour*	5	142
1 cup cake flour	4	113
1 cup whole-wheat flour	5½	156
Sugar		
1 cup granulated (white) sugar	7	198
1 cup packed brown sugar (light or dark)	7	198
1 cup confectioners' sugar	4	113
Cocoa Powder		
1 cup cocoa powder	3	85
Butter†		
4 tablespoons (½ stick, or ¼ cup)	2	57
8 tablespoons (1 stick, or ½ cup)	4	113
16 tablespoons (2 sticks, or 1 cup)	8	227

* U.S. all-purpose flour, the most frequently used flour in this book, does not contain leaveners, as some European flours do. These leavened flours are called self-rising or self-raising. If you are using self-rising flour, take this into consideration before adding leavening to a recipe.

† In the United States, butter is sold both salted and unsalted. We generally recommend unsalted butter. If you are using salted butter, take this into consideration before adding salt to a recipe.

OVEN TEMPERATURES

DEGREES FAHRENHEIT	DEGREES CELSIUS	GAS MARK (imperial)
225	105	¼
250	120	½
275	135	1
300	150	2
325	165	3
350	180	4
375	190	5
400	200	6
425	220	7
450	230	8
475	245	9

CONVERTING TEMPERATURES FROM AN INSTANT-READ THERMOMETER

We include doneness temperatures in many of our recipes, such as those for poultry, meat, and bread. We recommend an instant-read thermometer for the job. Refer to the table above to convert Fahrenheit degrees to Celsius. Or, for temperatures not represented in the chart, use this simple formula.

Subtract 32 from the Fahrenheit reading, and then divide the result by 1.8 to find the Celsius reading.

EXAMPLE:

"Roast chicken until thighs register 175 degrees."
To convert:

$175°$ F – 32 = $143°$
$143°$ ÷ 1.8 = $79.44°$C, rounded down to $79°$C

INDEX